CW01512745

ATLANTIC FURIES

ATLANTIC FURIES

THE WOMEN WHO RISKED EVERYTHING TO BE THE FIRST TO FLY

MIDGE GILLIES

SCRIBE

Melbourne | London | Minneapolis

Scribe Publications
18–20 Edward St, Brunswick, Victoria 3056, Australia
2 John St, Clerkenwell, London, WC1N 2ES, United Kingdom
3754 Pleasant Ave, Suite 223w, Minneapolis, Minnesota 55409, USA

Published by Scribe 2025

Back cover images: (Elsie Mackay) Chronicle/Alamy; (Lady Anne Savile) The Sketch; (Frances Grayson) Maine Historical Society/MaineToday Media; (Ruth Elder) Smith Archive/Alamy; (Amelia Earhart) Science History Images/Alamy; (Bessie Coleman) IanDagnall Computing/Alamy; (Mabel Boll) Smith Archive/Alamy

Typeset in Garamond Premier Pro by the publishers

Printed and bound in the UK by CPI Group (UK) Ltd, Croydon CR0 4YY

Scribe is committed to the sustainable use of natural resources and the use of paper products made responsibly from those resources.

978 1 761380 57 0 (Australian edition)
978 1 915590 52 7 (UK edition)
978 1 761386 48 0 (ebook)

Catalogue records for this book are available from the National Library of Australia and the British Library.

scribepublications.com.au
scribepublications.co.uk
scribepublications.com

To the Kelly family on both sides of the Atlantic
and in loving memory of Heather Kelly

CONTENTS

LIST OF AVIATORS x

MAPS OF FLIGHT PATHS xii

PART ONE

The Lure of the Atlantic

PRELUDE: June 1928 3

CHAPTER ONE: The First Attempts 15

CHAPTER TWO: Girls Will Be Girls 24

CHAPTER THREE: Queen Bess 38

FLIGHT CHECKLIST: A Memorable Nickname 47

PART TWO

Rich Girls Take to the Skies

CHAPTER FOUR: Amy Phipps and the Challenges of High Birth 57

CHAPTER FIVE: The Flying Princess 64

CHAPTER SIX: Elsie Mackay: From Interior Designer to Stunt Pilot 76

FLIGHT CHECKLIST: A Tendency to Tomboy 90

PART THREE

The Women Behind the Planes

CHAPTER SEVEN: Frances Grayson and Ruth Elder Square Up 101

CHAPTER EIGHT: Amy Guest: Thwarted Adventurer 110

FLIGHT CHECKLIST: A Well-Packed Picnic Basket 122

PART FOUR
1927, The Race Begins

CHAPTER NINE: Anne Savile and the 'Superfliers' 133
CHAPTER TEN: The Flying Matron Versus 'Miss America of the Air' 142
CHAPTER ELEVEN: The Weather Man 152
CHAPTER TWELVE: Missing 157
CHAPTER THIRTEEN: 'A safe and sane flight' 165
CHAPTER FOURTEEN: Winter Comes to Old Orchard 173

PART FIVE
1928, Round Two

FLIGHT CHECKLIST: A Handle on Husbands 195
CHAPTER FIFTEEN: Limbering up: Boll and Earhart in Cuba and Boston 207
CHAPTER SIXTEEN: Hinch and Mackay 213
CHAPTER SEVENTEEN: 'The most secret flight in the history of aviation' 223
CHAPTER EIGHTEEN: Ambiguous Loss 234

PART SIX
Crossing the Atlantic

FLIGHT CHECKLIST: Noteworthy Hair 253
CHAPTER NINETEEN: 'Violet. Cheerio.' 260
CHAPTER TWENTY: Crossing the Atlantic 272
CHAPTER TWENTY-ONE: Grounded: London, June 1928 281

PART SEVEN
1932, The First Woman to Fly the Atlantic Solo

CHAPTER TWENTY-TWO: Solo 293
EPILOGUE: Flight Debrief 315

ACKNOWLEDGMENTS 333

BIBLIOGRAPHY 336

NOTES 342

INDEX 389

List of Aviators

Lady Anne Savile (Princess Anne of Löwenstein-Wertheim-Freudenberg)
Flight Date: 31 August 1927
Route: Upavon, Wiltshire, UK to Ottawa, Canada.
Aeroplane: *St Raphael*
Crew: Leslie Hamilton and Frederick Minchin
Backers: self-funded

Ruth Elder
Flight Date: 11 October 1927
Route: New York, US to Paris, France
Aeroplane: *American Girl*
Crew: George Haldeman
Backers: Wheeling Aero Exhibit Company

Frances Wilson Grayson
Flight Date: 23 December 1927
Route: New York, US to Copenhagen, Denmark
Aeroplane: *Dawn*
Crew: Oskar Omdal, Brice 'Goldy' Goldsborough and Fred Koehler
Backers: Ancker-Grayson Aircraft Corporation

Hon Elsie Mackay (Poppy Wyndham)
Flight Date: 13 March 1928
Route: Cranwell, Lincolnshire, UK to Long Island

Aeroplane: *Endeavour*
Crew: WGR Hinchliffe, ('Hinch')
Backers: Self-funded

Mabel Boll
Flight Date: 26 June 1928
Route: New York, US via Harbour Grace, Newfoundland, Canada to Europe
Aeroplane: *Columbia*
Co-pilots: Oliver Le Boutillier and Arthur Argles
Backers: Self-funded and Charles Levine

Amelia Earhart
Flight Date: 17 June 1928
Route: Trepassey, Newfoundland to Southampton, UK.
Aeroplane: *Friendship*
Crew: Bill Stultz and Slim Gordon
Backers: Amy Guest

Amelia Earhart
Flight Date: 20 May 1932
Route: Harbour Grace, Newfoundland to Paris, France
Aeroplane: *Little Red Bus*
Crew: Solo
Backers: Various sponsorship deals

Note on names:
After their first use, surnames have, where possible, been used, unless repetition of the given name helps to avoid confusion.

I have followed the convention used in the worlds of flying and sailing by referring to ships and aircraft by the feminine form.

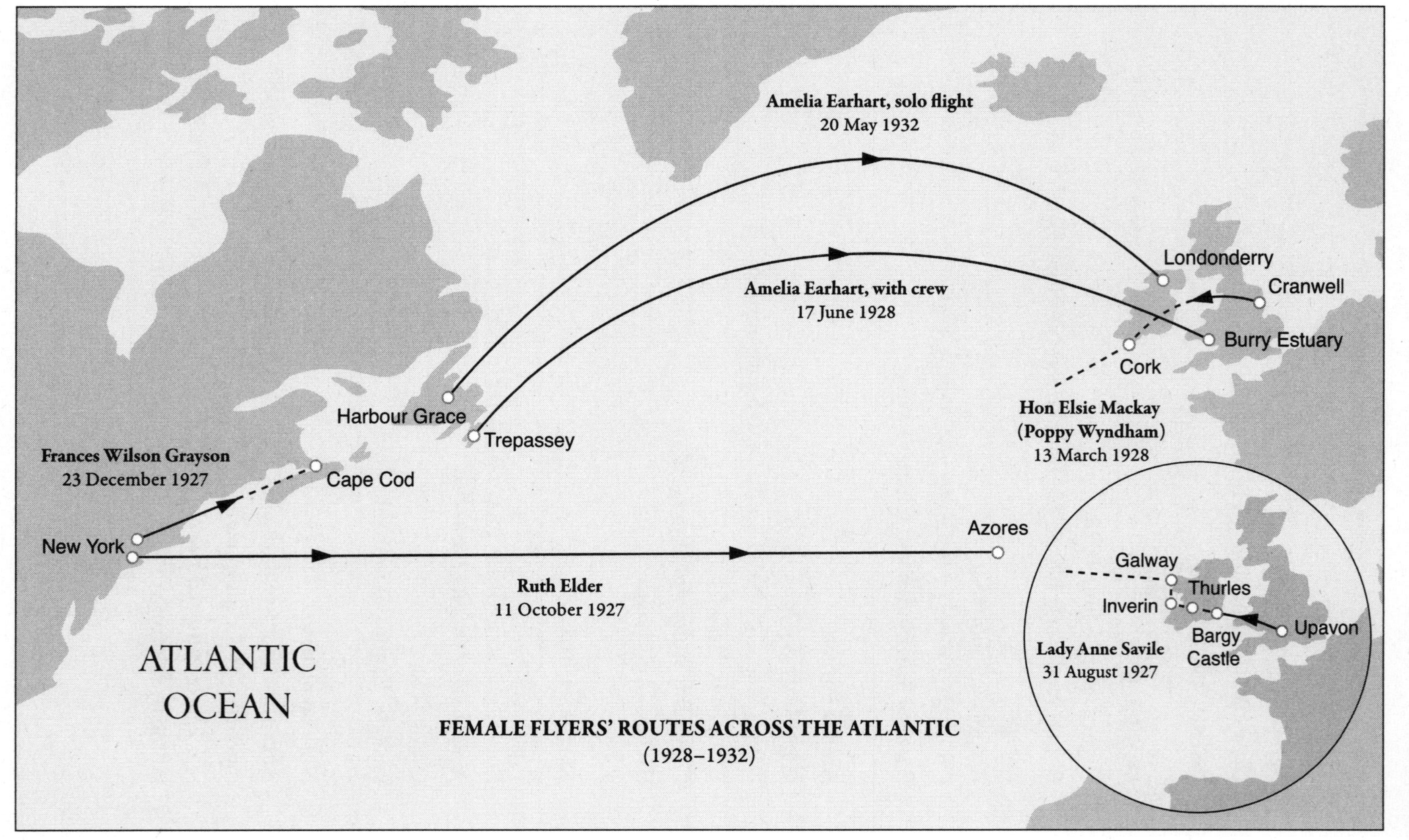

FEMALE FLYERS' ROUTES ACROSS THE ATLANTIC
(1928–1932)

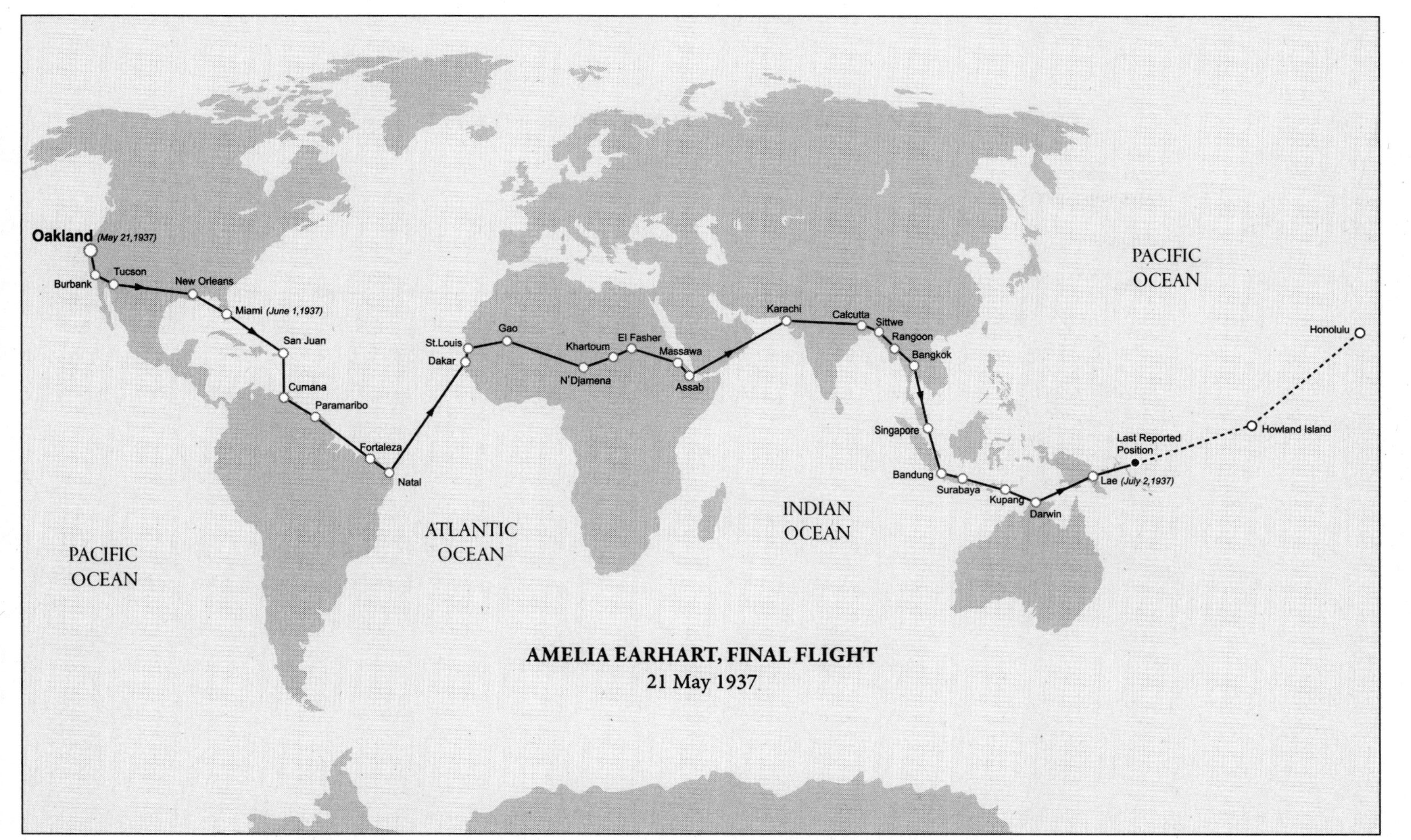
Oakland (May 21,1937)
Burbank
Tucson
New Orleans
Miami (June 1,1937)
San Juan
Cumana
Paramaribo
Fortaleza
Natal
St.Louis
Dakar
Gao
Khartoum
N'Djamena
El Fasher
Massawa
Assab
Karachi
Calcutta
Sittwe
Rangoon
Bangkok
Singapore
Bandung
Surabaya
Kupang
Darwin
Lae (July 2,1937)
Last Reported Position
Howland Island
Honolulu
PACIFIC OCEAN
ATLANTIC OCEAN
INDIAN OCEAN
PACIFIC OCEAN
AMELIA EARHART, FINAL FLIGHT
21 May 1937

PART ONE

The Lure of the Atlantic

PRELUDE

June 1928

Trepassey, Newfoundland, 3 pm, 4 June 1928

It was probably the most exciting day in the school's history and one that few of its pupils would ever forget. The deep rumble from the skies was the first clue that something unusual was above the fog.[1] The children leapt up from their desks to press their faces to the windows as the nuns tried to restore order.[2] But the teachers could not compete with the spectacle of an orange and gold plane circling the harbour, and the students abandoned their books to swarm past the Holy Redeemer Church and down to the waterside.[3] The adults, too, were unable to conceal their excitement and gathered on the beach as the plane touched down with the help of pontoons that made the aircraft look like it was wearing giant boots. The plane's name, *Friendship*, was stamped on its side in bold capital letters.

The small fishing community of Trepassey in a remote, eastern corner of Newfoundland had, over the years, experienced its fair share of unexpected visitors, but the Fokker F.VII represented a blast of modernity. Four hundred years before pilots began their quest to cross the Atlantic, sixteenth-century fishing fleets had used Trepassey as a supply depot before heading back to England after a season's fishing. It may have been French sailors who named the town using the word 'trepassé' – a reference to those who had passed on to the afterlife. The description echoed the shipwrecks that litter that part of the coast. Other nearby places, like Mistaken Point and False Cape, are even more blatant in pointing out the harshness of life on the edge of the Atlantic.

Trepassey is perched on the Avalon Peninsula, a title that gives it a mystical, Arthurian association and one that is entirely fitting for a region where some people still believe in fairies. Visitors to the settlement in the seventeenth century commented on how wolves mingled freely with domesticated dogs. The settlement passed to and fro between French and British control and was always vulnerable to attack by pirates who might suddenly appear at the mouth of the harbour – as the famous English pirate Black Bart did in 1720, forcing inhabitants to flee to the woods. The pirates burnt landing areas and houses and, according to one account, Black Bart took a local woman for his wife.

A decade before *Friendship* arrived, aviation provided the greatest hullabaloo since Black Bart's marauding visit when, in May 1919, three unwieldy US flying boats, each with a wingspan of 126 feet, supported by ten US warships and around 8,500 US naval crew descended on the harbour. The hungry men quickly stripped the shelves of the town's only shop before establishing their own tented canteen as a base from which to launch an attempt to be the first plane to cross the Atlantic – albeit skimming across the ocean like a pebble making several quick stops, rather than flying direct. The Curtiss NC-4 arrived ten days later in Lisbon, having travelled via the Azores. Its achievement slipped off the news agenda a week later when Alcock and Brown made the first non-stop crossing, setting off from Newfoundland's capital St John's, 157 km north of Trepassey. Eight years later, and three days after Charles Lindbergh had become the first person to cross the Atlantic solo, the Italian Francesco di Pinedo took off from Trepassey on the final leg of his 124-day, around-the-world trip.

*

As *Friendship* settled in the harbour on 4 June 1928, she was surrounded by rowing boats that tried to lasso her in a way that prompted one of the plane's occupants, Amelia Earhart, to describe them as 'maritime cowboys'.[4] During the flight east from Halifax in Nova Scotia to Trepassey, where they would start their bid to cross the Atlantic, Earhart had crouched in the cabin next to added fuel tanks. Now she crawled through to the cockpit to take photos of their reception and 'convulsed with laughter' at the mayhem.[5] She compared *Friendship*'s arrival to a 'rodeo' as twelve small boats frantically circled the plane.[6] A man stood in the bow of each, whirling a rope above his head as he prepared to lasso the plane. The aircraft's twenty-seven-year-old mechanic and co-pilot, Texan Louis 'Slim' Gordon climbed onto the pontoon and yelled at them to stop, but the noise of the small boats and the plane's idling motors swept his voice away with the wind.[7] Pilot, Wilmer 'Bill' Stultz was concerned that one of the ropes would get caught in the propellers or that the welcome party itself would drift too close to their deadly blades. The highlight for Earhart came when one rope hit Gordon and nearly knocked him off his perch. Eventually a Paramount cameraman[8] asserted order by circling them in his own launch as the town magistrate transported Earhart and Stultz to the shore in a rowing boat,[9] while Gordon followed after making sure the plane was properly secured. The crowd responded with three cheers. Earhart later wrote that she had never had a more entertaining half hour.

Friendship's arrival from Halifax caused a rumpus in a community more attuned to the quieter and more predictable comings and goings of fishing boats, but this was nothing compared to the shock which rippled through the onlookers as they realised that one of the crew was female and – even more shockingly – dressed in men's clothing.

*

Earhart, who was a few weeks shy of her thirty-first birthday, was a tall, lean – some might say gaunt – woman in brown jodhpurs and knee-high leather boots. She wore a helmet tied under her chin and goggles pushed onto her forehead. Local resident Laura Devereaux, who was ten at the time, remembers being shocked at what she was wearing but still thinking her 'lovely'.[10]

A cloud of white pinafores and aprons swept towards Earhart as the town's schoolchildren rushed to greet her. She assumed they'd been let out early to welcome the plane. In fact, they would be given a detention for abandoning their class and Earhart made the situation worse by later visiting the school and scandalising the nuns by wearing trousers. They were probably also nonplussed by her freckled and tanned complexion at a time when women of her class did their best to avoid any hint that they were used to spending time outdoors.

Fannie Devereaux ('Mrs D' as Earhart called her) was also overcome by the sight of a woman in breeches and couldn't resist touching her to convince herself she wasn't an apparition. Mrs D, who ran a general store from her wooden house, had a chance to observe her at close quarters when Earhart, Stultz, and Gordon spent the night at their home. Their daughter moved out to make way for them and Earhart was able to sink into a feather bed.

The three visitors sincerely hoped it would be a brief stay and that they would be back in the air and on their way to making Earhart the first woman to cross the Atlantic by plane as soon as possible. They had already been forced by bad weather to break their journey at Halifax and now they were trapped at Trepassey waiting for better conditions. Folklore claims that eastern Newfoundland is blighted by fog because God was so disappointed by his efforts that he used it to obscure his handywork. A more scientific theory points to the Gulf Stream colliding with the cold waters of the North.[11] As well as the fog, high winds, which would have aided their journey once in flight, made it too risky for *Friendship*, with its heavy load of fuel, to take off. As their enforced stay dragged on, Earhart, who had not packed a change of clothes, was forced to buy a 90c, green, checked, long-sleeved, and modest 'Mother Hubbard' dress and a pair of tan hose. She borrowed shoes, a skirt, and slip and washed everything else.[12]

The visitors had to concentrate to understand their hosts, who spoke with an Irish accent that would have been instantly recognisable 2,000 miles across the Atlantic in Waterford, Kilkenny, or Cork. Their speech was a legacy of the late eighteenth century when English fishing companies brought young men over – mainly to help with the summer cod catches. Interpreting the cadence, which still persists today, can feel like tuning out the static on an old wireless set.[13]

As *Friendship*'s crew settled in with the Devereauxs they had to get used to conversation peppered with Irish words and speech patterns and a hard 'd' or 't' used instead of 'th'. Earhart described the language as 'peculiar'; there were too many 'r's and often an 'oi' sound where one didn't belong. Her first meal was a dinner of chicken, dandelions, and 'badadoes' (potatoes), and her profession had been transformed from 'pilot' to 'poilet'.[14]

As well as sounding Irish, it may have occurred to Earhart, Stultz, and Gordon that Trepassey *looked* like Ireland, their nearest landfall: the landscape is vividly green, with a rugged coastline. When the mist descends it can feel as if there's a lid on the world, but when the sun comes out nothing's as bright as the sea and sky. Only the distinctive, jaunty, red and white Cape Race lighthouse, which honked out its mournful fog warnings to passing ships, made it feel more North American than Irish.

In Trepassey, Earhart, who was born in Kansas, deep in America's Mid-West, had a chance to observe at close quarters the Atlantic she was so desperate to cross. She was immediately aware of its power and how the coast was a 'graveyard of wrecked ships'.[15] Mrs D's house was full of hooked rugs, some made from cotton washed ashore twenty years ago from a lost ship.[16] Much of the silver she saw in the fishermen's homes bore the names of vessels that had disappeared in the Atlantic.[17] She might also have heard of the many superstitions that governed a community so dependent on the ocean's whims for their livelihood. They were visiting at the tail end of iceberg season, when it was common to see great bluey white edifices that could tower above a house and, like cloud formations, shift into all sorts of uncanny shapes, from fantastical creatures to holy figures, such as the Virgin Mary that was said to have floated through the narrows of St John's in 1905. The most famous iceberg, less than two decades earlier, was the one that sank the *Titanic* in 1912, killing over 1,500 people, just 400 miles off the coast of Newfoundland.[18] Cape Race was the first to receive the distress signal.

In other circumstances, Earhart would have enjoyed her stay at Trepassey. Her background as a social worker in Boston had made her comfortable around young people, and she relaxed in their company at Trepassey. She might have been on holiday with Stultz and Gordon as they played gin rummy, fished for trout, and held musical evenings. Their soirées were limited by Trepassey's modest resources: two gramophone records, a guitar harp, and a piano – from which Gordon extracted painful versions of 'Jingle Bells'. Earhart gazed out at the Atlantic and took photos of a place and people clinging to the very edge of the continent.

From the Devereauxs' house she could hear the sea, even if the fog stopped her from seeing it, and the susurrating waves from both Trepassey Harbour, and behind her in Mutton Bay, provided a rhythm as regular as a plane's engine. People who live in the Irish Loop, the potholed coastal route that meanders its away around Newfoundland's eastern peninsular, are fond of saying that it's possible to experience all four seasons in one day. Weather dominates their lives to the extent that they have words that could only hold currency in Newfoundland.

'Mauzy' denotes a warm fog and 'caplin weather' describes the wet, foggy days of June and July when the caplin fish spawn. It's then that great humpback whales prowl the coast and the water boils with fish, driven to the surface moments before a pair of mighty jaws appears to scoop them up and into its delicate pink mouth.

As the days stretched into nearly a fortnight, any pretence of a vacation faded in an agony of frustration. The three of them felt trapped and tormented by their individual demons. Gordon was the most easy-going of the three, a 'cheery, whole-hearted youth' as one description put it.[19] He had learnt his trade in the Army Air Corps as pilot and mechanic and after the First World War had amassed a particular knowledge of planes with three engines.[20]

Stultz had already been employed by two other Atlantic hopefuls: Mabel Boll and Frances Wilson Grayson. A British journalist described him as:

> . . . short, almost stiffly built. He has a face in which the features are advertisements of hardiness, every one short, stiff and sharp. His nose curves out almost pugnaciously, his skin has the weathered brown of old ivory, his eyes are the tawny colour of a lion's, and, though he is only 28, his hair is powder-grey, rising square off his forehead.[21]

He was known to resort to alcohol and Earhart grew increasingly concerned about his heavy drinking.[22] With 500 hours' flying under her belt, she hoped to take her turn at the controls, but the risks involved – made all too stark by the deaths of several crews who had attempted to cross the Atlantic in the past nine months – meant she would always have to bow to his expertise. Moreover, her flying had been mainly in single- or twin-engine planes and she lacked experience in flying solely by instruments, without the aid of landmarks. She had yet to be tested by the hypnotising combination of sky and waves alone.

However, her role as leader of the expedition was undisputed and had been set out in a legal document drawn up by an attorney on 18 May 1928 in which it was stated that, when *Friendship* arrived at Trepassey, 'if any questions of policy, procedure, personnel or any other questions arise the decision of Miss Amelia M. Earhart is to be final. That she is to have control of the plane and of the disposal of the services of all employees as fully as if she were the owner.'[23] Her authority was reinforced by the fact that the document was drawn up by an attorney authorised by Earhart's sponsor, the Anglo-American millionaire, Amy Guest, whose husband was British MP, Frederick Guest, cousin of the future wartime leader, Winston Churchill. Although it would be months before they finally met, Guest's involvement would change the course of Earhart's life.

What made the waiting so agonising for *Friendship*'s crew was the knowledge that a rival bid, with another female at its head, was ready for the off about 100 miles, as the Atlantic puffin flies, to the north of Trepassey, in the bustling fishing town of Harbour Grace. This competing team was also watching the weather for a sign that they could risk launching their heavily laden aeroplane out into the Atlantic.

*

While Earhart left letters, logbooks, and a whole treasure trove of other sources, Mabel Boll's motives are harder to fathom. We hear her voice in newspaper articles and find her name – in all its various permutations – in official records such as marriage licences and passenger lists.

Boll was born in Rochester, upstate New York, one of three children. Her paternal grandparents had been German, and her father worked as a bartender before prohibition made him redundant and he was forced to earn a living as a porter.[24] It was a modest home but her parents managed to send her to a convent school. One of her first jobs was as a clerk in a cigar store[25] and legend suggested that her striking blue eyes, blonde hair, and vivacious personality provided the opportunity to work in cabaret.[26] But when she married the businessman Robert Scott I, everything pointed to a life of steady domesticity and a gentle climb up the social ladder. They had a son together and lived in Atlanta for nearly a year in 1917, where he was in charge of the southern branch of a sugar company. From here they moved to Cuba.[27]

On the face of it, Boll had made good, but being the wife of a successful businessman was not enough. By 1920 the marriage was over and she was on her way to Europe, her profession described as 'artist', her residence in England, the Savoy Hotel.[28] Like many women in the 1920s, marriage had offered an escape route from a small-town existence but her next alliance changed her life beyond recognition and provided her the sort of power normally only enjoyed by men and women who had inherited wealth. Her second husband, Hernando Rocha (also known as Rocha Schloss or Rocha-Schioos) was a coffee planter or rancher from Colombia, South America, and gave her $1 million as a wedding gift.[29] She spent the money on diamonds, a chateau in the suburbs of Paris, and a villa on the French Riviera.[30]

Despite her humble upbringing, Boll instantly took to the persona afforded by this generosity. She liked to wear thirty-three diamond bracelets from shoulder to wrist on one arm when she attended parties and the jeweller Cartier once estimated that the gems on her left hand alone were worth $400,000.[31] It was reported that armed guards accompanied her on evenings when she was weighed down with her bounty.[32] One reporter marvelled at the tendency for diamonds to 'fairly leap out of men's pockets and fasten themselves on Mabel'.[33] She quickly became known as the 'Queen of Diamonds'. Rarely mentioned was her son, brought up by his grandparents, although she would drive to visit them in her green Rolls-Royce.[34] She paid them $50 a week on condition that her father refrained from working in a speakeasy.[35]

As one reporter put it, her sparkling appearance caused 'extravagant tales to spring up about her as thick as the pigeons around the New York Public Library'.[36] But she also ruffled feathers in France, where she unsettled the pecking order in the cafes, casinos, and clubs of Biarritz, Paris, and Nice. She preferred the company of men but became friendly with the Dolly Sisters, who shared her interests in gambling, flirting, and flying. Rosie and Jenny were Hungarian-American identical twin dancers, singers, and actresses who moved to Europe after the First World War where at least one of them became the lover of department store owner, Harry Gordon Selfridge.

Boll's obvious enjoyment of her wealth would probably have gone unremarked upon in a man; in a woman, her activities were pounced on by a press eager for salacious stories. She enjoyed attending boxing matches at Madison Square Garden at a time when it was unusual to see a woman in the baying crowd. One journalist noted astutely, 'Behind the casualness of her poise, one senses an eagerness on tip-toe for a new thrill.'[37] She liked to be noticed and when she visited Childs', a chain known for its affordable and hygienic restaurants, which became a national institution, she brought her own delicate teacup rather than drink out of a cruder piece of crockery.[38]

She clearly enjoyed turning heads, but flying – even as a passenger – was an unorthodox and highly dangerous way to ensure she was remembered for something other than her diamonds. She pestered pilots to make her dream of crossing the Atlantic possible and finally found her match in Charles Levine, who owned *Columbia,* built by his Columbia Aircraft Company. In June 1927, the plane had carried him from New York to the outskirts of Berlin, a feat that was over 300 miles and nine hours, six minutes longer than Lindbergh's transatlantic crossing and which bestowed on him the title of first transatlantic air passenger. The achievement was particularly satisfying for Levine because Lindbergh had beaten him to the prize of first solo crossing of the Atlantic.

Just as Boll is often described as 'flamboyant New York socialite' so Levine attracts phrases such as 'millionaire playboy'. He was a pugnacious, balding man whose father had made his fortune as a New York scrap metal dealer. Levine Junior amassed his own wealth by winning a contract with the US War Department in 1917 to buy and dispose of shell casings.[39] Boll and Levine were widely believed to be lovers,[40] and the way in which he casually places his hand on her lower back to assist her into the plane as *Columbia* prepares to leave New York for Newfoundland seems to confirm that intimacy.[41]

Earlier that year, on 5 March 1928, Boll had taken her make-shift seat in *Columbia* as a passenger on the first non-stop flight from New York to Cuba with Stultz at the controls. She assumed he would join her transatlantic bid and was furious that Earhart's team lured him over to their side.[42]

It is tempting to dismiss Boll simply as an attention-seeker, but her desire to fly the Atlantic was genuine. 'It's such an absurd title. But Queen of the Air! I should be very proud to deserve that,' she told reporters.[43] Her rivals took her seriously and the knowledge that she was planning a transatlantic attempt gave Earhart's team a heightened sense of urgency. In the summer of 1928, she was very much a contender.

Boll was about thirty-five when she landed in Harbour Grace. *About* because, as soon as she was old enough to know that age counted, she started to shave years off her birth date so that by the time of her death she'd lost six years.[44] Rocha had been killed in a car accident a few weeks before she arrived in Newfoundland, and she was now a very wealthy widow.[45]

*

Harbour Grace is situated at Conception Bay, about sixty miles northwest of St John's. In 1928, before it was largely destroyed by a fire started in 1944, the port was an energetic town that saw itself as competing with St John's to become the capital of Newfoundland. Local people welcomed flyers with enthusiasm and would wave white sheets and send up columns of smoke to pilots who appeared to have lost their way.[46]

Thousands came to see Boll arrive from Roosevelt Field, New York when they landed at Harbour Grace on the evening of Tuesday 12 June 1928. She had a cramped spot behind the cockpit but there was never any suggestion that she would take control of *Columbia*. She left that to Oliver Le Boutillier and relief pilot and navigator, Arthur 'Bert' Argles. Her first question was: 'Has the *Friendship* hopped off yet? Great! Our chances are even.'[47]

As the two teams waited on the very edge of North America, ready to embark across 2,000 miles of lonely ocean, they were acutely aware of what was at stake and of the many lives that had been lost trying to do what they wanted so badly to do. They knew that their names would be forever linked with four other women who had taken on the Atlantic and achieved varying degrees of success: Ruth Elder, the girl-next-door from Alabama; the Scottish socialite, Hon Elsie Mackay; Lady Anne Savile, at 63 the oldest of the contenders; and the wealthy real estate investor, Frances Grayson.

But, for Boll and Earhart, the priority was just being able to take to the air. As *Time* magazine put it: 'Both [teams] made false starts; both panted at the leash of bad weather.'[48]

CHAPTER ONE

The First Attempts

Twenty-seven years before Amelia Earhart and Mabel Boll waited at different ends of the Avalon Peninsula for weather conditions to lift, an Italian physicist and his assistant, George Kemp, were also battling against Newfoundland's irascible climate. In December 1901 Guglielmo Marconi was intent on proving that the Atlantic could be crossed by wireless telegraphy – the transmission of a message using radio waves rather than wires – and, like Earhart and Boll, hoped this new form of technology would bring the two continents closer.

Exactly what Marconi was planning puzzled the press, and the local people of St John's, as they gazed up at the abandoned TB isolation hospital clinging to the rocky outlet of Signal Hill as it leans out into the Atlantic Ocean. Marconi and his team laboured away in the weeks before Christmas and looked down to catch brief glimpses of the busy harbour, but mostly it was shrouded in mist.

The Italian with his neat moustache and elegant Norfolk jacket was obviously serious about his intentions – so serious that his venture was cloaked in secrecy. But the equipment he demanded – large sheets of zinc, two balloons and six kites – suggested a crackpot scheme, a venture somewhere between a scientific experiment and a children's party.

At the start of his career Marconi had abandoned his home in Italy for Britain, where enthusiastic investors funded the manufacture of radio sets capable of sending and receiving messages in Morse code. In 1897 he proved their effectiveness by propelling a wireless message across six kilometres of the Bristol Channel. The message read, 'Are you ready?'

The missive was as much a provocation as a question. If radio waves could cross open water – and if the distance could be extended from the Bristol Channel to an ocean as vast as the Atlantic – this achievement would have huge implications for the world. Marconi's wireless telegraphy presented a mortal threat to the telegraph companies who monopolised the way countries spoke to each other and who had invested huge sums in cables to facilitate that dialogue. Marconi's discovery also challenged the way warships and commercial vessels kept in touch. Wireless telegraphy promised to make signalling by light and semaphore as arcane as pigeon post. The safe delivery of a message across the Atlantic would be as significant for international relations and the world of communication as the first flights across the same stretch of water.

His experiment sought to overturn the widely held belief that electromagnetic (radio) waves travel in a straight line. Marconi believed that these waves tapped out in Morse code from an equally remote site, 3,500 kilometres (2,100 miles) away in Cornwall, on England's western coast, would follow the earth's curvature until they reached the other side of the Atlantic rather than following a straight line that threatened to bounce them heavenwards into oblivion.[1] Unlike the transatlantic pilots who would follow him, Marconi preferred to keep his plans secret in case his venture failed.

Each day Marconi battled up Signal Hill in the bitter cold, where local men had been enlisted to wrangle a series of balloons and kites into place to help keep the antennae upright in the powerful winds. Inside the deserted hospital Marconi clamped a headset to his ear and listened. At exactly the same time as Marconi and Kemp went through their daily ritual, scientists in Poldhu, Cornwall tapped out three dots – the Morse code for 'S' and the letter thought most easy to distinguish. They could only hope that their counterparts at Signal Hill were still listening and that the dots had not been blown away by Cornish storms.

Finally, on 12 December Marconi and Kemp both thought they detected the sound, 'dot, dot, dot'. However, it was hardly a ringing endorsement of the potential of wireless telegraphy and because communication across the Atlantic was so poor it took several days for the news to reach British newspapers. On page five *The Times*, Tuesday 17 December, noted: 'Most of the New York papers are apparently waiting for irrefragable proof that Signor Marconi has succeeded in obtaining signals from the other side of the Atlantic before commenting on the subject.'

As Marconi's key witness was also his assistant, who was hardly likely to query whether his boss had mistaken the keening of the wind for a message from Cornwall, that 'irrefragable proof' was never likely to appear, and eventually the newspapers were satisfied that, as a 'man of science', Marconi should be trusted.[2] He was back at Newfoundland in 1904 to install a wireless station at Cape Race, twenty miles east of Trepassey. It was this station that claimed to have been the first to have received the SOS plea from the stricken *Titanic* on 15 April 1912.[3]

Marconi's invention helped to modernise perceptions of the Atlantic. One such notion, that the vast expanse was made up of layers of debris captured like insects in amber, now seemed outdated. This perception relied on the nineteenth-century conviction that once you reached a certain depth water became so dense that it slowed the descent of objects. Items cast into the sea, therefore, found their own level, depending on their weight. This theory applied to bodies and, according to some believers, the added burden of a guilty conscience or the weight of sins would drag a corpse further towards the seabed.

An ocean the size of the Atlantic was awash with stratified debris: lost babies eternally separated from their parents, pious clergy floating above murderous pirates; ship's vermin looking down on unfortunate horses and cattle.[4] Marconi's achievement replaced this fanciful notion of a stretch of water littered with corpses arranged according to the value of their soul and brought a much more scientific approach to the understanding of the water that divided two continents..

Just over a decade later, Lord Northcliffe, who owned the *Daily Mail* and who knew a good story when he saw one, boosted interest in the Atlantic and how to cross it by offering a prize of £10,000 for the first non-stop flight over the ocean by a heavier-than-air vehicle, that is, excluding a hot air balloon or a zeppelin.[5] The start of the First World War paused the competition but Northcliffe re-issued his challenge at its conclusion in 1918. There were three rules: the starting point had to be Great Britain, Canada, Newfoundland (at the time a self-governing dominion), or the United States; the flight had to be non-stop, and to be completed within seventy-two hours. The War provided an unwitting impetus to the contest by advancing the capability of the aeroplane and produced a surfeit of pilots looking to earn a living and willing to risk their lives.

The British pilots John Alcock and Arthur Whitten Brown arrived in the summer of 1919 at St John's to make their attempt on the record in a modified, open cockpit First World War Vickers Vimy bomber biplane, which had been shipped over in crates and carefully reassembled for the attempt. Both men had served in the First World War, and both had spent time in enemy prisoner-of-war camps: Alcock in Turkey, after ditching into the sea, and Brown in Germany, having been shot down over France.[6]

Their expedition would assume epic proportions over the years – like the tales of Viking voyagers who left their homelands in Scandinavia to follow an uncertain horizon.[7] When, deep into their flight, rain turned to hail and then to snow, they noticed that the engines had lost their regular beat as the snow was blocking the fuel gauges. Brown felt he had no option but to pull off his mittens, stand up and pick his way through the supports and on to the wing. There was a moment when Alcock tried to stop him and they had a brief, mid-air tussle before Brown, who was still troubled by a wartime leg injury and walked with a stick, continued across the wing where his feet slipped on the icy surface. Painfully, he extracted a jack-knife from his pocket and chipped away at the ice, a few, perilous inches away from the propeller; the exhaust roaring in his face, his whole body tensed against the slipstream. He managed to clear the air intakes and make his way with care back to his seat. Brown was said to have repeated this feat five times.[8]

Alcock's response to a reporter, on their arrival about sixteen hours after leaving Newfoundland, summed up the extreme conditions they'd endured: 'We did not suffer from cold or exhaustion except when looking over the side; then the sleet chewed bits out of our faces.'[9]

On 21 June both pilots were knighted, but Alcock enjoyed his celebrity status for only six months. On 18 December 1919 he set out solo to deliver a Vickers Viking amphibian to Paris, where it was due to be exhibited at the Aeronautical Exhibition. But fog forced the plane down about twenty-five miles from Rouen and his skull was fractured on landing. He died in hospital, without having regained consciousness.[10] Brown never flew again after the death of his navigator.[11]

Despite the publicity in North America and Europe surrounding the achievement, Alcock and Brown's crossing failed to persuade many people that aeroplane was the best way to fly the Atlantic. Britain's Air Ministry had been lukewarm about the attempt and its only support came in the form of loaning wireless and navigation equipment. It saw airships as a safer and more reliable form of long-distance air travel. Less than a month after their flight, the Air Ministry's stately R34 airship, nicknamed 'Tiny' due to its huge size, crossed the Atlantic, though at a much more sedate speed – on average forty-three miles per hour.[12] The massive, hydrogen-filled vessel, crewed by thirty men bobbed its way to New York and spent three days in New Jersey before heading back to Pulham in east Norfolk. R34 achieved the first ever east/west flight – in four and a half days – and the first return voyage.[13]

It was to be another eight years, inspired by another prize, before a second aeroplane crossed the Atlantic – and this feat would be even more impressive because the crossing extended to France and was achieved solo. Raymond Orteig, who started life as a shepherd in the French Pyrenees, moved to New York, where he worked his way up from the role of bar porter to become waiter, head waiter, and hotel manager. Orteig saved enough money to buy the Lafayette and then the Brevoort hotels in Manhattan. He was so inspired by the way France and the US had collaborated during the Great War that he followed the *Daily Mail*'s example and offered $25,000 to the first aviator to cross the Atlantic. His challenge would require pilots to fly much further – between Orteig's two homes of America and France. They must achieve the flight, without stopping, in a heavier-than-air vehicle in one leg from Paris to New York, or vice versa. Initially, the competition was restricted to pilots who had fought on the Allied side in the First World War but this rule was lifted in 1924.[14] Orteig and Northcliffe were as consumed by the challenge of the Atlantic crossing as Elon Musk, Jeff Bezos, and Richard Branson would be a century later as they considered how their vast wealth might be used to extend human travel into outer space.

To begin with, even the most daring of pilots could not permit their imagination to stretch to Paris so long as their planes lacked the technical capability to go those extra miles. The fact that the first attempts ended in tragedy appeared to confirm the wisdom of this hesitancy, or even to warn of a *Titanic* level of hubris.

In September 1926 France's celebrated flying ace René Fonck, reputed to have shot down seventy-five planes in the First World War, thus making him among the most deadly of the Allies' pilots, was the first serious contender to throw his flying helmet into the ring.[15] On the morning of 21 September his S-35, three-engine biplane sat waiting on the runway at Roosevelt Field on Long Island. The luggage for the four-man crew included flotation bags in case they were forced down, as well as a hot 'celebration' dinner to be consumed when they landed in France and a last-minute order of croissants to boost their spirits before take-off.[16] A large crowd had gathered and stared in horror as the plane lurched into a ditch at the end of the runway. There was a moment's silence before an explosion rocked the air. Only Fonck and one other crew member managed to drag themselves away from the fireball.

Despite the horrific accident, the following April, Noel Davis, a former US Naval Air Corps pilot, and Stanton Wooster, a serving military pilot, planned the crossing in a Keystone K-47 Pathfinder biplane. The two men, who were worried about the heavy fuel load needed for the journey, tested the plane at an Army base in Virginia. On what was planned as its final test flight the Pathfinder struggled to gain height and suddenly lost speed before plunging into a pond. Both pilots were killed.[17]

The knowledge that they were flying cheek by jowl with such a flammable cargo haunted every pilot who attempted the Atlantic crossing. Take-off is one of the most perilous moments in any flight and the extra weight added by the fuel needed to make long-distance journeys threatens to destabilise the plane. Worries about the start of their journey were uppermost in the minds of the three American teams who were busying themselves with their own ocean preparations on Long Island in May 1927. Like modern Formula One teams, they finetuned their machines to push them to their technical limits, knowing that lives depended on these readjustments. Richard Byrd and Floyd Bennett were doing their best to repair their Fokker aircraft, *America*, which had crashed during a test flight. Byrd and Bennett were already national heroes after their flight to the North Pole the previous year (although doubts have subsequently been raised about whether they actually reached their destination). At Curtiss Field, an airstrip next to Roosevelt Field, Charles Levine's *Columbia* was also preparing to join the race. For many, *Columbia* was the favourite because it had already set an endurance record by flying for fifty-one hours without refuelling.[18] A year later Mabel Boll would be sitting in the same aeroplane at Harbour Grace waiting for the right weather to allow her to race Amelia Earhart's *Friendship* to Britain.

In the hangar next to Levine's, a twenty-five-year-old pilot called Charles Lindbergh was calmly tending to a monoplane, *Spirit of St Louis*, which had been specially designed for the crossing. Lindbergh grew up in Little Falls, Minnesota, the only son of Charles and Evangeline. His parents split up when he was seven and his father, who was born in Sweden, went on to be a well-known congressman who opposed America's entry into the First World War. Charles began engineering college but dropped out to learn to fly and quickly became one of a group of young men – and a few women – seduced by flying circuses that toured North America and Britain at the end of the First World War. He'd bought a Curtiss JN-4 ('Jenny') and made a living by offering short flights in the southern and Midwest states. In 1926 he became an airmail pilot and took advantage of new legislation that transferred air mail operations to private companies – a development that gave the commercial aviation industry the fillip it needed to carry America's mail across vast distances.[19]

While three different bids were gearing up at Long Island, Orteig's compatriots and former First World War veterans Charles Nungesser and François Coli were preparing to attempt the crossing from the more difficult east-west route – they would be battling against fierce winds blowing from the opposite direction. Although their plane was called the *Oiseau Blanc* (White Bird) they added a black skull and crossbones and a coffin, incongruously contained in a heart, on its fuselage. The implication being that a strong heart doesn't fear death.[20]

The navigator, Coli, appeared to reinforce their image as aerial pirates by wearing an eye patch.

They set off on 8 May, despite worrying reports of bad weather out at sea, and the following day French newspapers announced that they had landed in New York. However, these bulletins turned out to be premature and the wild celebrations that had erupted all over France turned into a vigil for their safe return. Extensive searches of Newfoundland and the eastern coast of America failed to find any sign of the aeroplane, and Orteig's $25,000 reward failed to rouse any information about their fate.

Meanwhile, the two pilots in the running to fly Levine's plane fought a very public battle. Lloyd Bertaud, an expert navigator and pilot, obtained an injunction restraining Levine from going back on his commitment to include him in the team, but his legal case was eventually dismissed. The unseemly battle placed Clarence Chamberlin in the pilot's seat but also gave Lindbergh enough time to complete his preparations and slip away on 20 May.

Lindbergh made it look easy. When, thirty-three hours, thirty minutes, and thirty seconds later – a pleasingly memorable time for the punctilious pilot – he landed at Le Bourget airfield and unfolded his six-foot-three-inch frame from the cramped cockpit of the *Spirit of St Louis*, he instantly became one of the most famous men in the world. Although Orteig's business was suffering from the US Government's prohibition on selling alcohol, he was, nevertheless, relieved to hand over the promised reward. Six men had died in attempts to win the prize and Lindbergh's success meant Orteig would have no more deaths on his conscience.

Lindbergh's achievement ignited Atlantic fever. Now pilots and their backers wanted to fly further and faster than *The Spirit of St Louis*. They wanted to cross the Atlantic from east to west and to push their engines beyond France. Among the accolades was one of the most sought-after titles: the first woman to fly the Atlantic.

CHAPTER TWO

Girls Will Be Girls

There was still heat in the Californian sun that day in December 1920 as Anita Snook, known as 'Neta' or 'Snooky', leant against her biplane at Kinner Airport on Long Beach Boulevard, south of Los Angeles.[1] She took off her helmet and rubbed the bridge of her nose where her googles had been digging in and wished that this was her final lesson of the day. Her assistant had already passed the leather coat, helmet, and goggles to her next student and was going through the mantra he was obliged to deliver to each passenger:

Don't touch the controls,

Don't put your feet on the rudder,

Keep your hands in your lap,

Don't look out from behind the windshield or the propeller's slipstream will rip off your goggles.

The customer, who was almost certainly male, asked whether the assistant would tell Snook not to go too high as he'd never been in a plane before and never with a woman at the controls.

Snook started to tuck her hair, which was still damp from perspiration, back under her helmet when a tall, slender young woman and an older man approached. The woman was wearing a simple, brown, well-cut suit and had arranged her hair in a plait coiled around her head. She had a scarf at her neck and carried gloves. The man wore a blue serge suit.

The woman introduced herself and, as she could see Snook was busy, quickly asked whether she would teach her to fly. While they chatted, the woman couldn't take her eyes off the plane and lightly stroked the tip of the wing. They agreed to meet the next day.[2]

Snook later said she had liked Amelia Earhart the minute she'd set eyes on her. She found her directness appealing and they quickly struck up a friendship that was more sisterly than one of instructor and student. Snook grew used to Earhart carrying something to read, which could be anything from a book about Islam to a volume of poetry by Christina Rossetti. They had their first lesson on 3 January 1921 and then went up when the weather would allow – often it was too foggy or windy for a novice. They enjoyed driving a borrowed open-top car with Snook's Great Dane standing on the backseat, his front paws resting on the front passenger seat, his massive head held high to catch the draft from over the windshield.[3]

Snook found Earhart to be meticulous in many ways – she washed the dishes *before* they ate and always left the part of an ice cream cone that had been handled by the vendor untouched.[4] But she never objected to getting her hands dirty when it came to the daily grime of maintaining a plane. She could be careless, though, like the time that she forgot to check that they had enough fuel.[5]

Snook and Earhart were lucky to have found one another at a time when female pilots were a minority and it was rare to come across an experienced woman as a mentor. As girls weren't taught practical subjects at school and hadn't been given the opportunity to learn about mechanics while serving during the First World War, they didn't have the knowhow to earn money in a hangar and usually weren't welcome in its male atmosphere. They couldn't fund their flying lessons by working as an engineer or, unlike many of the early record-breaking pilots, learn to fly in the armed services. However, although Snook was only a year older than her friend, she had enjoyed freedoms unheard of for most women in the first two decades of the twentieth century. In photos of the time she looks like one of the boys and was often referred to as such.

At the start of her career Snook couldn't afford her rail ticket to continue her training at Curtiss Flying School. Instead, at the end of September 1917, she took inspiration from the hoboes she'd seen 'riding the rods' – crossing America by clinging to the metal rods that supported the freight train's wooden cars. It was snowing when she grabbed the iron handle of one car and swung herself on board before climbing on top of the car until the speed and sleet became unbearable. When the train slowed for a water stop, she climbed down to surprise the brakeman and crew where they sat next to a potbellied stove. Later in her journey a friendly station manager warned her to hide her 'sparklers' (diamond earrings) – so she reversed them to conceal the stones behind her hair. She hid her $600 flying fees in her shoes.

As soon as she could, she bought a wrecked Canadian training plane, known as a 'Canuck' and had it shipped to her parents' home in Ames, Iowa, where she restored it in their backyard. In spring 1920 she made her first solo flight. She now had the experience and the plane to make a living from flying and in the summer she did just that.

The term 'barnstorming' evolved from the nineteenth-century word for touring actors who performed melodramatic pieces in makeshift venues such as barns. In the following century it came to mean pilots who swooped down to entertain local people before disappearing off to their next venue.[6] It was usually men who did the barnstorming – flying as low over farmers' barns as they dared – or who carried out mock air battles while women walked or danced on the wings or hung by their legs from landing gear, like aerial vaudeville acts. But Snook knew she had the technical skill to take the controls.

In 1920, just as American females were earning the right to vote, flying offered her a physical and commercial freedom most young women couldn't dream of. She received her official U.S. license for flying civilian aircraft in July 1919, and when the document stated the number of passengers she was allowed to carry as 'none' she boldly erased the 'n', so that it read 'one'. She and her biplane barnstormed through the Mid-West offering fifteen-minute rides for fifteen dollars. In her first contract with a fair, just like the one she attended as a young girl, she earned $1,000 for just two flights daily over three days.[7] Photos of her standing next to her biplane show her dishevelled, her flaming, curly hair making her look like a child's drawing of an aviatrix. There were no airports, but the mostly flat terrain transformed the entire Mid-West into a landing field and farmers usually greeted her warmly. She admitted that she got lost often but that the landscape's chequerboard of roads and railroads crossed by rivers offered useful clues.

With the approach of winter, she decided to move to a climate that allowed her to spend more time in the air. She dismantled the Canuck and shipped it to Los Angeles where she test-flew Winfield 'Bert' Kinner's Airsters in return for full commercial use of his airfield. This arrangement allowed her to transport passengers, perform aerial advertising stunts, and teach flying.[8] It was where she met Amelia Earhart.

*

The two women enjoyed rare freedoms at a time when American and British women were jostling for their place in a world that, at first, seemed to be closing in on them after the opportunities that had been presented when soldiers left for the front. Margery Brown, a journalist and pilot, epitomised the conflicting views surrounding women flyers. Her own eagerness to fly suggested that women had earned their rightful place in the skies, but her public comments warned that the character of the average female, whom she thought was too easily distracted, made them a menace in the cockpit.

Just as Lindbergh was known for his towering stature, most people remembered Brown for her diminutive size. At four feet eleven inches tall she barely came up to his armpit.[9] In some ways, she represented a champion for the new breed of female flyer. However, her rallying cry came with some caveats.

She had moved from West Virginia to New York in 1920 and was so inspired by Lindbergh's flight across the Atlantic that she took flying lessons and obtained her licence in 1927. Over the years she became a journalist who specialised in writing about flying and, after divorcing her husband in 1931, travelled the world. She was also one of the founding members of the Ninety-Nines, a professional organisation set up to support women pilots. The name originated from the initial ninety-nine women out of the 126 or so American licenced female pilots who signed up to the group in 1929. Earhart was its first president.

Curtiss Field became Brown's second home, and it was here that she carried out her informal surveys of male pilots' views on women in aviation. Her findings appeared in an essay, 'What Men Flyers Think of Women Pilots' (1929) and revealed a seething cauldron of disparaging male attitudes nearly a decade after Snook had first flown solo and many other women had demonstrated their skill in the air. Despite these achievements, the pilots Brown spoke to described women as too 'emotional'; they said they were likely to 'blow up' in a crisis and they didn't take aeroplanes seriously; flying was pointless because it was a skill women wouldn't be able to use in business and, besides, women usually only become involved in flying as a publicity stunt. One male pilot stated that a mere 10 per cent of women were clever enough to fly and another pointed out that the very same reasons of temperament that made women poor drivers of cars would hold them back in the air.[10]

Given how much Brown loved flying we might have expected her to jump to the defence of female pilots. However, rather than express surprise or anger, she pointed out that flying might help to curb some of women's failings, although she still had severe doubts about whether women were temperamentally suited to flying. The average American woman of the mid 1920s, she believed, had too much time on her hands and flying could be used to offer languid women a sense of purpose.[11] The modern woman needed a pastime that would absorb her energies and expand her social circles, something that would turn her away from 'weary dancing in a hotel tea-room, or in a stuffy night club'. Brown warned, though, that a law should be passed to ban mirrors in prominent corners of the plane as 'With a mirror in the cockpit, too many women would be far more interested in their looks than in their landings!' She worried that women were so prone to gossip that they would expect the plane to fly itself while they chatted.

It wasn't just attitudes that needed adjusting: planes were designed with a male physique in mind. A pilot of Brown's size had to stuff the cockpit with pillows to reach instruments; brakes and starters were positioned and designed for men and Elsie Mackay, one of the first women to gain her pilot's licence in the UK, had to have the seat in the cockpit of her DH6 moved to allow her to reach the rudder bar with her feet. The British journalist who reported on this added, 'She is dark, both of eyes and hair, has tiny and nervous hands, which one would think incapable of controlling a great machine.'[12]

It would be satisfying to think that modern aeroplanes are a better fit for women pilots but, as with so many other forms of transport, they are designed with a male user in mind. One of the female pilots interviewed for this book told how she always knew which aeroplane she'd been flying because of the position of the bruises on her legs that showed how she had been forced to stretch her calves to reach the rudder. In her book, *Invisible Women,* Caroline Criado Perez describes a vest designed for US Airforce pilots to help them determine whether they are facing up or down – a common challenge when visibility is poor or when flying at extreme heights. The kit is fitted with thirty-two sensors that vibrate if the pilot needs to readjust their position. About 20 per cent of the US Airforce are women and yet a review of the vest acknowledged that it works best on hairy, bony skin and less well on soft fleshy parts of the body. So, if you happen to have breasts and a smooth chest don't expect any help knowing which way up you are.[13]

*

The transatlantic flights by Lindbergh and Alcock and Brown were the two most significant moments in proving what this new form of travel could accomplish but, in a quieter way, pilots across North America and in parts of Europe were also showing how air power could bring people closer. In America, in particular, aeroplanes started to carry mail across vast distances and the flying circus that entertained ordinary people on their precious day off, while also helping wartime pilots to eke out a living, imbued flying with a sense of fun and adventure – although in a strictly gendered way. Earhart glimpsed her first plane at the Iowa State Fair in 1908. She was not impressed and, aged ten, was much more interested in a paper hat in the shape of a peach basket.[14] It was a decade later, when she was nursing injured servicemen in Canada, that she became intrigued by aeroplanes and would spend hours watching her former patients going through their steps at the local airfields. When she moved to California with her parents in 1920, she began to visit flying circuses and decided she wanted to learn to fly.[15]

Although women weren't allowed to fly in the First World War, they started to leave their mark in the skies in other ways. Harriet Quimby, whose image usually shows a face framed in a loose-fitting hood, was the first American woman to earn a pilot's licence issued by the world governing body, the Fédération Aéronautique Internationale (FAI) and became famous as the first female to fly the English Channel solo in 1912. Most people assumed she would fail, and a male pilot offered to don her purple flying suit and to fly in her place. She refused, but her achievement was overshadowed by news of the sinking of the *Titanic.* Three months later she and her passenger died when they were tipped out of her Blériot plane at an airshow near Boston. Neither of them was wearing a seat belt.[16]

In the same year that Quimby qualified, Hilda Hewlett became the first woman in the UK to earn her pilot's licence. Hewlett attended the National Art Training School where she learnt woodwork, metalwork, and needlework – an ideal triumvirate for anyone flying the early wood and fabric planes.[17] On the other side of the Atlantic Katherine Stinson sold her piano to pay for flying lessons and gained her pilot's licence in 1912, making her the fourth woman to do so in the USA, when she was twenty-one. Stinson was the first of her sex to fly for the US Postal Service before swooping and diving through stunts that were normally felt to be out of bounds for females. She was the first woman to loop the loop, a manoeuvre in which the aeroplane completes a full, vertical circle in the air. When pilots started to perform this stunt they believed it required special training and would practise hanging upside down for up to twenty minutes, suspended like bats in their plane, which was supported on trestle tables.[18] Stinson was also the earliest female skywriter and when, in 1915, she flew over Los Angeles at night and drew the letters 'CAL' (denoting 'California') using magnesium flares attached to her aircraft, she became the first pilot ever to carry out the practice by night.[19] She offered to serve her country when the US entered the First World War in 1917, but despite her achievements, she was rejected.

*

Flying could be as much an escape for rich women trying to avoid their destiny as it was for others fleeing a humdrum life or the prejudice attached to their gender or race. Ruth Nichols was the daughter of a Wall Street financier and lived in a mansion in Rye, twenty miles north of New York. Aviation was probably the last career her parents had in mind for her – indeed, they fully expected her to avoid a career altogether; to sidestep college and to marry as soon as possible. Her father, however, inadvertently stymied his own plans by paying for her to have a ride in an open-cockpit biplane, a First World War 'Jenny' that was passing through Atlantic City. Ruth, who was five foot, five inches, had never even been on a roller-coaster but the experience turned her world upside down – literally, as the pilot decided she should experience a loop the loop.[20] She underwent an existential conversion that persuaded her to duck marriage for the time being, and to attend Wellesley College instead. After her first year her parents tried to tempt her away from study by sending her to Florida for the winter but, again, the tactic backfired when she used her allowance to pay for flying lessons – something that would have been too expensive for most young women. She took her first solo flight in a flying boat and earned her pilot's license after graduating from Wellesley in 1924, making her the first woman in New York to do so. In January 1928 she completed the first nonstop flight from New York City to Miami with her original flying teacher Harry Rogers.[21] She became the only woman simultaneously to hold the women's world speed, altitude, and distance records for heavy landplanes and fully intended to fly the Atlantic solo.

As pioneering women flew further, higher, and faster than ever before, looped the loop, etched words in the skies, and wing-walked their way into the record books, their achievements were met with one of two responses. For some people, who read about these exploits in the newspapers or even watched them at a county fair or flying circus, their adventures could not be more thrilling. For others, women were straying into arenas that were too dangerous, too physical, and too public.

And it wasn't just that women were taking to the air; they were conquering other elements too. On 6 August 1926 nineteen-year-old Gertrude Ederle became the first woman to swim the English Channel and only the sixth person to make the crossing. Her body, smeared in a protective coating of sheep's grease and wearing a two-piece outfit of her own design, powered through the choppy waters. It was her second attempt at the twenty-mile stretch of open water and she sliced two hours off the previous record.

Ederle, who was born in New York to German immigrant parents, didn't learn to swim until she was nine but went on to win a gold medal in the 400-metre freestyle relay and bronze medals in the 100- and 400-metre freestyle races at the 1924 Paris Olympics. In June 1925, she became the first woman to swim the length of New York Bay; her time of seven hours and eleven minutes broke the previous men's record. She was given a ticker-tape reception in New York when she returned from crossing the Channel and US President Calvin Coolidge described her as 'America's best girl'. It was a label that could hardly have been more belittling for someone who had accomplished such an extreme feat of bravery. The crossing permanently damaged her hearing, and she spent much of her adult life teaching deaf children in New York City to swim, as well as appearing in vaudeville and, in 1939, at the New York World's Fair. She lived to be ninety-eight.

Until Earhart reached the height of her fame, she was sometimes mistaken for Ederle (and another pioneering pilot who would attempt to cross the Atlantic, Ruth Elder). Earhart was twice congratulated on swimming the Channel and commented with her usual wit: 'Elder, Ederle, Earhart – how thoughtless for us all to have names that begin with E.'[22] The confusion reveals how, in the public's mind, young women who achieved feats of physical daring were all too easily pigeonholed.

While Ederle was splashing her way through the record books French tennis player Suzanne Lenglen was leaping around the All-England Club with balletic abandon and a daring one-piece tennis dress cut above the calf and which revealed her forearms. She wasn't afraid to hurl her racquet to the ground in anger if she missed a shot and, unusually for a woman, she served overarm. Her father coached her to play with masculine aggression and would sneak her snifters of cognac between end changes. When Wimbledon resumed after the First World War, she beat seven-time winner, Dorothea Lambert Chambers, who, at forty, was twice Lenglen's age. The victory made her the first non-English speaker to win the tournament. She went on to win five of the next six Wimbledons, and in France became known as 'la Divine' and 'Notre Suzanne'. By the end of the 1920s she was one of the world's most famous sports stars.[23]

Elder, Ederle, Earhart, and Lenglen followed a generation of women who had been pushing against a door marked 'men only'. That door opened – but only a crack – as men disappeared to fight in the First World War and women were called on to drive ambulances and trams, deliver post, and work in factories, where they handled deadly ammunitions. The door in most cases was slammed shut again when soldiers returned, but a tantalising after-taste of what was possible lingered. Commercial flying offered a chance to explore a job that was physically and mentally challenging, although, for many of its proponents, female pilots were merely a means to an end. Advocates recognised that wives had an increasing say in how families travelled and how budgets were spent. What better way to prove the safety of flying and to win over these female influencers than by demonstrating that female pilots were as capable of breaking records?

The truth was that flying was still a perilous pastime. In 1926, 240 people were killed or injured in air crashes in the US – a huge figure considering just how few people flew at the time and how many crashes went unrecorded.[24] Freedom of movement, physical excitement, and danger seemed unnatural, even ungodly, but it was these very elements that made the new pursuit irresistible to a growing number of women.

As well as the comments collected by Margery Brown that women were scatty and generally not mentally and emotionally robust enough to be left alone with a plane, there was also widespread belief that women weren't physically capable. This concern became official following the first all-women transcontinental air race in August 1929 (which, despite the high calibre of the pilots, became known as The Powder Puff Derby). Several competitors reported acts of sabotage, and the interference reached a sinister point when one of the most accomplished pilots, a twenty-nine-year-old former sales assistant at a department store in San Diego, Marvel Crosson, died on the second day. Whether her death was due to foul play or more straightforward mechanical failure, Dr Louis Bauer, editor of the *Journal of Aviation Medicine* and the person responsible for drawing up the first medical rules governing civil aviation in the USA, insinuated that the blame lay with female pilots. He advised flying examiners to warn female pilots not to fly just before, during, or immediately after their period.[25] He added that biology had caused a number of recent crashes, although he didn't give specific examples and seemed to be relying on anecdotal evidence. The implication was clear – women's reproductive cycles added yet another factor to the weight of evidence against their right to be in the air.

Bauer's pronouncement wasn't seriously challenged until 1945, and during the Second World War doctors continued to cite examples of women fainting or becoming 'emotionally upset' during their periods as the cause of many crashes.[26] These official views put into words something that many male pilots had been muttering about for years. The attitude was particularly damaging for any woman considering the Atlantic crossing, as it left very few days each month when it was deemed safe to take to the air and this was without the added annoyance of waiting for the right weather. Earhart seems not to have been troubled by her own periods and towards the end of her life was gathering evidence to dispute the effect of the menstrual cycle on women pilots.

Twenty-first-century scientists have found that women's approach to navigation changes during their period and they can switch from sticking rigidly to a route to adopting a more intuitive, perhaps more risk-taking, strategy, depending on hormonal level. As one writer says:

> It's not a big deal – sex hormones affect many aspects of cognition, and we are all slaves to them. In fact, one interpretation of the testosterone study [in which a drop of testosterone on the tongue appears to improve women's orientation skills] is that the drop on the tongue simply made women navigate more like men, which wouldn't always give them an edge.[27]

By the time NASA was encouraging both sexes to enter space, menstruation was seen as less of a problem – although the fact that when, in 1983, Sally Ride was preparing to become the first American female in space her team of male engineers asked whether 100 tampons would be sufficient for her week-long trip still indicates a shaky knowledge of a woman's world.[28]

Hormones aside, women struggled to obtain the skill set needed to fly a plane. The notion of them in charge of something as masculine and mechanical as a plane challenged the widespread view of women as nurturing, home-based creatures, and these prejudices fed through into practical constraints. As Snook had discovered, many flying schools were reluctant to take on female pilots and individual instructors refused to teach them.

Some pioneers used their success as pilots to secure jobs with the new commercial airlines. After Ruth Nichols completed the first nonstop flight from New York City to Miami in a Fairchild seaplane, the manufacturers offered her a job selling the aircraft.[29] Louise McPhetridge (later Thaden) sold aeroplanes for Travel Air Corporation while learning to fly. She earned her pilot's certificate in 1928 and, in 1929, went on to become the first pilot to hold the women's altitude, endurance, and speed records in light planes at the same time.[30] Earhart claimed to have had twenty-eight jobs before she settled on the career that would make her famous. These included working in a telephone exchange, driving a truck, selling sausages, and helping in a photographic lab.[31]

While women pilots had been taking part in flying circuses, working behind the scenes, selling planes and tickets, other females, like Mabel Boll, had married well, or, as in the British cases of Ladies Savile, Heath, and Bailey, The Duchess of Bedford, and Hon Elsie Mackay, staked family money on their Atlantic dreams. Frances Grayson was unusual in that she had a successful career in journalism and then real estate to fund her flying obsession, but, even then, when it came to her Atlantic bid, she was fortunate enough to persuade a fabulously wealthy heiress to bankroll her. Earhart, too, was lucky that a frustrated member of the Anglo-American elite – Amy Guest – selected her as the vehicle for her own thwarted dreams of crossing the Atlantic. Thea Rasche could not have countenanced flying the Atlantic without the financial support of another American, Anne 'Fifi' Stillman, who wanted to spend part of her banking husband's wealth on buying the young German pilot a plane.

Pilots like Earhart, Elder, and Thaden were clocking up hours in the air, but their endeavours were kept strictly within the confines of the USA. Although Lindbergh made them dream of crossing the Atlantic it was the rich and, in many cases, titled, who had seen the Atlantic at close quarters – but from the deck of a ship, rather than the cockpit of an aeroplane.

CHAPTER THREE

Queen Bess

A photo taken at the first all-women transcontinental air race in August 1929 shows a motley line-up of ten pilots. Most are linking arms or have their arms round their neighbour's shoulders and look relaxed and happy. Three wear trousers; only Amelia Earhart is in a dress, and the rest are in baggy flying suits. The photo shows a range of heights and body types. In some ways the image is a good advert for the variety of women who enjoyed flying and of the support they gave one another in the 1920s. But one detail derails this impression – all the women in the photo are white.

In a period of vicious Jim Crow laws and racial violence, the photographer capturing this moment would have had to retreat so far into the distance to find a person of colour that his original subjects would have been reduced to a speck on the horizon. He would also have been forced to travel back in time, to 1926, to find the first African American woman to learn to fly.

Although Bessie Coleman never aspired to cross the Atlantic in a plane – that was a feat beyond even the imagination of a woman who had always favoured bold moves – her determination to travel to Europe to find someone to teach her to fly allowed future generations of African Americans to believe that they, too, had a place in the cockpit. While the white press largely ignored her achievements, newspapers such as the weekly *Chicago Defender*, which had a largely African American readership, followed her progress eagerly and made sure that her name stayed in the public eye long after her tragic death. Even though she was excluded from the upper echelons of society and spheres of influence such as publishing, real estate, and commerce, she found other networks to support her efforts.

Coleman was born in 1892 in Texas, part of a family of thirteen children, four of whom died in childhood. It is likely that her mother, whose parents were originally from Georgia, had been enslaved; her father was probably born free and three of his grandparents were native Americans – although in Texas this aspect of his heritage put him at even greater risk.[1] As a child, Bessie grew accustomed to the fear of lynching and mob rule against the Black population who lived a segregated life; they were forbidden from riding the same railroads as white people or using the same restaurants or hotels. Sipping from the same water fountain or using the same restroom was strictly forbidden. Somehow her father managed to save enough money from his wages as a labourer to buy a small plot of land in Waxahachie, thirty miles south of Dallas, in an area that survived, before the discovery of oil, through the backbreaking picking of cotton. From the age of six Bessie walked the four miles from home to her one-room wooden school building where it was soon evident that she was a stand-out pupil and particularly adept at maths.

Bessie's life became that bit harder when her father moved to Oklahoma – a state where his native American heritage attracted slightly less discrimination. Her mother stayed in Texas and took a job as cook-housekeeper to a white couple. Bessie was left to look after their home and to watch her younger siblings. Between these duties and the cotton-picking season, when school closed, her education became haphazard, although she continued to read books from the 'wagon library' that passed the house. When she was eighteen, she completed one term at the Colored Agricultural and Normal University before her money ran out and she was forced to return to Waxahachie where she made a living by taking in washing. Her chance for escape came in 1915, at the age of twenty-three, when her brother, Walter, who worked as a Pullman porter on the railway carriages that served passengers meals and offered sleeper accommodation, said she could stay with him in Chicago while she looked for a job.

Most Black women at the time earned a living as domestic servants because so many other jobs, such as working in a factory, were closed to them. Bessie, though, became a manicurist. Her choice was a canny one: it avoided the training needed to become a hairdresser and gave her the opportunity to tend to men's nails in barbershops, where she could earn greater tips and get to know more influential customers. By now she was a startlingly pretty young woman who mingled with the city's most influential Black citizens and who followed its politics though the pages of the *Chicago Defender*. The newspaper, which was founded in 1905, had a readership that was close to half a million – one of the highest among African Americans.[2]

While many Black people had moved north in search of a life with fewer prohibitions, racial tensions were still only ever just below the surface. In July 1919 they broke through that veneer when a young Black man was spending a rare moment of leisure on a home-made raft that drifted into an area of Lake Michigan usually reserved for white bathers. A group of swimmers stoned him until he fell into the water and drowned. The tragedy led to four days of rioting in Chicago during which thirty-eight people died. Only torrential rain and the arrival of the National Guard were able to put an end to the horror.

It was against this backdrop that, Bessie, now twenty-seven, finally settled on the course that would define her life. Two of her brothers had served in France during the Great War and one, John, turned up at her work and began teasing her about the superiority of French women and how they even flew planes. It wasn't the first time he had goaded her in this way, and it clearly hit a nerve.

But there was no one to teach her to fly: all the instructors were white and refused to take her on. She turned to Robert Abbott, editor and founder of her favourite newspaper, the *Chicago Defender* for advice. Abbott, whose paper had been extolling France as a country that led the world in aviation and was less racist than North America – although Josephine Baker had yet to stamp her mark on Paris – urged her to head to Europe. She would need to learn French and he would provide her with a reference. Bessie's husband, whom she'd married, unexpectedly, just before her twenty-fifth birthday and who was fourteen years her senior, didn't seem to figure in her plans.

Bessie took Abbott at his word: she enrolled in a language school and found a job as a manager of a chili restaurant. Abbott helped to finance her ambitions, and she seems also to have been supported by other male admirers. In November 1920 she sailed for France and settled into a seven-month course at the École d'Aviation des Frères Caudron at Le Crotoy in northern France. It must have been a lonely existence as her French was still rudimentary and she had to walk several miles each day from her lodgings to the school. But eventually she gained her FAI licence, a qualification recognised throughout the world and one that marked her as the first Black woman ever to gain the licence.

When she returned to New York in September 1921 as a qualified pilot her success was recognised in *some* white newspapers. The *Chicago Herald* offered to interview her but only if she agreed to pretend to be white – instead, she took her sister and niece with her to avoid any attempt to 'pass'.[3] Only the *Chicago Defender* ran a full profile and shared her ambitions to help 'men of the Race' who could fly. The newspaper also bestowed on her the nickname of 'Queen Bess'.

But it was not enough simply to be able to fly; she needed to be able to make a living from her skill and, for a Black woman, that meant being able to produce the thrills and spills only a flying circus could offer. She booked a second passage to France to continue her training and after two months travelled to the Netherlands where she met the famous aircraft manufacturer, Anthony Fokker, and tried some of his planes. Probably with his blessing, she travelled to Berlin where Pathé News filmed her visit, and she flew over the Kaiser's palace. When she returned the *New York Times* commented she was 'said to be the only negro aviatrix in the world' and described some of the planes she had flown in Europe.[4]

Abbott helped to arrange an air show at Curtiss Field, which was billed as honouring the Fifteenth Expeditionary Force's contribution in the Great War but whose main purpose was to showcase the first public flight of a Black woman in the USA. After her appearance on 3 September, it was noted how many people of colour were far more eager to go up in a passenger plane than was usual at such an event. In October she took part in the Negro Tri-State Fair in Memphis when 20,000 spectators attended the three-day event, including an exhibition of stunt flying by Coleman.

The two events secured her role as an aerial performer, and she signed a contract to star in a full-length feature film. However, her career in movies floundered before it had even begun. The false start was due either to her temperament or because she was asked to appear in an early scene as a figure who seemed too close to a parody of a poor woman of colour from the South.

Her main goal had always been to open a flying school for African Americans, and she used money from her endorsement of the Coast Tire and Rubber company to buy an early Curtiss JN-4 'Jenny'. She planned to reveal the aircraft on 4 February at the opening of Palomar Park when a crowd of 10,000 was expected, but moments after she took off from Santa Monica to fly the twenty-five miles to the fairground her motor stalled and she nose-dived into the crowd. She was knocked unconscious, broke a leg, fractured three ribs, and her face was covered with cuts. But despite her obvious pain many spectators were furious that the fair had been cancelled; some even thought the accident was divine retribution for her audacity at flying on a Sunday.

Even though she was physically unable to fly because both her body and her plane had been crushed, she placed an advert in the *Eagle* newspaper to promote the Coleman School of Aeronautics. She started to give lectures at the Young Men's Christian Association in Los Angeles and to show film of her flights in the US and Europe. But her stock was falling in Chicago and Abbott featured her less in his newspaper. Finally, she was able to secure a series of lectures at schools and movie theatres, as well as exhibition flights in her home state of Texas. Here she swooped and dived to within a few feet of the ground, she looped the loop, rolled across the skies and swept through figures of eight while the crowd below gasped in fear and admiration. In August she appeared at the former San Antonio Speedway where Liza Dilworth, a local African American, became the first woman of colour to parachute from a plane when she stepped off the wing of Coleman's machine. By the time Coleman was due to perform outside Wharton, south-west of Houston, Dilworth refused to repeat the jump – either due to fear or because she was ill – and Coleman found someone else to fly the plane so that she could take Dilworth's place. At Waxahachie she performed in front of a mixed audience, and although Black and white spectators were restricted to different areas, Coleman insisted that they enter through the same gate. In Orlando she threatened to withdraw unless people of colour were allowed to join the onlookers.

She eventually found a benefactor in Edwin M. Beeman, heir to a chewing gum fortune, who gave her the final payment for her plane.[5] She was due to headline the Negro Welfare League's annual Field Day in Jacksonville, Florida on 1 May. A twenty-four-year-old white mechanic, William D. Wills, flew her new plane from Love Field in Dallas to Jacksonville, but the Jenny was so poorly maintained that he had to make two forced landings on the way.

The strict segregation laws meant that Wills had to lodge in another part of the city from Coleman and she and John Betsch, the publicity manager from the Negro Welfare League, had to pick him up and drive them to Paxon Field early in the morning. She asked Wills to take the controls while she scanned the field for a good spot from which to jump. At five feet, three and a half inches, she was too short to look over the edge of the fuselage with the safety belt secured and so she left it unfastened.[6] Wills took the plane up and circled for five minutes at about 2,000 feet before edging up to 3,500 feet and then preparing to land. He was doing 80 miles per hour when the plane suddenly surged to 110 miles per hour before nosediving. Onlookers described the plane flipping upside down at 500 feet, throwing Coleman out of the cockpit and sending her somersaulting through the air until she hit the ground. Wills struggled to bring the plane under control, ploughing through a pine tree before crashing into farmland. Rescuers, including Betsch, rushed to the scene. In an effort to calm his nerves, Betsch lit a cigarette with a match that set fire to the gasoline fumes and engulfed the plane in flames. He was arrested and held in jail for several hours.

Although rumours persist that the plane had been sabotaged, Coleman and Wills died because she couldn't afford a plane that had been properly serviced. As a Black woman of limited means, she didn't have a team of mechanics and other advisors around her and had to travel by segregated, slower trains. Coleman died because, like all female pilots at that time and now, she was travelling in a machine designed with a man's physique in mind – and wasn't wearing a seatbelt so that she could see over the fuselage.

Over 5,000 people attended her funeral service in Jacksonville, including hundreds of school children who had heard her speak the day before. When her coffin arrived in Chicago an estimated 10,000 people filed passed to pay their respects. Her legacy was slow to take off but has burned more brightly in recent years. Coleman has been remembered by various groups of pilots who fly over her grave at

Lincoln Cemetery in Chicago annually. The city honours her through Bessie Coleman Day (2 May) and in 1995, the US Postal Department issued the Bessie Coleman stamp. At Frankfurt Airport, Bessie Coleman Strasse meets Amelia Earhart and Thea Rasche streets at a roundabout that then takes the driver on to Rita Maiburg Strasse, named after the first female captain of a commercial passenger airline.

In 2023, Coleman became part of Mattel's 'Inspiring Women' series of Barbie Dolls. She arrived in moulded form five years after Earhart but cuts more of a dash in her military uniform and looks more lifelike than Earhart. Her ambition was, she said, to 'make Uncle Tom's cabin into a hangar by establishing a flying school' and, while she didn't achieve this in her lifetime, she inspired future generations of pilots of colour.[7]

Although she hadn't ever wanted to fly the Atlantic and her goal was to create a flying school for African Americans, she left her mark in ways that could only ever be different from the legacy of women like Earhart, Boll, Savile, Mackay, Grayson and Elder. She crossed the Atlantic twice by ocean liner, an achievement in itself for someone of her background, in pursuit of a skill she couldn't be taught in her home country. The white press of the day tended only to report on the activities of Black Americans if they were criminals or sportsmen, but she harnessed the interest of the African American press such as the *Chicago Defender* which, unlike their white counterparts, weren't as obsessed with her marital status and her hair. While she wasn't ever likely to secure a column in a publication like *Cosmopolitan*, as Earhart did, or to sign book deals, she took her message to the grass roots: to schools; movie theatres, particularly in Georgia and Florida;[8] the vaudeville circuit; churches; and, on one occasion, a pool hall.[9] Her speeches have been described as part of a rhetorical tradition by Black women that includes the impassioned words of nineteenth-century abolitionist Sojourner Truth. Although little survives of Coleman's spoken words it's possible to feel their ripples through the reports of standing ovations, like the one she received at the Metropolitan Baptist Church in New York, which had a congregation of around 2,500,[10] after she described how she planned to open a flying school.[11]

Coleman didn't have the same networking opportunities as white female pilots, who had organisations like the Ninety-Nines, and she failed to find a manager who could protect her in the way that Putnam did Earhart. But she, nevertheless, knew the importance of a memorable photo that would pin her in the reader's memory. She was usually pictured on, or by, a plane – as if the two were inseparable. She wore an army uniform of shiny boots, puttees, olive-coloured trousers, and leather coat. The Sam Browne belt was a daring choice – not only did the accessory accentuate her slender waist, but it also suggested the rank of 'officer'. When Mae Jemison became the first African American woman in space, in 1992, she took a picture of Coleman with her as she orbited the earth in the space shuttle *Endeavour*.[12]

Flight Checklist: A Memorable Nickname

Charles Augustus Lindbergh was never going to be a natural 'Charlie', a 'Chuck', or a 'Gus'. He was too serious-minded and too much of a loner for that. As a barnstormer he had briefly been 'Daredevil Lindbergh' but shed this title once he became a transatlantic contender.[1]

The tradition of nicknames and abbreviations was common in the armed services, where they helped to foster a sense of belonging and could be barked out when speed was of the essence. Often, they lived on in Civvy Street. Mackay's co-pilot, Captain Walter Hinchliffe was known as 'Hinch', 'Ray', or 'Walt'; Frances Grayson's navigator Brice Goldsborough as 'Goldy'; one of Savile's pilots, Captain Leslie Hamilton was the 'Flying Gypsy', because he was always on the move,[2] or the 'Flying Taximan';[3] and Amelia Earhart's co-pilots were Louis 'Slim' Gordon and 'Smiling' Bill Stultz (the latter may have been ironic).[4] But for most airmen, these pet names were reserved for behind the hangar door. Once a pilot gained fame, or notoriety, they were more likely to have a nickname inflicted on them. After Lindbergh crossed the Atlantic the burgeoning press took every opportunity to pour hyperbole on the fresh-faced, handsome pilot. He was the 'Human Meteor', the 'Flyin' Fool', and the 'Kid Flyer'.[5] Each moniker moved further away from Lindbergh's true character, but the one he appeared to hate most was 'Lucky Lindy' because it ignored the painstaking preparation that had gone into his flight: luck had very little to do with his success.[6]

'Lady Lindy' was an obvious nickname for Earhart because she bore a striking resemblance to him, and because she wanted to cross the same stretch of water that he had already conquered. Such nicknames made it easier for America's growing legions of newspaper and magazine reporters and radio commentators to conjure up a vivid picture in just two words. As Thea Rasche, the young German pilot who dreamt of conquering the Atlantic in 1927 would discover, alliteration also helped. Predictably, she became the 'flying Fraulein'.[7] Elinor Smith, who at sixteen became the youngest pilot to receive her flying licence, was the 'Flying Flapper of Freeport'.[8] Swimmer Gertrude Ederle was known by her trainer as 'The Kid' because of her age, and as 'Queen of the Seas' by the public after she swam the Channel.[9]

*

The practice of bestowing on public figures – and public objects – a nickname reached its zenith in the 1920s, which is probably not surprising for a decade that earned its own epithet: the 'Roaring Twenties'. It was a period when Europe and America were grappling with the aftermath of a devasting conflict before trying to come to terms with a brave new world of mechanisation, mass communication, and greater leisure time in which to enjoy sport, movies, and music. For the USA, there was a confidence to that roar as it sped past its European counterparts who were still recovering from the destruction. America became a place of mass production and consumerism. Once wartime restrictions on construction were lifted, new buildings erupted all over the nation, many clawing their way high into the skies. There was a boom in new homes that, in turn, fuelled demand for telephones, radio sets, as well as what today we call 'white goods'. All these things needed names.

Sales of newspapers soared in the Twenties and most big cities had more than one publication that filled their pages with adverts for shiny new goods. It was also the decade of the tabloid, titillating its readers with items about sport, celebrities, and crime. As well as reading about their heroes, Americans also listened to their exploits on radio sets, which were fast becoming an essential piece of furniture.

Nicknames didn't just make it easier to convey an image in a word or two, they highlighted what really mattered. Crime, boosted by the prohibition of alcohol in 1920, sport, and entertainment were each of great interest to the average person on the street. Mobsters with names like 'Big Jim Colosimo',[10] 'Scarface', 'Bugsy' (meaning to lose control),[11] and 'Waxey Gordon', so-called for his ability to remove someone's wallet undetected as if it were coated in wax, made money from prohibition and toted submachine guns that could fire 800 rounds a minute – though admittedly not always with great accuracy. The fast-firing weapon was so impressive that it had two nicknames: the 'Tommy gun', named after its inventor, General John Taliaferro Thompson, who perfected the weapon just as the First World War was ending,[12] and the 'Chicago typewriter', after the city where they were so often deployed and because of their rat-tat-tat soundtrack.[13] These criminals were chased by federal agents like Richard 'Two Gun' Hart who, in the topsy-turvy world of the 1920s, was Al Capone's brother.[14]

'Babe' Ruth, so called because of his baby face and initial innocence, hit his sixtieth home run of the season in 1927 – a record that stood until 1961 – in a sport that was slowly emerging from its status as a pastime that few people watched because it was played in the afternoon when everyone was at work. Baseball's growing popularity was helped by this plethora of nicknames, not just for players but for their clubs. Ruth played for the Boston Red Sox, New York Yankees, and Boston Braves, while 'Chick' Gandil, 'Happy' Felsch, 'Swede'

Risberg, 'Lefty' Williams, and 'Shoeless Joe' Jackson turned out for the White Sox.[15]

The new forms of transport that were making the country smaller also had names, which made them sound thrilling and romantic. When, in 1925, Pennsylvania Railroad decided to call its fast freight trains by names rather than numbers they came up with titles such as 'The Challenger', 'The Trailblazer', and 'The Flying Cloud'. The *Latrobe Bulletin* said approvingly, 'The train with a name, has become something as is a ship with a name – a thing of personality to the crew and to the public.'[16]

The aeroplanes that took on the Atlantic also conveyed a message. Amy Guest chose *Friendship* for Amelia Earhart's first attempt as a way of stressing a hopeful message of uniting the countries on either side of the ocean. When Earhart crossed the Atlantic solo she did so in her single-engine Lockheed Vega 5B *Little Red Bus*, which made her jaunt sound playful. Putnam, who was usually known as 'GPP', 'GP', or 'Gyp', by friends, was opposed to naming the plane in case it took away from the Amelia Earhart 'brand'.[17] Privately, once they were married, Earhart often referred to him as 'Simpkin' after a character in a book she remembered from childhood. Simpkin was a cat who kept mice under upturned teacups to play with in idle moments.[18] He often joked that he was 'Mr Earhart' but in private referred to her as 'A.E.'.[19]

Frances Grayson's Sikorsky amphibian had the romantic title *Dawn*, which suggested the start of a bright new future, for women, perhaps. Savile's Fokker was named *St Raphael* after her beloved mother's maiden name.[20] Ruth Elder flew in a yellow Stinson Detroiter called *American Girl*, which summed up her own lively take on life: she was the epitome of the 'it girl' – a term novelist Elinor Glynn had created to describe a young woman who had an undefinable charisma that made her attractive to both sexes.[21] Mabel Boll hoped to cross in a Wright Bellanca, a plane that had already been named *Columbia* by its owner, Charles Levine, but which was unofficially renamed *Miss*

Columbia because it was better for publicity and also put Boll – 'Queen of Diamonds' – centre stage.[22] Levine's own nickname was less than flattering. He was called the 'Flying Junkman' because his father had been a scrap merchant and Charles had made his fortune by trading in unwanted shell casings during the Great War.[23]

That the planes' pilots and passengers also needed special names, beyond those printed on their pilot's licence, demonstrated the extent to which these flyers were the new celebrities, on a par with singers, movie stars, sports men and women, politicians, and mobsters. As a group they were known, derogatorily, as 'Fly Girls'. In the 1970s and 1980s the media was still referring to the first female astronauts as 'girls' or 'ladies in space'. Collectively, they were often known as the 'Glamornauts' and NASA's 'eye-popping space gals'.[24] Later journalists were just as interested in the astronauts' age, hair colour, and marital status as reporters in the 1920s were hungry for the same details about the fly girls.

Although women in the 1920s were gaining greater independence, there were still few in the public eye. Most of those who gathered nicknames were in the world of entertainment. Clara Bow, the cupid-lipped actress who shot to fame in the movie *Wings* about pilots from the First World War, was known as *the* 'it girl' after she starred in the film, *It* (1927), an adaptation of Glynn's novel. Earlier in her career she had been known as the 'Brooklyn Bonfire'. Blues singer Ma Rainey was said to owe her first name to her husband and 'Ma' to be a play on his name, 'Pa'.

When it came to 'girl flyers', a nickname usually described the pilot's family background, profession, or physical characteristics – her age, clothes, or hair – and it could change depending on the angle the reporter wanted to emphasis. After Louise McPhetridge (later Thaden) spent 196 hours and six minutes in the air in August 1932, she and her co-pilot, Frances Marsalis were transformed into 'flying matrons' and their plane a 'flying boudoir'.[25] They were both in their mid-twenties at the time, and when Marsalis died in a plane crash two years later she underwent one final transformation to become the 'famous girl aviator who gave her life to her love for planes and speed'.[26] Frances Wilson was also described by the *New York Daily News* as 'the flying matron' when she was thirty-five.[27] One wonders at what age a woman became a matron and what other factors might be involved in the word choice – Thaden, Marsalis, and Wilson had all been married, for example, although Grayson was divorced. It was rare for the age of a male pilot to be included in a press report.

Ruth Nichols, who would have taken on the Atlantic crossing if it hadn't been for a crash that nearly killed her, earned her nickname, the 'Flying Debutante', from her parents' wealth and was also known as the 'Flying Salesgirl' because of the way she promoted air travel.[28, 29] Likewise, Savile was known as the 'Flying Princess', but The Hon Elsie Mackay was content for her friends to call her 'Poppy'.

Bessie Coleman's nicknames reflected her character. She was 'Brave Bessie' and 'Queen Bess'.[30] Mabel Boll's nickname was usually 'Queen of Diamonds', but she was also sometimes known as 'Mysterious Mabel', due to her reluctance to talk about her past. She was especially coy about her age and, on one occasion, said she was thirty-two, despite having a nineteen-year-old son.[31] Ruth Elder, by contrast, had a form of headdress named after her: young women took to emulating her by wearing a brightly coloured bandana, and it became known as the 'Ruth Ribbon'.[32] Newspapers also called her 'Miss America of the Air' and the 'Flying Flapper'.[33] Mildred Doran, the only female to enter the Dole Trans-Pacific Air Race of August 1927, was known by her profession and became the 'Flying Teacher' or 'Flying Schoolmarm'.[34] Doran was lost in the race where the 'Pineapple King' James Dole offered $25,000 to the first pilot to fly from California to Hawaii, in an effort to emulate the Orteig prize.[35]

Neta Snook, who taught Earhart to fly, was known at the Davenport Aviation School as 'Curly' because of her unruly hair – a nickname that could have applied to a man. She trained alongside young men like 'Tex', from Texas, and 'Babe', who enjoyed childish pranks; there was also a 'Spud' and a 'Mort', but no reason was given for their nicknames.[36] When Earhart was a teenager at school she was known as 'Butterball' or 'Butter' – probably an ironic reference to her slim physique.[37] In Britain, when Amy Johnson, who would become the first woman to fly solo from England to Australia in 1930, was training to become a mechanic and learning to fly, she was given the nickname 'Johnny'. These sorts of private nicknames confirmed that someone had been accepted into a group. They were affectionate and implied a level of respect. The names used in newspapers and magazines were more flexible and represented an attempt to shoehorn a pilot into a preconceived narrative. At a time when families handed down first names to the next generation there was also a need to find alternative handles to differentiate people with the same first and last names. Public nicknames helped to keep a pilot in the spotlight but newspapers, like schoolground bullies, often had a knack of highlighting the very element the recipient wished to conceal – this was especially true for women in a decade when great store was placed on age and beauty. There was always someone trying to fly further, higher, or faster; and a catchy nickname could play a part in catapulting a pilot beyond their nearest rival or relegating them to a lower rung on the celebrity ladder. This was probably why, when she married in 1931, Amelia Earhart made the bold decision not to change her surname. By then her full name had become a valuable marketing brand.

PART TWO

Rich Girls Take to the Skies

CHAPTER FOUR

Amy Phipps and the Challenges of High Birth

The Phipps family was all packed and ready to sail the Atlantic, just as they had for the last six years running. The plan was to spend the summer at Knebworth House, a gothic, turreted mansion set in Hertfordshire grounds grazed by deer and framed by horse chestnut trees, rented from the novelist Sir Edward Bulwer-Lytton.

But 1898 would be different. Twenty-six-year-old Amelia, known as 'Amy', the eldest of the five Phipps children, had put her foot down. She had decided to stay in New York to train to be a nurse. The headline in the *Pittsburgh Post-Gazette* expressed approval: 'Miss Amy Phipps and the Useful Path She Has Chosen', but her parents were unimpressed by her alternative holiday arrangements.[1]

The Phipps family was all about being useful and Amy's father, Henry, known as 'Harry', had proved himself so useful that he had risen to become one of the wealthiest businessmen in Philadelphia. Harry, the son of immigrants from Shropshire, had caught the wave of post-Civil War industrial expansion that produced a fretwork of roads and rail roads across the continent and changed the skyscape of cities with ever-taller buildings. But Harry, whose father had started out by selling shoes from the back of a horse-drawn cart, never lost the fear that his wave of good luck might at any moment collapse under him. In his early years he had the clean-cut movie-star looks of a young John Ford and grew up in a neighbourhood called Barefoot Square in Allegheny, now part of Pittsburgh. The address acted as both a reminder that his father's skill as a cobbler fed the family and as a warning of their proximity to the gutter.[2]

Barefoot Square introduced him to a life-long friend and future business associate, Andrew Carnegie. The Carnegies had emigrated from Scotland and Andrew's mother did piece work for the Phipps' shoe business. Harry and Andrew grew close over conversations snatched behind the cobbler's shop, where they plotted their escape from poverty. Harry studied at night school to become an accountant and then used his new skills in the burgeoning steel industry that fed the insatiable needs of the railroads. Andrew, too, had hitched his ambitions to steel and railroads and rose quickly through a series of shrewd investments and wheeler-dealer manoeuvres on both sides of the Atlantic. The fate of the two childhood friends was sealed when Harry joined Andrew's Union Iron Mills in 1865 and later became the second largest shareholder in the Carnegie Steel Company.[3] The two men shared an ingrained work ethic and a burning desire to pay back the results of their own hard work through philanthropy. The Phipps and Carnegie families also liked to holiday together in Britain.

Harry gradually grew into a grey-bearded elder statesman who needed a cane to support his short frame and whose hair was unkempt and his suit sometimes a little too tight.[4] He married Annie Childs Shaffer in 1872 when he was thirty-three and his bride eleven years younger. Annie took a while to adjust to married life and in contemporary accounts sounds like a lonely, anxious woman who found it difficult to manage the servants and became obsessed with her children – the first of whom, Amy, was born in 1872.

At the start of their marriage Harry was often away on trips, but later Annie joined him, and their family album is studded with photos in exotic settings like the Alhambra Palace in Granada, Spain, where they donned Moorish robes and head-dresses, and of Annie wearing a mantilla and holding a fan. They bedded down in tents along the Nile and visited Moscow. As a family, they travelled as far as Rome, India, and Burma (now Myanmar).

Crossing the Atlantic became a regular occurrence for Amy, although often she was doing it in the opposite direction from her father. Between 1891, when the family sold their house in Pennsylvania, and 1903, the Phipps had no permanent home and flitted between America and Europe. They leased mansions like Knebworth House; North Mymms Park, a Jacobean stately home near St Albans; and Beaufort Castle in Inverness-shire, built in 1880 in a baronial style. In each of these temporary homes the family, including the girls, indulged their love of the outdoors, of riding and playing sport. Although they held country house parties, when Annie dressed in the latest fashion designed by the House of Worth, she had no pretensions to be a Vanderbilt, Astor, or Churchill.[5]

Amy's niece, Peggie Phipps Boegner later wrote:

> There is no doubt that Aunt Amy Phipps Guest was the most original and imaginative member of our family. I always thought that she should have been a man – she was so forceful and so absolutely fearless. I have seen her riding sidesaddle on a borrowed horse, suddenly turning away from the rest of the hunt and urging her horse over an enormous fence taken at short range.[6]

*

At the end of the nineteenth century there were few outlets for a rich young woman like Amy who wanted more from life than to travel in style and wait for a suitable husband. War was one of them.

When, in 1898, the US supported the Cuban War of Independence against its Spanish coloniser, the intervention captured a nation's imagination as Americans sympathised with people struggling against a faraway dominion – as they themselves had against the British. Newspapers reported unsparingly on the humanitarian crisis, and when Amy Phipps decided she wanted to help, the *Evening World Herald* praised her in its headline: 'Heroic Daughter of Carnegie's Partner With Millions in her Own Name Shows Her Colors'.[7]

Amy, together with another rich young woman, Helen Long, whose father was one of the wealthiest men in New England, had decided they were willing to forgo their summer. In Amy's case she would be missing out on being presented at Court and visiting Scotland. Instead, the two had 'doffed the silk and satin of society and donned the stuff that is meant for wear in the service of the sick' to work as nurses on a hospital ship, and imagined themselves ministering 'under the blazing tropical sun off the coast of Cuba'. Both 'belles' were now wearing blue print dresses and white caps and had enrolled in St Luke's nursing school. Amy's parents did their best to persuade her to change her mind by promising a visit to Rome and reminded her that her gown had already been prepared for her royal introduction.

Amy's act of rebellion was catnip to the press. The *Evening World Herald* described her as a 'golden haired girl of 18' (she was in her late twenties), 'athletic, winsome, fun-loving, frank-faced American, with her dainty figure and her beautiful face'. She had 'fluffy' chestnut hair and stood five foot seven inches tall. She was worshipped by plenty of young men and set to inherit $3 million. The newspaper also recorded that she was a strong swimmer, rode to hounds, and enjoyed golf. But she was keen to play down her nursing duties:

> No, please don't make me out a heroine – this is nothing at all. I'm simply following out what I want to do. Surely if the men can

> give up home and loved ones and all the comforts of life to face death, our women can afford to endure a few discomforts.

The journalist pointed out that Amy's brother, Jay had sailed for Britain: 'Here is the strange end-of-the-century antithesis. The man goes a-pleasuring; the woman goes to war.'[8]

Ultimately, though, Amy was denied the chance to experience the blazing tropical sun of Cuba, and her father managed to dissuade her from boarding a hospital ship. His argument was simple and difficult to refute: if she really wanted to help the wounded, he and her mother would pay for two trained nurses to work at the army hospital for the duration of the war.[9]

Instead, Amy was destined to follow the traditional path of so many of her rich contemporaries and married Frederick Guest, third son of Lord and Lady Wimborne, at a 'very smart wedding' at St George's, Hanover Square, London in the summer of 1905.[10] He was serving in the 1st Life Guards, and bride and bridegroom were in their early thirties. Their wedding presents were 'very costly' and included a tiara and diamond ornament from the bride's parents, a diamond necklace from the Carnegies, and a large diamond and turquoise ornament from the Aga Khan, spiritual leader of the Nizari sect of Ismaili Muslims and a well-known figure in aristocratic circles.

The Queen noted that Amy's parents were well known in London because they had spent several seasons in town and many autumns in Scotland. Amy's wedding reinforced existing ties with 'distinguished English families' and her siblings had already married members of the British aristocracy.[11]

To celebrate the union, the American society portraitist John Singer Sargent was commissioned to paint Amy's picture. She probably sat for the artist, who was at the very height of his fame, in his Tite Street studio in Chelsea.[12] Amy looks languid, perhaps even bored, in her loose-fitting, diaphanous dress, two rows of pearls appearing pinkish against her alabaster skin. In one hand she's holding a straw hat; in the other she's scooped up a black and white King Charles spaniel. She's depicted standing in front of trees, and the decorative balustrade, probably one of Sargent's antique props, immediately suggests the grounds of a country park. The painting, almost five feet tall, was exhibited at the Royal Academy. About a year later Sargent produced a second painting of other members of the Guest/Phipps family.[13]

The paintings aim to portray an image of contented opulence, but Sargent was growing weary of what he described as these society 'mugs' and during a sitting would dart behind a screen to relieve his frustration by sticking out his tongue.[14] In hindsight, this behind-the-scenes rebellion provides a metaphor for the different expectations of both parties in the Phipps/Guest marriage.

If Amy's parents had read the *Los Angeles Express*'s account of the wedding, rather than the more obsequious versions in the British press, they would have been worried about their daughter's prospects. The American newspaper presented a much more rumbustious picture of their new son-in-law than his elevated ancestry and military CV suggest. The newspaper reported that Freddie's fellow officers in the Life Guards were wondering whether he would 'turn over a new leaf and lead a more commendable existence' now that he was married. The article continued: 'Guest is a handsome fellow, with a soldierly bearing superior even to what Londoners exact [sic] in the guardsmen, whom the music hall entertainers dub "potted meat," and he has a Lothario record in India as well as England.' Amy, by comparison, was 'serious, fond of books, a woman of high ideals, and determined to be different from the ordinary run of feminine humanity'. 'When a girl of her ilk is smitten it is always a hard case, and it is often the veriest dandy who attracts her.'[15]

According to the paper, Amy had fallen for Guest when she saw him riding across Coronation Park in Delhi during the Durbar that was held between late 1902 and January 1903 to celebrate the succession of Edward VII. His fellow officers pointed out that he was 'the foremost flirt in Asia and warned her not to trust his flatteries; but she went her own way'.[16] Amy, for her part, thought that a husband would allow her to fulfil yet another dream that her father had forbidden. Inspired by the British expedition of 1903, in which Sir Francis Younghusband, effectively invaded Tibet, Amy made it clear that she longed to become the first white woman to enter the sacred city and capital of Tibet, Lhasa.[17]

Once married, though, Freddie restricted their travels to shuttling between their family homes on either side of the Atlantic. In 1910, after three attempts, he finally became an MP for East Dorset. He returned to Parliament after the war and in 1923 was elected to the Stroud constituency and to Bristol North in the general election of the following year. Probably the nearest Amy came to danger was in Kenya with her husband and the Swedish big game hunter Baron Bror Blixen. Blixen, whose first wife was *Out of Africa* author Karen Blixen, organised opulent safaris for customers such as the Prince of Wales and wealthy Americans like the Vanderbilts.[18]

But Amy hadn't given up on her dreams of adventure and her next plan would be more ambitious even than tending to the sick in far-off Cuba. Her parents no longer had the power to hold her back and it would take different tactics to persuade her from risking her life by climbing into the cockpit of a heavily laden plane in a bid to become the first woman to fly the Atlantic.

CHAPTER FIVE

The Flying Princess

Although by the 1920s no woman had ever flown across the Atlantic, millions of female passengers had crossed the ocean by ship. Between 1860 and 1900, 14 million people emigrated from Europe to the US to escape poverty or persecution,[1] while a much smaller number made the trip in the opposite direction to see the sights, make business transactions, in search of better health or for old world charm.[2] By the second half of the nineteenth century the nouveaux riches – and the Phipps family (which Amy Guest had been born into) certainly fell into this category – were keen to see their daughters presented at Court. John Peyton, who travelled to London during the American Civil War to secure arms for the Confederates, likened the ships that plied backwards and forwards to 'shuttles in a loom . . . these gigantic steamers flying to and fro between Europe and America are weaving nations closer and closer together'.[3] For wealthy families like the Phipps, the crossing was as regular a part of their year as waving their children off at the start of a new term at boarding school.

The ships that crested the wave of the new century were equipped with anti-rolling devices and during a calm period it was possible to forget that you were at sea. But even the best berth could not protect a passenger from the Atlantic's worst weather, when fog was so dense that a crew member had to blow a whistle every thirty seconds to warn other vessels of their proximity. The sky could also conjure up menacing waterspouts and uncanny cloud formations that mesmerised passengers with mountain ranges and snake-like fingers reaching from heaven, as if a celestial being was poised to scoop up presumptuous ships.[4] Wealthy women fliers like Boll, Grayson, Guest, and Mackay had witnessed the power and unpredictability of the Atlantic from the deck of a ship and, if they allowed their imagination to wander, they could envisage just how much more frightening the ocean could be if you were flying above it in a plane. Indeed, Mackay's father had made his fortune from ships, and she had even designed rooms on twelve P&O liners that now plied the ocean. But for pilots like Earhart and Ruth Elder, who came from more humble origins and who had no cause to cross the Atlantic in a ship, the fogs and eerie cloud formations were beyond imagination.

On a ship, the wealthy were able to recline in lavish bedroom suites and sit on mahogany chairs as they ate meals which, because galleys had been moved nearer to the dining saloon and stewards didn't have to negotiate open decks to deliver courses, were no longer soaked in sea spray. The invention of the fridge also meant food stayed fresher for longer and shipping lines were able to provide gargantuan supplies. In 1895 the *City of New York*, for example, which carried 1,420 people, set off with provisions that included: 1,150 chickens, ducks, and turkeys; 700 dozen eggs; 5,000 oranges; 7,000 pounds of sugar; 3,000 gallons of fresh milk; and 2,812 bottles of ale.[5] Happily, there were also more toilets to rush to when, as still happened with reliable frequency, passengers were struck down with seasickness. Some doctors recommended bromides of sodium and potassium or injections to combat this side-effect of ocean travel. Others suggested caffeine or cannabis for 'sea headache'.[6] Electric bells, fitted in the first-class cabins, were useful for summoning assistance.[7]

Savile had sailed across the Atlantic several times before, in January 1913, using the voyage to America to test her 'self-levelling cot' – a bed she'd designed to stave off seasickness. There was considerable curiosity about her invention but in raising awareness of the contraption she also risked reviving interest in her scandalous past. Indeed, some newspapers made only a fleeting reference to the device before launching into a reprise of the sorry tale of her brief marriage. Her presence in the USA, the *Times-Dispatch* of Richmond noted unashamedly, 'serves to recall the extraordinary career of her husband, the late Prince Louis of Loewenstein-Wertheim'.[8]

The newspaper then went on to remind readers, in great detail, that she had married her prince against the wishes of both families. Her father, the Earl of Mexborough, objected to his daughter's union with the younger, penniless son of a small German principality who, the paper said, came from 'one of those houses that exercised petty sovereignty until the overthrow of the Holy Roman Empire and which retains to this day the right of mating on a footing of equality with reigning dynasties of the Old World'.[9] The prince's family, so the paper claimed, disapproved of the match because it was erroneously believed that Anne's mother was Jewish, whereas she was, in fact, Catholic; her husband converted to Catholicism, and Anne married in a Catholic church. It was the sort of dynastic quagmire that could never occur in the New World and the paper relished every detail.

Ludwig Löwenstein-Wertheim-Freudenberg (several versions of his name were used in the press) lived in a Bavarian schloss and was a handsome man with a waxed moustache but was so deeply in debt, according to press reports, that he had to resort to 'marriage brokers' who introduced him to Savile. The couple married in the Spring of 1897, when she was thirty-three. The wedding was a grand affair in a church draped in the Bavarian colours of red and white and attended by many members of the European aristocracy. In a move that was seen as thrillingly modern, the Pope sent his Apostolic benediction by telegraph.[10] The ceremony must have sparked memories of Queen Victoria's nuptials – the most famous wedding between a member of the British aristocracy and a German from a principality so small it could easily become lost in the crease of a map.

But Savile and Löwenstein were no Victoria and Albert. Their marriage soured within months as Ludwig fell prey to blackmailers who threatened to reveal lurid details about his past. The prince appealed to his father-in-law, but the ageing Earl refused to step in. The prince had no option but to slip out of the country, leaving his debtors to advertise in the columns of the *Evening News* for leads as to his whereabouts.[11] London solicitors Plunkett and Leader placed ads in Britain and abroad and even employed private detectives to search for him.[12] Their appeals hinted that he was fleeing an unspeakable scandal, leaving his wife to defend his honour as best she could from their marital home in Park Lane, which was a gift from her mother, and to make assurances that she had been in regular contact and that suggestions of 'foul play' were 'ridiculous'.[13]

The wayward prince was doubly embarrassing for the Mexborough family because Anne's older sister, Mary Louisa had, the year after Anne's marriage, when she was thirty, also made an ill-advised union. Walter Burton Harris was, on and off, a *Times* correspondent in Morocco, between 1887 until his death in 1933. He also dabbled in espionage. Harris came from a reputable, ship-owning family; he had one brother who was an MP and another who was knighted, but Walter preferred a more peripatetic lifestyle and disguised himself as an Arab to write about north Africa. He spoke fluent Arabic, and his hazel eyes, dark complexion and shaved head – but for a foot-long lock emanating from the crown – allowed him easy acceptance as a local man.[14] Harris's lengthy absence from London and his openly homosexual lifestyle in Tangier meant it came as no surprise to those who knew him well that his marriage was annulled in 1905.[15] Lady Mary swore an affidavit that Harris was unable to consummate the marriage and that 'such incapacity is incurable by art or skill and will so appear upon inspection'.[16]

The aftermath of the Spanish-American squabble over Cuba, which had offered a tantalising glimmer of escape for Amy Phipps, provided a conclusion to Savile's torture about her wayward husband. The Treaty of Paris in December 1898 ended the war but, while the US agreed to allow Cuba its independence, the US decided to deny Philippine nationalists their freedom. The decision led to bitter fighting with Filipinos that far exceeded the bloodshed of the Spanish conflict.[17]

On 1 April 1899 – a date that seems to add to the sense that the family was being mocked – the *Army and Navy Gazette* reported that Löwenstein, who had been acting as Honorary Aide-de-camp (ADC) to American General, Marcus Miller, had been killed in fighting between the Americans and 'insurgents' near Manila.[18] Even his death was clouded in mystery and it was unclear how he had found himself in the line of fire or even why he was there in the first place. A report in *The New York Times* on 27 March 1899 further muddied the waters by suggesting he had been working as a spy for the German Government. A few months earlier, Savile's mother died, leaving an estate of £163,047 (worth about £17.2 million today).[19]

The humiliation for the Mexborough family must have been profound and it's easy to imagine the whisperings that followed the two sisters around London. But there was no sign that they would retire from public life. Like most widows of high birth, Anne became involved in the usual charities: the poor, children, orphans, and wounded soldiers. But she also re-discovered a taste for London parties. In 1905 she held a 'charming little dance' at her 'nice' house in Upper Belgrave Street. Lady Mary was staying with her for the season, and both wore stunning dresses and impressive 'brilliants' (diamonds).[20] It was the same year that Amy Phipps married her British husband in London, and her new relatives, the Churchills, were present at the ceremony. Another party suggested that Savile, too, had a taste for the more physical side of life and, in 1911, she arranged for a special floor to be laid in the ballroom of the Grafton Galleries so that one hundred guests could indulge in the current craze of roller-skating.[21]

There was no sign of Society shunning the sisters; indeed, their notoriety seemed only to have added to their appeal. Anne was on the edge of the infamous Marlborough House Set, a coterie of wealthy men and women who buzzed around the Prince of Wales, later King Edward VII. The group of politicians, lawyers, and other powerful men and women was named after his house in Pall Mall and shared a love of horse racing, card playing, and country house life.

Anne's royal connections came in handy when she visited New York in 1913, accompanied by her agent and footman, in a bid to publicise her patented anti-seasickness bed. But, although Queen Mary had used it in 1912 and journalists across America reported Anne's visit, few investors wanted to back it.[22] The contraption, which looked more like a form of medieval torture, consisted of a cot fixed to a gyroscope suspended from the ship's bunk. Soon Anne started to lose interest in inventions that were tethered so firmly to the ground. Instead, she had become captivated by conveyances that, at their most basic, resembled an airborne wooden crate strapped to a toboggan.

*

William Rowland Ding had only been a qualified pilot for a matter of weeks when, in May 1914, he agreed to fly Savile, now 50, from Hendon, North London, across the Channel to Calais for what she described as a pressing social engagement.[23] Hendon still had a village atmosphere in the early decades of the twentieth century but it was starting to attract anyone interested in the emerging flying craze. The area was conveniently close to London and had been associated with flying since 1909 when a local instrument manufacturer, Everett, Edgcumbe, built an aeroplane there and flying schools and manufacturers followed.[24]

Ding learnt to fly at the Beatty School, next to other flying enthusiasts such as designer and manufacturer Handley Page.

He was far from the stereotypical image of a dashing pilot. His flying helmet trapped a jowly face and Roman nose. His long leather jacket, belted at the waist, made him look like a clumsily assembled package. When Savile's car rolled up at the grass airfield she appeared, by comparison, as if she was about to encounter the night air after a glamorous ball. She wore heavy furs and an elegant hood that framed her delicate features perfectly. A voluminous velvet muff warmed her hands and shimmered like liquid. She looked every inch the princess.

Her footman unpacked the rugs and expensive pieces of luggage that were piled into the two-seater 110 HP Handley Page biplane. Ding said later that she evidently viewed the air crossing as she would a train journey.[25] The concept of travelling 'light' was alien to Savile, who had recently returned from Egypt, where she had been a passenger on a flight from Cairo to Luxor, taking photos as she went.[26]

Her decision to fly the Channel, if only in the passenger seat, followed Harriet Quimby's solo crossing two years earlier. Savile's jaunt was newsworthy because of her social status and because she was part of a growing number of wealthy British women keen to escape to the skies. Their fascination with flying – although focused on an individual endeavour – matched the earth-bound fervour of the suffragettes who were campaigning for votes for women. Newspapers that reported Savile's trip to Calais also featured 'Wild Scenes outside King's Palace' as suffragettes attempted to send a deputation to George V. A photo showed a police officer lifting Emmeline Pankhurst several inches from the ground as he manhandled her away from the protest.[27] Savile's flight shared the same page with accounts of entries into the *Daily Mail*'s £10,000 transatlantic competition.

Ding didn't have an easy journey after they left Hendon at 8.00 am on Thursday 21 May and fog forced the plane down at Eastbourne.

They set off again in the afternoon and Ding took 'his precious charge' several hundred yards out to sea.[28] At Folkestone he struck out on a diagonal line for Calais – about thirty-four miles away – and made the crossing in a record fifteen minutes, flying at a 'terrific pace' of, according to some accounts, an average speed of 138 miles per hour.[29] They landed at 4.20 pm with 'slight damage' at Beaumarais, near Calais. Savile boarded the evening train for the Hôtel de France et Choiseul in Paris,[30] and the next day Ding flew back to England to take part in an aerial derby at Hendon.[31]

Savile enjoyed the experience so much that she immediately signed up for daily flying lessons at Beatty's.[32] As one paper put it, 'Being a fearless horsewoman and practised motorist, she is not troubled by "nerves", and finds flying at high altitudes an excellent tonic and a certain cure for headaches and neuralgia.'[33] Another stated that she intended to buy her own plane.[34] 'Never did I enjoy better health,' she told one journalist, 'and never did I feel so hungry. The complexion does not suffer in the least, and the physical exertion required is very small indeed.'[35]

But by the summer of 1914 aeroplanes were no longer just flimsy vehicles for short hops around Britain or, at a stretch, across the Channel or beyond. Instead, governments were beginning to see their potential as killing machines. And, three years into the Great War, trying to have an aeroplane built – particularly if your husband had been a German – was likely to land you in hot water. But that was exactly what Savile did in September 1917.

It may have been that she had forgotten that her marriage to a German had, technically, made her an 'enemy alien' and that she needed a permit to travel more than five miles beyond her registered living quarters, or perhaps she simply thought those sorts of rules didn't apply to her. Or maybe she was just bored and desperate to own an aeroplane. Whatever the reasons, she made no attempt to obtain a travel permit when she left her home in Upper Belgrave Street, Piccadilly to travel to her sister's house, Scarcroft Lodge near Leeds. She must have known she was breaking the law because, when she travelled to Manchester on 27 September, she registered at the Victoria Hotel as 'Evelyn Ellis' and gave her address as the fictious 118 Porchester Terrace in London. Her visit appeared even more sinister when she telephoned a nearby aeroplane manufacturer to ask whether they could build her a 200 horsepower aircraft capable of carrying four passengers. She added that delivery must be quick. The factory manager informed the police, and a detective arrested her in the hotel reception.[36]

When she appeared in court the Scottish newspaper, the *Daily Record* carried the story on the front page next to patriotic photos of dashing soldiers who had been killed at the front, officers saluting volunteers and nurses raising money for the armed forces. Savile, by contrast, is shown smiling and encased in her leather coat, a flying helmet framing her thick eyebrows. The headline states, 'Lady and the Aeroplane' and the caption reads, 'Ann Lowenstein, believed to be Princess Lowenstein, a German Princess remanded under Alien Order'.[37]

It was pointed out in court, where she was allowed to sit on the magistrates' bench and appeared 'erect and stately',[38] that, while it was not illegal to buy an aeroplane, Savile's inquiries couldn't be seen as anything other than suspicious. Circumstantial evidence was stacked against her: she was a German princess buying a plane capable of crossing the North Sea at a time of national peril. It didn't take much imagination to place an escaped German officer behind her in the cockpit, highly sensitive documents tucked into his flying suit.

She claimed she wanted the plane to carry out war work and explained that she had been given a verbal permit from an 'an officer of high rank' in the Air Board to allow her to visit aerodromes and to fly in an aeroplane. When her brother, the Earl of Mexborough, was called to give evidence he described her 'craze for flying' and the family's disapproval. It was this disapproval that had led her to subterfuge. He said her only connection with Germany had been occasional visits during her two-year marriage. She had no anti-British leanings, and she was referred to among the family as 'John Bull'. A letter from Father Bernard Vaughan, who knew the defendant well, was read out and confirmed her patriotism. She was fined twenty-five pounds for each of the two offences and ordered to pay three guineas in costs. However, the publication *John Bull* was not impressed and wrote in its 'Candid Communications' page:

> MADAM, - Accept my congratulations. If you had not been a lady, the widow of a German prince, and with what we call 'high English family connections', you would have received six months instead of being fined £50 for that little attempt of yours . . . I notice that you entered the Court by way of the Magistrates' staircase. If I had had anything to do with the case, you would have left via the steps to the cell.[39]

That same year, Savile lost the pilot who had flown her to France. Ding's aerial stunts had transformed him into a flying celebrity and postcards bearing his likeness sold well. But at one display at Leeds on 12 May an extravagant loop placed too much strain on the wings and they crumbled, sending the plane hurtling to the ground, watched by 1,000 horrified spectators. Ding, who was married with a family, died instantly.[40]

*

Savile was granted a certificate of nationalisation in June 1918, a few months before the end of the war with Germany.[41] Public awareness that she had once been married to a German prince, which had been reawakened by her visit to the magistrates' court, faded and peacetime released a flood of qualified pilots looking for work. Those flyers now had regular race meetings to compete in and Savile became a fixture at these events, which had the atmosphere of an equine point-to-point. Newspapers such as *The Times* started to devote several column inches to the flying contests on their sports news pages, where reports earned their place side-by-side with polo, rugby, and cricket. Although Savile took flying lessons, there is no record of her having secured her licence; instead, she preferred to experience the visceral thrill of being in the air but with someone else at the controls. From the early 1920s, that companion was Captain Leslie Hamilton, MBE (Member of the Order of the British Empire), DFC (Distinguished Flying Cross).

Hamilton, also known as the 'Flying Gypsy' and the 'Sky Taximan', cut a romantic figure.[42] Despite his impeccable RAF background, he often flew short hops in lounge suits – a fact that was remarked upon in the press. His grin and tightly fitting clothes, which made him look as though he had grown out of them but not had time to buy replacements, gave him a boyish air. He had also gained a reputation as a stuntman and in the winter of 1924 caused a sensation by landing a plane on the ice at St Moritz. He then towed the Scottish Earl of Northesk and the Hungarian Prince Odescalchi at forty miles per hour as they held on to a bar attached to a rope in a form of aerial, frozen-water skiing.[43]

In September 1922 the *Edinburgh Evening News* pictured Savile in the cockpit of an airplane reaching down to grasp the hand of her retired nanny who had turned out to wish her well at the start of the 810-mile Round Britain King's Cup Race from Croydon to Glasgow and back again.[44] The newspaper pointed out that she was flying under her maiden name but, in saying that she was sixty-eight years old, inflated her age by a decade. This was the first of what became an annual event to encourage the development of light aircraft and their engines. Twenty-one planes started the race, which took in Birmingham and Newcastle on the way to Glasgow, and Manchester and Bristol on the return leg. Savile and Hamilton were among eleven who finished the two-day route. They landed at Croydon Aerodrome, which had been transformed into an 'Epsom of the Air', as crowds followed the planes' progress on giant wooden boards like the runners and riders' signs at a horseracing event.[45]

The land-based races were relatively safe as it was comparatively easy to guide a fabric and wood plane to earth, but crossing a long stretch of water like the Channel was a different matter. When Hamilton and Savile went missing on Saturday 22 August 1925, after leaving Lympne on the Kent coast at 4.20 pm the day before, it must have been an excruciating ordeal for his wife to read headlines such as 'Princess in Aeroplane – Mystery of Journey to Paris – Machine Missing'.[46] Officials at aerodromes on both sides of the Channel scanned the skies for the biplane.[47] St Inglevert, the first French air station on the London-Paris route received news from a semaphore station at Cap Gris-Nez that a plane had been spotted flying south at 4.45 pm but there was no further news from ships who were wirelessed to keep an eye out for the pair.[48] Just before 6.00 pm on Saturday, after an all-night search, Croydon Aerodrome received news that the plane had landed in a wood on Friday evening, near Beauvais, thirty kilometres from Paris. Hamilton had repaired the plane and resumed their journey, although he failed to let the authorities know.[49]

For Savile, the adventure confirmed that forced landings were survivable, perhaps even part of the thrill of flying. She was now held in its maw. To Hamilton, it was a way of life and a way of living; the skies were much more peaceful than they had been in the Great War but flying still brought danger – especially as pilots pushed their engines further and harder.

Savile had the funds to indulge her passion and her disregard for the law showed that she couldn't shake her compulsion for flying, even when she'd seen from the cockpit just how dangerous it could be. Her family, like Amy Guest's, was particularly unhappy about her exploits in a plane, but she was determined to find a way to stay in the air, no matter the risks.

CHAPTER SIX

Elsie Mackay: From Interior Designer to Stunt Pilot

Although Elsie Mackay was thirty years younger than Savile, they had much in common. Both came from wealthy families, both worried away at the edges of what women were allowed to do and both had troublesome marriages, although the unsuitability of their husbands was resolved in different ways.

Both gave their closest male relatives the run-around. Savile's brother was constantly having to rescue her from scrapes and Mackay's father, Lord Inchcape, chairman of the steamship company, P&O, and one of the richest men in Britain, didn't dare take his eyes off her. He was close to Elsie, his third and, it was said, favourite daughter but frequently had to dash home from abroad or from the family's home, Glenapp Castle, near Ballantrae in Southwest Scotland to untangle a mess of her making.[1]

Mackay's family wealth had been much more recently acquired than Savile's and was soaked in seafaring. Her paternal grandfather had owned and captained a number of ships in Arbroath, northeast Scotland, and part of his business was to transport Irish immigrants across the Atlantic to Newfoundland. Another strand involved shipping flax from Russia to make rope and canvas and the first time James Mackay, the future Lord Inchcape, accompanied his father on a journey he was eight, and joined a voyage to the distant port of Archangel in Russia. For him the Atlantic was associated with business, but also tragedy. He had nearly drowned during the Archangel expedition and the Atlantic had taken his father, leaving him an orphan at the age of eleven.

An eye for detail, a fierce work ethic, and the expanding British Empire allowed Mackay to leave these modest beginnings and enter a world where his influence reached the highest levels. He was at the very heart of the British Empire just as the new Suez Canal was opening India up for European businesses and proved himself such a zealous public servant that Lord Morley offered him the title of Viceroy of India.[2] The cabinet refused to promote a man who had risen through the clerical ranks and, undaunted by the snub, Mackay expanded his commercial interests, becoming director of the Great Western Railway (GWR) and chairman of British India. In this latter role he negotiated the amalgamation with Peninsula and Oriental Steam Navigation (P&O) and became chairman in 1914. His long years of service garnered a slew of awards, culminating with the title of Viscount Glenapp.[3]

But, despite his travels, he would always have one foot in Scotland, and it was on a visit home to recover from typhoid that he reconnected with Jane Paterson, a friend of his sister's from Arbroath and an engineer's daughter. They married in 1883, allowing him to avoid the trials of the 'fishing fleet', the eligible young women who travelled to India 'fishing' for husbands among the administrators, businessmen, and soldiers who had made their lives there. Jane understood that her new husband had come from a very different background from the men he now worked with, that he had attended Elgin Academy rather than a public school and concluded his education aged fourteen. He had spent his spare time gazing out at a grey North Sea, rather than at a verdant family estate.

Elsie, who was born in Simla, India, in 1893, existed in many worlds but mainly in the bracing, rugged freedom of Southwest Scotland and the more constricted world of Mayfair. Her Scottish home was Glenapp, a romantic baronial castle that her father bought in 1917. The building was designed by a Victorian architect from Edinburgh and inspired by a Sir Walter Scott view of Scottish life. A team of servants fussed around its sandstone battlements and kept fires burning in its wood-panelled rooms where guests did their best to shake off the Scottish damp. Many of those visitors arrived in limousines, and included maharajas and rajahs Inchcape had met during his years in India, who alighted wearing painfully thin saris and shalwar kameez. Gardeners tended Glenapp's dark firs, lush rhododendrons, and giant redwoods and groundsmen made sure there were plenty of grouse in its 15,000 acres for visitors to chase around the loch and forests in the August hunting season.[4] Inchcape worked from a turreted office overlooking the Mull of Kintyre, where he loved to sail his yacht, *Rover*. His desk mirrored his orderly mind – everything had its place. He hated anyone to interfere with his routine and had a special 'touching' drawer so that any grandchildren who ventured into his study could restrict their rummaging to a designated area.[5]

Although Mackay was educated in a convent in Belgium, she loved the outdoorsiness and freedom of Glenapp: the chance to dance Scottish reels, to ride horses, and later, like the pilot in John Buchan's *The Thirty-Nine Steps* who chased Richard Hannay through the same remote terrain, to swoop over the area's rugged landscape. She careered round the lonely roads in her silver Rolls-Royce,[6] past ancient ruins and a craggy coastline saturated with stories of smugglers and characters like Sawney Bean, the sixteenth-century highwayman who was said to waylay travellers and dine off their bodies in the cave where he lived with his family. If she paused to glance out to sea from Ballantrae she would see the lonely granite island of Ailsa Craig and the coast of Ireland, a landscape she would one day fly over in her most famous adventure.

Her love of speed and danger were all the more striking because she was so tiny and her slightly protruding front teeth gave her the air of a schoolgirl who refused to succumb to braces. Before she discovered flying, she got her thrills at the wheel of her Rolls-Royce or Bentley or perched high up on her favourite 'hunter'. She had a brief career as a film actor under the name 'Poppy Wyndham' and appeared as a jockey called Tricot Blue (sic) in *The Great Coup*, shunning stunt doubles to mount the horse herself and race against two male professionals.[7] Although women weren't allowed to compete professionally, she threw down a challenge to the world of horse racing: 'I am quite willing to ride for anyone who will engage me. A licence for a first race is not necessary for a man jockey so why can't a woman test her skill in the same way?'[8]

Her lifestyle was at odds with commentators such as Major Oliver Stewart, an ex-RAF pilot, who wrote in his 'Air Eddies' column in *The Tatler*:

> Their [women's] interests and energies are being wasted on some such activity [of flying], and they will be persuaded to mend their ways only when they have learned the truth that the lip-stick is mightier than the joy-stick.[9]

Like many well-to-do women of her age, Mackay felt a compulsion to take up nursing as a way of proving her support for the war effort. In retrospect, her parents may have wished they had followed Amy Phipps' family's example by forbidding their daughter from having anything to do with wounded soldiers. Instead, Mackay's mother, invited the damaged young men into their house, Seamore Place in Mayfair, where their neighbours included the Rothschilds, and which they converted into a convalescent home.

Mackay, must have made a startling addition to the convalescent home. When she wasn't trying to cheer up the wounded she enjoyed the social whirl of London, especially, as her mother's poor health meant she often had to deputise for her. When Mackay fell in love it was said to be one of *the* romances of the First World War.[10]

The Inchcapes could not have envisaged that their daughter would be attracted to someone like Captain Dennis Wyndham and, in so doing, created the ingredients for a 'war wedding adventure in which the principals are a wounded officer and peer's daughter'.[11] At the time Wyndham was a lieutenant in the Royal Flying Corps and the Wiltshire regiment and perhaps, like Amelia Earhart who was nursing officers in Toronto at around the same time, Mackay became intrigued by flying when she heard about it from a man she was coaxing back to health.[12] Even without the allure of the air, Wyndham was different from most of the men she had met. He was South African, Catholic, a boxer, and an actor who had been gassed in France[13] and who towered above her.[14] When he asked Lord Inchcape for her hand in marriage, he refused. Inchcape was dismayed by his prospective son-in-law's connection with the stage and may also have been concerned about the £1 million his daughter had inherited on her 21st birthday in 1914.[15] The soldier was moved to another hospital, and she took to her bed for six weeks.[16]

But the couple became secretly engaged and planned what the papers, who delighted in the story, described as a 'runaway marriage'. The lovers, aware that they were being chased by the military police because Wyndham's leave had been cancelled, headed for a restaurant in Coventry Street, just off Piccadilly Circus, where they took several people into their confidence. Their accomplices lent them clothes and they changed into their disguises in a telephone box. In her later account there is a sense that Mackay enjoyed the thrill of the chase. 'My husband entered a box in uniform and came out in mufti. I had had a tailor [sic] costume on order at a shop which I was able to send for and change into,' she later told reporters. They jumped into a cab and the taxi driver, who was in on the secret and 'behaved like a brick', drove them to Willesden Junction where they boarded a train for the North.[17] At Crewe they felt it would be 'safer to travel among these lads' and bought third class tickets, obviously a thrilling novelty for the bride.[18] The 'Tommies' were delighted by the chance to outwit the authorities and several offered to lend Wyndham their uniform.

They had intended to stop at Gretna Green but 'the blacksmith business did not appeal to us'[19] the groom said later, referring to the tradition of couples eloping to the border town where a blacksmith would seal the marriage by striking his anvil. Instead, they carried on to Glasgow where they took advantage of Scotland's more relaxed marriage laws. When they called at St Aloysius Church the priest assured them that they could get married on the spot. A verger and an old lady, who had popped in to pray, acted as witnesses. Afterwards they telegrammed their friends to tell them the news and then took a train to Euston where the bridegroom was arrested by a provost-marshal.

'That P.M. was a splendid fellow,' Wyndham said later. 'He took us both to his house, and served us with a capital breakfast.'[20]

No action was taken, and he was invalided out of the Army.

Not surprisingly, no mention of Mackay's elopement appears in Lord Inchcape's official biography. The whole episode, which was covered so fully in the press, was deeply embarrassing to someone who had become a pillar of the establishment. A wedding in a Catholic church was probably not the worst aspect. Although Scotland at that time was a sectarian country divided by religious affiliations and the Inchcapes were Protestants, Inchcape was not motivated by faith and even spoke out against the observance of the Sabbath that precluded travelling by train, playing golf or tennis, reading papers, or going on a charabanc outing – in short, anything 'which is a source of pleasure or interest to the people on the Lord's Day'.[21] He was probably more troubled that his favourite daughter was marrying a man who didn't have a steady job.

After the war, Wyndham continued his acting career and Mackay took to the stage and appeared in two silent films, both of which were screened in 1920. In *The Tidal Wave* she plays Columbine, an artist who is saved from the sea by a fisherman who falls in love with her. After she is plucked from the water, her long, curly hair falls around her face in a way that makes her look attractively dishevelled. Her role in *The Sun of David* is unclear but the plot revolves around a rabbi adopting an orphan who becomes a boxer and fights the man he thinks killed his father. It was about this time that she left her dog, a borzoi, known for its slim elegance and long snout, alone in her West End flat with a window open. It's easy to see this oversight as proof that she was unwilling, or incapable, of imagining a scenario when things go wrong. But, the dog, seeing his mistress walking down the street, jumped thirty feet to its death. It was said that Mackay's grief was uncontrollable for weeks.

She was also having to contend with a failing marriage and in 1922 applied for an annulment after it was found that neither party had been in Scotland for the fifteen days required by the special wartime marriage act.[22] By July that year she had resorted to her maiden name and appeared to have returned to the Inchcape family fold.[23] In May she had travelled with her father on the new White Star liner, *Majestic*, at the time the largest ship in the world, when it completed its first eastbound crossing of the Atlantic. The voyage took five days and thirteen hours and passengers were treated to daily displays of 'fancy swimming and diving' and a game of water polo.[24] Mackay, who was a keen swimmer, enjoyed a dip in the emerald and coral pool daily.[25] She and her father were together again at Cowes in July when she wore a 'byzantine-red coat and hat' on board his yacht, *Rover*,[26] and in December she travelled with her parents to India.[27]

She was starting to take an interest in the family business, too, and while Savile had been most concerned about reducing seasickness, Mackay concentrated on making the ships' interiors look more like the comfortable homes the passengers had left behind – at least those in first class. Mostly her style indicated a desire to turn the ships into floating versions of Glenapp.[28] The first-class smoking room in the *Viceroy of India* resembled the great hall of a castle with its huge fireplace, oak panelling, crossed swords and a royal coat of arms.[29] The swimming pool, the company's first indoor pool, mimicked the recently excavated public baths at Pompeii, boasted classical columns and a gallery from which spectators could glance down at the swimmers.[30]

When it came to flying, though, Mackay was not content simply to sit in the passenger seat and, on 14 August 1922, she became one of the first women to obtain her pilot's licence when she lifted her de Havilland biplane into the skies over Stag Lane Airfield in Hendon.[31] It was ten years since Harriet Quimby had become the first woman to cross the Channel and Hilda Hewlett the first British woman to earn her pilot's licence. By 1922 there were still only about twelve qualified English women pilots, according to *The Vote*, a suffragette newspaper that praised Mackay for learning to fly in just six months.[32] She quickly gained a reputation as a steady and reliable pilot, unlike the so-called 'flying flappers' who dabbled in the sport. Her reputation was acknowledged, when in 1925, she became the only woman on the Advisory Committee of Pilots to the Air League.[33]

There were other stories, though, that indicated that Mackay was a fearless – perhaps even foolhardy – pilot. Captain E. C. D. Herne, one of her flying instructors, told *The New York Times* that, as the paper put it, it was a 'marvel ... she has never broken her neck'.[34] He recounted how during one of her first lessons, when they were 10,000 feet in the air, she had shouted through the connecting tube, 'Say, Hernie, loop her round the other way.'

Her request was that, instead of pointing the plane's nose up and climbing into a gentle arc, or 'loop', he should steer the plane towards the ground. This manoeuvre would place the wheels of the landing carriage on the inside of the loop and exert a huge strain on every strut and wire. Herne checked they were both properly strapped in and did what she'd asked – perhaps he was galled by her confidence and wanted to teach her a lesson. He watched the wings tremble under the strain like a flag in a gale. Then Mackay's safety strap snapped; she caught the bracing wires inside the cockpit just as her body swung outside the plane. Herne struggled to land and when they were safely on the ground, he noticed that her hands had been cut to the bone in her efforts to cling on. Despite her injuries she said she would repeat the exercise once she was fitted with a stronger safety belt.[35]

Although the anecdote sounds far-fetched, it's significant that such a story of daring-do was told about a female pilot. Sir Alan Cobham, who made his name as a long-distance pilot and who gave Mackay lessons at Stag Lane, was also impressed by her and allowed her to fly some of the bigger planes.[36] She might have been content to push herself to fly larger and faster machines and to try out more daring stunts, had it not been for Lindbergh's crossing of the Atlantic. According to one friend, she was inspired by his visit to England in 1927.[37] The American had not expected such an enthusiastic welcome from his British supporters but when he arrived at Croydon Airport the crowds were as big as they had been at Le Bourget, where he had landed in France. 'Barriers were swept away like matchwood' and when a member of the crowd snatched his helmet Lindbergh made no attempt to hide his anger.[38] He had to fight his way through the crowd and when he addressed the well-wishers he described the reception as 'a little worse than Le Bourget, or, I should say, better.'[39] Thousands lined the streets as he passed through central London; he met the Prime Minister, Stanley Baldwin, at Number Ten Downing Street and King George V at Buckingham Palace. It was at the palace that the King was alleged to have asked him, 'There is one thing I long to know. How do you pee?'[40] He was the guest of the Astors at the House of Commons, where MPs rose to honour him. As a prominent pilot, Mackay may well have been at one of the social events he endured.

*

Captain Walter Hinchliffe – known as 'Hinch', 'Walt', or 'Ray' – was also inspired by Lindbergh and saw the landing at close quarters when he and his wife happened to be in Paris. Hinch, whose life and career would soon be perpetually entwined with Mackay's, joined 150,000 people at Le Bourget airfield to welcome *The Spirit of St Louis* on May 21 1927[41] as Lindbergh emerged through the glare of popping camera lights, car head lamps, and the airfield's own illuminations.[42] The successful crossing, later likened in its significance to a moon landing, had a deep effect on most of those who witnessed it, but it was especially significant for Hinch who told his wife, 'How I envy that man, he has done something.'[43]

Hinch is a difficult character to pin down – even his place of birth is uncertain. His pilot's licence from the Royal Aero Club states that he was born in Liverpool and that his date of birth was 11 June 1894. Significantly, this document was produced in 1916 – two years into a vicious war with Germany. Other sources, however, assert he was born in 1891, 1892, and 1893. The document issued by the FAI looks as though it has been tampered with and his daughter, Joan, in her introduction to his logbook, gave his date of birth as 10 June 1894 (this is confirmed by his 1921 passport).[44] Not only did he get younger with the passing years but his birthplace also migrated – the 1911 census gives it as Munich in Germany. It's understandable that an ambitious pilot such as Hinch would be keen to shed any connection with a country he spent several years trying to battle into submission.

He had learnt to fly in 1912 at Brooklands aerodrome in Surrey, a site where the rich could indulge their love of both fast cars and aeroplanes, and studied medicine and dentistry at Liverpool University in 1919.[45] He also described himself as an 'artist', like his father.[46] His Army Records state he spoke German fluently.[47] According to family lore he was a competitive athlete and particularly good at boxing, cricket, putting the shot, horse-riding, and swimming. He loved animals and, as a boy, turned the cellar of his family home into a hospital for the neighbourhood's sick cats. Like Mackay, he owned a borzoi, although his avoided defenestration and instead accompanied his master in the cockpit for occasional flights.[48]

Hinch served with the Royal Artillery for two years before joining the Royal Naval Air Service (RNAS). In his FAI photo he is sitting in a cockpit, goggles pushed on top of his head, handsome, yet unsmiling, his brow furrowed as if his blue eyes can see into the future. Over the next two years he worked as an instructor at RNAS Cranwell in Lincolnshire, in the East of England. Some days he would take as many as fourteen men through their paces, often jotting down scathing comments in his logbook such as: 'has no idea of flying', 'lacks confidence in himself', 'OK though windy', and 'temperament unsuited'. Frequently he would record their subsequent deaths – either on active service or during accidents while flying in the UK.

But another side to the unyielding instructor also emerges from between the stark lines of his logbook. Here is a man who enjoys 'buzzing' soldiers crossing the aerodrome as a way of 'putting the wind up' them, who can see the humour in a mechanic who jumps onto a roof to avoid an out-of-control plane, and who amuses himself by 'chasing' trains from the air. He's a careful navigator but one who can also appreciate the perspective that only a pilot can see, 'the wonderful sunset effect', for example. When he takes Lieutenant Commander Tsen-Li Ching, aide-de-camp (ADC) to the president of China, for a flight he records his passenger's thanks for 'initiating him to the Paradise of Heaven'.

He had clocked up a total of 1,250 flying hours in thirteen months when, in January 1918, he was released from his duties as an instructor to fight in a war that, unbeknown to its combatants, was in its final year. Everything changed on the night of 3 June 1918. He was flying a Camel 3307 over the forest of Lieppe, close to the France/Belgium border. He was alone and on the hunt for German Gothas, although it was difficult to see anything through the ground mist and without the help of a moon. A searchlight picked up the shape of an enemy 'machine' and in the battle that followed Hinch crashed through the treetops, fracturing his skull and injuring his face, probably from being hurled against the metal of the twin Vickers machine guns.[49] At least that's the version in Hinch's own logbook. Other accounts suggest a less heroic end to his frontline services in which he was attempting to fly a Camel, which had been damaged after a forced landing in a cornfield by another pilot, back to base. In this version, the left tyre came off during take-off causing the plane to turn over and badly injuring Hinch. Whichever account is accurate, the reality was that he lost the sight in his left eye as part of the crash and wore a patch for the rest of his life. He received the Distinguished Flying Cross and Air Force Cross for his service, and his logbook recorded that he was back in the air by 3 August and felt no 'ill effect' as he looped the loop over Hendon and soared along the Thames at Richmond. A few days later he felt 'fit for active service again'[50] and 'Quite OK now, ears well back, tail up!!'[51]

The terrifying accident meant Hinch concluded his RAF career as a hero, but it also disguised a record that was far from unblemished. In June 1915, the year he was promoted to captain, he was arrested and charged with stealing a motorcycle and sidecar belonging to a fellow officer from a farm and with taking a meteorological barograph from the Air Ministry.[52] The charges were dropped due to lack of evidence but left a permanent cloud over his reputation and his commanding officer described him as an 'undesirable character'. In August he resigned his commission from the West Lancashire Division, but, despite this fall from grace, he married Dorothy Taylor in Salford,

Manchester in September. However, a year before Elsie Mackay would resort to the same get-out, the marriage was annulled – in Hinch's case because his bride had been under the age of consent.[53]

Despite his disability, his flying experience meant he was snapped up by fledgling commercial airlines and he worked for the Royal Dutch Airlines, KLM, and later Imperial Airways. Although flying round Europe on ad hoc missions sounds romantic, it brought with it a weighty responsibility. One incident that brought home that responsibility for Hinch, and in which he was lucky to survive, occurred when he stopped over on his way to an exhibition flight near the Dutch–German border. As a crowd gathered to take a closer look at the plane, several people were forced against the propeller, which suddenly backfired, killing a thirty-five-year-old woman and a ten-year-old boy; a man, also thirty-five, died later from his injuries. The crowd turned on Hinch and his crew members and the husband of the woman produced a revolver. Hinch and the other airmen fled to a car and drove 200 miles back to Amsterdam. Members of the mob were locked up and Hinch returned to the plane under military escort. The minister who conducted the boy's funeral wrote to Hinch to ask what would be done for the victim's parents who were 'poor working people'. We don't know how he replied, but he kept the letter in his logbook.

By 1927 the horrible incident was far in the past and probably only remembered by those who had been directly affected by it. But Hinch can't have failed to have been troubled by it. Like his wartime experience, and the friends he had lost in that conflict and in other flying accidents, it was part of his backstory. Very few pilots had gone through what he had gone through or witnessed what he had seen. He was one of the world's most experienced flyers and had spent a total of 9,000 hours in the air.[54] At Imperial Airways he made the daily flight between London and Paris and was known for his ability to fly in bad weather. His logbook for this period ends with cuttings about the extraordinary feat of Alcock and Brown who had just flown the

Atlantic. Clearly their achievement had had a big impression on him but his personal experience of flying included many tragic examples of how things can go wrong. Flying for him was always a matter of weighing up the risks and the rewards. That equation became even harder to judge once he had more than just his own personal safety to consider.

Flight Checklist: A Tendency to Tomboy

As a young girl growing up in Kansas, Amelia Earhart was a scruffy, outdoorsy type in dirty breeches. When she went fishing with her granddad she wore blue jeans and a farmboy hat.[1] She was the sort of child Willa Cather might have been thinking of when she described Sally Harling in *My Ántonia* (1918) as a 'tomboy with short hair ... uncannily clever at all boys' sports'. Or she could easily have been the matter-of-fact Scout in baggy overalls from *To Kill A Mockingbird*.

Earhart liked all kinds of sports and games and wasn't afraid to try those not considered proper for young ladies, although she wished that she had been taught the basic skills to allow her to be good at them. Horse riding was a case in point. Whereas Phipps, Savile, and Mackay had grown up with a stable full of animals to choose from and the best riding tutors, the nearest Earhart and her younger sister, Muriel, got to a horse was one belonging to their neighbour. They would sneak him lumps of sugar, but he was too 'sleek and too tall' for them to climb onto his back.[2]

Amelia so wanted to be sitting on top of a horse that when a fat delivery animal stopped at the house one day she managed to clamber on board using the curb and the wagon harness. She had to be lifted down but was desperate to repeat the experience. She got her chance when she visited friends whose father ran a butcher's. When business was quiet, they were allowed to sit on the old horses who pulled the delivery trucks. Amelia particularly enjoyed riding the 'heavy-footed sorrel' who would buck for no good reason.

She shocked her grandmother by habitually running home from school and jumping over the fence. Further shock was caused by the Earhart girls' 'gymnasium suits' – a sort of bloomer that were the first of its type seen in town.[3] They wore them on Saturdays to play in and felt 'free and athletic' but also were outcasts among the little girls who 'fluttered about' in skirts.[4]

When she went sledging, she refused to sit upright and insisted on lying flat. She later said this method saved her life because it allowed her to slide straight through the front and back legs of the horse pulling a junk man's cart that appeared as she careered down an icy slope.

The two sisters confidently put footballs on their Christmas list because they didn't need more baseballs and bats. They got what they asked for and Muriel also managed to procure a gun, but it was quickly confiscated. When it was reinstated, she progressed from target practice at bottles sitting on the fence to culling rats in the barn while Amelia, aged six, constructed a trap out of an old orange crate to catch chickens that strayed into their garden from next door. They also built a roller-coaster.[5]

Earhart enjoyed school because of games and the mud pies. She relished the expeditions up and down the bluffs of the Missouri River and in and out of the sandstone caves. She was excited, rather than scared, by the whirlpools in the river's yellow depths that had once swept away bridges and engulfed the lowlands.

But she was not someone who went blindly into danger. She had an imagination. One of her favourite games was to sit in an abandoned horse-drawn carriage kept in her grandmother's barn and, together with her cousins, to create faraway, hair-raising adventures. She fuelled these fantastical trips by reading ferociously, and through car journeys with her father, who spent long hours on the road as part of his job as a lawyer for the railroads. He would often take her with him as they shuttled between Kansas City, Des Moines, St Paul, and Chicago.

Earhart classed flying as a sport. In August 1927, nearly a year before she became a household name, she was interviewed for a newspaper feature about women and aviation. At the time she was working as a social worker in Boston and was also on the board of Dennison Aircraft Corporation, which had just opened Boston's second airport at Atlantic. She was 'teacher, social worker, sportswoman and airplane pilot'.[6]

'New England has some of the best yachtswomen and sportswomen in the world,' she declared. 'I am surprised that more New England women have not gone into flying as a sport. Why is it? ... I started flying as a sport. I had ridden horses, played tennis, enjoyed yachting and all that – and flying, by the way, is much akin to sailing.'[7]

Earhart may have had more opportunity to run wild as a child because she wasn't watched over by servants but, generally, wealthy American families seem to have allowed their daughters more freedom than their British counterparts. When she was young, American-born Nancy Langhorne (later Astor), who married into the British aristocracy and became a politician herself, liked baseball and boys' games and later shocked her British husband by riding a motorbike. The Phipps girls made the most of the vast gardens and country estates they lived in on both sides of the Atlantic. They took easily to the British pastime of hunting, and Amy Guest was known for her fearlessness riding side-saddle. When newspapers described her as a debutante, they pointed out her prowess as a swimmer, golfer, and rider to hounds, as much as her good looks.

Elsie Mackay couldn't stop moving – the faster the better. Horse riding combined her love of animals and speed.[8] She started riding at the age of five and would have loved to have competed as a professional jockey, if the rules had allowed. Images of her perched high up on a horse for a film part make her look tiny, but unafraid.

She dashed around the country in her silver Rolls-Royce and threw herself into Scottish reels when she was staying at Glenapp. For a short period during the First World War, she was a driver attached to a training squadron at Northolt, in the suburbs of North West London.[9] It was so common to see her 'big Crossley burning up the Uxbridge-road with a load of brass-hats [officers]' that, in an effort to slow her down, she was forced to downgrade to a smaller car. She ended her wartime career driving a Douglas motorbike.[10]

Earhart bought her first car, a Kissel roadster that she called the 'Yellow Peril' (after its canary-coloured paintwork) or 'The Kizzle', and that summer drove her mother from Los Angeles to Medford, Massachusetts where Muriel lived.[11] The 7,000-mile cross-country road trip took them through some of the country's most spectacular scenery, including Yosemite and Yellowstone national parks but, given that cars were not yet designed for long-distance travel, this was a gruelling expedition and when the Yellow Peril chugged into the more remote towns it usually attracted a crowd. Hours of driving must have been even more trying for Earhart since she suffered from chronic headaches due to sinus problems and eventually had to have an operation to alleviate the pain.

In the early days of flying, merely sitting in an open cockpit represented a physical activity in which you were buffeted by the wind and your whole body was forced to accommodate the plane's jolts and surges. For Savile, there was no conflict between the physicality of flying and travelling in style. Flying was a fashion statement, and she enjoyed choosing colours that co-ordinated with the plane. Like the Duchess of Bedford, who took to flying because it eased her tinnitus, Savile found that being airborne cured headaches and neuralgia and gave her a healthy appetite.[12] She had flown over the Channel at least twice and experienced the terror of a forced landing in woods, but she'd also gazed down through the shimmering heat of the Nile and had the sublime experience of viewing the Valley of the Kings from above.

Lady Mary Heath was another wealthy pilot – although she was born in Limerick, western Ireland, as Mary Peirce-Evans and the title 'Lady' only came courtesy of her second husband, Sir James Heath. She had also done much to promote the idea that it was possible to be feminine and take on daring exploits in the air. She found space in her plane for six dresses, a fur coat, and tennis rackets when she became the first woman to fly solo from Cape Town via Cairo to London in 1928. When she landed in Cairo, Amy Guest's husband Frederick castigated *The Times* for its muted coverage and pointed out that most of the terrain she had flown over was jungle or bush and that her chances of rescue if she had been forced down were only a little less hopeless than if she had been crossing the Atlantic.[13] Unlike Earhart, she eschewed masculine clothes and did her best to make her achievements sound effortless, letting everyone know that she had eaten chocolates and read a novel as she followed the Nile to Cairo.

When she arrived at Le Bourget she told reporters:

> It is so safe that a woman can fly across Africa nowadays wearing a Parisian frock and keeping her nose powdered all the way ... Really it was not hard. When my powder blew off I simply clamped the joystick between my knees, held my mirror with one hand, and powdered with the other, and I did it many a time with a lion, a giraffe, or a herd of elephants gazing up at me.[14]

But Heath's contribution to flying amounts to much more than beauty tips. She first flew solo in 1925 and then campaigned to overturn the International Commission for Air Navigation's 1924 ruling which determined that physiology alone meant commercial pilots carrying passengers must be male. She wrote to the commission offering herself as a guinea pig in medical tests to challenge this ruling and in the first three months of 1926 she put herself through the rigorous training required for the B licence. The commission rescinded its ban in May 1926. She and another Irish pilot, Mary Bailey, both secured several world altitude records.

Heath achieved all of this despite a tragic start to life. When she was only one year old her father beat her mother to death and was then declared insane. She had gone on to study at the Royal College of Science in Dublin and, like Mackay, served in the First World War, riding a Harley-Davidson motorbike as a dispatch rider for the War Office. She was a talented sportswoman and competed at an international level in javelin throwing, discus, shot putting, and the high jump, while also campaigning through the Women's Amateur Athletic Association (WAAA).

As vice-president of the WAAA she encouraged, whenever she could, women to take part in sport. At the eighth Olympic Congress in Prague, 1925, she delivered a paper entitled 'Women's Participation in Athletics' in which she set out the advantages of physical exercise for women, though insisting on safeguards against over-exertion, especially during adolescence, when girls, she thought, might damage their ability to bear children. She subsequently compiled a report on the opinions of schoolmistresses and doctors on games for females in England, which concluded that the benefits outweighed any drawbacks, provided that there were proper safeguards. These views were included in her book *Athletics for Women and Girls* (1925), which offered advice on training for the various track and field events.

Ruth Elder managed to combine stylishness with the practical side of being a pilot. She liked to wear a masculine ensemble of brogues, 'knickers', a tie, and a shirt. However, she had a habit of re-applying her lipstick at moments of extreme peril and stressed that one of the highlights for her of crossing the Atlantic was to go shopping in Paris.

There seem to be no tomboyish tendencies in Frances Grayson's childhood and yet she thrived in male-dominated worlds: real estate and leading a trans-Atlantic flight. Mabel Boll's childhood is so shrouded in mystery that it barely exists. It is impossible, though, to imagine her building a chicken trap or careering down a snowy slope. It's much easier to conjure her up as a little girl sliding along in her mother's high-heeled shoes, lipstick applied with wild abandon, perhaps an ostrich feather in her baby doll hair. And even then, she must surely have been dreaming of diamonds.

Flying in the 1920s was a physical pursuit and, even if women pilots chose to mask its masculine side with a colourful scarf or a touch of lipstick, there was no disguising the fact that they were battling the elements and taming a forceful machine. Typically, their early lives offered a taste for the outdoors or a need to move fast – whether on horseback, by car, or motorbike. But nothing gave them quite the thrill of sitting in an aeroplane and, once experienced, it was difficult to shake the flying bug.

PART THREE

The Women Behind the Planes

CHAPTER SEVEN

Frances Grayson and Ruth Elder Square Up

In the summer of 1927 two well-dressed women met in the elegant, echoey Beaux Arts splendour of Manhattan's Pennsylvania Station. To an outsider the pair may have looked as though they were about to embark on a shopping trip to nearby Macy's. They were both in their mid to late thirties and both had round, plump faces that the cloche hat of the time did little to flatter. It was the presence of a third person – a man who was almost certainly dressed in the sort of smart suit that an attorney employed by two wealthy clients could afford – that suggested this rendezvous was more significant than the start of a day out in New York.

As both women owed their fortunes, in different ways, to the development of the railway and the wealth it brought to cities like New York, it feels right that this first encounter took place in a paean to mass travel. But Frances Grayson and Mabel Ancker had come to Penn Station to discuss flying, a means of travel that would eventually leave rail travel standing and precipitate the destruction of the cathedral to railways in which they now stood. Air travel as a way of transport for the ordinary person was still decades off and today the focus of the meeting was how to achieve the first crossing of the Atlantic by a woman in a plane.[1] Within minutes of meeting they realised they were both enthralled by aviation and three weeks later Mabel Ancker invested in Frances Grayson's project.[2] Grayson would be on the ground, supervising the bid at close quarters, and would eventually take her seat in the aeroplane that she hoped would cross the Atlantic, while Ancker would return to her home in Denmark, from where she would receive regular bulletins on the expedition's progress.

Ancker had brown eyes and wore glasses, although she removed them when her photo was being taken; her hair was mousy and her small mouth and eyes set in a chubby face.[3] But this rather frumpy exterior hid a life that at thirty-seven had been drenched in scandal – much of it paraded through New York courts and eagerly recorded by journalists in the city and beyond. A noble venture such as backing the first woman to cross the Atlantic in a plane might go some way to expunging her chequered past.

Even the question of her parentage was open to debate – was her father really Pittsburgh steel manufacturer, Charles Spang and her mother his wife, Rosa?[4] In a court case of 1904, Mabel, then a teenager, said that until recently Charles had been known to her as 'Uncle Charley' and that she had been brought up by a family called Willis. She told her lawyer that he had 'dandled' her on his knee and said that one day she would be rich enough to sign cheques for $300,000.[5] The truth was that Mabel was born to Charles and Rosa three years before the Spangs married but this was a fact they were keen to hide.[6]

Mabel was forced to reveal her early childhood in an attempt to secure her release from a sanatorium in Yonkers that her parents had banished her to.[7] They took the drastic action to protect her from what they saw as the sinister influence of her French teacher, who was said to have 'an unnatural' and 'degrading' hold over her charge.[8]

After the case had been dragged through the legal system – and the newspapers – the Supreme Court in Brooklyn declared: 'She [Mabel] is not, and I think never was, insane. But she is disobedient and unfilial, and is subject, when permitted her freedom, to a vicious influence, and is easily led.'

She was remanded back to the sanatorium.[9]

Her parents decided to put her in the care of a woman who became her legal guardian and in 1911 took her to Europe for five years to shield her from further unsuitable influences in North America. Mabel returned in 1916 and married thirty-six-year-old Johann Crome, from Copenhagen. He was known as 'Fritz'[10] and described as a pianist[11] and 'newspaper man'.[12]

When Charles Spang died in 1919,[13] Mabel received $20,000 a year and Rosa was left $4 million.[14] But, following Rosa's death in 1919,[15] aged, seventy-six, it emerged that she had bequeathed around $2 million to set up a charity to support the care and education of children, leaving Mabel with $10,000 a year, in addition to the $20,000 a year Charles had left her. The ensuing case, in which Mabel's lawyers did their best to prove Rosa had been of unsound mind, painted a picture of a disturbed and cruel woman who held sway over her husband and servants from the grandeur of their home in the Waldorf Astoria.[16] One doctor described how she kept a young man to sing to her,[17] and a nurse spoke of how Rosa had complained within earshot that her husband was never going to die and that she would have to shoot him.[18] A second nurse said Rosa refused to buy Charles night shirts and moaned about the cost of the medicinal alcohol used in his bath. She remembered hearing Rosa tell him, 'You are blind and you are going somewhere soon. I hope you will have a front seat there [hell] and a short poker.'[19]

At the same time, journalists took the opportunity of the contested will to point out that, after two years, Mabel had divorced Crome in an act that required the approval of the King of Denmark and married another Danish suitor, Aage Ancker. She and her husband, who was described variously as a merchant, landowner, property developer, concert singer, sportsman, and riding or music teacher, lived in a remote mansion, Karlebogaard, near Hillerød, thirty-seven kilometres north of Copenhagen.[20] When the disputed will was finally settled in 1924 Mabel received nearly $2 million,[21] and the couple bought a second home in Aiken, South Carolina.[22]

In Denmark they set their minds to creating a Xanadu that reflected their wealth and their interests. From the outside, the house they commissioned was all gleaming white 1920s elegance set in formal gardens of neatly trimmed hedges, ornate wrought-iron gates, and geometrical parterres. But the inside felt more like a dolls' house that children – perhaps after a sugar-fuelled birthday party – had been allowed to decorate.

They toured the world to collect items with which to furnish their home, and the sixty-four rooms quickly became as cluttered and mismatched as the exterior was clean and crisp. The Anckers slept in a room decorated with Victorian wallpaper foraged from London and climbed a gilt-edged staircase that had taken their fancy in Venice. They listened to music in a room embellished with Louis XIV-style furniture, while other rooms were lined with centuries' old Chinese rice wallpaper, its vivid red adding yet another splash of colour to the house's conflicted palette. Everywhere there were panels that slid to one side to hide objects, often just for the fun of concealment, and the library had a door that led to a secret passageway. It was as if the owners couldn't decide on their favourite historical period.[23]

Personally, Ancker was also trying to settle on an identity. The Ancker surname was the fifth she'd used and would not be the last.[24] By the mid 1920s she had secured independent wealth but still seemed to be trying to decide on which side of the ocean her loyalties lay. She was beguiled by flying and the possibilities it offered. Enabling the first woman to cross the ocean in a plane promised to unite her interests in one noble venture and finally to attach prestige, rather than scandal, to her family name.[25] Perhaps it would also dismiss, once and for all, the judge's pronouncement that she was 'easily led'. What better way of proving that she was her own woman than by investing in a bold and imaginative venture of conveying the first woman across the Atlantic in an aeroplane? Mabel found her match, in her enthusiasm for aviation and, to a lesser extent, financial reserves, in Frances Wilson Grayson. Although Grayson did not have Ancker's millions she was, nevertheless, very wealthy and, unusually for a woman at the time, had made her money through her own endeavours, rather than inheritance.

She was thirty-five when she started planning her crossing, shortly after Lindbergh's success in 1927 – twenty-eight years younger than Savile, the oldest of the women hoping to conquer the Atlantic. It seems unfair, then, that parts of the American press dubbed her the 'Flying Matron'.[26] Others were more balanced and described her as 'Long Island businesswoman and feminist'[27] or 'Long Island Girl Flier'.[28]

It's true that Grayson's stature and figure didn't suit the 'flapper' styles of the 1920s and that she sometimes appeared upholstered in her tightly belted coat and cloche hat that accentuated a forehead, which was officially described in her passport application as 'broad'. But in other ways she had an energetic sparkle. In one photo, she is perched on the front of the new Sikorsky amphibian aeroplane she had commissioned, her thick legs dangling from the pontoon, a smile playing over her face as she gazes into the distance. In another she grins straight at the camera as she stands on weighing scales while five men cluster round her, hands on hips, or notebooks open, calculating how her dimensions will affect the finely balanced plane she hopes will deliver her across the ocean.[29] Here is a woman not afraid to be weighed in public.

Grayson was born in Cherokee Village, Arkansas and grew up in Muncie, a city deep in Indiana, which had blossomed due to the discovery of natural gas. The arrival of the railways helped make

Muncie a transportation hub and her father, Andrew Wilson, who had previously been a farmer, ran a grocery store where he served workers from the automobile factories.[30] The town was so typical of a middle-American community that sociologists Robert and Helen Lynd used it for their field work in *Middletown: A Study in Contemporary American Culture* (1929).

Frances's mother, Minnie, died when she was three, leaving her widower to raise the family single-handedly. Frances received music lessons so that she could accompany her brother, a talented singer, but when he died young there seemed no point in continuing her studies at Chicago Musical College. Instead, she studied recitation and drama at Swarthmore College and became popular as a local actress and singer who performed at garden parties and soirées.[31] She continued to perform after her marriage to local postmaster, John Brady Grayson, in September 1914 when his job took them to Virginia. Newspapers described her as 'pretty and talented'[32] and as a cousin of Dr Cary T. Grayson, physician to President Woodrow Wilson. She was also earmarked as a 'prominent local suffragist' and supported the cause by performing in *War Brides* on the lawn of local dignitaries.[33] She began to tour the Northeast theatres and eventually divorced her husband in 1922.[34] After their split she moved to New York where she worked as a freelance journalist. She was still giving her job as 'actress' when she sailed for France and England in 1924 but she eventually discovered a talent for real estate.[35] By the time she had become interested in flying she had opened an office at 1 West Thirty-Fourth Street and her name was regularly appearing next to her male competitors on the list of property deals secured in a highly competitive market.[36] Within four years, and by the time Lindbergh had crossed the Atlantic, she had sold $2 million worth of property in two years and was living in the grassy village of Mineola on Long Island.[37]

As the allure of property deals started to pall, she spent more time at Curtiss Field where pilots were planning long-distance flights.

When Lindbergh landed in France, she needed no further incentive and began touring aeroplane manufacturers. She also got to know Igor Sikorsky, who had emigrated from Russia after building primitive bombers for his country during the First World War. Although his name would come to be closely associated with the development of the helicopter, in 1927 he was working at College Point, Long Island, on a large amphibian plane for a South American customer. He gave Grayson flying lessons and, while she learnt a lot about how the plane worked, she never got round to flying solo.[38] By this time, she had also become a Christian Scientist and her faith gave her an extra determination, some might say intransigence.[39]

Three weeks after meeting Ancker at Penn Station the two women agreed to join forces and formed the Ancker-Grayson Aircraft Corporation; Frances was president and Mabel vice-president.[40] The venture was a 50/50 enterprise and they contributed $20,000 each, although other sources say Ancker put in the lion's share of $38,000.[41] This covered the cost of building the plane, the crew's salaries, maintenance, fuel and oil, and sophisticated instrumentation in an aircraft that, one newspaper stated, would have a 'commodious cabin ... [with] a chair, a bed and a combination dressing table and writing desk' for Grayson, who would accompany the crew. This seems rather fanciful and may have been prompted by the sheer size of the plane, which had an enormous wingspan.

*

Ruth Elder and Frances Grayson hadn't meant to become archrivals – and, in truth, they were always very supportive of one another – but the timing of their Atlantic bids meant the press couldn't resist turning their individual struggles into a race against one another. Their backgrounds and their physical appearance made them ideal opponents.

Elder enjoyed joking with newspaper reporters in her high-pitched Alabama voice that she wanted to fly to Paris because of the pretty evening gowns she could buy there. Like a movie star, her appeal was enhanced by the fact that she was unattached and there was no romance between her and her co-pilot George Haldeman who was married with a three-year-old son.[42] Elder was someone men could dream of asking out on a date and young women could emulate as they tied up their hair in 'Ruth's Ribbon'.

Unlike Earhart, Boll, and Grayson, she was from the South and, although the details of her early life were slow to emerge, she came from a humble home that she was clearly keen to leave behind her. She was the third of seven children, and her father struggled to earn enough to support his family. In 1910 they moved to Texas where he worked as a farm hand before returning to Anniston in Alabama to earn a living as a moulder in a pipefitting shop.[43] Elder escaped as soon as she could and, through a series of jobs, from selling lingerie in a department store to working as a dentist's assistant – all of which she kept secret from reporters once she was famous – turned up in Florida.[44] Here, in 1925, Haldeman taught her to fly and introduced her to a friend, fruit grower and fellow flyer, Edward Cornell. The two men had toured the country in 1923, giving joyrides to anyone who would pay, and in 1926 made a similar jaunt as agents of the Waco biplane company.[45] They then approached T. H. McArdle, a retired business man from Florida who had made his money from real estate, and the trio pitched the idea of a transatlantic flight to a group of financiers from Wheeling, West Virginia who could see how a beautiful young woman could harness the potential of the twin emerging industries of movie-making and aviation.[46] Footage of Elder could be sold to Hollywood and her daring feat of crossing the Atlantic would raise further sponsorship money. The investors, who remained anonymous, set up Wheeling Aero Exhibit Company and invested $35,000 in a plane.[47]

The press could not have designed a more photogenic poster girl for aviation if they had tried. Grayson's stolid personality and physique only served to heighten Elder's appeal to readers. But Grayson had one major advantage over Elder – she had nothing to hide. And Elder knew that it was only a matter of time before the one aspect of her private life she was desperate to keep under wraps would bubble to the surface.

CHAPTER EIGHT

Amy Guest: Thwarted Adventurer

Amy Guest's relationship with her in-laws had always been fraught and might best be summed up by an unfortunate event that occurred in the summer of 1908, three years after her wedding.

Amy's husband, Freddie, and his brother had rented Burley House near Oakham in the East Midlands from the estate of parliamentary 'father of the house', George Finch, and had invested large sums of money in gussying up and extending the eighteenth-century mansion.[1] One of the improvements was a new central heating system. The next day a large party of friends, relatives, and political allies, including FE Smith, a fellow MP, and Winston Churchill, who at the time was President of the Board of Trade, arrived.

Freddie was acting as Churchill's private secretary and, given that there were at least two other ambitious politicians staying at the mansion, it's safe to assume that a lot of parliamentary gossip was exchanged over cigars and port before everyone retired to bed. At about 1.00 am they were awoken by the sound of a distraught maid urging everyone to evacuate the building. As they tumbled out of their beds a fire, thought to have been started by the newly installed heating system, began to lick its way through the West Wing. The visitors, most in their night gowns and pyjamas, gathered on the lawn, where some took the opportunity to scramble into what items of clothing they had been able to snatch as they fled. The strange, half-dressed group of aristocrats and servants could only watch as the blaze devoured priceless tapestries and oil paintings, as well as historic letters from Oliver Cromwell. Churchill saved his red despatch box and other departmental documents, before working with the Guest brothers and Smith to try to staunch the flames until the fire brigades from Oakham, Melton Mowbray, and Stamford arrived.

As news of the event reached London, Churchill's fiancée, Clementine feared for the life of her husband-to-be. But it was exactly the sort of scrape he enjoyed and a full-page drawing in *The Illustrated London News* later depicted him on the roof next to three axe-wielding firemen. Sparks and flames provided a menacing backdrop as he helped to cut the lead from the roof in a vain attempt to feed the hosepipes into the stricken house. Churchill's stripey pyjamas are clearly visible under his coat.[2] According to the report, he made several forays into the building to salvage precious treasures and emerged grimy with smoke and with smarting eyes. He just managed to clear the building, carrying two monumental busts, when the roof collapsed. The fire brigade had access only to a small reservoir and after ten minutes the water failed and more had to be carried from a mile away. The fire blazed on for several hours until it burnt itself out. There were no injuries, although the house's west wing was destroyed, and Smith lost his entire wardrobe.[3]

By the time Winston and Clementine married at St Margaret's Church in Westminster six weeks later, the catastrophe had been transformed into a comic anecdote that served to highlight the bridegroom's daring do. Newspapers reported how, among the many expensive wedding presents – a silver bowl; the Prime Minister's gift of ten volumes of Jane's Austen's novels bound in crimson Morocco and tooled in gold; engravings; and mezzotints – a glittering fireman's helmet sat in pride of place atop a rosewood escritoire sent by Sir Edward and Lady Sassoon. For Amy, who was still new to the British upper classes and its strange sense of humour, the elaborate waggery must have felt humiliating.[4] We don't know for sure whether she was present when the fire broke out, but, either way, her attempts at fulfilling the role of hostess had been transformed into a joke that looked set to run and run. Luckily, she and her husband could leave for a two-month cruise on the yacht of their friend, Lord Lonsdale, accompanied by another American heiress, W. K. 'Anna' Vanderbilt and her third husband.[5]

*

Feeling awkward or bemused by public school humour was something young American wives had to get used to when they crossed the Atlantic and Amy was one of several brides who married into the British aristocracy during the late Victorian and early Edwardian period. On 1 July 1905, *The Queen* newspaper noted: 'The annual influx of Americans into London is at its height just now. One meets them everywhere – those who are "touring England," those who are doing the season, and those who are just resting for a day or two before going off to the Continent.'

While British newspapers were proud that so many American heiresses liked the idea of settling down with an earl or a duke, the trend rankled reporters on the other side of the Atlantic. In 1921, the *Nebraska State Journal* ran a feature with the headline, 'Billion Hard Cash leaves America by Marriages'.[6] The newspaper estimated that in the last thirty-five years over $1 billion had been squirrelled out of the US via marriage settlements. It ran a photo of Amy Phipps as someone who typified this trend. She was sixth on the paper's list of American women who now lived abroad and her investment, so the paper claimed, amounted to $6 million.

According to one estimate, between 1870 and 1914, one hundred American women married British aristocrats in a trend that the English journalist William Stead described as 'Gilded Prostitution'.[7] Amy joined the ranks of well-known American socialites who had dipped their beautifully gloved hands into exquisite purses and extracted rolls of dollar notes to help out struggling members of the British aristocracy.[8] The flipside of this arrangement was that it offered newly rich Americans an entrée into the higher echelons of British society, although they usually had to endure jibes about their accents and customs. It was widely believed, for example, that Americans got by with few, or no, servants and that the size of their families suggested they might be resorting to birth control.[9] They were portrayed as speaking with a nasal twang, no matter where they came from within the USA, and of using expressions such as 'I'm pretty crowded just now' when they had had enough to eat.[10]

Rich American women had been brought up differently and this could often feel threatening to their European equivalents. They were able to speak to men with greater confidence because they had not been segregated from an early age – as happened in Britain when boys were sent off to boarding school – and many were better educated and better travelled than their British counterparts.[11] For the new American wives, like Amy, it was often a shock to find that they were living in poorly heated, badly plumbed mansions in which the decision to take a bath triggered a military-style operation to ferry buckets of hot water from one end of the house to the other. American wives also found it difficult to grasp the power dynamics that existed among servants 'downstairs'.

Amy observed at close quarters how Winston Churchill had been helped by the Wall Street wealth of his American mother, Jennie Jerome, whose union with Randolph in 1874 was seen as one of the first significant transatlantic marriages.[12] Amy also shared certain characteristics with Nancy Astor. Both their fathers had made a fortune from the boom in railway building and as a young woman Nancy visited England three times before settling in London after her first unhappy marriage led to divorce.

Astor became friendly with other Americans living in the capital, such as Consuelo Vanderbilt, who married and then divorced the Duke of Marlborough. Like Amy, Astor had her portrait painted by Sargent and was presented at Court in the year that Amy married. She eventually settled down with American-born Waldorf Astor, whose father bought the couple the country house of Cliveden in Buckinghamshire as a wedding gift and which she used, together with their London house in St James Square, for what today would be called 'networking'.

Politicians Joseph Chamberlain, Sir Lyon Playfair, and Sir William Harcourt all forged unions with American women and both Amy Guest and Astor were married to Conservative MPs.[13] American women weren't used to the constant political gossiping that went on at most dinners and house parties but Guest and Astor did much to further their husbands' careers: Guest, through financial support, and Astor, through campaigning and, reluctantly at first, fighting to win Waldorf's seat herself following the death of his father. His father's demise had led to his elevation to the Lords and meant he had to stand down from his Plymouth constituency in 1919. She was elected with a majority of 5,000 votes.[14]

Amy's wealth gave Freddie, who was a third son, the funds he needed to enter politics, although his political career was not as glittering as his cousin Winston's. Four months after finally gaining a seat in Parliament he was expelled for breaking the rules about how much could be spent during an election campaign; a court hearing also suggested he had intimidated tenants and their families.[15]

While he was preoccupied, Amy transformed their London home, Aldford House at 26 Park Lane, into a private hospital with fifty beds for British officers. In 1918 she handed it over to the American Red

Cross so that surgeons from the medical corps of the US Navy could treat both officers and men. The building took up a whole block and had an elaborate roof garden and lawn.[16] After the war Freddie worked hard to boost Lloyd George's financial standing but his fundraising efforts relied too heavily on the honours system and led to scandal in 1922, but not before, in 1920, he was appointed to the Privy Council, which meant he became 'The Right Honourable'.

Amy, like many Americans marrying into a rich British family, found it difficult to establish a role within the aristocratic clan that she had joined. Her assimilation was further complicated by subtle political allegiances that made her feel like an outsider. And then there was Christian Science.

Mary Baker Eddy had established the Church of Christ, Scientist in New England in the second half of the nineteenth century. Her beliefs were based on her conviction that continuous study of the Bible had cured her of long-term illnesses and the effects of a near-fatal accident. Her personal experience convinced Eddy that Christianity had the potential to rescue others from sickness. Drugs and medicine were, therefore, superfluous, although some followers turned to them if all else failed. Eddy distilled her philosophy into a book, *Science and Health with Key to the Scriptures*. 'Students', as they were called, of the religion read a Bible lesson every day and studied Scripture and Eddy's writings. They often went to church twice daily.[17]

Amy followed her mother's lead and became a Christian Scientist – although, as was the case with her parents, Amy's husband had no interest in the religion.[18] Her devotion was another reason to set her apart from her in-laws who, like many British members of the upper echelons, viewed Christian Scientists as odd and austere. In the novel, *Queen Lucia* (1920), the first of E. F. Benson's Mapp and Lucia series, Benson extracts maximum comic mileage from his character, Mrs Quantock, who leaps from fad to fad and who briefly alights on Christian Science.

> The inhumanity of that sect towards both herself and others took complete possession of her, and when her husband complained on a bitter January morning that his smoking-room was like an ice-house, because the housemaid had forgotten to light the fire, she had no touch of pity for him, since she knew that there was no such thing as cold or heat or pain, and therefore you could not feel cold.[19]

The religion's most famous follower in Britain was Nancy Astor who, with her abhorrence of alcohol and reputation for aloofness, seemed to epitomise what many saw as the church's censorious and joyless view of the world. She was the first woman to take her seat in the House of Commons – Constance Markievicz was the first female to be elected but she did not take up her seat because she was an Irish Republican. Churchill's parliamentary sparring with Astor only served to confirm the Guest family antipathy towards this modern religion. The alleged repartee between them often lacks verification but confirms the general impression of how the Churchill clan viewed women like Astor. In their two most famous exchanges she is said to have told him, 'If you were my husband, I'd poison your tea,' to which he is reported to have responded, 'Madam, if you were my wife, I'd drink it!' and, when he asked her what disguise he should wear to a masked ball, she supposedly replied: 'Why don't you come sober, Prime Minister?'[20]

Astor and Guest both felt like outsiders, and Christian Science provided a certainty for those who found themselves in an alien world. Astor, who had to adapt to the barrack-room bullying of the House of Commons, said she took solace in her religious beliefs.[21] Frances Grayson was also a Christian Scientist and thrived in the male-dominated world of real estate and then aviation. It may have been her belief in the power of prayer that gave her a distorted view of the risks she faced when she set off across the Atlantic.

*

From the start, Amy did her best to assimilate into her new family and wrote a sweet letter from a hotel she was staying in in Bembridge on the Isle of Wight to Winston Churchill after he announced his engagement to Clementine Hozier. Amy admired her beauty and charm and hoped that only good fairies would come to their wedding. Winston thanked her for her kind wishes.[22]

Churchill's wife Clementine disliked 'the Guest tribe' and often found Amy maddening. She stayed with them in Leicestershire where the two families went hunting and the Churchills shared the Guests' house, Templeton in Roehampton, during the winter of 1919–1920. On 7 February 1913 Clemmie wrote to her husband from Burley-on-the-Hill: 'Amy is kind, but more Suffragetty, Christian Sciency, & Yankee Doodle than ever. Poor Freddie is a Sheep in Lion's clothing.'[23] Winston was shocked by the way Amy treated her husband and how she was said to fly into jealous rages if she felt he was spending too much time talking to other people.[24] Winston warned his wife, 'Clemmie, don't you ever behave like Amy. If you do I'll leave you right away.'[25] He was just as outraged at a dinner party when Amy ordered a valet to remove her husband's clothes from their bedroom and locked him out because she thought he had been flirting with another woman.[26]

By December 1921 Amy's fears appeared to have had some basis and Winston wrote to Clemmie from Cannes saying, 'Freddie is pursuing the beautiful Miss Gellibrand who is here staying with a minor French Royalty. He even talked to me of matrimony – after disposing of the Amy problem – I replied sepulchrally that she was young enough to be his daughter, & that ten years wd carry us both to the brink of the sixties. Also that he wd lose his office if he lost his Amy. So there's a problem! Don't make chaff about it.'[27]

The 'office' she referred to was the role of Secretary of State for Air, to which Lloyd George appointed Freddie in 1921, partly as a reward for his loyalty. Although the position was not a cabinet one, it delighted Freddie, who was a keen pilot, and allowed him to appoint Sir William Sefton Brancker as Director of Civil Aviation – a wise choice that helped to put Britain at the forefront of development in aviation. Freddie spent the rest of the 1920s in and out of power and making his anti-socialist stance the backbone of his political ethos.

In fact, the Guests' marriage was over two years before Winston had written to Clemmie about her concerns: in July 1919, they agreed to a secret separation that gave Amy custody of the children. The arrangement only became public in 1936 when their first son, Winston, named after his father's beloved cousin, realised he wasn't, technically, an American citizen – a fact that constituted a major drawback for anyone who planned, as he did, to pursue a career in politics.[28]

Amy said later, in a letter to Churchill following her husband's sudden death in 1937, that during the eighteen years in which they lived separate lives, the children had been a great support.[29] She added that at the start of their separation Freddie had wanted to marry someone else and Amy had said she would divorce him after a certain period of time and if his new wife was a suitable person for the children to visit. However, the children were upset by the idea and Freddie abandoned the suggestion.

Amy did all she could to make it easy for them to see their father and he would stay with her to be near them. She expressed regret that she had been unable to make the marriage work. But in the next sentence she revealed the nature of their relationship when she added that Freddie had asked her whether she would go to South Africa with him because he had a chance of becoming governor. She agreed but he added that if she could donate £50,000 to the Government, they might consider it. In the end Amy felt, as things weren't going well between them, it represented a risk. She also didn't want to be far from her parents who were old and infirm, or to leave her sons in England. She was sorry she had let Freddie down and ended the letter by saying that she had always hoped they would be reconciled.

The exotic family trips she had enjoyed as a young girl were cut short by marriage. In 1923 she became an American citizen and, by 1927, like Frances Grayson, Mabel Ancker, and Ruth Elder, she was looking for adventure.[30] Her children no longer relied on her: the youngest, Diana, was eighteen; Winston was twenty-one; and Ray twenty. Sargent's proud young woman in her diaphanous white dress and pearls, a straw hat in one hand, a lapdog in the other was now a rather plump older woman who rarely appeared in photos and certainly never by herself.

The tomboy, who had grown up riding horses and playing in the grounds of her family's sprawling homes on both sides of the Atlantic and whose rich parents had denied her wish to nurse American soldiers fighting in Mexico, was now fifty-five and spending more and more time in America. She felt at ease in Palm Beach, where the Phipps cousins could play together on the beach and at the end of the day be driven home in a wicker rickshaw to their Spanish-style, coral stone home surrounded by purple bougainvillea, yellow allamanda, and pots of orange and yellow nasturtium. The children could catch fireflies to decorate the girls' hair and there were no vicious British aristocrats to worry about, only the alligators that, by and large, knew their place.[31]

Or there was Westbury on Long Island's moneyed 'Gold Coast', where her brother John ('Jay') lived with his wife, Margarita ('Dita') and their four children. The Charles II-style mansion was built in 1906 by the English designer George A. Crawley and sits in 200 acres of formal gardens, landscaped grounds, tennis courts, and polo fields.[32] Dita disapproved of Freddie and of Amy's brother-in-law, Bradley Martin, and felt their drinking habits and sense of humour were a bad influence on her husband, Amy's brother, Jay.[33] But, despite this disapproval, Westbury was a haven for Amy.

Amy had long been interested in flying, not only because of

Freddie, but also her brother, Jay, who had been due to be posted abroad as a pilot in 1918 when the war ended.[34] As an Anglo American, she was acutely aware of Lindbergh's achievement. But more than her disintegrating marriage and her frustrated sense of adventure, what may have trigged her desire to become the first woman to cross the Atlantic was, according to family legend, news that a woman called Rosa Lewis was planning to get there first and Amy didn't feel that so great an honour should fall to someone who, in an account by Amy's niece, was described as 'a nightclub hostess'.[35] The flaw in this theory is that the most famous Rosa Lewis of the time was the proprietor of the Cavendish Hotel in Jermyn Street, just off Piccadilly Circus, who would have been forty in 1927. She left school at twelve and clawed her way up from scrubbing floors as a kitchen maid to become a renowned cook and caterer-at-large to aristocrats in their home. She married a butler but divorced him after he mismanaged the venture she had poured her money into and took over the Cavendish where royalty and aristocrats from both sides of the Atlantic and the Bright Young Things of the 1920s could conduct their affairs safe in the knowledge that their secrets stayed with Rosa. She visited New York in 1926 and wafted through customs with a trunk load of champagne. Evelyn Waugh caricatured her as Lottie Crump in *Vile Bodies* and British TV immortalised her as *The Duchess of Duke Street* in the 1970s BBC TV series.

'The king's cook' was well known in the USA and it wouldn't be surprising if Amy had actually met her, but it's a stretch to call her 'a nightclub hostess'. What seems much more likely was that Amy was worried that Mabel Boll – the 'Diamond Queen' – was on track to represent America as the first woman to cross the Atlantic in a plane. Her father had been a bartender in Rochester and she herself had made a living as a showgirl.[36] The confident, twice-married New Yorker, who led an independent life and enjoyed the pleasures money could bring, was the antithesis of the woman Amy had in mind when she thought of the person who deserved to hold the title of first female to join her two home countries by flight.

Amy, who in her youth had travelled to Egypt, India, and Burma, and who, on her marriage, dreamt of being the first white woman to enter Lhasa, started to wonder if her destiny lay in the grey expanse of the Atlantic.

Flight Checklist: A Well-Packed Picnic Basket

A pilot packing their lunch for a transatlantic flight in the first half of the twentieth century had many factors to consider. For a start, they could be in the air for over twenty hours but there wasn't much space and most of that was taken up with fuel. They needed food that would help them concentrate and not make them ill – ideally, the snack would represent a little treat when they most needed a morale boost. Sandwiches were a firm favourite.

Alcock and Brown took 'specially prepared sandwiches', chocolate, coffee, and ale with them when they crossed the Atlantic in 1919. 'We are carrying enough to give us quite an aerial banquet. I suppose I shall be butler and everything, for Alcock will be too busy flying the machine to get the food out,' Brown explained to *The Mail.*[1]

Savile and her two-man crew packed sufficient rounds for two days. Mackay had to swear the staff of the George Hotel near Grantham to secrecy when she supervised the preparation of enough sandwiches for two people over three days. They also filled vacuum flasks with chicken and turtle soup, tea, and coffee.[2]

Elder and Haldeman appeared to have been less concerned about the weight of their provisions and, according to one account, carried nine pounds of food. This was actually half of the amount they had originally planned[3] and included four dill pickles, six turkey and Swiss cheese sandwiches, two quarts of coffee, one quart of beef tea, one gallon of water in three canteens, six bars of chocolates, a pound of raisins, and a few oranges, all neatly arranged in a basket that they placed behind their seats.[4]

'The Woman's Day' column assumed Elder had assembled the feast herself:

> Any girl who can start flying across the Atlantic with a picnic lunch of turkey sandwiches, dill pickles and some chocolate bars, gets a salute from my new beige velour bonnet! I smiled with a tear behind the smile when I read in my morning's paper an itemising of the food which pretty Ruth Elder stowed in her plane just as she hopped in to begin her long and lonely trek.
>
> It might have been a school girl's picnic basket, a box for a box social, or a sorority spread. It was fine that a girl who made turkey sandwiches and bought dill pickles got through! It took courage to be really interested in appetizing food when such a jaunt was before one! Most men throw in some beef cubes and let it go![5]

There's a sense of nationalistic pride behind Elder's choice that's also present in French pilot René Fonck's carte du jour. As he sat waiting on the runway at Roosevelt Field on Long Island in September 1926 his crew's luggage included a hot 'celebration' dinner to be consumed when they touched down in France and a last-minute order of croissants to boost their spirits before take-off.[6]

Lindbergh studied Fonck's menu and decided to take only essentials, plus a few concentrated tinned rations, as used by the Army, and a little extra water. No croissants or hot celebration dinner for sensible Lindbergh.[7] Instead, he opted for five sandwiches (the fillings aren't recorded and some accounts put the number at four).[8] When

Frank Tichenor of *Aero Digest* queried whether he had sufficient, Lindbergh replied laconically: 'If I get to Paris I won't need any more, and if I don't get to Paris, I won't need any more, either.'[9]

Frances Grayson's team packed sandwiches on each of their three attempts from Old Orchard in Maine and each time they were reduced to munching them on their way back to Maine, like a school trip that's been called off because of the weather and everyone decides to tuck into their packed lunch.[10] On the third attempt the hotel proprietor was so convinced that they wouldn't be returning that he'd sent the staff home for the night and was forced to ask his wife to prepare their dinner.

In the summer of 1928, Mabel Boll's three-person team planned to take twenty-four chicken and twelve ham sandwiches, four quarts of bouillon, sixteen oranges, two gallons of water, and an undisclosed number of chocolate bars.[11]

Flyers learnt from polar explorers and one item most packed, and which would be a mainstay of an arctic voyage, was pemmican. This concentrated fat and protein mixture looks a bit like a Christmas cake but without much taste. It's high in calories and would sustain a pilot as they waited for rescuers after a forced landing.

In today's modern airports, pre-flight snacking in enclosed, unnaturally lit terminals is part of the ritual of departure. We cram in an average of 3,400 calories between check-in and arrival at our destination as we search for satisfaction.[12] This gluttony is partly driven by boredom, but the constant grazing may also be a quest to wake up our taste buds and once on the plane the food and drink always seems to lack their usual levels of saltiness and sweetness.

Record-breaking flyers, by contrast, could never be certain whether their pre-flight meal would be their last – not just in the sense of a condemned man facing their final repast – but because their departure might be delayed for several days, even weeks. In effect, they could have several 'last suppers' and might become more reckless with their choices as boredom set in. If they had tried every dish a small town had to offer then they might be tempted by cuisine, such as clams, often linked to food poisoning – a complaint that no long-distance flyer wants to contemplate in a cramped cockpit and before the invention of sick bags.

In her account of her first crossing, *20 Hrs., 40 Min.*, Earhart makes light of the monotonous diet they faced as they waited for meteorologist Doc Kimball to give them the all-clear.[13] The waiting had started in Boston, where they distracted themselves by trying out restaurants of every nationality they could find until the weather improved. When they finally set off for Newfoundland, they had packed sandwiches and a big thermos of coffee for 'the boys' and a smaller one with cocoa for Earhart. Delays meant the sandwiches and drinks twice had to be dumped. Earhart had her first snack when they landed at Halifax. She enjoyed an orange, waiting in the rear of the plane, behind the cockpit, while Stultz and Gordon went on a recce. They took off again but fog forced them back and they decided to land at Trepassey. Amelia munched on a ham sandwich in her space at the rear of the plane while 'the boys' sorted out accommodation.

'We seem to have endless ham sandwiches,' she noted in her logbook.

She eventually realised that the lack of variety was their own fault, and they should have explored further. The Copley Plaza Hotel in Boston had arranged the picnic for what was described, for reasons of secrecy, as a 'fishing trip'. But the hotel had put all the ham sandwiches on the top layer and the crew failed to dig deeper: 'Later, to our chagrin, we discovered that below were similar layers of delicious chicken and tongue sandwiches, hard boiled eggs and much beside. We never had the courage to determine exactly what else there might have been.'

By the time they were ready to leave Trepassey those sandwiches must have felt like a gourmet dinner. She, Stultz, and Gordon grew to loathe the canned rabbit they were served in Newfoundland. When Stultz first tasted it, he commented, 'Here's something they caught last year – something that couldn't get away.' The first time they tried fish it was from a source that had been in a tin for a year and Gordon was told it was the only thing available and that even the eggs would be fishy because of the chicken's diet. He'd already suffered from food poisoning in Boston when he was rash enough to eat clams just before their departure. In Trepassey he had resorted to chocolates 'by the package and [he] seems to thrive'.

A few days later, on 9 June, they had lamb stew for lunch. Earhart complained that the local people thought the only way to cook it was by boiling. She started to fantasise about a chop, but at supper they had fresh salmon that, she conceded, was 'delicious'. However, she noted, 'We are just managing to keep from suicide.'[14]

When they finally set off, they abandoned the large thermos and kept the smaller one for the boys' coffee. She decided she wouldn't drink – unless they came down.[15] Their remaining provisions consisted of:

> 2.5 gallons mineral water (half the amount they'd loaded at Boston);
>
> Three 'elephantine' egg sandwiches constructed from Trepassey's home-made round loaves;
>
> Eight or nine oranges from their original supply;
>
> Two tins Drake's oatmeal cookies, which Earhart admitted, were a 'luxury'.
>
> Emergency rations:
>
> Pemmican;
>
> Bottle of Horlick's Malted Milk tablets;[16]
>
> Hershey's chocolate.

They appeared to have left behind a ham sandwich, a detail that has been handed down in Trepassey folklore, as if it represented an act of deliberate wastefulness.[17]

The oranges proved to be a surprising source of nationalism. Earhart described them as 'under-nourished little bloods' from Spain, whereas those they'd brought all the way from Boston were from California and 'sturdy'.[18] She ate only three and a dozen malted milk tablets on the entire journey.

Coffee was essential for most transatlantic crews because it warmed them up and kept them awake. However, they were mindful of how tricky it was to urinate in a flying suit. Men could use a relief tube, but it was much harder for women and, although this was impossible to verify, it seems probable that some female flyers resorted to a form of adult nappy. Others may have knelt on the seat to use the sort of funnel that female festival goers make use of. Either way, it must have been uncomfortable.

When, four years later, in May 1932 Earhart attempted to fly the Atlantic solo, she left Harbour Grace with even fewer provisions. She carried just one can of tomato juice which she punctured and sipped through a straw.[19] Her choice of beverage was unusual in the 1930s but commonplace today. Tomato juice represents 27 per cent of all drinks ordered in aeroplanes – even by people who wouldn't go near it on the ground.[20]

The reason for this tomato preference may be because of the food's magical ability to preserve taste when the lower air pressure and humidity, as well as the noise, makes most food taste bland. According to research, high altitude food loses 30 per cent of its flavour.[21] Tomatoes and other foods like Parmesan cheese, anchovies, and Marmite, however, are rich in umami, an amino acid, that helps to preserve taste. So maybe there is reason behind many air passengers' instinct to reach for a Bloody Mary.

Earhart's plane wouldn't have been flying as high as modern

aircraft and wasn't pressurised. She wrote in her logbook that she wore 'little rubber ear stops' sent to her by Commander Richard Byrd's wife, Marie, after he had used a pair in his transatlantic flight in 1927 and was the only member of the crew who could hear when they touched down.[22]

In fact, Earhart's stripped-down planes, which lacked the upholstery of modern airliners, would have produced even more of a racket. While food can taste less salty and sweet if you're consuming it in a noisy environment umami becomes more intense. It's also thought that stress can ramp up the effect of umami. So, while risking her life in a rattling aeroplane, she was unwittingly creating the perfect conditions in which to enjoy her tomato juice. If only she could have spared the extra grammes and poured the juice into a cut-glass tumbler it would, suggests the research, which advocates that 'proper' cutlery, crockery, and glassware enhances our sensory perceptions, have tasted even better.

PART FOUR

1927, The Race Begins

CHAPTER NINE

Anne Savile and the 'Superfliers'

On Wednesday 31 August 1927 the Archbishop of Cardiff found himself in a limousine with three other priests, being swept across Salisbury Plain through the early morning 'ghostly mist' towards the remote airfield of Upavon in Wiltshire.[1] When he arrived, he met two pilots, Lieutenant-Colonel Frederick Minchin, dressed in a dark tweed suit,[2] and Leslie Hamilton, in a double-breasted lounge suit, earnestly discussing the weather.[3] The identity of their female passenger who, it was rumoured, *might* accompany them was still a secret 'for fear of her relatives stopping her flight'.[4]

Neither of the pilots had slept much and asked to be called at 3.00 am.[5] Their aeroplane had been fuelled the night before and stood waiting, but the strong easterly wind made take-off impossible. Both pilots had experience of what at the time were considered long-distance flights and Minchin had flown from London to Egypt in three days.[6] Hamilton, the 'Flying Gypsy' whose most noteworthy flight had been the King's Cup and crossing the Channel,[7] jumped into a waiting car to tour the eastern sections of the airfield while spectators on Salisbury Plain watched as his headlamps swept the perimeter. On his return he consulted Minchin, and they agreed to attempt a take-off in another direction and forty men manoeuvred the plane to a new starting position. The journey had already been delayed once when the Air Ministry failed to grant a certificate of airworthiness to the plane. No one wanted a further postponement.[8]

Minchin and Hamilton had made no secret of their plans to fly the Atlantic to the Canadian capital of Ottawa but had laid a careful paper trail away from their financial backer. In early July it was rumoured that Captain Robert McIntosh might take the third seat on their Fokker monoplane and that they would return after landing in Ottawa.[9] A few weeks later they were reported to be planning a trip from Clifden in Ireland to New York where they would refuel before heading for Vienna.[10] Next they gave Dublin as the expected starting point.[11]

They were both conscious that they were in a race and that several other pilots were planning a crossing. Hinch and his backer Charles Levine had ambitions to be the first aircraft to cross from East to West. Levine had already become the first passenger to cross the Atlantic in a plane and now wanted to win this second record. News of their imminent departure may have prompted Minchin and Hamilton to leave sooner than planned.

*

As if it wasn't startling enough that three priests should spill out of a limousine on a blustery airfield, it emerged that the other passenger in the car was Savile, who had left her home in London at midnight, before picking up the clergy in Devizes. Servants reported that she was 'out of town' as her relatives, led by her brother, the Earl of Mexborough, were desperately trying to stop her boarding the plane. She took up a position under the wing in the weak sunshine as the archbishop sprinkled holy water on the Fokker F.VII. The aircraft was much more elegant and comfortable than anything else Savile had flown in, despite the crammed space due to the extra fuel tanks that had replaced the normal seats. It had three engines and two robust front wheels made by the Palladium Tire Manufacturing Company.

Savile was wearing blue velvet breeches in a subtle contrast with the sky-blue fuselage.[12] Her yellow leather flying jacket and high-legged yellow boots lined with black fur echoed the plane's golden wings.[13] She knelt to kiss the episcopal ring and the archbishop raised his hand, saying 'God bless you all. May you have a safe journey. We shall not forget to pray for you.'[14] He squeezed Minchin and Hamilton's shoulders affectionately.

Savile appeared confident about the outcome and told a reporter: 'During the journey I shall probably take a turn in the pilot's seat and in piloting the machine.'[15]

When asked if she was nervous, she replied: 'No, but I am excited. Could I be anything else? I am looking forward to the trip. I feel quite confident in the pilots and the machine. I am proud to be the first woman to attempt the crossing. It is a great adventure.'[16]

With that she took up her position in her wicker chair, which was tucked behind the eight cylindrical fuel tanks, loaded with 800 gallons of petrol.[17] According to one account, she also had an army cot so that she could rest and it may have reminded her of the anti-seasickness bed she had designed for crossing the Atlantic by ship. Next to her, she placed a small attaché case and a scarlet hat box. According to some later reports, that luggage included $200,000 worth (about $3.6 million today) of family diamonds and jewels, which she couldn't bear to be parted from. The same report suggested that Hamilton had packed 600 one-pound notes that he intended to sell once they landed in America. If each crew member signed the notes, it was thought they would be able to re-sell them for twenty-five to thirty dollars each.[18]

At 7.30 am Hamilton and Minchin eased the aeroplane, with its heavy load of fuel, 1,020 yards along the field, and on its second attempt, just as they were running out of runway, they coaxed the *St Raphael* into the air, narrowly missing an ambulance and a line of fir trees before clearing the road, which was three feet lower than the aerodrome.[19] A down draft from a nearby hill rocked the fuselage but the plane over-rode it in a way that must have given the crew confidence in their engine.[20] Members of the RAF, who were stationed nearby, had risen early and let out a round of cheers as the *St Raphael* finally departed. On board they carried a week's army rations and sandwiches for two days, a collapsible rubber boat and enough fuel for forty-four hours.[21] The *St Raphael* had a maximum speed of 130 miles per hour and a cruising speed of 100 miles per hour.[22] If all went well they were due to land in Ottawa between 7.30 and 11.00 pm, British Summer Time and would become the first plane to cross the Atlantic from east to west.

Hamilton had said that he considered the first three hours of the flight to be the most dangerous because of the heavy load of fuel they were forced to carry, since crossing the Atlantic from Europe meant a pilot had to battle *against* strong head winds and cross-air currents, rather than taking advantage of them.[23] This was one reason why no one had yet achieved the crossing in a heavier-than-air vehicle in this direction, although two airships had managed the feat: the British R34 in 1919 and the German ZR3, which flew a more southerly course.[24]

As *The Times* explained to its readers, if a plane had an air speed of 100 miles per hour (as the *St Raphael* did) and was flying eastward with a tail wind of twenty miles per hour it could achieve a speed of 120 miles per hour. The same plane flying in the opposite direction would only be able to manage 80 miles per hour. Over a distance of 2,400 miles, a plane flying to Europe would take twenty hours, whereas an aircraft heading for North America would be in the air for thirty hours. The plane flying westward would consume twenty gallons of fuel an hour and must carry 200 gallons (1,400 pounds) – and that added weight would make it trickier to fly, especially at take-off.[25]

The *St Raphael* was carrying 795 gallons and expected to be able to fly for forty to forty-two hours at one hundred miles per hour, leaving four to six hours of petrol to spare. If her speed dropped to ninety miles per hour it would be touch and go whether they could reach Ottawa but there should be plenty of fuel left in the tank to make Newfoundland, although the east coast of America held its own particular challenges of disorientating fogs and ice. The plane was also likely to be affected by winds that could change quickly and make it difficult to calculate speed – a vital component of navigation. And all this when the pilot was at his most exhausted. It was no wonder that papers concluded: 'so far as airplanes are concerned the North Atlantic is still a one-way street.'[26] If Savile made it across the Atlantic she would be not only the first woman to fly the Atlantic but also her plane would be the first to cross the ocean from east to west.

The princess's departure wasn't just a horrible surprise to her family, but also stole a march on other pilots, who had hoped to be the first to cross the ocean from Europe to America by airplane.[27]

Wednesday 31 August

At first, *St Raphael* appeared to be making good progress and was reported to have reached the Irish coast shortly after 10.00 am, although there was some concern about her speed – which was estimated at a sluggish seventy-five miles per hour at ground speed.[28]

10.03 am: Captain Harvey of Bargy Castle, County Wexford saw her flying at 500 feet in a NW/W direction. One wonders if Minchin thought about his home in central Ireland as they sped over the green fields below.

10.40 am: She passed over Thurles, County Tipperary, flying at a very low altitude due to fog.

Shortly after midday Civic Guards at Inverin, a village in Connemara, spotted her heading due west, at a height of 1,000 feet. She continued along the Galway coast, before turning out to sea between Gorumna Island and Inishmore (the most northerly of the Aran islands). She was over the Atlantic and 'flying well'. The weather was fair but showery.[29]

9.44 pm: A tanker, *SS Josiah Macey* sighted her halfway across the ocean at latitude 53.150 and longitude 29.45.[30]

Thursday 1 September

6.00 am: Reuters received a telegram saying a white light, an international distress signal, had been spotted by a Dutch steamer, the *Blijidendijk* 420 miles East South East of New York and reported to Cape Race, near Trepassey.[31] The signal was thought to have been sent by a plane flying in an easterly direction. If it was the *St Raphael*, she was seriously off course.

11.45 am: Reuters reported that a plane thought to be the *St Raphael* had been seen over Saint-Malo, Quebec. This was later found to be a different plane.[32]

2.30 pm: An agent of the Canadian National Railways at Pigou River, Quebec Province sighted a plane but was unable to identify it.[33]

Crowds started to gather at Newfoundland's capital, St. John's and barrels of saturated oil were placed at Harbour Grace, ready to be lit as beacons to guide the plane to safety.[34] Wireless stations, lighthouses, and customs houses were told to be vigilant.[35] The Canadian Government steamer, *Beothic*, returning from its annual Arctic trip, was ordered to keep an eye out for the plane on the Labrador coast and Gulf of Saint Lawrence.[36] United States ships in the Atlantic also scanned the skies.

'Hinch', who was planning a crossing with Levine, was not optimistic about their chances: 'I'm afraid they have not got anywhere near Newfoundland. They have probably flown well north of it, where they would be over land for some hundreds of miles. I hope they will do it.'[37]

This assessment from such an experienced pilot must have been a blow to the families and friends of Savile, Hamilton, and Minchin.

Weekend of 3/4 September

It was rumoured that the plane had been sighted over Labrador.[38]

*

Newspapers, including *The New York Times*, reported that Minchin and Hamilton were single.[39] This wasn't strictly true. Minchin's wife had divorced him four years earlier after he had abandoned her on their wedding day in 1922 never to return. It also transpired that Hamilton had separated from his wife of six years, Barbara, who was reportedly so beautiful that she could silence a room simply by entering it. When news reached her in Paris of his plans, she sailed to New York with a maid to use the crossing as a means of reconciliation. She left the city abruptly to catch the early train north after two weeks of waiting.[40] In Ottawa she managed to evade reporters by pulling a large hat over her blonde bob and checking into a suite at the Chateau Laurier under the name of 'B. Gower'.[41] When reporters eventually found her the twenty-six-year-old was described as looking 'drawn and white'.[42] She did her best to sound casual about the couple's separation:

> Oh, there's nothing to that report. It is nonsense. I've heard it before.
>
> I have absolute faith that Leslie will be found. Both he and Colonel Minchin are regarded not only as superfliers, but as men of tremendous personal courage and resource in a difficult situation.
>
> Leslie has been in so many tight corners in his time and has come out of each with flying colours that I feel absolutely sure that he will be found. He and Colonel Minchin are an ideal team. Leslie is dashing and never worried, while the Colonel is calm and cautious.
>
> I am frightfully disappointed for Leslie's sake and for all their sakes that they did not reach their objectives, because I know that Leslie had counted on being the first to cross the Atlantic from east to west.[43]

But as the hours after their expected time of arrival ticked by, she refused to leave her hotel room where the wife of the Canadian Director of Civilian Aviation, John A. Wilson, kept vigil with her.[44] An ambulance waited at the landing field and prayers were said for the *St Raphael* at St Patrick's church.[45]

By Tuesday 6 September an 'unremitting' search had found no sign of the aeroplane, and *The Times* concluded that, 'unless their lives have been saved by some altogether extraordinary piece of fortune ... it is to be feared that one more tragic and gallant failure must be added to those which have already taken a heavy toll of adventurous spirits.' The leader added that the tragedy was more 'intense' because 'the very place and manner of the disaster must for ever remain unknown'. However, the writer urged that it would be wrong if the 'easily imaginable terrors of such a fate, by the very excess of distress which they must excite in the mind of the public, should cause an outcry against all such attempts.'

It went on:

> Who, however, would wish to condemn or even blame the spirit of those who dare the hitherto unaccomplished? It is the innate impulse to attempt the apparently impossible which makes man only a little lower than the angels ... The men – and women – who make them [the attempts] have just that element of the heroic which touches a chord in every human heart ... Flying, it is true, remains risky, but a number of disasters, terrible and distressing though they be, do not mean that it is become more so ...

The writer made the distinction between 'the unjustifiable rashness' inherent in 'stunt flying' and the need for pilots to consult their conscience when planning a risky flight. Every pilot should be asking themselves, 'How will my effort contribute to the future of aviation?'[46]

Other newspapers were less measured and called for an end to all attempts at a crossing. *The New York Times* noted that, as hope turned to despair, Savile was in danger of becoming the second woman – after Mildred Doran – to be lost in an ocean crossing. Fifteen people had died in attempts and many more during take-off or in test flights.[47] William Lyon Mackenzie King, Prime Minister of Canada, said his parliament might consider banning such attempts – although how this would be enforced was unclear.[48]

The Catholic News on 10 September 1927 speculated that the plane had been brought down by engine trouble or thick fog. It ended its report by reminding readers that Savile's mother had left her 'some remarkable jewels'.

In November, Hamilton's wife, Barbara, applied to the courts for her husband to be declared legally dead but her application was denied as the plane had only been missing for ten weeks.[49] He was finally presumed dead in January, and Savile a few weeks later. The date was given as on, or after, 31 August 1927 at the last time the plane was believed to have been seen at 9.44 pm by a ship in mid Atlantic.[50]

A year later, on 31 August 1928, tangible evidence appeared of the plane's fate when the Palladium Tire Manufacturing Company identified the markings of an aeroplane wheel found off the coast of Iceland as being one of their products. *St Raphael* was fitted with exactly such wheels.[51] Probate was granted in 1948 when her effects were valued at £19,766 5s (about £1 million today). These were left to the 7th Earl of Mexborough.

The disappearance of *St Raphael* at the end of August 1927 did nothing to quell Atlantic fever. Indeed, the hope that the plane may have managed to conquer a large stretch of the ocean might have encouraged many would-be contenders. Two separate teams, both led by women, were already deep into plans for their crossings, despite the onset of autumn. The next east-west bid by a woman was also only six months in the future.

CHAPTER TEN

The Flying Matron Versus 'Miss America of the Air'

Old Orchard Beach, near Portland in Maine, is roughly 100 miles (161 kilometres) north of Boston, and in the autumn of 1927 was as fun-loving and cosmopolitan as Trepassey was hardworking and insular. Both looked out onto the same Atlantic and for both the ocean provided a living. In Newfoundland the sea meant one thing – fishing; in Old Orchard the beach transformed the town into a seaside resort and one of its most famous attractions was the Jack Rabbit. The giant rollercoaster, one of the biggest on the east coast, transported holiday makers sedately over rows of shiny new motor cars parked on the seafront below before hurtling them down past the sand until the train started to climb again towards views out to Saco Bay. The terrifying vehicle epitomised the roaring twenties – it gave passengers the chance to let off steam before they returned to their generally humdrum lives. The casino at the end of the wooden pier offered a similar release – either via gambling or by listening to the most recent music.

It was the arrival of the railroad that pushed the small settlement into the modern age, but it was the wide, open beaches that broadened its appeal in the twentieth century to revellers from New York, Boston, and even Canada. Visitors came to knead their toes into the wet sand, to enjoy the local lobsters, to treat themselves to hot dogs, and, in the 1920s, to pretend they were drinking real alcohol, rather than a prohibition alternative. But for aviators, Old Orchard's biggest attractions were its position on the east coast and its miles of natural, sandy, runway.

The origins of the resort's modern elegance stemmed from a catastrophic fire that had taken hold one warm summer's evening in August 1907 when the town was heaving with visitors. The flames were so persistent that they leapt the Boston and Maine Railroad tracks that had brought such prosperity in the first place.[1] During the course of six hours the blaze destroyed seventeen hotels, sixty cottages, and several houses. An undisclosed number of people died.[2] Firemen were still dampening down the embers four months later. The metaphorical afterglow never quite left the resort and there was a sense that pleasure and death were closely linked at Old Orchard. Even the original elegant pier of 1897 had only lasted 156 days before its twin pavilions were swept away by a northeast gale.[3]

In June 1912 Old Orchard was described as 'An Eldorado of Refined and Select Amusements'[4] and for several seasons 'Pecks Prancing Ponies', 'the longest and most thrilling ride in the world' provided a 'merry go round straight' on which women perched in a decorous, side-saddle fashion, as they were transported forward, rather than round and round.[5] But the resort also offered wide streets and comfortable hotels, such as the Old Orchard House, whose tiers of windows and fluttering flags kept guard over the beach.

Just as the railroad had transformed Old Orchard so the aeroplane promised to open another chapter in its history. At low tide, the town's firm sand provided a runway almost three times the length of Roosevelt Field and without the bumps and jolts that made the New York surface so troublesome. Old Orchard's convenient location on the globe also gave it an advantage. It was positioned at a point on a

Great Circle – the magical, coveted line that allows a pilot to follow the fastest route possible across the Atlantic, in other words the arc that forms the shortest distance between two points on the globe.

The resort's final advantage for flyers was Harry M. Jones – a pilot who was part airman and part promoter – and who was responsible for putting the town on the aerial map. Jones was a big, flamboyant man who often wore plus fours, a flat cap, and bow tie and who offered flying lessons as part of the resort's range of amusements. He appreciated that flying was a good way of advertising products and people. A local businessman, Robert Hazzard, paid for Jones's hangar and his first plane. Jones's part of the arrangement was to use his biplane as an aerial billboard in which the word 'SHOES' was painted in giant letters on the underside of one wing and '$4' on the undersides of the top deck of wings.

Jones also liked to dress up as Father Christmas and to drop presents to needy children, and persuaded the governor of Maine to create a special position that made him the state's first airborne police officer.[6] When fog prevented Lindbergh from landing at nearby Scarborough on 24 July 1927 as part of his good-will tour across America, it seemed fitting that he should head for Old Orchard instead and that Jones should welcome him. *Spirit of St. Louis* was carefully backed into Jones's hangar and guarded by local policemen.

For several years Jones transported customers from Old Orchard to Scarborough in a return trip that cost twenty-five dollars for two passengers. In the summer of 1927 Frances Grayson joined his list of flying pupils and confided to him that she hoped to use the resort as a stepping off point for an Atlantic crossing.

*

By early September New York was full of rumours that a flight 'under direction of women' could start in three weeks. Grayson and Ancker were thought to have organised an expedition in which a woman would act as 'commander and relief pilot' and it was believed they would leave New York for Oakland, California before continuing on to Seattle and Honolulu on their way to Japan.[7]

But less than a fortnight later newspapers switched their attention to Ruth Elder when diligent reporters discovered that the pilot had been married not once, but twice. Through tears she implored them: 'Married girls in New York use their maiden names – why shouldn't I?'[8]

The press seemed most titillated by the fact that she had overlooked the existence of her current husband, Lyle Womack, who was twenty-five and worked as a salesman. He was broad-shouldered with thick hair.

At first, Elder tried to pass him off as a 'very dear friend of mine' and denied they had ever been married but her sister put the record straight and, inconveniently, Lyle himself turned up in New York as his wife prepared to embark on a bid to cross the Atlantic.[9]

Elder, who was involved in final tests at Roosevelt Field before she set off with George Haldeman, defended the omission tearfully: 'American women believe that a married girl's place is in the home and not the cockpit of an aeroplane ... I don't want to turn them against me to outrage their belief of the girl's place in life.'[10]

Frances Grayson, whose preparations were covered in a column next to the story about Elder's surprise husband, sounded calm and unemotional by comparison. Her Sikorsky amphibious plane, *Dawn* had been specially built for long-distance flights and she would be flying the ocean 'not for a thrill' but to 'help re-establish confidence in aviation [after tragedies such as the disappearance of Savile's plane]'. She was described as a 'young business woman' and sitting in the lobby of the Waldorf-Astoria, where the parents of her business partner, Mabel Ancker had spent their final, unhappy years, she was 'smartly gowned in tan, and speaking in a refined manner' for her first interview – although, generally, she was 'adverse to publicity'. She told the reporter:

> Caution is necessary in making a flight across the ocean, the recent disasters have proven that. I'm not making a race of it to be the first woman to do it. I don't believe in rushing a thing like this. There will be nothing hasty or haphazard in my flight. I intend to be convinced that every bit of the plane is in tip-top shape ... this is not to be a stunt.[11]

She described the plane's J-5 Wright Whirlwind motors and its radios and explained there was no need for a rubber boat because of the amphibious nature of the plane. She was inspired by Savile's bid and the need to 'show that their sacrifice has not been in vain'.[12] She wished Ruth Elder 'loads of luck'. What she didn't point out was that *Dawn* had been developed at breakneck speed and had flown on her maiden flight just seven days after assembly.[13] A week later she took *Dawn* up so that photographers in an adjacent plane could snap pictures but when she opened a door in the cockpit to afford them a better view the wind ripped it off its hinges and it fell to earth somewhere over Long Island.[14]

By the end of September Elder and Haldeman were ready to take their Stinson Detroiter to Paris. Both *American Girl* and Grayson's amphibious *Dawn* skulked in their hangars at Curtiss Field, as mechanics and instrument experts fussed over every nut and bolt, lavishing care on them like expensive racehorses. Originally Grayson and Ancker had wanted to have both a female navigator and pilot on their team but conceded that the most experienced of both were male.[15] *Dawn*'s pilot Wilmer 'Bill' Stultz and navigator Brice 'Goldy' Goldsborough worried about an oil leak and both teams were concerned about the weather and the fast-disappearing 'flying season'.[16] In one photo Grayson stands sternly between the two men, holding an arm of each. It is not an affectionate pose; rather, she looks like she is preventing them from running off.

Goldy was a natty dresser and often wore a bow tie or a double-breasted suit. He had a long nose and deep-set eyes that made him look permanently worried. Newspapers noted that he wore 'suspenders' (braces) *and* a belt – an indication, perhaps, of just how risk-averse he was.[17] He first became interested in radio before the First World War and joined the navy as a way of mastering the relatively new science. He rose to become chief petty officer in command of a radio station in the Far East and served in the Great War.[18] The expertise he gained in the early years of his career allowed him, with two other men, to set up the Pioneer Instrument Company of Brooklyn, which was responsible for inventing the earth induction compass which Lindbergh used when crossing the Atlantic. The instrument was at first seen as more reliable than a traditional compass and as offering the pilot the chance to maintain a heading over long periods of time. One of its key features was that it used a wind-driven generator to create an induction field that produced a variable current as it interacted with the Earth's magnetic field.[19] Goldy sold his 405 shares in the company earlier in 1927 to concentrate on the challenge of flying long-distance over water.

As the flight's official documents reached their expiration date Haldeman was forced to return to Custom House to renew them while Stultz and Goldy were keen to head north, where they wanted to take *Dawn* out at Old Orchard's famous beach. But the weather would not let them risk the three hours to Maine, and Elder and Haldeman only managed around sixty minutes in *American Girl*. On 10 October the *New York Times* declared: 'Women now air rivals' but the truth was that both teams were simply fed up with the weather.

*

On 10 October people strolling along the beach at Old Orchard just after 5.00 pm stared open-mouthed at the unannounced arrival of an enormous, blue and yellow aircraft. The plane had stars and stripes painted on the outer surface of each upper rudder, and the Danish flag on the inner surface to honour the home countries of the plane's two financiers. It circled the pier before preparing to land.[20] One report said that 500 people had waited all afternoon for her arrival.[21] An enormous harvest moon rose, as if to confirm that something otherworldly had just arrived in Maine.

Grayson, who had started the voyage in the seat next to Stultz at the controls, retired to sit on the edge of a leather chair at the rear from where she began to write the story of what she hoped would be their crossing.[22] Hazzard stepped forward to greet them on behalf of the governor and Jones put his hangar and equipment at their disposal.

There was only one hotel, the rattlingly empty Brunswick, which was still open as the holiday season drew to an end and it had to be hastily dusted down so that the visitors could warm themselves round the fire. As news of the strangers' arrival leaked out a shivering crowd of several hundred people gathered at the hangar to welcome Grayson, Stultz, and Goldy. They couldn't have had any idea how long they were settling in for at Old Orchard and what familiar faces they would become at the out-of-season resort. *Dawn*'s spin around the Bay, depending on the weather, became as familiar as one of Jones's joyrides.

*

As October started to lengthen, Elder and Haldeman were going through a similar rigmarole in New York until, suddenly, on 11 October 1927, they were off.[23] As the headline in the *Manchester Guardian* put it, 'Miss Ruth Elder and a Man Piloting "the American Girl"'.[24]

The weather forecast predicted 600 miles of bad weather at the start of the voyage. *American Girl* carried just one engine and a small wireless set with a range of twenty-five miles but its main advantage over expeditions such as Savile's and the future flights by Grayson and, in 1928, Earhart and Mackay, was that *American Girl* was following a more southerly route. This meant that, while they were aiming for a non-stop crossing, Elder and Haldeman would not be as alone as the planes heading over the Grand Banks, off Newfoundland, and the treacherous northern Atlantic. They would also have the vital handhold of the Azores to grab on to if they ran into difficulty mid ocean. The downside was that *American Girl* was most heavily laden at the start of the flight, when she faced the most perilous part of the journey over water, and very soon in darkness, with little chance of rescue if she came down. And if she made it through these first few hours, she would face two nights over sea.

Elder was dressed as if about to play a game of golf on a very cold and exposed golf course. She wore a plaid green and red sweater, thick stockings, Oxford shoes, tan-coloured light woollen plus fours, and a multi-coloured hair band.[25] Haldeman resembled her caddy on that same freezing course and wore a dark blue lounge suit and grey cap. Elder carried a basket of provisions and a blanket – and looked as if she was heading off for a picnic. Both pilots snuggled into a fur-lined one-piece, army flying suit and carried rubber, inflatable life suits, which had drinking water and a can of emergency rations in their pockets. They hadn't bothered with a rubber raft because Elder thought they had little chance of being picked up if they had to abandon the plane. They did, however, have a Very pistol and lights, as well as navigation flares and a large knife with which to cut their way out of the plane if they needed to escape after landing on water. They also had two pounds of sugar cubes, which a physicist had suggested could be a useful way to generate heat.[26]

Much store was placed on Elder's attention to her looks, and she was said to be carrying a miniature vanity case in the pocket of her knickerbockers. She accepted a small Bible from her mother and, although she professed not to believe in luck, wore a Chinese ring that was said to bring good fortune, which a female friend had pressed on her. She had also packed a doll mascot cat called Felix and a lucky rabbit's foot.[27]

Their plan was to follow the steamship shipping lanes and fly entirely by instruments. They would head due south for about 1,200 miles before changing course to north-east to steer for Paris. The 3,600 miles would be the longest distance ever flown over water. They carried 520 gallons of petrol and twenty gallons of oil – thought to be enough to keep them going for 4,400 miles. The fuel was stored in tanks in the wings and fuselage and 140 gallons in twenty-eight cans which, when emptied, would be dropped overboard. Each tin was painted red and carried the names of both pilots.[28] They planned to take turns at the controls and the press seemed to have been briefed to describe Elder as 'pilot' and Haldeman as 'co-pilot'.

It was Haldeman who had grown tired of waiting for the wind to change direction and, with only an hour of daylight left, kissed his wife goodbye and jumped into the plane. Elder had been pacing around, nervously repeating, 'I'm very happy, I'm very happy' in a mechanical way, with a mixture of anxiety and excitement.[29] She threw a final kiss to the crowd and waved before being helped into the plane.

Haldeman taxied along what was considered one of the worst runways that an Atlantic flight had left from that year. The plane bounced across a mile of yellow sand edged with grass and lined with people, cars, and a smattering of planes on the ground and in the air. He opened the throttle and, when he was sure he had squeezed as much speed out of the engine as possible, lifted *American Girl* into the skies.

He was easily making eighty miles per hour when he turned to the southeast. He cleared the telegraph lines that had nearly tripped up Lindbergh and sailed over the nearby golf course where players, more modestly dressed than Elder, stared up at the sky. The bright orange-yellow plane, with NZ 1384 painted in black letters on its wings, left

Roosevelt Field, Long Island for Paris at 5.04 pm.

As news of their departure reached Old Orchard, Grayson speeded up her own preparations, but commented:

> There is plenty of room over the Atlantic for two women and plenty of glory for a lot of them. We believe that we have an entirely different purpose from Miss Elder's ... The work will not be hurried and there will be no semblance of a race.[30]

After the intense press attention and excitement, the leading actor had suddenly left the screen. Newspapers felt bereft: 'The first American girl to attempt the long flight over the North Atlantic to Europe was somewhere out at sea last night, her plane speeding through the darkness and ahead of her one of the most dangerous passages ever attempted.'[31]

Reporters knew that *American Girl* was flying towards her biggest challenge, just as she was roughly halfway across the ocean. *The New York Times* was blunt with its readers: 'There is a storm which will strain her plane and the skill of her pilot to the utmost.'[32]

CHAPTER ELEVEN

The Weather Man

Throughout their preparations Elder and Grayson, and later Earhart and Boll, were acutely aware of the presence of one man who stood, like a referee at a boxing contest, between them and their ambition to cross the Atlantic. It was he who talked to them earnestly about the risks they faced, urging them to wait for perfect weather out at sea, no matter how calm conditions seemed on land. And it was he who pleaded with them not to risk everything on a foolish assault on a stretch of water over which the weather was notoriously difficult to predict.

James H. 'Doc' Kimball spent his working day in a staid business suit, sitting behind a desk in his high office eyrie in the thirty-two-storey Whitehall Building at the southern tip of Manhattan, overlooking the Battery and Upper Bay. Despite his discreet profile, he played a key part in every record-breaking flight across the Atlantic in the 1920s and 1930s. It was Kimball who called Lindbergh to tell him that the weather was as good as it was going to get on the morning of 20 May 1927. It was to Kimball that Amelia Earhart's team turned in the summer of 1928 when *Friendship* was weighing up the pros and cons of leaving Newfoundland – and Kimball whom Boll focused her wrath on when she felt she had been excluded from his priceless insights. Kimball is namechecked in every biography of a famous pilot and every account of a major Atlantic attempt.

His behind-the-scenes importance became evident, when, in April 1931, Kimball, the assistant meteorologist of the New York office of the US Weather Bureau, was a guest of honour in New York at a dinner given by eight of the men and two of the women who had survived the Atlantic. Lindbergh sat on one side and Amelia Earhart commented, 'We couldn't get along without him.'[1] He was 'gentle, grey-haired, looking somewhat older than his 57 years' and 'moved to tears by the demonstration [of affection]'.[2] Richard E. Byrd presented him with a flag he had carried for Kimball across the Atlantic and in his trips to Antarctica.

Although 'Doc' was a common nickname in the 1920s, often used to denote those in charge, or who took a particularly analytical approach to a problem, for example a baseball coach, Kimball's qualification was genuine and he earned his PhD from New York University at a time when weather forecasting was a new, but increasingly important, science. In the first half of the nineteenth century the Smithsonian Institution had helped to establish an observation network in which reports were gathered by telegraph, and by 1849, 150 volunteers across the US were submitting bulletins. On the outbreak of the Civil War in 1861, 500 weather stations were sending in regular observations. The invention of the telegraph made it possible to relay information about what the weather was like as it moved, generally, eastwards. Suddenly, the idea of forecasting the weather became a possibility.

President Ulysses S. Grant recognised that only a government agency had the discipline to gather these observations promptly, at regular intervals, and with the greatest accuracy. The army's Signal Service Corps was the ideal organisation until 1890 when the role moved into civilian hands under the aegis of the newly created US

Weather Bureau, which was part of the Department of Agriculture.[3] By the start of the new century the US was exchanging weather information with Europe, in 1901 the Service provided three-day forecasts for the North Atlantic, and in 1926 the Air Commerce Act ordered the Weather Bureau to provide advice for civil aviation.[4]

Harold Gatty and Wiley Post later described Kimball as 'the guardian angel, guiding spirt, and foster father of flyers who take it upon themselves to dare the ocean'. When, in 1931, they prepared to cross the Atlantic as part of a round-the-world flight, they received weather reports from him three or four times a day and gathered for a 'council of war' in Kimball's office daily. Standing next to his drawing board, he urged them to pace themselves so that they weren't worn out on the first leg of the journey. Gatty felt 'the hypnotic influence of the meteorologist's quiet but business-like manner'.[5]

Kimball, who himself had never flown and who earned $4,000 a year in his government post, concentrated on preparing charts for the weather at sea, although he was fully aware of the scant material he had to work with.[6] 'How is it possible to make a scheduled flight over 3,000 miles of water, when the only information available is the routine observations of from only 10 to 20 ships rarely in locations where they are most needed?' he moaned.[7]

But he also weighed up the personalities of the prospective flyers, 'his boys and girls',[8] as keenly as he measured the isobars he drew on the Atlantic charts that he spread out before them on his office desk.[9] He refused to advise anyone whom he felt lacked the right personality and the right equipment to attempt the Atlantic – which may have been why he had such an uneasy relationship with Mabel Boll. By contrast, he approved of Ruth Elder's co-pilot, George Haldeman: 'He knows what he wants to do and how to do it. If anyone can work his way through the bad weather ahead of him he can do it. But he will have rough going.'[10]

As Haldeman and Elder prepared for the flight Doc urged them to fly over the low-pressure area at about 15,000 feet and to shimmy through the fog and rain.

*

On Tuesday evening, 11 October 1927, about 400 miles from New York, the ship *American Banker* spotted *American Girl* flying 'fast and low through a clear moonlight night'.[11] And then silence.

Five hours after take-off there was nothing but conjecture about her whereabouts. Had she taken to higher airspace to avoid the storms, making her all but invisible to the fifteen to eighteen passenger, mail, and freight ships using the two-way shipping lane that linked New York and the Channel ports during their flight?[12] Kimball was surprised that no ship had spotted her yet. Large steamers crossing from Europe, including the *Homeric*, *Ile de France*, and *Leviathan*, were all thought to be in the area. He was disappointed that the *Mauretania* and *Ryndam*, which were sailing to the southeast of Newfoundland, had not detected any trace. Steamships from Glasgow and Scandinavia were believed to be too far north to encounter *American Girl*.

Perhaps the strong crosswinds had pushed her away from the shipping lanes and Elder and Haldeman had taken Kimball's advice and tried to skirt the bad weather by heading south. Or maybe unexpectedly fine weather had catapulted them ahead of schedule? The storm, which was 600–700 miles off the European coast, had slacked and the wind was calming down from gale force to fifteen miles per hour. According to Kimball, 3.00 am New York Time, was the earliest they might be seen over land, and he speculated that, if conditions became really rough, the plane might come down in Spain.

Kimball, as a non-flyer, could not have imagined what the two pilots were going through – and not just for one night, but two. Flying a plane in 1927 for long periods of time meant hours of concentration and the constant awareness that the smallest lapse in that concentration could prove fatal. It wasn't the mental strain alone but the physical element. Watching the instrument panel's 'little dancing dials' for hour after hour places an unbearable exertion on eyesight, even more so when flying in darkness or over water, where there is nothing to even glance at as a calming contrast.[13] The tension doesn't just come from the physical effort of watching the instruments but from the mental burden of computing what the dials are telling you. The pilot is constantly assessing the banking and turning of the plane, the angle of ascent and descent, the height above sea level, the revolutions of the motor, the oil pressure, and whether the three compasses are presenting a united front. He or she must also make sure the engine is ticking along at the right speed to conserve fuel, which involves calculating drift to see how it will affect speed. Monitoring all of this in the darkness is even more taxing because you must have complete faith in your instruments, even though your natural impulses may be screaming at you to ignore what your eyes are telling you. Only your instruments can accurately say whether the plane is on an even keel, and the right way up, and following the correct course. All of this while the plane is being jolted and bumped by a raging storm and the engine is so loud that you have to shout to make yourself heard.

Kimball was correct in assuming that *American Girl* had dipped south of the major shipping routes, but he couldn't have guessed just how far south she'd gone.

CHAPTER TWELVE

Missing

Although by the early morning of 13 October the storm had largely burnt itself out, the Dutch registered oil tanker, *SS Barendrecht*, which was on her way to Texas from Rotterdam and about 360 miles northeast of the Azores, was still rolling in heavy seas. At 7.45 am the mate on watch spotted from the bridge what he thought was an unusual bird to the northwest. After studying the shape, he realised there was nothing avian about it.

'It was coming fast,' he said later.[1]

When it became obvious that he was looking at a plane, most of the crew emerged to gawp at the unusual sight and to cheer it on its way. They had no idea the aircraft was in trouble until it swooped low to drop a packet that fell short of the tanker. A second message hit its target and read, 'How far are we from land and which way? – Ruth Elder.'

It took several minutes for the crew to check their exact position and to paint the answer on the deck, 'True south, forty west, 360 miles, Terceira [an island in the], Azores' – information that, to Elder and Haldeman, must have felt agonisingly slow to appear.[2]

Once they had read the message the plane moved away, before turning and heading straight for the tanker, all the time dropping lower and lower until it ditched in the sea. The crew watched as two people climbed out; the female figure stood on one wing wearing her bulky inflatable life-saving suit and the man appeared on the other wing in his flying clothes. Elder, who was always so conscious of what she looked like, could not have been wearing a less flattering outfit. When it was inflated, the suit gave her giant, shapeless limbs and a torso further enlarged by one massive pocket. Only her head appeared to be the right size. The suit was designed to be able to keep the wearer afloat for several hours.[3]

The tanker put out a small boat and rode the heavy swell to get as close to the sinking plane as she could. The seamen shouted out inquiries about whether they could swim and, when the couple said they couldn't, the tanker crew prepared to fling lines to them.[4] Elder told them to save Haldeman first since she was wearing her inflatable suit. Both caught the lines and tied them round their bodies; they were soaked but in good spirits.

The ship's captain, who is described in accounts by his surname of Goos, was clearly smitten by his unexpected female passenger and lent her his cap and cabin.

> You would have thought she was just coming aboard to pay a sociable call. I was much more excited myself. As she came overside she put out her hand man fashion and said, 'Thank you very much captain'. Then, as George was following, she stepped aside, took out a lipstick and a small mirror and began to see how she looked and to fix herself up.[5]

The two pilots persuaded Goos to try to rescue *American Girl* and *SS Barendrecht* edged closer to the sinking aeroplane, which now had a broken wing. But as the plane scraped the ship's side there was a puff and a big bang, followed by two explosions before the aeroplane burst into flames shooting up as high as the bridge. One crew member noted that it was fortunate that they weren't carrying petroleum. The crew had no option but to release the line and watch the waves swallow what had been the pilots' home.

It was only at this point that Elder broke down. She said later:

> What a pity that we couldn't have saved the *American Girl* after she had carried us safely through so much bad weather. It was just like watching an old friend drown to see that plane go down. But I suppose we ought to be thankful we are here and able to talk about it.[6]

She consoled herself by drinking tea brewed by the crew, although it was so strong that she had to ask for an extra cup of hot water to dilute it.[7] She slept badly in the narrow bunk and was troubled by dreams that she was still in the plane, battling against the storm, until she was woken by her own cries and realised that she was safe.[8]

News of their rescue travelled ahead of them and hundreds of people gathered on the shore of the island of Fayal in the Azores. Others took to roofs to search for the first sign of the tanker. Among the crowds were three German airmen and their passenger, a crop-haired Viennese actress called Lilli Dillenz, who were waiting to take off for Newfoundland.[9] Bad weather had delayed them further at the Azores.[10]

Elder arrived at the island in plus fours, a red jumper, and a leather jacket, and had replaced her usual head band with Goos's cap. She was still wearing her Chinese ring, but her mother's bible, the lucky toy cat, and her passport were all at the bottom of the ocean. Everyone tried to shake her hand as she arrived on shore and she responded with an automatic, 'Thank you. I thank you. I thank you.'[11]

At the press conference in Horta she brushed off talk of the storm but said she had started to become anxious when the oil pressure gauge showed 'a derangement'.[12] Haldeman explained how, after just a few hours, the weather turned into a 'frightful storm' and no matter how high they climbed they were unable to leave behind conditions that 'lashed the battered plane in the most terrifying fashion'.[13] For eight hours they were buffeted by rain and gales which smashed one of the plane's fuel reservoirs. Heavy sleet turned to ice on the plane, and they took turns to throw some of the fuel overboard. One unlikely version, which recalls the first crossing of the Atlantic in a plane when Brown edged along the wing to chip away at ice, claimed that she had crawled out on to the tail of the plane to balance the machine.[14] It seems much more probable that she shuffled *inside* the fuselage to the rear of the aircraft but even this manoeuvre, within the comparative safety of the aircraft, doesn't sound as though it would have achieved much.[15]

When the storm had finally abated, they could no longer be sure where they were and feared they would have to bring the plane down onto the water at any moment due to lack of fuel. Haldeman took her higher to make it easier to scan the waves for a ship and it may have been this action that heated up the oil-starved engine and led to the fire that destroyed the aeroplane.

Elder laughed and chatted to the admirers who swarmed around her at the press conference. She insisted she planned to launch a new attempt on the Atlantic as soon as they returned to New York from Paris. She was adamant, perhaps with a nod to her Austrian rival, that she would not consider any offer to star in a movie if it interfered with her goal. Or perhaps she hoped to plant the seed of a future career in the mind of any impresario reading her words.

*

The New York Times received 2,000 phone calls from worried readers inquiring if anything had been heard of the plane.[16] Grayson was sitting in her car outside the hangar at Old Orchard when she discovered that they were safe. She was sopping wet, having just inspected her own plane, which had been bounced around the beach by the heaviest waves to strike the Maine coast in ten years. Until that moment she had appeared depressed but the good news lifted her mood and she was heard to say, 'Thank God!' and to repeat over and over, 'I'm so glad.'[17]

On the day that *American Girl* had been ploughing her way through the skies, Stultz and Kinkade, the Wright motor expert, had been putting *Dawn* through her paces. They were particularly concerned about how she would perform with the heavy load of fuel needed to get them across the Atlantic. Sand and water were used to mimic the weight of a fully fuelled aircraft as the pilot got used to the much longer runway afforded by Old Orchard's beach, compared to Roosevelt. Kinkade tinkered around with the port engine after these test flights and in the evening Maine's governor and his wife arrived to christen the plane. Prohibition meant that a decorated bottle of local Poland Springs water was hurled against *Dawn*, in place of anything alcoholic.[18] The fact that the governor's wife, standing on a chair, was able to break the bottle, which was wrapped in the plane's colours of blue and gold ribbons, over the prow with one blow was seen as a good omen but the mood soured after the ceremony when she issued a statement urging Grayson to postpone: 'The hazard of the enterprise, however, and the question as to its fruits lead me to express what I believe to be the earnest entreaty of Maine women that you may decide to wait.'[19]

Grayson replied graciously and emphatically on behalf of her crew and Ancker: 'In urging me not to go I feel that you have assumed as great a responsibility as if you had advised me to go. The *Dawn* will awaken American women to greater efforts and bind together the women of two continents.'[20]

Knowing that Elder and Haldeman were safe – and that the title of first female to cross the Atlantic in a plane was still up for grabs – seemed to galvanise Grayson into action and she left her car to return to *Dawn* where the plane was battling a combination of equinoctial storm and the towering moon tide. In a borrowed overcoat and knee-length rubber boots, which she had snatched from the hangar door, and which soon filled with sea water, she struggled to the plane. She ordered more ropes to secure *Dawn* and herself took up a shovel to dig out the landing gear as it disappeared under sand deposited by the persistent waves. From time to time the sea broke over the 'boat' part of the 'flying boat' in a 'swirling mass of green foam and flotsam'.[21] The salt water sprayed the twin motors and seaweed draped itself over the golden wings, as if the ocean was trying to claim the plane for itself.

The bitter cold meant that the team of the *Dawn* worked alone and without the curious onlookers who usually gathered to keep an eye on their endeavours. 'All along this chill frontier not a soul was to be seen except the little knot of dripping, straining men …'[22] Pilot Bill Stultz, in a blue serge suit, and navigator, Brice 'Goldy' Goldsborough, in golf clothes, led the team, burying huge timbers in the sand to which they could fix ropes to tether the plane and prevent it being swept out to sea.

Grayson asked anxiously when the tide would reach its high point. At noon she was told the waves should start to recede in thirty minutes, but the sea showed no sign of retiring. A fifty-gallon barrel of valuable fuel started to bob out to sea and Goldy and then Stultz waded after it. Both were knocked off their feet but managed eventually to retrieve the cask.

When the waves finally retreated, the team built a temporary wooden runway from which to move the plane to the safety of the upper beach. They finished late at night. Kinkade examined the engines and ripped back the tarpaulin to gently blot up moisture that had gathered on the cylinders. The engine had survived. Goldy, Stultz, and Libinski, the Sikorsky mechanic, examined the plane with forensic care, while another man from Sikorsky shovelled away the sand that had gathered on its floor. The fact that the plane had been fully loaded with fuel probably saved it by anchoring her down.

Once Grayson was satisfied there was no water in the fuel lines or carburettors, she allowed herself to relax. One reporter commented that she 'sought her powder puff and seemed to gain confidence with it.'[23] She returned the borrowed boots and overcoat, wiped mud from her feet, and appeared untroubled by a ladder in her stockings. She drove back to her hotel for a hot bath and ordered the same for the crew. Tomorrow might be the day they left for Denmark.

American Girl's rescue off the Azores made the front page of *The New York Times* and established a record for the longest flight over water and the longest flight ever by a woman. It was estimated that Elder and Haldeman had covered 2,633 statute miles and the figure may have been much greater due to their efforts to skirt round a storm. They were 1,000 miles short of Lindbergh's distance to Paris and 1,200 miles below Chamberlin and Levine's flight to Germany.[24] When they were forced to ditch, they were only about 700 miles from Europe and, if the oil pipe hadn't broken, they would surely have made the Atlantic crossing.

Elder's husband, Lyle Womack, who had been against the enterprise from the start, was ecstatic when he received a message from his wife saying that she was safe. From Balboa in Panama he told reporters he had only been able to sleep for a few minutes and had been living at the cable office: 'If Ruth had been lying dead in a casket and then got up to put her arms around me I wouldn't feel any different than I do now.'[25]

He added that he was sorry she hadn't succeeded but added that he would not have minded if she'd only got as far as Sandy Hook in New Jersey.

But, amid all the plaudits about their bravery and stamina – particularly in flying over water for two consecutive nights – many commentators pointed out how very lucky *American Girl* had been to stumble across a ship that happened to be in the area. A few were angry at the risks that a pilot – particularly a female one – had deliberately put herself through.

A jokey letter to *The New York Times* from the vaudeville performer and wit, Will Rogers, concluded a round-up of international news with 'Ruth Elder, that dutiful and home-loving wife, says "save the lipstick first". So the plane was lost.'[26] Religious leaders were affronted by her gall. Rev Dr Christian F. Reisner asked his congregation at the Chelsea Methodist Church in New York what was to be gained by her pluck. 'Are we not in danger of women finding highest glory in being as near like men as possible? They may lose their crown as "queens" in this work-a-day world where they have ruled for so long.'[27]

Many women, while praising her courage, nevertheless saw the attempt as foolhardy. Eleanor Roosevelt thought it 'very foolish' and Winifred Sackville Stoner, founder of the League for Fostering Genius, commented: 'a good typist is of much more service to humanity.'[28] Stoner, who had criticised Gertrude Ederle for crossing the Channel when it was possible to make the journey by boat or plane, clearly missed the point of such expeditions.

Since record breaking was also about national pride, it was not surprising that the German newspaper *Zwölf Uhr Blatt* criticised Elder's 'overweening presumptuousness [in that she] imagines all the world and powers of nature are hers to command'.[29] *The Irish News* was even more vehement and said a woman had 'no business' attempting such a flight. 'She is a married woman. Her husband wisely remained at home. If Ruth has any sense left she will join him now and keep house for him.' The paper advised that the other American woman waiting to make the same crossing (clearly a reference to Frances Grayson) should be taken home by her relatives and if they 'used a slight rod to tame her ardent spirits, no one would censure them too severely.'[30]

Even the German pilot Thea Rasche said that men were better pilots and still made the best tutors for their female counterparts. Ruth Nichols was more ebullient in her praise, although she commented that it was rather late in the season to make such an attempt.[31] Everyone seemed to agree that it was, indeed, rather late in the day. Only Frances Grayson appeared undaunted by the approaching winter.

CHAPTER THIRTEEN

'A safe and sane flight'

The threat of winter gave *Dawn*'s crew an added impetus and in the days after Ruth Elder's failed attempt Old Orchard hummed with activity and anticipation. Ivor Sikorsky himself, moustachioed and serious in his thick coat, tie, and hat, arrived from New York to inspect the plane after the deluge. The weather was sunny, and Grayson announced that they would attempt to leave on Saturday 15 October 1927. The Brunswick Hotel managed to put together a banquet at short notice and 'Lady Grayson', as she had become known among local people, took the opportunity to make a speech in which she hit back at her critics who described her plans as foolhardy.[1] Orders were given to wake the crew at 5.30 am but pilot Stultz and navigator Goldy had spent much of the night chewing over the weather data as it arrived from steamships already out in the Atlantic. The reports persuaded the team to postpone. They went back to bed and Sikorsky returned to his factory at College Point.

On Sunday 16 October Goldy plotted the storms out in the Atlantic and when it got dark sat on his little hotel balcony with his sextant to add the stars to his chart.[2] He was particularly concerned about the strength of the wind, which could force them to consume too much fuel. Grayson used the spare day to visit Portland where she bought two cans of dark blue paint and attended the Episcopalian church. On her return to Old Orchard she climbed into a tatty pair of overalls and started to repaint the upper half of the flying boat. She was still working away at 4.00 pm, perched on one of the wheels, when a delegation from the local Board of Trade turned up. She frowned at their arrival, expecting them to remonstrate with her, but, instead, the head of the Board made a speech telling her to 'go to it' and presented her with a bunch of red roses.[3]

By Monday 17 October *Dawn* had been sitting fully fuelled for two days. Grayson had examined the plane carefully for storm damage and ordered that the paint applied to the upper portion be rubbed smooth with emery paper to reduce resistance caused by the constant attack from sand. Each joint and crevice was washed with petrol to eliminate any grains that had crept in. A huge vacuum cleaner would be brought in to suck out sand from the plane's interior before take-off.[4]

No storms were reported out at sea. Goldy and Grayson pored over the charts he had meticulously drawn and which he now spread out on the floor of the Brunswick for them to peer at on their hands and knees. Grayson said the decision was up to the navigator and pilot and the two locked themselves in a room to analyse the maps further. A representative from the Sikorsky company was called in and a moment later tapped on Grayson's door.

'The flight is on,' he told her.[5]

Kinkade was already on the beach, swinging the 'props' (propellers) and listening to the 'sighing compression of the twin Whirlwinds [engines]'.[6] Grayson took a few bites of breakfast and dashed off some telegrams before paying the hotel bill for her and the crew. Each departure was like this, and they had to assume they would not be returning. One thing was different this time: she had slimmed down her extensive luggage to just two small pasteboard boxes. In one preposterous report it was claimed she would be wearing a rose-pink silk negligee under her flying suit and silver slippers with very high heels.[7]

At 9.30 am, when the tide was low, the mechanics cranked the handles on the starters, which produced a shrieking sound; the propellers began to turn, and the two engines leapt into action. The crew boarded and waited for the plane to warm up. Stultz and Goldy's wives were there to wave them off as the sound of the engines' roar competed with the ocean's waves.

Once ready, *Dawn* taxied down as far as the supports beneath the pier where she was turned to face Pine Point. Stultz let the engines idle before opening up the throttle and the plane hurtled along the sandy runway. A car beside them on the beach tried to keep up; Kinkade was clinging to its running board, gripping his stopwatch in one hand to judge when Stultz, according to their test flights, should attempt lift off.

'Pull her up, Bill; pull her up!' he cried.

Dawn achieved lift-off but was only able to gain about a further ten feet and just as she was approaching Cabbage Island, further northeast along the coast, onlookers noted vapour escaping from the plane's rear as Goldy released 260 gallons of precious aviation fuel. This allowed the plane to climb higher, but jettisoning the fuel had meant they had no hope of attempting the Atlantic crossing and had to return to base.[8]

Later, Stultz said she had been too nose-heavy and Goldy added that when he'd tried to retract the wheels for a landing the mechanism had stuck. Sikorsky was summoned to look into the problems, and it was thought that the recent storm may have damaged part of the equipment. Grayson argued that the aborted flight was not the fault of the plane or crew but because a few gallons of fuel had been placed too far forward in the aircraft. She cabled her business partner, Ancker in Denmark, to put her in the picture and said she hoped to be in Copenhagen within a week and would refuel at either Valentia in western Ireland or Croydon Airport in Britain.

Fifty gallons were moved from the nose tank and transferred to five-gallon cans that were stored in the rear. Ironically, the team was helped by the discovery of 300 gallons of high-quality aviation fuel in the beach hangar. The barrels had been left by Elder and Haldeman when they had thought they might begin their journey from Old Orchard.

Following repairs, *Dawn* performed well in test flights, but Stultz was starting to have doubts about her capability to cross the Atlantic with the load of fuel needed to feed two engines. His concerns seemed justified when a second attempt on Tuesday 18 October failed at a similar point, only this time the plane settled on the water and had to be escorted back to the hangar through one-and-a-quarter miles of sea.

The weather was still poor on Sunday. Grayson ordered seventy-one gallons to be drained away and the crew decided to try a take-off in the opposite direction. Very few spectators bothered to show up at 6.00 am for yet another attempt but Grayson lent out of the cabin window to embrace Goldy and Stultz's wives before the plane taxied to Pine Point to begin its race towards the pier. The two wives stood awkwardly in their smart New York coats and shoes on the wet sand next to Kinkade, who was more relaxed in a jumper and shades. Each raised an arm in salute as they watched the plane starting to climb after just a mile. She then made an emphatic left-hand turn and disappeared in a northeast direction.

'It seemed for the first thirty minutes as if all three of us in the plane were in the thrall of a charm,' Grayson said later. 'None of us spoke; none of us moved. I have never experienced the feeling before. I know now I never will again. We seemed dedicated to a great adventure. Then something broke the spell. It was all over. We moved and talked to each.'[9]

For several hours they flew smoothly and continued to gain altitude. Coincidentally, the first ship they spotted was a Danish freighter, the *Luchana* on her way from Boston to Europe. The sighting must have felt like a good omen.

Grayson sent two messages via Goldy who was hunched over the radio. The first to her father in Muncie read 'love to all the people back in Indiana'. The second was to the wives of Goldy and Stultz and said they were hard at work. A third was for Mrs Calvin Coolidge in Washington:

> I greet the first lady of my country first from the *Dawn*. I am off after six months' preparation, confident in the success of my two-fold purpose: to prove the amphibian plane the logical one for transatlantic commerce and to prove that woman has her place in the advancement of the science of aviation.

The fourth was intended for the Queen of Denmark:

> Your Majesty knows ere this that one of the women of your great land, Mrs Ancker, helped to make this expedition possible. Confident of success we salute you beneath the glorious October sun. Four hundred [and] thirty-seven years ago Columbus sailed westward in his wooden ships. Today we are sailing eastward in an all-metal ship of the air. Columbus discovered America. We hope to discover a new method of transatlantic commerce – the amphibian plane.[10]

A fifth message thanked the people of Maine for their hospitality.

Given its weight, it was a significant choice to take the radio, but it wasn't long before they were relieved at their decision – and not just for the opportunity to send messages composed for posterity.

The trance-like atmosphere in the plane disintegrated as they approached the treacherous Newfoundland waters. At one point *Dawn* entered a cloud where it hit an air pocket and started to shake violently before dropping to within a few feet of the water. Grayson and Goldy frantically ditched three five-gallon tins from the window to lift the plane above the waves.

By the time they had reached a point thirty miles south of Sable Island, a slim, crescent-shaped slither of sand covered in tufts of marram grass 300 kilometres (190 miles) southeast of Halifax, Nova Scotia, the atmosphere in the cabin had become tense. The area, which resembles little more than an eyelash on the map, was famous for its thick fogs, unpredictable currents and for the number of ships that had been wrecked there.

Dawn was 500 miles from Old Orchard across the Atlantic when Grayson realised from the motion of the plane and from glancing at the compass mounted at the top of the instrument panel that the dial had swung from east to west.[11] They were travelling in the wrong direction. Goldy was in the radio nook and for several minutes was also unaware of the decision to change course. When he emerged Stultz told him that they could not continue in such weather without gaining altitude but this was impossible because of the direction of the wind; he had altered course to find calmer air. They flew westward for thirty minutes but failed to gain height.

Grayson was about to manoeuvre her way to the cockpit to confer with Stultz when the exhaust pipe on the port motor started to belch puffs of white smoke. The needle of the tachometer, which shows the numbers of revolutions made by the engine per minute, vibrated violently before dropping to zero. The engine slowed and began to lose power. The damaged engine had knocked out the tachometer and Stultz had no way of knowing how quickly the engine was turning.

At the same time the weather worsened. In that instant the dilemma moved from which direction they needed to follow in order to gain height to whether they could make it back to Old Orchard or should ditch in the sea. They decided to try to find the most recent ship they had spotted, *Coahoma County*. Goldy issued an SOS and managed to speak to the ship's captain who agreed to retrace his steps to meet them. He told them that if they decided to land they should do so to the leeward of the vessel. Stultz and Goldy's wives happened both to be in the operations room of the naval radio compass station at Cape Elizabeth when Goldy's message of their predicament came through.[12]

Although the sea was smooth, the wind was still keen and the sky darkening. As the three of them huddled together to confer about what to do raindrops pelted the cabin.[13] They decided to put their faith in the starboard motor and limped back to their starting point in six hours, compared to the four hours it had taken them to cover the same distance on their departure. The struggling engine blew a black cloud of oil back that covered the stars and stripes and the Danish flags on the left-hand rudder. As they readied for landing, they had to poor soup and coffee over the hydraulic landing gear to lubricate it.[14] By this time the left motor was barely turning over and the wings and body were covered with a heavy coat of oil.

Newspaper reporters noticed that the relationship between Grayson and Stultz appeared 'somewhat strained' on their arrival in Maine and on Monday they took a long walk on the beach together.[15] Stultz later said Grayson had 'played up like a brick' and left the decision about whether to turn back entirely to him and Goldy.[16]

The latter retreated to the Brunswick Hotel and refused to be drawn into the debate over Stultz's action. But even the hotel offered less than its usual warm welcome as the proprietor had been so sure that the team wouldn't be returning that he had dismissed the maids, waitresses, and cook. The chef refused to return, saying he would not delay his annual deer hunt another day. Instead, the proprietor's wife had to prepare lunch.[17]

A new engine had been ordered to replace the faulty one and a through-express train would stop just long enough for it to be unloaded, but as Kinkade started to examine the plane it became evident just how close to disaster the expedition had come. He discovered that a valve had broken in the head of a No. 2 cylinder and had fallen on the piston head. The upward stroke of the piston had transferred the broken part back to its original position. Had the valve not been returned to its position by the next stroke of the piston, the engine would probably have exploded, sending bits flying into the other engine and causing *Dawn* to either burst into flames or to plunge into the ocean. Kinkade also reported that the broken engine had only two gallons of oil left and the remaining thirteen gallons had leaked over the rudder and supporting struts.

Old Orchard was 'muffled to the ears against the hint of Winter' to wave off *Dawn* as she returned to New York on Sunday 30 October.[18] The end of the month also marked the end of the team's contract and Stultz used the moment to declare he was 'through' with any plans to take *Dawn* across the Atlantic.

'I have been paid up until last night and I hold no ill feeling toward Mrs Grayson. She has repeatedly refused my resignation with a plaintive cry that I was leaving her in a bad fix,' he told reporters.[19]

He said he had received many offers but would not fly 'blind' over the ocean. He added that *Dawn* was 'the best flying craft I have ever handled. Too much cannot be said for it. With good weather, it will be get through. But without me.'[20]

But there was no sign of good weather and winter seemed just around the corner. Surely, for Grayson, whose motto had started out as 'safe and sane' this was the end?

She shared her thoughts in a typed statement delivered to reporters at a few minutes' notice. In it, she said she had discussed *Dawn*'s performance with Sikorsky and more tests would be needed before a decision was made, although a transatlantic flight before Spring was unlikely. Having read the statement, Stultz said she was wise to postpone the flight, but added: 'I do not feel, however, that the tests of which she speaks are needed. We know what [sic] the plane will go, but we also know that it cannot be flown in adverse weather.'[21]

CHAPTER FOURTEEN

Winter Comes to Old Orchard

Throughout the northern states of America people were being nice to one another. In New York, Clarence Chamberlin, who had flown the Atlantic with Charles Levine as his passenger, was playing Santa to several hundred children in Beekman Street Hospital. Another Father Christmas – Saint Nicholas's immigrant status temporarily overlooked – was chatting to 300 immigrants and one hundred visitors in the detention room at Ellis Island. The city's jails were putting on a special entertainment for its prisoners – 600 of whom were women, which was a third more than last year and one hundred of whom had been convicted of shoplifting in the last month.[1] Newspapers warned its readers not to be tempted by bootleg alcohol during the festive season. Remember, the articles said, illegal booze could lead to upset stomachs and, in the worst case, an agonising death. In Boston, thirty Syrian and Chinese youngsters were taking a final bow at their end-of-course Christmas drama, *The Other Wise Man,* organised by Denison House.[2] Amelia Earhart had joined the settlement the year before and worked closely with the children, who were all under the age of fourteen.

But amid all the bonhomie one story drove a shard of tragedy through the festive celebrations. The *S-4* was a government submarine that had been going about its business on Saturday 17 December when it chose exactly the wrong moment to surface off Provincetown, Cape Cod. In a horrible quirk of fate, it bubbled up through the water just in time for a US Coast Guard destroyer to ram it, shunting the damaged submarine back down below the waves. As most other people started to wind down for Christmas, a team of rescuers desperately fought to save the forty-man crew. The six occupants trapped in the torpedo room had tapped out a morse code message in which they had asked desperately, 'Is there any hope?' The rescuers had replied, 'There is hope and everything possible will be done' but, in the season of hope, bad weather was snatching back that most prized commodity.

When considered in the light of the tragedy unfurling off the East Coast, the message carried on the sides of the buses that sped down Fifth Avenue in the dry, mild weather spoke a horrible understatement.[3]

'Christmas cheer everywhere. Don't spoil it for anyone with an accident.'[4]

*

After *Dawn*'s three failed attempts, Frances Grayson was desperate for a break from the whole transatlantic circus and to clear her mind. She needed, too, to consult with Mabel Ancker, who, 'unlike most women, has not dropped our project but continues to back me'.[5]

In early November Grayson set sail on the *Majestic* for Europe and used the crossing to study the air and ocean currents. Her findings convinced her that a plane could only make the same journey in several hops. In Berlin, where Ancker was staying, Grayson told the Associated Press: 'No non-stop flights across the ocean for me,' adding, however, that she was just as determined to make the crossing, although, presumably in several stages.[6] She was impressed by the German aviation industry and a representative from Lufthansa informed her she could refuel at their aerodrome in Iceland. She told reporters: 'It is nonsense to say you can't fly in Winter. An expedition like ours, if it is worth anything at all, must be so organized that we can go independently of the seasons.'[7]

She denied that she had fallen out with Stultz saying: 'It takes a stout heart and implicit faith to make a trip like ours and when I discovered that my pilot had faltered somewhat I felt it was only fair to release him.' She added that she would probably have 'heated arguments' with Goldy and other crew members for 'the rest of our days, but we will also remain the best of friends until the end'.[8]

In France she toured hangars at Le Bourget Airfield and flew as a passenger with a French pilot who took her over Paris and its suburbs in a trip that lasted about thirty minutes.[9]

*

The announcement from Curtiss Field, on 7 December, that she planned another imminent assault on the Atlantic came as a shock to everyone – including her crew. Investigations into why *Dawn* had stumbled in previous bids had begun in early November and most people expected Grayson to wait until at least mid-January to make a new attempt.

There was the all-important factor of who would pilot the plane after Stultz's departure. Bernt Balchen was the ideal candidate. Described as 'the last of the Vikings', he was born in Norway and served as a cavalryman in the Finnish Army in the First World War before training to fly in the Norwegian Naval Air Force. This, and his inclusion in two expeditions led by Roald Amundsen, gave him important experience of arctic conditions. When Grayson approached him, he had just flown the Atlantic with Byrd.[10]

In early November, Grayson said he had accepted – orally at least – but friends countered that he would not commit until he had had a chance to test the plane. While Grayson was waiting at Curtiss

Field for Balchen, Clarence Chamberlin took *Dawn* for a spin. He said she handled well, and he was known to want to fly the Atlantic again but was adamant he must run the expedition himself.[11]

By early December a new pilot, Lieutenant Oskar Omdal, who was on leave from the Norwegian navy, was putting *Dawn* through her paces.[12] Omdal, thirty-two, came from a large, well-to-do family and was described by *The New York Times* as a 'slender, blue-eyed, blond young chap' known as a 'skilled "cold-weather" pilot'.[13] He had been a member of Amundsen's party, which had tried to fly to the North Pole in Dornier-Wahl airplanes and a mechanic on his expedition, from Spitzbergen to Alaska, over the north pole in the dirigible *Norge* in 1926. Amundsen had praised the young pilot's expertise and the part he played in monitoring the engines over seventy-one hours with barely any sleep.[14] He was highly recommended by his friend, Balchen.

The second, key member of the crew was already in place, but came from a far less privileged background. One incident in his youth stands out as an early example of his resilience. When Goldy was a ten-year-old boy he had fallen down a four-storey elevator shaft at the back of a drugstore where he worked in his hometown of Sioux City, Iowa.[15] He was lucky that he survived with just a broken leg. The story about a boy from a poor family who endured his misfortune with great bravery and had to stay in hospital for four weeks touched the hearts of readers of his local paper and strangers subscribed to a fund that raised eighty-one dollars (about $2,839 today) for him as he lay recovering in hospital.[16] When a reporter visited him the boy seemed stunned at the generosity of strangers.

'Gee, what will I do with all that money? Well, you can search me,' and Brice [Goldy] looked very much puzzled.

'What's the matter with putting it in the bank,' he added after a pause.[17]

As he sat once more in *Dawn*, but this time wearing a thick, fleece-lined flying suit and boots and fur-lined helmet, waiting for take-off from Roosevelt Field in the fading light of Friday 23 December 1927, he may have thought back to that terrifying moment when he stepped out of the drugstore lift and found himself plunging into darkness.

*

Grayson had decided to make for Harbour Grace and, as Mabel Boll and Amelia Earhart would the following year, use its position on the very edge of the continent as a jumping off point for her attempt on the Atlantic. This would mean flying through the night so that they would be approaching Newfoundland in the early morning and give Omdal valuable experience of flying by instruments at night.

Goldy aimed to hold the 'ship' to a dead reckoning course for the first 1,200 miles. 'Dead reckoning' is a means of navigation, originally used by ships, in which the navigator estimates the position of the aircraft based on a combination of factors. These factors include compass readings; the time when the readings were taken compared to the time when the plane set off; and air speed, which might need adjusting for wind velocity. Flying over water is particularly challenging because there are no landmarks, no friendly flags or washing lines to indicate the direction of the wind, and no snaking rivers to reassure you that you are where you think you are.

Fred Koehler, from the Wright Aeronautical Company, would be monitoring the engines for the first leg of the flight to Newfoundland. On the face of it, he was the least interesting member of the crew since his role was simply to babysit the Wright Whirlwind engines until they got to Harbour Grace. Once there, he would overhaul the engines before returning to the safety of the Wright plant and leave the Grayson, Goldy, and Omdal team to attempt the Atlantic crossing. However, while he was only hitching a ride for the early stage of the trip, he, too, had a life of adventure behind him and one the other crew members may not have been aware of. Before joining Wright, he had spent eight years with the Stinson Aircraft Company in Detroit. During five of those years, he had piloted air mail between Chicago and Omaha. He was a loner and hadn't seen his brother Edward for seven years. When they last met, Fred had said he'd clocked up an impressive 4,500 flying hours but was tired of being in the air. He was born in Newark and in the past had also been a motor racing driver. [18]

There was plenty of room in the cabin to move around and Grayson was expected to take the controls from time to time.[19] Omdal, who was used to flying within the Arctic circle, played down the hazard of ice forming on the wings. He was convinced that the only parts of the plane vulnerable to freezing were at the front and these had been treated with a glycerine coating to prevent sleet and heavy mist turning to ice.

Goldy had been plotting courses and studying the storm paths for days. He expected there would be good weather over the Atlantic but, although the United States Weather Bureau was no longer able to offer reports due to lack of funds, Doc Kimball told him bluntly the crossing would be foolish.[20] The Canadian Government and British Air Ministry would provide weather reports, based on the system worked out by Kimball during the summer. Goldy also hoped to use a radio to receive weather updates from ships and shore stations and to send progress updates. The radio was said to have a reach of about 1,000 miles at night.[21]

As dusk fell on Friday 23 December at Roosevelt Field, Omdal fussed over Grayson's zip like a parent making sure a small child was properly protected from the cold. Just before they set off, she tucked a small automatic pistol into the pocket of her flying suit. This was, in itself, not an unusual detail, as Ruth Elder had also taken a gun, but, in Grayson's case, reporters were quick to jump to conclusions about her firearm. She laughed when one asked whether it was a 'badge of authority for the commander of the expedition' but then grew serious for a moment as she reflected on the fate of the *S-4*. She was clearly allowing herself to imagine what it would be like to be trapped inside the metal fuselage of the *Dawn*.

'With a gesture and a shrug she spoke of the horror of a prolonged period of suffering with no hope to relief before death intervened.'[22]

She also appeared disturbed by a statement from Stultz that to take off in such weather would be suicidal.[23]

Goldy's wife, Gertrude was there to wave him goodbye with her seventeen-year-old stepson, Fred, who was studying at the Technical High School in Brooklyn. She had noticed that Goldy had been behaving strangely for several days. After returning on 21 December from a meeting with Grayson, he paced the floor for nearly two hours. When Gertrude questioned him about the wisdom of the flight, he denied there was a risk, but she noticed that his hands were clammy and worried that he had some premonition of how the expedition would end. Later that night he took her in his arms and asked her not to leave him, although this was never likely, and cried that he could not live without her.

When he returned home the next day he was again in an agitated state and told her they would take off tomorrow (23 December). She asked him, 'quite vehemently, "Do you think the damned woman is worth risking your life for?"'[24] He denied that he would be risking his life. They packed his kit and went to bed at 2.00 am, although Goldy seemed very agitated and clung to her throughout the night, only managing a few hours' sleep before he left the house at 9.00 am, struggling under the weight of maps, charts, parachutes, flares, and the rest of his luggage.

She joined him at the airfield at 4.00 pm but found he was acting 'very peculiarly' and was so absentminded that he nearly walked into a propeller. On the three previous occasions when she'd seen him off, he had been content simply to wave goodbye but this time he returned several times to kiss her.[25]

As she watched the plane disappearing into the setting sun, she had a very strong feeling that she would never see her husband again. She had dinner with a friend but at 7.30 pm became very cold and had to be put to bed. Her friend covered her with blankets and gave her two glasses of wine to try to warm her up, but it took two hours before the chill left her. She went home and seemed to recover.

Dawn left at 5.07 pm carrying 595 gallons of fuel, enough to last about eighteen hours.[26] Goldy had plotted a course that allowed them to hug the coastline and to use lighthouses as an aerial breadcrumb trail from Long Island to Nova Scotia.

A report from a French cable station at Cape Cod at just after 7.00 pm suggested the plane was making one hundred miles per hour but from there it faced a 250-mile 'water jump', between Cape Cod and Yarmouth, out of sight of land.[27]

Dawn should have reached the Nova Scotia coastline by midnight but the Chebucto Head wireless station in Halifax Harbour had heard nothing from her. At Harbour Grace, where she was due at 7.00 am, a wet snow was falling.[28]

The next day, Christmas Eve, Gertrude received an envelope in the post at her home at 54 Logan Street, Brooklyn, marked 'not to be opened until Christmas'.[29] Inside she found a cheque for $500 (about $8,800 today). That her husband had the presence of mind – in the midst of all the flight preparations and his mental turmoil – to ensure her Christmas gift arrived suggests a thoughtfulness and attention to detail.

Christmas was a miserable time for the crew's family. Omdal had been staying with his cousin in Brooklyn since September and his cousin put a brave face on matters and said Oskar had flown boats to safe landings in rough water many times in the last ten years. The pilot's sister, who also lived in New York, remained confident.

Dawn's disappearance made the front-page lead for Grayson's hometown newspaper, the *Muncie Evening Press*, where her father, Andrew Wilson still ran a grocery store. Frances had written to him a few days before the flight telling him 'not to worry about anything' and urging him 'don't give anything to the papers – they're such a bother'.[30] In fact, he was finding reporters to be a useful support and was sleeping at his shop so that he could read the latest reports from Associated Press as soon as the *Muncie Star* received them.[31]

At first he remained optimistic about the plane's chances, commenting that the aircraft was built to float for two weeks and they had plenty of supplies.[32] But, as hope faded, he told reporters gloomily, 'If she'd have alighted on land they'd probably have heard something of her before now.'[33] The Christmas dinner planned with Frances's brother and other relatives to celebrate her success had to be hastily abandoned.

On Christmas Day, Gertrude and Frank went to the midnight service at Trinity Church in Brooklyn to pray for Goldy.[34] Out to sea, strong northwest winds, reaching gale force at times, started to whip up the ocean. Efforts were made to contact Mabel Ancker to secure funds for a search.

There had been no word from *Dawn* for twenty-nine hours and two relief expeditions were hastily assembled. One, led by William Winston of the Curtiss Flying Service, set off carrying food and vacuum flasks of hot soup and coffee and followed the coastline to Cape Cod.[35] If he found the plane floating on the sea, he planned to land next to it or, if the sea was too rough, to try to drop supplies to her. The team refused to accept the $500 Christmas cheque Goldy's wife had immediately offered.[36]

George Wies, who was taking part in an endurance test for a Stinson-Detroiter monoplane, also joined the search. By 27 December, the mine-laying destroyer, *Mahan*, which had been helping to salvage the *S-4* submarine, was told to help.[37]

On Monday, 26 December it was reported that a radio message had been picked up by a government station on Sable Island from *Dawn* on 9.45 pm Friday, a time when it would have been feasible for her to be in that position. The listener heard a 'spluttering' message that 'something had gone wrong', but storm interference meant nothing more was discernible.[38] Gertrude was delighted and said that it would allow her a little sleep before, she hoped, more good news arrived in the morning. When she wasn't at home with her stepson she visited her mother on Long Island.

As the hours of waiting wore on, she asked the Associated Press, in a terrible echo of the plea from the trapped submariners: 'Is there any hope? Why haven't there been any messages from the plane. Oh, I wish I could be with my husband now, even if he is dead.'[39]

The next day Canadian officials said they were now dubious that the message picked up on Sable Island had come from the stricken aeroplane.[40]

On Tuesday 27 December, Washington ordered an airship to join the search and around thirty-seven crewmen, many of whom had been called back from Christmas leave, responded. The *Los Angeles* floated over Times Square 'looking in the night like a gray cloud riding a high wind'. She passed over Curtiss Field, where the searchlights were directed downwards 'carrying a ghostly acre of light swiftly eastward over the black landscape'.[41] The dirigible concentrated its search twenty miles due east of Cape Cod and planned to cruise northwest towards Sable Island. It would then do an about-turn to retrace *Dawn*'s route. The Weather Bureau reported they would face high winds, fog, scattered rains, and snowstorms.

The same day Ancker told a *New York Times* reporter over the phone from Berlin:

> I am sure they will be found. Naturally I am very anxious, but without any reason perhaps than intuition I am convinced they are alive and must have landed on some desolate place on the coast or on an island, and will be heard from in the next two days.

She added that Grayson had not told her she was going to leave and that she was 'extremely surprised' when she read of her departure in the papers. She felt sure that 'at this time of the year' they had not intended to attempt the Atlantic crossing, but only to make the New York–Newfoundland flight as a trial. 'I'm sure if Mrs Grayson had intended to try the Atlantic crossing she would have advised me.'[42]

Aviation specialists were divided over what would happen to a seaplane like *Dawn* if it was forced down at sea. Ivor Sikorsky said that its metal composite boat-like hull would keep it afloat indefinitely, although he was puzzled that there had been no radio message from Goldy.[43] One theory suggested they were hiding out, waiting for the weather to clear, and that the reason no radio message had been heard was that the oil had frozen and the generator was refusing to turn.

Others were less optimistic and thought *Dawn*'s eight-inch clearance meant it could easily be swamped in rough weather.[44] Chamberlin, who had flown this route, pointed out: 'Ice forming on their wings would bring them down very fast no matter where they were.'[45] As usual, Stultz was blunt in his assessment: 'Ships are coming in from Europe two or three days late and all broken to the devil, so what chance would the *Dawn* have in that kind of weather?'[46] Sikorsky faced criticism about the unusual design of the outrigger tail of the plane, which some commenters believed might have broken off.[47] Kimball had told Grayson she was 'very foolish to start at this time of year and [said], while I admire her courage, I think that she should have postponed the attempt. The chances of success I believe were not better than one in ten.'[48]

Captain Hugh A. Grant, a former Superintendent of the Meteorological Department of the British Navy and an authority on Atlantic weather, referred to the storms 'convulsing' the North Atlantic at this time of year. He drew attention to the threat of fog and how its arrival robbed the pilot of a horizon to help them steer. Gusts of wind would make instruments difficult for Omdal to trust. 'He may then be flying in the most extraordinary and dangerous altitudes without being aware of it unless the plane is such that it is always stable and will keep an even keel independent of the pilot's efforts.'[49]

As the days since their departure lengthened and tipped into a new year, the tone and the grammar of these comments changed subtly from conditional guesswork to the past tense. Even the most hopeful and optimistic had to admit that, given the terrible conditions and the lack of contact for so long, *Dawn* must have been lost.

The tragedy was all the more painful and senseless because there was no rival team considering a crossing in the middle of winter. Taking into account the dire warnings, and the conditions that were self-evident simply by glancing out of the window, why did the crew feel compelled to venture out in such hostile weather?

Of the four people on board, Koehler would have had least say in the decision. He'd been at Wright for about a month and as a recent recruit was unlikely to have carried much clout in discussions about whether he left his humble boarding house in New Jersey that Saturday before Christmas. Besides, he was only going on this first leg of the journey. When they got to Newfoundland he could head back to his safe life.

Omdal may have believed that the conditions could hardly have been any worse than those he had experienced on his previous polar expeditions. Perhaps he felt he had a chance to make his name and was too proud to raise a note of caution.

Goldy's motives were most complicated. He'd worked closely with Grayson for several months now and had endured with her the long delays at the out-of-season Brunswick Hotel in Old Orchard, where they waited for the weather to change. Together with Stultz they had experienced three fraught take-offs and landings and in their final attempt must have felt they were on their way. Grayson clearly had some emotional hold over him.

Then there was the money. The evidence shows that Goldy was

a wealthy man. When probate was filed in May 1929 it was revealed that he had left an estate of $64,040.13 (over $1 million today). Gertrude would receive $21,346.71 and his son, Frank, $42,693.42.[50] The process of probate also revealed that he had a contract for an annual salary of $6,000 to be paid until 30 June 1933, regardless of whether he was alive or dead.[51] But pilots and navigators who were part of record-breaking attempts in the 1920s and 1930s often found it impossible to retire – not just because of the adrenalin rush and the prospect of making history – but because of the financial gains. Many, like Goldy, came from humble beginnings and were tempted by the financial rewards and the chance to provide lock-tight security for their families. Who can blame them? Goldy knew all too acutely the difference money could make. The little boy who fell four storeys down an elevator shaft had been stunned by the kindness of strangers; as a grown man he had learnt how his technical skill as a navigator offered the chance of security for his wife and son, although he always tussled with the unimaginable personal risk he was taking.

Grayson's motivations are less clear-cut. She had no need for money and no dependents to provide for. However, some hint at her driving force is evident in a statement she left to be published only in the event of her disappearance when she set off from Old Orchard for the third time in October. The declaration, which runs to around 500 words, reveals her strong religious conviction, as well as her struggles with self-doubt:

> Waiting.
>
> Who am I?
>
> Am I a little nobody? Or am I a great dynamic force – powerful – in that I have a god-given birthright and have all the power there is if only I will understand and use it?
>
> Sometimes I am torn between the knowing I have a great, living, breathing power of understanding my heritage and

again I take cognizance of worldly values. Then I become a little nobody.

This morning, as I sit here at a window and look out over a turbulent gray ocean – gray fog, gray clouds, all is gray – and the lashing of the waves, the rain, the wind remind me that it is almost November and the world says, 'Impossible to fly any more this season.'

The Weather Bureau folded their maps and said, 'impossible weather. No more flying this season.' And then I take account of the many discouraging delays – shall I listen to the warnings of an unbelieving public or shall I listen only that 'voice within'?

...

Quit?

Shall I let wise worldly heads, wise aeronautical sages influence me?

Shall I?

Are they right? Can it be that I am wrong? Wrong after these many months of listening to that still, small voice.

I cannot – I will not believe I am wrong ...

I have but to maintain faith and courage and know I am right – that I am wisdom because I am of Him who is all wisdom.

She continued, stating that 'Things do not just happen' and that it was not chance that she had met Ancker or chosen the amphibian plane at random.

Before contracting for this ship which is to carry three lives I listened to that still, small voice ...

I am who or what I really am, a little nobody or a living, forceful power to carry out part of His great plan.

I will win.

I must not quit too soon.

> Success is just ahead and the clouds between must disappear.
> I will wait.[52]

We are unlikely to know exactly what happened to *Dawn*, but we do have a first-hand account of what it was like to be in the Atlantic the weekend the plane disappeared. Captain F. F. Summers, of the British Naval Reserve, was on his way from Liverpool to New York when the ship he was master of, the White Star liner *Albertic*, was hit by a northwest gale and frequent snow squalls that lasted from noon on Saturday until 4.00 am on Sunday morning. He described how, close to Sable Island, Newfoundland, the crew faced winds of sixty-five to seventy miles per hour and snow so thick that, at times, it was impossible to make out the ship's bow from the bridge. He had received radio messages to keep a 'bright lookout' for *Dawn* but saw nothing.

It was one of the worst days he had ever spent on the Atlantic and snow turned to ice as soon as it landed on the deck, so that the seamen struggled to keep their footing. The sea was, he said, 'running with rollers from thirty to forty feet high, and if any airship, no matter how well built, had gone down in it the waves would have broken the craft to pieces in less than fifteen minutes, no matter how many pontoons were attached to it.'[53]

Dawn's cabin and cockpit were often compared to a boat, and its windows were made of the type of thick shatter-proof glass used at sea. The parts of the flying boat employed for flight were fitted so that, when it was floating on water, they would be out of reach of ordinary waves. She carried pneumatic boat flares, smoke bombs, and rockets to help rescuers locate her and a rubber boat in case the crew needed to evacuate the plane.[54] But all of these features were geared towards 'normal' seas, not the kind of thirty to forty foot 'rollers' described by Summers. It would have been ridiculous to even contemplate launching a rubber boat in such conditions.

The other item we know was on board was the pistol that reporters noticed Grayson slipping into her flying suit just before take-off. Did she have the time to go through the torment of weighing up whether she should take her own life rather than face the same fate as the submariners who, in all likelihood, were a matter of miles from where *Dawn* hit the worst weather?

Or was the pistol wielded for some other reason? Gertrude seems to have thought so and made her views clear via an intermediary when, in March 1928, she went through the painful processing of having her husband declared legally dead. An unnamed person, authorised to speak for her, let slip to a journalist that Gertrude believed Grayson had told the crew there would be 'no turning back this time'.[55] The informant continued: 'Here's what I think. You know she carried a revolver. Everybody knew that she was determined to go that time.'[56] The informant cited the turmoil Goldy had shown the night before the flight, 'Mrs Grayson certainly exercised a sinister influence over him.'[57]

He or she went on to say that they had heard the story of a hunter who had a shack on Cape Cod and that he had seen the plane circling, and, to the informant and (he or she claimed) Gertrude, this suggested the crew was arguing about whether to continue. Gertrude confirmed her husband's strange behaviour the night before but seemed annoyed that her theory about Grayson had emerged. She did not deny it, one paper said, but it has to be noted that this is not the same as saying she confirmed it.[58] Nor did this detail emerge during the seventy-eight-page record of the hearings of the New York County Surrogates' Court in December 1928.

It's worth considering the four players in this final act and how they might have responded to the crisis. Omdal was at the controls. He was on leave from the Norwegian navy and had taken part in two expeditions led by Amundsen. He was used to operating in a highly disciplined environment in which the chain of command was clear cut. Who did he think was in control now? Surely, he can't have submitted to Grayson, simply because she was paying his salary? Would any of the three men have given way to a woman – even such a driven woman and a woman with a gun? She was easy enough to overpower, if it came to that. Goldy had been with her in a plane before when she insisted they carried on. Then it had been Stultz, as pilot, and the all-too evident mechanical fault, that had persuaded her to turn round.

Koehler is an unknown quantity. With 4,500 flying hours under his belt, he was, by far, the most experienced pilot in the plane, as well as being well-attuned to how the engines were faring. Did the other three crew members know of his vast experience and, if not, surely, he must have used this moment of extreme peril to reveal his background?

While the evidence from Gertrude and from Grayson's father cannot answer these questions, the Surrogate Court proceedings shed light on *Dawn*'s final hours. The lengthy investigations make extensive reference to newspaper reports of the time from ships who were in the area, but the most convincing evidence emerged from a reporter called G. H. Evans who interviewed Captain Comeau and other crew members of the British schooner, *Rose Ann Belliveau* for *The New York Times* of 3 January 1928. They told him that on 23 December 1927, at about 7.30 pm, they heard the whir of an airplane overhead, then a splash as the plane hit the water. They were eighteen miles off Nauset Beach, Cape Cod.[59]

The newspaper described how the wind was blowing a moderate gale, and the schooner was shipping water heavily. Louis Thibodeau, chief mate, was on watch on the poop deck.

'I could not make it out at first,' he said. 'I turned to the wheelman, who was looking about amazed as if something had struck him.'

Thibodeau fetched Comeau and the cook and three other seamen followed. After the splash it took about five minutes for the noise to fade. Another man at the wheel said he was frightened when he first heard the noise as it seemed to be directly under the spanker boom, where he was standing. He heard the motor churning for ten minutes.

Comeau said they were powerless to offer help as they were doing at least ten knots and it would have been 'suicide' to put a small boat over the side. As a professional sailor he carefully marked the point at which they had seen the plane. The *Belliveau* continued to Salem to wait for better weather. It was only when he read the newspapers that he made the connection and become convinced the plane had been *Dawn*.[60]

Unbeknown to Gertrude, her stepson, Frank, had a premonition on the morning after take-off that the plane had nose-dived into the sea off Cape Cod.[61]

Dawn's final moments must have been horrific. If, as seems likely, the fuselage started to ice over it would have added catastrophically to the plane's weight. Omdal would have struggled to control the aircraft, to see anything and to read his wildly fluctuating instruments. Plunging into the icy sea must have been beyond terrifying. It's almost worth hoping that the shatter-proof glass burst and that the ocean flooded in through the windows so that it was all over quickly.

PART FIVE

1928, Round Two

Flight Checklist: A Handle on Husbands

'Back among the piney woods, the corn patches and the moonshine, away back in the billy-billy section of northern Georgia, where the Tallulah River crashes silver out of the Blue Ridge and the little town of Clayton perches on the one-track railroad to civilisation ...' a long-forgotten scandal was springing back to life.[1]

The newspaper feature's headline, 'First Facts from Georgia About Her Arrest for Goings-on with a Preacher, and Why the Scandal Hid for Five years' confirmed that readers of this lavishly illustrated and syndicated feature were in for a juicy tale. The photo that accompanied the article confirmed this impression and showed a 'Georgia [religious] Revival' in which a young woman is led into a river. She's flanked by two men who are in shirt sleeves – as if to emphasis the seriousness of God's business. One has a towel thrown over his shoulder, like a waiter about to serve a fine wine, rather than someone poised to dunk a convert. The older man raises a hand to the skies. Behind them crowds of other young converts block the bank; the men among them have their arms crossed menacingly.

It was at exactly such an event, in 1923, that a travelling evangelist, the Reverend Shuford Jenkins, had shown up amid the 'piney woods and cotton patches'.[2] Since the Blue Ridge Mountains still regularly rang with the sound of sermons preaching hell and damnation, and because there was nothing much else to do for entertainment, most of Clayton's 300 souls turned up to hear him.[3] The 'girl-wife' (she was just sixteen, later reports said seventeen) of the local schoolteacher, Claude Emmett Moody, was among those who joined the eager spectators.

When she wasn't listening to sermons, this young woman, so the gossip went, liked to take her pony and trap into the woods to gather mountain laurel, rhododendrons, and wild honeysuckle. So, the gossip continued, Rev Jenkins also enjoyed similar nature walks and, on at least one occasion, their paths crossed. These al fresco wanderings led to such febrile gossip that the schoolteacher and his wife fled town, and the preacher also hurried on his way. Their departure was followed by a meeting of the Rabun County Grand Jury at which Mrs Moody and Jenkins were found guilty of improper conduct.

The matter might have faded quietly into the background of the Blue Ridge Mountains had it not been for Mrs Moody's subsequent career. After fleeing Clayton, she returned to Alabama, divorced Moody and married Lyle Womack. It was only when someone recognised her picture in one of the newspaper accounts of her Atlantic bravery that the connection was made. Some of Clayton's inhabitants felt proud of Ruth Elder's achievements; others could only remember her nature-loving reputation and the indictment that still sat on the county record books.

*

Like every other record-breaking pilot, Ruth Elder made the most of her fame and was touring the US with Haldeman. In November, New York City had given the 'girl aviator' a reception costing $333.90. The price tag was just a third of the cost of the scroll presented to Lindbergh as part of almost $72,000 lavished on welcoming him.[4] On her arrival at the port of New York Elder was dressed in a Parisian suit of dark blue jersey, a deep, velvety silk black hat and a black satin coat trimmed with black fox fur at the collar, sleeves, and bottom. A cluster of orchids adorned the collar, and she wore a string of pearls.

Womack, the husband who had slipped her mind at the start of her Atlantic adventure, had left Panama, where his father made hats, to greet his wife, and approached the *Aquitania* in a tug with other members of the mayor's reception committee, Elder's sisters and an aunt. Husband and wife embraced, and he lifted her and a bunch of roses that was almost as big as the flyer off her feet. He later claimed that he tried to kiss her but that she refused saying,[5] 'don't be a damned fool'.[6] Instead, she patted his hand as they sat on the boat and he grinned, allowing her glory. It was the greatest moment of his life, he said, except the day, two years ago, when he had married her in May 1925. Womack had given her purpose again after her first teenage wedding went so disastrously wrong. They lived in Florida, where her husband played his part in introducing her to flying and the businessmen who financed the new form of transport. They also spent time in Panama where dashing Air Force pilots confirmed her growing fascination with aviation.[7]

The couple spent the next few hours in New York negotiating awkward questions from journalists keen to interpret every gesture. The consensus was that 'from all outward appearances the greeting was affectionate',[8] although Lyle violently objected to being called 'Miss Elder's husband' and rather weakly pointed out that he had played football and was middle-weight boxing champion in college. He seemed 'rather excited and at times embarrassed, but kept pretty much to himself'.[9]

At the reception at City Hall Elder blushed 'like a school girl' and managed, in a choking voice, to tell the mayor, in front of 10,000 people, 'My heart sticks in my throat. But I want you to know how much I thank you. It is more than we expected.'[10] She was shocked when told she could secure contracts worth $200,000.[11] When a reporter asked if she would give up flying, she said, 'I've washed lots of dishes' and that she didn't intend to return with Lyle to Panama.

She continued that a husband, although 'just wonderful' and 'awfully broadminded' should not interfere with his wife's career, 'whether it be flying, writing or banking'.[12] The only subject she refused to talk about was clothes.[13] In the evening she attended a production of the *Ziegfeld Follies* at the New Amsterdam Theatre. She and Haldeman were introduced to the audience and bowed from their seats as the crowds cheered and clapped. Lyle was not with them.

Nor did he accompany his wife when she went to a musical comedy followed by the Equity Ball at the Hotel Astor; he was also absent when she attended a dinner at the Colony Club that went on until 1.30 in the morning. Elder was steered through this social whirl by nineteen-year-old Marjorie 'Bubbles' Oelrichs, a young New York beauty who was known for her clear complexion and who advertised Pond's Cold Cream.[14] *Vogue* compared her perfectly arched eyebrows to butterflies. Her name appeared on the Social Register, a remnant of the Gilded Age in which ancient families were listed for their lineage and standing in society. Bubbles obviously had no intention of allowing a husband to burst her plans for Elder.

Newspapers either portrayed Womack as a killjoy who sulked in his hotel room at the towering St. Regis, from where he could look down on the city's bright lights his wife was enjoying, or a henpecked husband who rushed around carrying out errands which, some reporters suspected, had been invented to make him look as though he had a part to play in her new celebrity life. He made no attempt to hide his opposition to her flight but denied there was 'any coolness' between them.[15] In a leader headed 'Mr Ruth Elder', *The Washington Post* declared that many people felt sorry for 'this Canal Zone resident'.[16] The reference to the Panama Canal, which had opened in 1914 and was controlled by the USA, made Womack sound even more out of touch and un-American.

By mid-November he had decided to return to Central America, insisting he had a 'date' with his wife there after she had completed her lecture tour. Elder did not linger on the New York pier to see him off but left hurriedly for a 'business conference'. Womack told reporters: 'People can forget all this talk about our being separated. I've had a long, serious talk with Ruth and we understand each other. There's nothing in the talk of separation.'[17]

It was during her vaudeville 'lecture' tour that, as soon as she crossed the state border into Georgia, Elder's first marriage, and her alleged nature walks with Reverend Shuford Jenkins in the Blue Ridge Mountains, returned to bite her. The minute she stepped off the train at Atlanta, she was arrested by Clayton's Sheriff on the basis of the five-year-old warrant and the whole sordid story of the itinerant preacher, the sixteen-year-old 'girl bride' and the claim of improper conduct burst across the nation.

At first Elder refused to answer the phone and said her doctor had told her to sleep until 10.00 am but finally she provided her side of the story in a letter. She described the event as a 'harmless buggy ride', although she may have exacerbated the situation by adding that they had been sitting on a hillock admiring the scenery when a man approached, driving some cattle. Jenkins, afraid at being seen alone with a young woman, ran into a nearby patch of trees. Elder drove home but found she was snubbed by her neighbours and decided to return to her family in Alabama. Her agent called the emergence of the claims 'the worst holdup I ever heard and is nothing short of blackmail'.[18] She paid the $500 in bail.

Womack was having an even rougher time in the press. A feature in the *Chicago Daily Tribune* entitled 'Folks who get into the limelight sidewise: A handful of obscure celebrities who bask in reflected glory' was harsher still.[19] The waspish article began by saying that, next to Father Machree, who may have been a character in an Irish song, Womack 'is today probably the most widely known obscurity in the world: also the most obscure celebrity'.

> O, there were a few little odd jobs. Like sitting behind the palms in the foyers of smart hotels, killing time while his wife occupied the throne chair at the centre of the speaker's table in the big ballroom across the hall. Or elbowing policemen so that he might get within whispering distance of Miss Elder. What he wanted to whisper was that she stop flying and come home. The answer was 'No'.[20]

By March 1928 the same paper was reporting that Womack was back in Balboa in Panama and was 'lonesome'. Friends told the paper that he believed Elder would not join him but denied either was considering divorce. She was busy doing screen tests. Rather pathetically, he pointed out the number of kisses on a letter she had sent him.[21]

By September 1928 Womack announced he would be suing for divorce and alleging cruelty which, at the time, was a common ground for divorces in the USA.[22] From Hollywood, Elder said her husband had given her no warning of the proceedings or of the grounds, but added the news did not 'stun' her.[23] From Panama, Womack claimed that he had lost weight, was finding it hard to work and that his health had suffered. He said that Elder's transatlantic flight had caused him sleepless nights and 'much embarrassment' when she failed to kiss him on her return to New York.[24] On top of all of this, the whisky distillery where he worked in Panama had been destroyed by fire.[25]

His response to the humiliation he had endured was to run off to sea. Shortly after he filed for divorce, he joined an expedition led by Richard E. Byrd. The ship would sail from New Zealand to the South Pole and Womack seemed happier than he had been for months. He commented that Antarctica could hardly be colder than his estranged wife.[26] He would be working as a fireman to replace the original crew member who had had to leave due to ill health. It would be difficult to imagine a more rugged choice of role by which to prove his masculinity. The decision must have been even sweeter because the expedition was led by a famous aviator.

His name also appeared in a report in *The New York Times,* 13 April 1929, as one of twelve of Byrd's crew who had returned from their stay in Little America, the tiny settlement on the Ross Ice Barrier, for a break from the polar winter. They were treated as heroes when they landed in San Francisco.[27] He was further vindicated two years later when the Secretary of the Navy was authorised to confer medals on Byrd and other members of the Antarctic expedition. Womack's name appeared in *The New York Times* among those who would receive the honour.[28]

In the year that Womack was returning triumphantly from the South Pole, Elder married her third husband. Walter Chauncey Camp Junior was a movie producer and son of a famous American Football journalist and Yale coach. He was himself a former Yale half back and widower who was fourteen years older than Elder. By then she was also an actress, while still flying, and she telephoned her reply to his proposal during the famous 'Powder Puff Derby' of August 1929, when leading female pilots, including Earhart, raced across North America. But she later told reporters, 'I'm through with the limelight. From now on it'll be simply Mrs Walter Camp'.[29] However, in November 1932 she filed for divorce, citing cruelty.[30]

She was not alone in failing to find a husband who, in the 1920s and 1930s, was content to support their wife in such a high-profile venture. The six women who tried to cross the Atlantic by air in 1927 and 1928 amassed at least fifteen marriages. Other record-breaking female pilots also saw the value of multiple husbands. Heath, for example, married three times. These are startling figures when divorce, although less rare than before The Great War, was still unusual on both sides of the Atlantic. It didn't go unnoticed in the press, and the *San Francisco Examiner* ran a feature with the headline, 'Do "Air-Minded" Women Make Unsatisfactory Wives?' in which it examined the matrimonial lives of the women who tried to cross the Atlantic by plane.[31]

It seems unlikely that Savile could have managed her flying expeditions with a husband in tow and he had proved an inconvenience long before his mysterious death during fighting between Americans and 'insurgents' in the Philippines (he was acting as Honorary ADC to the US general and seems to have been caught in the line of fire, although rumours soon emerged that he had been a spy). Elsie Mackay's youthful marriage was an embarrassment and quickly annulled and Frances Grayson could not have become a successful real estate tycoon and led the *Dawn* expedition if she had stayed with her postmaster husband John Grayson. They were divorced in Virginia on grounds of incompatibility and, in a phrase that has a very modern ring to it, Frances always said her husband remained one of her best friends.[32]

Boll used each of her marriages as stepping stones to wealth, glamour, or high profile. Only her fifth union – to a New York harpist – seemed to offer no obvious catapult to high income or standing. During the late 1920s she was a close companion of Charles Levine, who was married to long-suffering Grace, and they shared a love of money and flying. Boll travelled with him to France in 1928 and discovered that the country's respect for glamour and aviation suited her. Three of her weddings would take place in Paris.[33]

She had also been known in Dallas, Texas as Mabel Bach, or variations on that theme like 'Mibsie Bach/Mach', 'Nibsie Bock, Bach, Basches or Bache or Mrs Bale M Bache in New York'.[34] She only ever admitted to her marriage to Lieutenant Albert Bache under extreme duress, such as when she was being questioned in court about non-payment for a lavalier – or 'Y' shaped – necklace diamond given to her by Bache.[35]

*

Before the First World War, divorce in England and Wales was still tainted by the whiff of scandal and it was usually only the rich who could afford to go through with it. Couples had to prove adultery or violence. In the first decade of the twentieth century there was just one divorce for every 450 marriages. Divorce increased immediately after the war as some returning men found it hard to settle down or discovered that their wives had been unfaithful. A sudden rush into what would prove unsuitable unions also led to an increase in divorces.[36] The Matrimonial Causes Act 1923 meant that either partner could petition for divorce on the basis of their spouse's adultery, whereas in the past only the husband had been able to do this.[37] There were more courts where you could seek a divorce and more financial help to do so (particularly after the Poor Persons' Procedure of 1914).[38] According to the Office for National Statistics, the total number of divorces in England and Wales was 577 in 1913. The figure increased to 3,522 in 1921 and 4,018 in 1928 before climbing slowly to a peak after the Second World War.[39]

Divorce followed a smoother trajectory in the USA, where it was governed by state rather than federal law. Reno in Nevada, where Ruth Elder moved to divorce her third husband, Walter Camp, in 1932, gained a reputation for 'quickie' divorces. Husbands and wives in the US could use the same grounds to file for divorce (unlike in England and Wales). At the start of the twentieth century there were 0.9 divorces per 1,000 Americans a year and this remained fairly constant until the start of the First World War. By 1928 the rate had climbed to 1.7 divorces per 1,000 Americans, helped by the new taste of freedom afforded women during the war and a booming economy, which always made leaving a marriage less daunting.[40]

Elder and Boll's failed marriages attracted headlines in a way that probably wouldn't have applied to their male counterparts. Revelations about Elder's first two marriages certainly caused her distress and distraction but later in life she, like Boll, appeared to relish the way a marriage or divorce could return her to the newspaper columns.

Earhart showed no signs of *needing* a husband and wasn't willing to risk bad publicity in choosing the wrong one. She became engaged to Sam Chapman, a dully reliable industrial heating engineer, who worked for Edison Electric in Boston,[41] in 1923 but refused to wear his engagement ring.[42] He visited her as they waited for the weather to change in Trepassey in June 1928 and in photos of that time he looks as bored as everyone else. But there was never any danger that a forgotten husband or beau would crash out of the closet to embarrass Earhart. Guest, who had deliberately chosen to back a woman of propriety to become the first woman to cross the Atlantic, had made sure of that.

George Putnam, whom Earhart usually referred to as 'GP', 'GPP' or 'Gyp', was another reason that she didn't face as many romantic rumours as other pilots. True, unlike Elder and Boll, Earhart paid little attention to her looks, but that was not sufficient to prevent newspapers speculating about her love life. Putnam put a stop to that by proposing.

He was forty-one when he first met her, tall and goodlooking in a professorial way. He usually wore a suit and glasses. At the time he was married to Dorothy Binney, who was heiress to the Crayola Crayon fortune, and they had two sons.[43] He had served as a lieutenant in the field artillery during the First World War and always loved exploring the remotest parts of the world. In 1926 he joined an expedition to Greenland by steamship and radioed daily accounts to *The New York Times*. Putnam was a close friend of Richard E. Byrd and used his family publishing company to produce accounts by famous pilots and explorers including Byrd. His biggest success was Lindbergh's book about his Atlantic flight, *We*, that proved to be a bestselling account of his Atlantic crossing.

Putnam's relationship with Earhart blossomed when she joined him and his wife at their home in New York State as a way of giving her the space she needed to help her write her account of her first attempt to fly the Atlantic, *20 Hrs., 40 Min.* Dorothy and Putnam divorced in 1929, but he had to propose six times before Earhart agreed to become his wife.[44] She finally consented in a Lockheed aircraft factory in Burbank.[45]

Earhart was blunt about what she wanted from their marriage. For her, unlike many of her rivals, marriage was a serious consideration, and in a pencilled letter composed before their secret marriage in Noank, Connecticut, on 17 February 1931, she reminded Putnam of aspects of their relationship that troubled her and which they had already discussed. She handed him the 'sad little letter', with its spelling mistakes and crossings out, just before the ceremony at his house.[46] The original draft reads:

> Dear Gyp
>
> There are some things which should be writ before we are married – things we have talked over before – most of them.
>
> You must know again my reluctance to marry, my feeling that I shatter thereby chances in work which means most to me. I feel the move just now as foolish as anything I could even do. I know there may be compensations but have no heart to look ahead.
>
> On our life together I want you to understand I shall not hold you to any mediaeval code of faithfulness to me nor shall I consider myself so bound to you. If we can be honest about affections for others which may come to either of us the difficulties of such situations may be avoided.
>
> Please let us not interfere with the others' work or play, nor let the world see our private joys or disagreements. In this connection I may have to keep some place apart – when I may retreat from even an attractive cage – to be myself
>
> I must exact a cruel promise and that is you will let me go in a year if we find no happiness together. (And this for me too).
>
> I will try to do my best in every way and give you fully of that part of me you know and seem to want.
>
> A.[47]

Putnam received a version that differed only slightly from the above and includes her reluctance to marry, the offer of an "open" marriage and the reference to the "attractive cage".

It's important, however, not to view Earhart as a cold fish for whom the physical side of a relationship didn't matter. An undated, pencilled note, presumably to herself, shows that it clearly did. In it she describes 'marriage (sexual fulfilment)' as 'like the entrance from a dark cool beautiful wood into a scorching plain, devoid of vegetation', although likening sexual satisfaction to a barren landscape may be interpreted in several ways.[48]

Despite her cautious tone in her letter to Putnam the couple seemed uniquely matched among aviation's unions. Putnam, who would go on to marry twice more after Earhart's death, loved flying and didn't resent his wife's time in the air. Indeed, he always had an eye for the commercial aspects of her career. It was he who massaged the time of her first Atlantic crossing to make the title of her account of it sound better and it was he who persuaded her to endorse Lucky Strike cigarettes – although she didn't smoke and later regretted the promotion.[49] Earhart, for her part, never faltered from her desire for an independent career. She refused to be referred to as 'Mrs Putnam' – although some newspapers couldn't bring themselves to observe her wishes – and there was never any suggestion that she might be called home to do the dishes.

CHAPTER FIFTEEN

Limbering up: Boll and Earhart in Cuba and Boston

In January 1928 Calvin Coolidge became the first American president to visit Cuba while in office; President Obama would be the second – in 2016. The visit was an arduous one for Coolidge, who was known to relish his leisure time and who, it was said, worked no more than four and a half hours a day. Cuba was the only foreign country he visited during his presidential tenure, from 1923 to 1929.

Coolidge and his wife, Grace, took the presidential rail car, which lacked air-conditioning, in a thirty-two-hour trip to Key West, Florida, before boarding the *USS Texas* battleship for the 100-mile, overnight trip to Havana. In Cuba the president, usually dressed in three-piece suit and silk hat, endured daily temperatures of around twenty-six degrees centigrade and relative humidity of 74 per cent.[1] Prohibition in his home country meant he also had to find a way to decline, without offending his hosts, the alcoholic drinks he was bound to be offered so that he was not seen to be flouting American law – even if he was, technically, under a different jurisdiction. His biggest challenge came at the ranch owned by the Cuban president,

General Gerardo Machado y Morales. All eyes were on Coolidge as a waiter, wielding a huge tray of crystal cocktail glasses upon which rested a well-shaken daiquiri, approached from his left. As the temptation bore down on him, he pivoted to his right, supposedly to admire a portrait on the wall. As the tray closed in, he wheeled a further ninety degrees to engage Machado in an intense discussion about the beauty of the landscape. By the time he had completed a full circle the tray had moved out of the danger zone, and it was as if he had never glimpsed it.[2]

While Coolidge was doing his best to avoid alcohol, the prospect of a refreshing cocktail, mixed with pure, unadulterated ingredients, may well have served as an added incentive for Boll, Levine, and Stultz as they planned the first non-stop flight from New York to Cuba.

When Lindbergh robbed Levine of the chance to be first across the Atlantic, Levine snatched another record by becoming the first *passenger* to make the trip. Levine's role, like Savile's, was kept secret – even from his wife, Grace, who only realised he would accompany Chamberlin when the plane took off in front of her, leaving her sobbing on the runway at Roosevelt Field. Her husband, dressed in a pin-striped, blue business suit, his bald head hatless, had slipped into the cabin in what everyone assumed was a final farewell to Chamberlin.

The couple were reunited in early September when Grace and one of their daughters joined Charles at the Savoy Hotel in London.[3] A photo in a newspaper account shows him wearing the hat he left behind and holding his daughter in his arms. But the fond reunion was short-lived and Charles remained in Europe, forcing Grace to cable him from their house in Bell Harbour, Long Island, to urge him to come home immediately – by boat. *The New York Times* reported that she and their two children were anxious for his return as soon as possible and that the business was suffering without him. Immediately above the news story, the paper ran a short item about how Charles had been spotted in a Russian restaurant in an exclusive quarter of Paris. His companion was Boll, 'the young American who is anxious to make the transatlantic flight'.[4]

Just over two months after the disappearance of *Dawn*, Stultz found himself again part of a crew of three but this time he was much more of a gooseberry and they were heading south. Again, he was beholden to a rich woman but on this occasion it was Levine who carried most clout. As before, they were waiting for the right weather but at least they were heading towards a warm climate, rather than the fog and ice of Newfoundland. Now Stultz was flying a tried and tested aircraft. The Bellanca monoplane, *Columbia* had already proved her worth by carrying Levine and Chamberlin to Germany; now she was being asked to fly to Cuba.

Although any take-off, especially of a plane loaded with fuel, is perilous, as he sat, warming up the engine at the army site at Mitchel Field, Long Island, Stultz must have felt that he was in a safer position than in the moments before any of the three take-offs in the heavily laden seaplane at Old Orchard. He'd received a report from Doc Kimball at about 10.00 pm on 5 March 1928 saying that, apart from a small area over South Carolina, the entire route to Cuba looked clear.[5] There would be a full moon, too, illuminating their way due south down the Atlantic coastline to a point in Florida directly opposite Cuba.

At the all-clear from Kimball, *Columbia* was wheeled onto the field and her tanks filled with 250 gallons of fuel.[6] Levine and Boll were summoned and arrived with Mabel's mother. Mabel wore a tweed suit with 'divided skirt' (perhaps culottes), camel hair coat, and brown cap and brought two suitcases, a hat box, and a large vanity case. She and her luggage were squeezed indecorously into the plane where she took an improvised seat behind the main fuel tank.

The plane needed only a short run-up before, at 11.36 pm, it took to the air. Stultz circled the field once or twice and then headed south – the sort of calm departure any professional pilot relishes. They hoped to cover the 1,400 miles in about fifteen hours in a journey that would make Coolidge's trek to Cuba seem, by comparison, like a lengthy and exotic expedition. Perhaps to stress the difference they carried no food, simply a thermos of coffee.

Boll was still most famous for her jewels, but she was also gaining a reputation as someone who was desperate to cross the Atlantic in a plane and was willing to pay any amount of money to do so. She was said to have offered Levine 500,000 francs to take her with him to Germany[7] and, when he declined, tried to tempt Captain Robert McIntosh with 100,000 francs (other accounts say £800)[8] to pilot her over the ocean.[9]

The flight to Cuba was almost too easy as they cruised at an average speed of one hundred miles per hour. When they touched down at 1.36 pm under 'balmy' skies, only a handful of people were there to greet them whereas, a month before, Lindbergh had been mobbed.[10] Boll was annoyed that they had to wait for the customs and immigration officials to turn up. She was further irritated when no one recognised them at their hotel, despite Boll pointedly wearing her flying helmet. They had failed to make reservations and were not expected. It may have been this apparent anonymity that prompted her to announce that she was planning to fly from New York to Paris that spring.[11]

While Boll was very publicly setting her sights across the Atlantic, Amelia Earhart was enjoying one of the most stable periods in what had so far been a nomadic life. She returned to the Boston area in May 1925 and, at first, taught English to foreign students at a Harvard University summer extension programme. Then she worked as a companion in a hospital for people suffering from mental illness, but she didn't enjoy the job and the pay was low.

In August 1926 she applied to join the Women's Educational and Industrial Union in Boston. One of its goals was to help women find work and to support them in other ways such as training and

Amelia Earhart during her stay at Trepassey in Newfoundland, 1928. The sight of a woman in trousers caused consternation among some local people. *(National Postal Museum)*

ABOVE: Lady Anne Savile's retired nanny wishes her well at the start of the 810-mile Round Britain King's Cup Race from Croydon to Glasgow and back again in 1922. Savile took part with pilot Leslie Hamilton. *(Smith Archive/Alamy Stock Photo)*

RIGHT: Bessie Coleman, known as 'Queen Bess' and 'Brave Bessie', proved an inspiration in the battle against discrimination when she became the first African American woman to obtain an international pilot's license. *(IanDagnall Computing/Alamy Stock Photo)*

Ruth Elder, in front of *American Girl*, holds the picnic packed for her transatlantic crossing. She wears the colourful bandana, known as 'Ruth's Ribbon', which became popular among her young, female fans. *(GRANGER — Historical Picture Archive/Alamy Stock Photo)*

Planes weren't designed for women and Elsie Mackay's heels helped her to get to parts of the machine that she might otherwise not have been able to reach.
(Chronicle/Alamy Stock Photo)

Captain Walter Raymond Hinchliffe, or 'Hinch', was one of the world's most experienced pilots, despite having lost an eye in World War I. *(The New York Times/Headpress)*

Elsie Mackay's flying suit helped her to keep warm, especially when she and Hinch faced snowy conditions on take-off from Lincolnshire, 13 March 1928. *(ANL/Shutterstock)*

Frances Wilson Grayson perches on *Dawn*, the Sikorsky amphibian plane she had commissioned for long-distance flights. *(Courtesy of the Boston Public Library, Leslie Jones Collection)*

Charles Levine (left) and Mabel Boll at Croydon, 27 August 1928. They were considering a transatlantic crossing, but pilot and mechanic Bert Acosta had doubts about sharing the ride with Boll. *(Smith Archive/Alamy Stock Photo)*

Friendship's pilot Wilmer 'Bill' Stultz and Louis 'Slim' Gordon (right, co-pilot and mechanic) relax in the Ye Olde Cheshire Cheese pub on London's Fleet Street, shortly after their arrival in June 1928. *(Louis E. 'Slim' Gordon Special Collection)*

Amelia Earhart was constantly in the spotlight when she arrived in London. She looks uncomfortable in fashionable 'flapper' garb standing to the right of her sponsor, Amy Guest, who is with her sons, Winston (left) and Raymond before they leave for Ascot. *(Courtesy of Purdue University Libraries, Karnes Archives and Special Collections)*

Amelia Earhart became famous for her 'tousled' hairstyle. Here she receives a haircut from an old friend, Carl Dunrud, at his Double Dee Ranch in the mountains of Wyoming, summer 1934. *(Courtesy of Purdue University Libraries, Karnes Archives and Special Collections)*

education. As part of the membership process, its director wrote to Sam Chapman asking for a reference about Earhart's 'scholarship and capabilities'. He ignored the additional request of how he knew the applicant (they were engaged) and scribbled on the back of the letter an endorsement that, while it begins in a rather grudging tone, concludes with glowing pride: 'Miss Amelia M Earhart is all right. I have known her four years and she is a very dear friend of mine. She is a good scholar and is capable in any field that she may claim.'[12]

*

Earhart took up her post at Denison House in 1926 and the combination of the social work she carried out there and flying proved a satisfying fusion, although no one at work knew she was a pilot. Denison was Boston's second oldest 'settlement' and grew out of the British idea that 'settling' in a deprived area was more effective, and helped to break down class barriers in a way that visiting the poor at home could never hope to. In America these settlements were mainly run by educated women who offered activities such as English lessons and entertainment for children. The building was on the edge of Chinatown and surrounded by warehouses and what had once been grand residences. The centre was particularly popular with Syrian, Chinese, Italian, Greek, and Irish families.

Earhart loved getting to know people new to the US. She particularly enjoyed meeting them in their homes and trying their way of cooking.[13] She was fascinated by teaching English as a foreign language and started with a co-worker to write a book on the subject. How much more could be done, she pondered, if there were sufficient funds to help immigrants?

She joined the Boston Chapter of the National Aeronautic Association, and her name started to pop up regularly in articles promoting aviation and women pilots. She agreed to help judge a nationwide competition, run by the National Playground Association, to find the best model aeroplane and wrote to Ruth Nichols about forming what would become the Ninety-Nines, to support women pilots.[14]

This pattern of squeezing flying in between work might have continued for several months had it not been for a phone call one afternoon in April 1928. Being called to the telephone was a rare occurrence but Earhart didn't want to be distracted from one of the most chaotic moments in the day. Denison House was swarming with children of all ages who had just finished school and were being funnelled into after-school activities. It was her responsibility to ensure that they arrived at the right room and that the tutors were ready with bats and balls, art supplies, dressing-up boxes, or whatever else they needed to entertain eager youngsters. She also had to negotiate with children who had decided they'd rather paint than play games or who wanted to join a sport activity rather than go to their drama class. When someone arrived to tell her that she had a phone call she initially said she was too busy, but the messenger insisted that the call was urgent.

The unfamiliar voice at the other end of the line said: 'Hello. You don't know me, but my name is Railey – Captain H. H. Railey.'[15]

*

Back in New York, Boll revealed that a few months ago she had offered Hinch $25,000 to fly her across the Atlantic but that he had written to say others were prepared to pay double and, because he was poor, he was obliged to accept the highest fee. He went on to advise her on the importance of fixing the most propitious time to set off and of picking the best aeroplane.[16]

Boll chose this moment to make the letter public because Hinch and his co-pilot Mackay had recently made their own attempt on the Atlantic. Given the drama that unfolded, his advice about the weather would turn out to be horribly prescient.

CHAPTER SIXTEEN

Hinch and Mackay

By the end of 1927, Hinch had clocked up over 8,000 hours as a pilot. The fact that, of the thirty-four years he had lived on earth, he had spent almost one whole year in the air, made him one of – if not – *the* most experienced pilot in the world.

It wasn't just the longevity of his life in the skies; his career was all the more impressive because of the range of planes he had flown and the weather conditions he had encountered. Flying had kept him at the forefront of world events. He had lost his left eye as part of a terrible conflict and the patch he wore represented a constant reminder of that horrible experience. When that war ended, he knew no other way of making a living.

Over the next few years, he flitted between Britain and mainland Europe. His logbooks become scrapbooks of his adventures, full of mementos of his travels: photos of Dutch women in national costume with elaborate head dresses, colourful tickets from airshows, business cards, invitations to official dinners, postage stamps from France, receipts from hotel rooms he's stayed in in Berlin, Zurich, and Vienna, a ticket to a play in Hamburg, a postcard from Cologne. There are photos of fellow pilots and of his two Borzoi dogs, Kazan and Erka, 'two non-paying passengers'.

At first, he was mainly based at Blackpool, in the north-west of England, but then he flew passengers to the first air traffic exposition in Amsterdam in 1919, which aimed to rekindle Dutch interest in flying and which became a meeting point for pilots who had served in the War and a tourist attraction in its own right. Like many other ex-RAF pilots, Hinch also eked out a living through joyriding. He picked up some work for the new state airline of KLM Royal Dutch Airlines and carried the first mail delivered by air between England and the Netherlands. He became a well-known and popular character who got into the habit of performing three loops as soon as he spotted the KLM head offices.[1]

The name 'E. [Emilie] Gallizien', personal secretary to KLM's general manager, first appears as a passenger in his logbook on 7 August 1920.[2] She's accompanied by a friend, H. Mensink, on the trip from Maaldrift to Schiphol. They fly above the clouds and the effect is 'most picturesque with sun shining upon the clouds', although Miss Mensink is 'rather ill'. He takes the same two women up in April 1921 when they return the plane to Amsterdam after a demonstration at Dordrecht. Hinch uses the opportunity to do some 'stunting', which makes poor Miss Mensink ill again. In view of how his relationship with Emilie is to develop, it is hard to avoid the impression that Hinch is showing off to impress her. Even the comment in his logbook that the flowers at Haarlem make the landscape look like 'one immense Turkish carpet' might be interpreted as the observation of someone who is falling love. Later that same month Emilie flies with him from Amsterdam to Croydon and back on KLM business and her name starts to appear regularly in his logbook, to the point where it is barely remarked upon. He calls her 'Millie' or 'M' and she refers to him as 'Walter' or 'Ray'.[3] She never seems to suffer from airsickness. She accompanies him on a night flight to Rotterdam and in another job in which he has to drop 30,000 pamphlets over The Hague – most of which cling to the rudder.

From April 1921 she often fills in his logbook for him, which is the sort of duty a pilot would only delegate to someone they trust completely. It is also a particularly kind action to perform for someone worried about eyestrain.[4] In July 1923 they marry in Croydon and settle down in nearby Purley.

Hinch's work as a pilot at the start of the new decade allows him to exploit the benefits of flight – whether for commercial, entertainment, or emotional reasons. In 1922 he starts to fly for Daimler and to carry newspapers across the Channel – a load which is heavy and makes it harder to manoeuvre the plane. In May he flies a passenger from London to Paris and they receive the name of the derby winner over the wireless – his passenger in the front seat is disappointed by the outcome. On another occasion he takes a couple to the spot where their son was killed in the war.

His passengers include Sir William Sefton Brancker, Director of Civil Aviation, whom he flies from London to Paris and from London to Rotterdam, and Sir Samuel Hoare, Secretary of State for Air, whom he takes from Croydon to Cologne. Both men are acutely 'air-minded' and convinced of the future of aviation; both are interested in his views on navigation and weather reports.

From his vantage point in the pilot's seat, Hinch has a unique view of how the world is changing and the part aviation is playing in bringing people together. He flies over the battlefields where he had once witnessed desperate dog fights and a few months later delivers a Persian blue cat to Berlin. He transports the Rani of Jodhpur, who is observing purdah, and her retinue, in the greatest secrecy. Other passengers include four Egyptian pashas and their wives, and on another occasion the Canadian-born comic actor Beatrice Lillie who was making a name for herself in London's musical reviews by parodying the stagey singing style of old-fashioned performers.

He is both in the middle of politics and above it. In the summer of 1925, he takes Charlie Cramp, Secretary of the Railwaymen's Union, from Stag Lane in North London to Paris. The following year he picks up copies of the *Daily Mail* which have been printed in France to circumvent striking British printers. On several occasions he bears the huge responsibility of moving vast amounts of gold around Europe at a time when people have lost faith in currency. In 1923, as Germany suffers crippling hyperinflation, he transports a representative of the German Reichsbank from Croydon to Cologne with £100,000 in Marks on board. The money, which was destined to pay German wages, had previously been flown from Berlin to Amsterdam and then on to London as a way of evading the French authorities who had arrested a pilot making an earlier trip.

On another occasion a passenger, who also happened to be an engineer, sends him a note as they are travelling from London to Paris because he is worried that a high-pitched noise is a mechanical fault. Although Hinch can't hear it he performs an emergency landing. When he still can't detect the noise, he reaches under the backseat to find a box of day-old chicks on their way to a French poultry fancier.[5]

He delivers cameras for a world enthralled by moving images and takes members of a BBC orchestra up over Croydon in November 1925 to see whether it is possible to broadcast from the air. In a practice flight the fog is so thick that he has to climb to 8,000 feet and glide down with the engine off while the musicians play jazz. On the day of the broadcast the concert goes well, despite a slight background engine noise. The second half of the programme is delayed by a broken oil pipe.

He's frequently in the press for these unusual flights and, in July 1924, for breaking the record for the length of time spent cumulatively in the air – eight months – and total distance flown. Journalists want to know his views on flying.

But being an on-call pilot is not an easy job for a father and husband. He's at Le Bourget for his daughter Joan's first birthday on 26 September 1924 and sends her a postcard to wish her many happy returns. He spends one Christmas alone in Lyons. Over the next three years he sends regular postcards from around Europe and sometimes as far away as Cairo. He normally writes just a line, dashed off from a hotel room or as he is waiting for the weather to clear. Sometimes the postcard shows a beach where he was forced to land or the hotel where he is staying, a cross marking his room. The notes have the quality of a modern text or WhatsApp message. 'Hope your temper is better than it was this morning'; 'hope to be back with you tomorrow. Love Father'; 'how is your sniffy cold?'; 'Proceeding probably to Belgrade in "Miss Columbia" with Levine today. Hope you are being a good little girl. Love Father'; 'Flying back in a few minutes & hope to see you before you are in bed.'[6]

Nineteen twenty-seven is a momentous year. He flits back and forth across the Channel. In May he and Millie watch Lindbergh land at Le Bourget and later that summer he takes Joan up for her first flight. At the end of July Levine is one of six passengers he flies from London to Paris. He plans to fly back to England and then across the Atlantic. 'Situation most complicated' he writes, gnomically, in his logbook.[7] He returns to Paris the same day, after deciding not to 'steal away in *Miss Columbia*' and then delivers Levine on 1 August to the Bucknall Races before showing him round Cranwell Aerodrome as a possible starting point for a transatlantic crossing.[8]

Watching Lindbergh arrive after his Atlantic crossing may well have sown in Hinch the idea of making his own attempt on the ocean. Whatever the inspiration, he took six weeks leave of absence from Imperial Airways to fly for Levine,[9] although he was less than impressed with Levine's crossing, which had smashed Lindbergh's two records of distance and time in the air. Hinch recorded in his flying log that the time was 'disappointing'.[10] Levine had fallen out with his pilot Chamberlin and with his replacement, Frenchman Bertaud Drouhin. He had also got into trouble with the French authorities for illegally flying his plane from Paris to Croydon. He was clearly not the most reliable person to have in a cockpit.

The tension between Hinch and Levine is palpable in a short news film entitled, *The Farewell Message from Mr Levine and Captain Hinchcliffe* [sic] (1927). The two men stand side by side on a stage in front of a theatre curtain. They both wear sharp, double-breasted suits, although Hinch's stature and bearing make him look more dapper than Levine who was slightly round-shouldered. They smile awkwardly at one another and Levine plays with a hat as he reads hesitantly in his New York accent from cue cards. After thanking Britain for its warm welcome, he concludes: 'In Captain Hinchliffe and the *Columbia*, an American plane, I am convinced I have found the ideal Anglo/American alliance ... Cheerio.'

Released from the straitjacket of his script he offers up a surprising, charming smile that highlights his piercing eyes.

Hinch replies in his clipped, upper-class accent. The patch over his left eye dominates his gaunt face. His mouth appears to be overcrowded with teeth.

After lines such as 'I value very highly the privilege of being allowed to take a man such as Mr Levine, who I esteem so very highly, upon a flight of this nature' he pauses, sways slightly and looks awkwardly at his feet, as if discomforted by his script.

He will be 'delighted', he continues, to spend 'those very interesting hours in such close proximity to Mr Levine' and he can see 'absolutely nothing' to prevent their arrival at our destination' – another beat, a sway, and a glance at this feet – 'but I really see no reason why we should not succeed.'

At the end of his speech the men turn and shake hands stiffly:

Hinch: 'And Good luck to Mr Levine and the *Columbia*.'

Levine: 'And to Captain Hinchliffe – one of the greatest pilots in the world.'[11]

The temperamental contrast translated to actions at Cranwell as they waited for nearly a fortnight, with Hinch rising early each day to see if the weather suited an Atlantic crossing. On a rainy 17 September

Levine had been called to set off on their momentous flight but took one look at the weather and went straight back to bed. Hinch, aware that the much more important factor of the wind was ideal for as much of the route as he could gauge, stormed into Levine's bedroom and insisted he get up. 'Something of a scene' followed and one of Hinch's relatives urged him to thrash Levine.[12] The standoff was defused, with the help of a £2,000 cheque for Hinch, and he later commented:

> Levine is one of the nicest men I know, and also one of the bravest, but he cannot make up his mind yes or no. I admit I was very much in the wrong this morning. He told me this afternoon frankly that he did not want to go because of the press of business, and I answered that he should have told me so instead of blaming it on the rain and the field.[13]

After the outburst Hinch persuaded Levine to aim for a less ambitious record before attempting the Atlantic, and they set off for India on 23 September 1927. On the first leg from Cranwell to Vienna Levine tried to take the controls and the engine suffered several air locks.[14] From Vienna they flew to Ravenna and then eventually over Vesuvius but when they left Rome for Bucharest the engine cut out completely after take-off and they just managed to clear some high-tension wires in a forced landing after which the left wheel collapsed and the undercarriage gave way. Hinch concluded that the plane and engine had been 'totally neglected' by Levine and his mechanic.[15] This experience, along with the news that Levine intended to take Mabel Boll on their east/west adventure, convinced Hinch that it was time to end the partnership – even though the decision would also mean turning down £10,000 in fees.[16]

The split with Levine left Hinch in a predicament. He was such an experienced pilot that Imperial Airways couldn't not accept him back, but their welcome was lukewarm. His bosses had been reluctant to allow his leave of absence in the first place but, when he threatened to resign, found they had no option but to let him go temporarily. When he returned to work after the Levine interlude, he was frequently kicking his heels around the hangar while other, less experienced pilots, were given work. In a job where flyers were paid for their hours in the air the financial impact was devastating. The loss of income was even more troubling for Hinch because he had dipped into his own funds when working for Levine and the prospect of further earnings from an Atlantic bid had persuaded him to commission a house, Hock Huis, in the then quiet, village-like area of Peaks Hill, Purley, just over a mile from Croydon Airport.[17] Imperial Airways had its base there and the site was fast developing into a hub for international air travel. Passengers flew to and from Le Bourget and some of the trappings of a modern airport were starting to appear: a hotel, terminal building, and control tower.

By the time Hinch decided he could no longer work with Levine, Millie was pregnant with their second child. He was torn between the need to provide for this expanding family and his fear, which he shared only with his wife, that he might lose the sight in his remaining eye and would no longer be able to fly. His health had been a nagging worry ever since his accident and in his logbook he recorded whenever he was required to have a medical – often with comments such as 'Too soon!!' (28 May 1927) or 'medical examination once more!' (30 August 1927). The industry publication *The Aeroplane* had been forced to issue a correction after it wrongly stated he was ineligible for a pilot's licence because the Air Ministry deemed his disability meant he was not fit to carry passengers. This false claim carried the implication that this was why he was forced to work abroad.[18] *The Aeroplane* article was a reminder that the medical board might change its mind in the future and that he might lose his livelihood at any moment.

Crossing the Atlantic was still one of the most dangerous journeys a pilot could make. By September 1927 twenty-four people had been killed or went missing in the attempt or during test flights.[19] Hinch was known to disapprove of women being involved in such ventures and had turned down $25,000 from Boll to carry her across the ocean.[20] It would take a persuasive young woman from Scotland, and her irresistible financial offer, to make him think again about the Atlantic.

The difference in their backgrounds was most evident when the Hon Elsie Mackay met Captain Walter Hinchliffe, DFC, at lunch at the London Ritz in October 1927. The appearance of the petite socialite and the tall, battered pilot with a patch over one eye must have caused a certain frisson even in an establishment known for its discretion.[21] The Ritz, which opened in May 1906, was the height of sophistication. Its Louis XVI furniture, gold leaf mouldings, and carefully placed palms spoke of an opulence that could not have been further from Hinch's home in Purley. If he needed a reminder of the largesse Mackay could offer, he had only to glance around him. The hotel, a six-storey confection with a Parisian-style arcade and Beaux-Arts exterior overlooking Green Park, also managed to convey another important subtext: discretion.[22]

Mackay had been thinking carefully about who would make the best pilot to accompany her across the Atlantic and had taken soundings from friends such as Anthony Johnson-Wreford, a flyer who had had to abandon plans for his own Atlantic crossing due to a war wound.

The presence of Mackay's bank manager at the Ritz showed she meant business and her offer proved difficult to resist. She would leave the choice of plane up to Hinch and pay for him to fly to the US to buy it. He would receive eighty pounds a month (some accounts say one hundred pounds),[23] plus expenses. Just as importantly, she would insure his life for £10,000 so that Millie and their two children would be provided for.[24] In return, she demanded absolute secrecy about the expedition and an agreement that she would co-pilot the plane.

The proposal had other factors in its favour. Mackay was a talented pilot and much more level-headed and committed than Levine; it would take more than a rainy day to persuade her to abandon an attempt, and Hinch's previous experience with Levine meant he had already planned the Atlantic crossing meticulously.

In December he had a chance to see the ocean at close quarters when he travelled to the US by liner. Hinch's working relationship with Levine meant that reporters were convinced his trip was somehow connected with the millionaire: perhaps he was chasing money or even threatening to sue him, or maybe Mabel Boll, who was known to be looking for an aerial chauffeur, was trying to persuade Hinch to fly her across the Atlantic. The British pilot denied all these theories and offered the far-fetched excuse that his crossing was to alleviate an attack of quinsy (an inflammation of the tonsils).[25] The arrival of his second child, he explained, meant his visit to the US would last just three days. It was noted, though, that during that short time he visited Curtiss Field and had a good look at a Stinson Detroiter monoplane which carried a factory price of $12,500.[26] Despite his protestations, the fact that the company's secretary, William Mara, was at his side suggested that Hinch was on a shopping expedition. In January he resigned his post at Imperial Airways and was officially engaged as Mackay's personal pilot.[27]

CHAPTER SEVENTEEN

'The most secret flight in the history of aviation'

On Thursday 8 March 1928 the *Daily Express* splashed the headline, 'Peer's Daughter to Fly the Atlantic' across its front page. It was wrong. But its instincts were right, and it was this unerring nose for a story that had made it Britain's best-selling newspaper.[1]

Elsie Mackay and 'the most secret flight in the history of aviation' dominated the front page of the *Daily Express* six times in the following eleven days.[2] While one of the paper's dogged reporters stalked the airfield at Cranwell in Lincolnshire, his counterparts kept an eye on Mackay's movements in London and Scotland. Their scrutiny forced Lord Inchcape's daughter to go to extraordinary lengths to throw them off the scent and conceal her plans to fly with Hinch to New York. For a start, she rang the editor and threatened to bring an injunction against the paper.[3] Even very close friends were unable to confirm the rumours that Mackay, now thirty-five, was part of a plan to cross the Atlantic in a bid to make the first, non-stop, east to west crossing in an aeroplane. Officials at Cranwell were also unclear about who would be in the plane and exactly where it was heading.

In Lincolnshire, the *Express*'s reporter watched as a golden-winged 'machine' circled the 'bleak aerodrome'. The reporter, perhaps mishearing an informant or squinting in the gloomy March weather, could only make out the name *Adventure* painted on the fuselage above the union flag. It was a good guess, and not too far from the correct name of *Endeavour*.

He was more accurate on other points: that extra petrol tanks had been installed in the wings and that other supplies would be carried in aluminium cans which, because of their lightness, shaved valuable pounds from the plane's weight. The contents of the tins could be tipped out in two minutes to lighten the load still further and bring extra buoyancy to the wings.

On 9 March, the day after the *Express*'s febrile lead story, the paper carried two other items connected to the attempt. Diligent readers working their way through the newspaper over their marmalade and toast would have found a short story buried on page three. Here they could read a few paragraphs about Princess Mary and Viscount Lascelles leaving Victoria station on the first leg of their overland journey to Cairo. Mackay was there with her brother-in-law, deputy chairman of P&O Cruises, to wave the princess off in place of her father, and ailing mother, who were holidaying in Egypt. Her appearance was an act of misdirection designed to throw both the press and her family off the scent.

The bluff continued with her tone of outrage when she spoke to a reporter from the *Yorkshire Evening Post*:

> I am very annoyed at the whole matter. I have only a very small financial interest in the project, which is an attempt to establish a new record for a long flight. I know Captain Hinchliffe and the pilot who is accompanying him. He has allowed me to go up on several of the tests. As you know, I have a pilot's certificate, and am very fond of flying, but I have never handled the control without Captain Hinchliffe being there.[4]

However, she was not quite so dismissive in a statement for the *Express*'s air correspondent:

> It is quite true that I have been up in every test flight of the machine, including a seven hours' test with Captain Hinchliffe. It is also quite true that I have helped to finance the venture. And I would give anything to go on the Atlantic trip ___! [sic][5]

Hinch explained that he wished she could have accompanied him but that this was impossible because the petrol cans were too heavy for a woman to manoeuvre when it was time to replenish the fuel tanks. He said that Mackay had put up some of the money for the flight but that his friend Gordon Sinclair would be co-pilot. Sinclair had been laid low by an operation and Mackay had been called in to help with the test flights. He conceded that he did want to cross the Atlantic but aimed to attempt a long-distance flight over land first. Somewhere like Karachi (then part of India, now in Pakistan) might be a good destination, or he might simply circle Cranwell in an attempt to break the world endurance record. The plan to fly to India fitted in neatly with the conditions under which he had bought the Stinson Detroiter. William Mara had originally been reluctant to sell Hinch the plane and changed his mind only when Hinch insisted the aircraft would be used solely for a record trip over land.

Mackay and Hinch's explanations might have been more convincing had it not been for the fact that Hinch's New York manager, John Gillespie, had let slip that they had had to abandon an Atlantic attempt due to 'premature publicity'.[6] What did ring true was Hinch's wariness of women pilots. He had spent most of his life in the testosterone-soaked world of flying and had turned down Boll, plus her $25,000 offer to take her across the Atlantic.[7] There was no reason to expect him to like Mackay who had, in many ways, enjoyed an easy ride in life. She clearly had the wherewithal to fund the expedition, but could he trust her as a pilot? During his war years of training young airmen Hinch had been brutally honest about their talent – or lack of it – now he had the chance to observe a young woman's ability in the air.

Endeavour was shipped over from the US and re-assembled by Vickers' engineers under close scrutiny from Hinch. The Stinson SB-1 Detroiter was an elegant, high-winged monoplane. She had a sleek, steel fuselage with an enclosed cockpit and heated cabin. The pilot had the benefit of dual controls, wheel brakes, and an electric starter. As well as these useful additions, the Detroiter was also beginning to build a name for herself as a reliable machine. In August 1927 William Brock and Edward Schlee flew their Detroiter, *Pride of Detroit*, from Harbour Grace to England on the first leg of their attempt at a world flight and got as far as the Pacific. The model was in the news again when Ruth Elder chose a yellow Detroiter, *American Girl*. The plane had the further advantage of a single Wright Whirlwind 220 horsepower J-5C radial engine. This was the same engine that had powered Lindbergh across the Atlantic and its association with the pilot gave it a talismanic allure.

Endeavour's tests flights started in earnest in mid-February 1928 and the plane had her first flight in England at Brooklands aerodrome, Weybridge, southwest of London, on 18 February. At 4.15 pm that day Mackay took the plane up for her second flight. *Endeavour*'s size alone made her an imposing machine. She had a wingspan of nearly forty-six feet and her height of eight feet dwarfed Mackay's tiny frame. She flew her for an hour, but on this occasion Hinch was assessing her skill as a pilot, rather than the plane's capability. He declared her flying 'very good' – which was praise indeed.[8] Several minor adjustments were made to the plane, including the repair of a leak in her airspeed indicator.

Over the coming days, he put *Endeavour* through her paces, correcting every fault he found, as they flew between Brooklands,

Croydon, and Hendon. At Hendon, on the very edges of North London, he picked up Mackay who took her place in the cockpit to the left of him and in front of a large fuel tank that replaced the usual six passenger seats. If the plane had a light load she could manage a top speed of 121 1/2 miles per hour. On 21 February Mackay flew in mist using her compass and Hinch rated her 'V.g.'. The next day he noted in his logbook, 'E.M. flew compass courses very well' and on 24 February she flew the entire way from Brooklands to Cranwell, an hour and twenty minutes 'without any trouble'. There was no wireless on board because, like most seasoned pilots, Hinch believed the extra weight wasn't worth it as technology was still rudimentary and reliant on a ship being close by if they ran into trouble. He was also concerned about the risk of fire should a spark from the set ignite fumes from the fuel tanks.

They had chosen Cranwell because it was so familiar to Hinch and because its runway was one of the longest in Britain. Although their starting point meant they would have to cross the breadth of England before they even glimpsed the Atlantic it did mean that the most perilous moments of the journey, when the plane was awash with fuel, would be over land, rather than choppy seas. Her heavy load made it unlikely that she would fly straight for Ireland but would, instead, avoid the Welsh mountains by heading north to the Peak District and then over the coast of North Wales before crossing to southern Ireland.

Hinch's most recent memories of Cranfield were of trying to get Levine out of bed and onto the runway for an Atlantic bid the previous September. This unprofessional behaviour had persuaded the RAF that civilians should no longer be able to use the airfield for similar flights. It was only after Mackay used her influence to secure a meeting with the Secretary of State for Air, Sir Samuel Hoare, whom Hinch had also met when he flew him from Croydon to Cologne, that they were granted permission to use the airfield – but only for one week.[9]

The tests continued and towards the end of February started to focus on how the plane handled when fully fuelled.

On 25 February 1928 Hinch noted the following calculations:

Petrol 350 X 7	- 2,450lbs
Machine [aircraft]	- 2,320
Crew [i.e. Elsie] 8 stone	- 112
Crew [Hinch] 11 1/2 stone	- 163
	5,045 lbs
20 gals oil at	
10 lbs per gal	- 200
	TOTAL: 5, 245lbs[10]

Over the next few days, he tested the turn and bank indicator, which shows the plane's position relative to the ground and how quickly it is turning, and found it 'quite useless' and lacking in mercury. He was also worried about an aileron. He had intended the afternoon flight on 28 February to carry them through the night for twenty to twenty-four hours but, while the machine took off well, the engine pump gave out after two hours and they landed in the dusk. The turn indicator was still 'useless'. The engine pump was overhauled and tested. But he was pleased with his co-pilot. 'E. flying perfectly – turns very accurate but occasionally drops nose too far.'[11]

The next day, 29 February, he and Mackay were in the air again at noon and she took the controls for four and a half of the five hours. The engine pump was successfully emptying the main tank, and they felt relaxed enough to have an in-flight lunch and to allow Mackay to snooze for the thirty minutes she wasn't in charge of the plane. Hinch noted in his logbook, and repeated to Millie, 'My confidence in the success of our venture now 100%.' He was reassured enough with the plane's performance to allow her name, *Endeavour* to be painted on the machine.

Everything seemed set – only the weather was failing to align. On Friday 9 March hail battered the windows of the tall, yellow-stoned former coaching inn, the George Hotel at nearby Leadenham, which became the team's unofficial headquarters. Although national newspapers said they were using the George Hotel in Grantham, all evidence suggests that they were, in fact, staying in a village that was only four miles from Cranwell. It was much easier for visitors to come and go unnoticed than at the hotel of the same name at Grantham. The team may have known that the building already had a strong link to adventurers since T. E. Lawrence (Lawrence of Arabia) was said to have scribbled parts of an early draft of the *Seven Pillars of Wisdom* in its restaurant.[12]

Every evening for the first two weeks of March Hinch, Mackay, and Sinclair pored over the charts and discussed the weather reports that were phoned through, just as Frances Grayson and her team had at Old Orchard. Mackay was accompanied by her close friend, Sophie Ries, who signed the guest book, a maid, and chauffeur. Often, Mackay and Ries would be driven back to London but always returned first thing the next morning.[13] When they stayed over they shared a room and Mackay made a point of keeping to herself so that she didn't attract the attention of the other hotel guests; sometimes she would take her meals in her room.[14] 'Mr Porter', who was known to be an American and probably a mechanic, was also present and Hinch's wife Millie made frequent visits.[15]

The hail turned to snow and persisted over the next days as Hinch and Mackay agonised over whether the conditions were bad enough to delay them. Hinch was known to be desperate to take the record and believed there were as many as twelve expeditions from countries including Poland, France, and Germany who could get there first. For Mackay the most compelling reason for them to set off quickly was so that her family didn't find out and try to stop her. Her brother and brother-in-law had already tried to deter her, and her sisters had made

Hinch promise not to join her on such a reckless flight.[16]

Her sister, Margaret said later:

> She had promised definitely not to go on the flight with Capt. Hinchliffe and we never dreamed that she would do so ... We had hoped that the news of Elsie's flight would be kept from her parents, but I am afraid they will see it in the newspapers out in Egypt.[17]

*

In the second week of March, the Picture House in Grantham, a tall, elaborate building that had opened in 1916 and whose façade of Doulton ceramic tiles looked out onto St Peter's Hill, was showing *Love's Greatest Mistake*, a silent movie and thrilling romance about a beautiful girl who leaves a small town to seek adventure in New York. It seems unlikely that Hinch and Mackay arrived early enough on the evening of Monday 12 March to watch it.[18] Instead, after the second showing, they slipped into the cinema to study a film of *Endeavour* taking off. They had arranged for the footage to be shot to give them a perspective, other than from the cockpit, of how the plane handled at this crucial moment in the journey. Although both Hinch and Mackay had hidden their identity, the manageress and projectionist recognised Hinch who, perhaps to throw them off the trail of their imminent departure, said they would return the following night for a second screening.

Mackay, whose clandestine (and later annulled) wedding had taken place in a Catholic Church in Scotland, also managed to attend an evening service at St Mary Immaculate in Grantham. She had been to the church on the previous Sunday and on Monday evening asked Father Arenzen to hear her confession.[19] She also arranged to take communion early the following morning, Tuesday.

Just before midnight Hinch made a request to Cranwell that a working party of aircraftsmen be on duty the next day to help him set off.[20] The night porter was asked to wake Mackay, Hinch and Sinclair at 4.00 am, but they were already up when he knocked on their door. No one had slept and it seems that they finally confirmed at 2.00 am that Sinclair would not be part of the team crossing the Atlantic. They didn't talk much as they left the hotel. Mackay wore a flying suit, leather coat, and silk muffler.[21] She carried her flying helmet as she hurried through the entrance and into one of two large saloon cars waiting outside.[22]

An hour later Father Arenzen opened the door to a woman clutching a small leather case. Together they walked in the darkness the few steps to the church. It was bitterly cold outside and can't have been much warmer inside.

Mackay could not have found a more appropriate place in which to consider the enormity of what she was about to embark on. A photo from about that time shows a high-ceilinged, imposing church, institutional in its rows of pews that no doubt gave off a background aroma of wood polish. Large oil paintings hung on the side walls, tilting inwards as if they were trying to catch what was being said as Mackay took communion and received the priest's blessing in the dim glow of the altar light.

The two figures were tiny in the vast church and further dwarfed by the statues around them. Mary and Jesus were twice human height and the Catholic tradition of painting them with realistic skin tones added another layer of hyper reality. Behind the altar the four apostles gazed down at them in white marble and stone.

Mackay knelt in prayer for a long while below a giant wooden cross suspended above them. Arenzen said later that she was agitated and on the verge of tears.[23] 'One thought,' he said, 'of the soldiers who took communion before going into battle.'[24]

They returned to his study and, with what seems like an extraordinary lack of tact, the priest said he hoped she would fare better than Savile. She simply smiled and waved to him as she rejoined Hinch who had been waiting in a car outside the church.

*

When the two vehicles arrived at Cranwell Mackay sat well back in one, while the two chauffeurs stood guard outside ready to ward off anyone who approached. As *Endeavour*'s engine warmed up Hinch waited for the final weather report. When it arrived, he read it through carefully and walked over to Mackay.

'Everything is all ready now,' he said. 'The report seems good and we have this east wind.'[25]

They spoke for a few minutes before she left the car, and they shook hands with Sinclair and other airfield officials who wished them good luck. Mackay waved from the side window of the plane and Hinch needed all of the runway's three miles to gain enough speed to lift the heavily laden machine off the ground. *Endeavour* turned first to the east, into the wind, before climbing slowly in a wide circle and then heading to the west.[26]

They left Cranwell at 8.35 am. The first reliable sighting of the plane was at 11.30 am at Kilmeaden in County Waterford, a few miles inland from the southeast coast of Ireland. They were next spotted by the lighthouse keeper at Mizen Head, County Cork, on the southern west toe of Ireland at 1.30 pm. A steamship then reported seeing them 170 miles off Ireland.[27]

They were expected in the skies over Newfoundland on Wednesday at 8.00 or 9.00 am. By Thursday anxiety in Britain had reached fever-pitch and sightings of the plane off Newfoundland occurred, at their most frequent, every twenty minutes. But in New York there was less concern since the secrecy surrounding the expedition led some to believe the *Endeavour* must have chosen a different route.[28] On Friday 16 March a couple in Maine were certain they had seen a plane coming down.[29] By Sunday 18 March Lord Inchcape was reported to be on his way back from Egypt.[30]

Doubt remained about who had stepped into the plane with Hinch. Gordon Sinclair and Mackay's friend, Sophie Ries, were nowhere to be seen. Millie, looking homely with a sensible centre parting, was pictured on the steps of their house and said diplomatically that it was 'more than likely' that Sinclair had gone with her husband.[31] It may, in fact, have been a last-minute decision to leave Sinclair behind to lighten the load. Hinch and Millie's young daughter, Joan, with her shoulder-length hair, stood awkwardly between her mother and Mrs Sinclair who was visiting from her home in North London so that the two wives could be together.[32] Joan went to bed believing that her father was on one of his routine London–Paris flights.

A spokesperson at Lord Inchcape's house in London told the *Express* that Mackay had left the house at 8.30 am and that if she was not back by teatime she would not be home until very late. The reporter was assured that she was still in London and that there was no foundation to the rumour that she was flying the Atlantic, in fact she was preparing to join her parents in Egypt.[33] But, as the days with no news of *Endeavour* passed, it became clear that the Atlantic had claimed two more victims.

The final photo of Hinch and Mackay was, appropriately, taken by a woman photographer, Dorothy Grainger, who helped to run a studio with her husband in the small Cambridgeshire village of Burwell. The photo accentuates Mackay's tiny stature as she barely reaches Hinch's shoulder. Both pilots wear high boots, and both are smiling but Mackay's smile looks more genuine. She seems, too, to be holding a snowball in her left, gauntleted hand.

Five years later, in 1933, Grainger sent a copy of the photo to Mackay's mother. The secretary who acknowledged the gift said that, because it was the final image of their daughter, it would be one of her most treasured possessions.[34]

CHAPTER EIGHTEEN

Ambiguous Loss

A family therapist first coined the term 'ambiguous loss' in 1973 for a grief in which the subject of that loss is nowhere to be seen.[1] The person or child has disappeared. They may have been kidnapped; walked out of the door one day never to return; been declared missing, presumed killed in action; were thought to have been at the site of a terrorist attack such as 9/11 or a natural disaster, like a tsunami, or a passenger on a trip like Malaysian Airlines Flight 370 that suddenly slipped off the radar screen. Their disappearance for their friends and family is agonising because, to use a lay person's term, there is no 'closure'; no final goodbye, no funeral, no end to hope. How do you mourn someone you can't be sure is dead, when succumbing to grief can feel like a loss of faith or an act of betrayal?

The thought of what might have happened to them or how they might have died only adds to the torture. Did they die instantly – perhaps in an explosion or from a sniper's bullet? Or was theirs a slow, agonising death? Were they stranded without water or food, or braced for their plane to hit the sea or for their space shuttle to burn up in the furnace they knew was moments away?

As the days after their take-off lengthened Millie refused to give up hope and believed that her husband and his co-pilot must be seeking refuge in a desolate spot where it was impossible to communicate with either Britain or North America.[2] While her mind flitted between the various scenarios she joined the ranks of other friends and families of transatlantic crews who were now gripped in the web of ambiguous loss. Elsie Mackay had managed to convince her brother and three sisters that she would not join Hinch. Two days after they had left, her sister, Margaret, clearly bewildered, told reporters:

> No message of any kind has been received by me or my husband from my sister. All we know we have learned from the papers ... We are praying that the favourable weather conditions which are reported for a flight from east to west across the Atlantic may be maintained and that they may land safely somewhere.[3]

While the family did not have to contend with today's black hole of social media, they still had to avoid – if they chose to – the press's obsession with every facet of the pilots' last days. We can only hope that they didn't see a letter in the *Daily News* from a reader who objected to Father Arenzen's comment that Mackay's act of taking communion was similar to the same devotion shown by soldiers before going into battle. Miss I. F. Fox of Lifton in Devon wrote sternly: 'There is a difference in quality between hazardous acts undertaken at the strict call of duty and hazardous acts undertaken from purely personal motives.'[4]

Hinch's parents, who lived in Liverpool where his father was an artist, barely managed to sleep for more than an hour while they waited for news. His mother had a vision in which she saw her son flying low over the ocean before encountering a large white cloud, which she took to be a good omen. Her husband, too, dreamt that he saw 'Ray' reaching America with a woman. Mrs Hinchliffe commented that it was strange that their son should leave on the 13th as he was so superstitious that he refused even to stay in a hotel room bearing that number. She added:

> I do not think it is the will of Providence that he should have dropped down in the ocean to his end. He went through the war and suffered a lot, and I do not think that Providence means that his end should be in this way. Although things look black we have not given up hope that he is alive.[5]

Gordon Sinclair, the pilot who hoped he might be on *Endeavour*, assumed the job of answering the door to the many callers – mostly reporters – who wanted to interview Millie. He was probably there when, two days after the take-off, one of the Inchcapes' chauffeur-driven cars, with a crest and monogrammed 'I' on its side arrived to return various spare parts that hadn't been needed for the flight. A large box and a covered object that looked like a propeller were moved to the Hinchliffes' garage. This seems like an extraordinarily tactless thing to do, a bit like the uniform and final remains of a soldier being returned to their family.[6] But worse was to come.

Meanwhile, the press tried to track down Mackay's close friend, Sophie Ries. Like other friends and family of the two pilots, she was finding it difficult to cope with their loss. Every false hope or reminder of their disappearance was painful – not just for those close to them but to others who had suffered something similar. On Saturday 17 March, the *Express* devoted a whole page to 'The Tragedy of the Atlantic Waste'. The gallery of photos featured Savile with Minchin and Hamilton and Grayson, Goldy, Koehler and Omdal. Mackay was shown embracing one of her beloved dogs next to an inset of Hinch.

But hope never quite died. Four weeks after *Endeavour* disappeared Millie was comforted by the fact that April was the time when remote parts of Canada became passable again.[7] Several people in Newfoundland swore they had heard *Endeavour*'s distinctive Wright

Whirlwind engine overhead. In August a beachcomber found a tightly corked bottle on the North Wales coast at Flint. Its message, written on a page ripped from a notebook, said, 'Goodbye all, Elsie Mackay and Captain Hinchliffe. Down in fog and storm.' The handwriting was sent to London for analysis and was declared a 'crude and cruel hoax'.[8]

The message-in-a-bottle trope would also crop up in the stories of the two other women who had disappeared trying to cross the Atlantic by plane. In January 1929 a man plucked a small bottle out of Salem Harbour in Massachusetts; inside he found a piece of paper with the words: '1928. We are freezing. Gas leaked out. We are drifting off Grand Banks. Grayson.'[9] Since *Dawn* had disappeared at the end of 1927, the message was initially thought to be a hoax, although it gained some credence when Grayson's friends said they recognised her handwriting.

In May 1928 Reuters news agency reported that a boy had picked up a bottle on the beach at Watch Hill, Rhode Island. Inside, a message, written in pencil, read:

> Hamilton and Minchin quarrelled over the course; struck water, sinking fast: can see light in distance; think off Block Island [about 9 miles (14km) south of Rhode Island]; everything out of order now: ship good for a few seconds yet. [signed] Princess Lowenstein.[10]

The message was due to be compared with a specimen of Savile's own writing but no verification or denial was ever given.

In 1938, an even more bizarre story emerged about Mackay's fate when Mary St Claire from *The Australian Women's Weekly* interviewed her former husband Dennis Wyndham in his West End flat. The actor told St Claire how he had been on set at Elstree Studios making a film with Will Hay when a former employee of the P&O cruise line had asked to see him. The officer had travelled from Falmouth after returning from a voyage to South America. He told Wyndham how, when he was visiting Lima, Peru he had heard a story about 'a mysterious English woman, living the life of a hermit in a little bungalow on the outskirts of the town'.[11] She was said to have made a home there for more than nine years and yet no one knew her name.

The officer visited the bungalow several times but was never allowed in. On his last attempt he glimpsed a face and immediately recognised it as Mackay, 'though she looked very wan and weary'. Wyndham told St Claire that he was convinced that his former wife was alive and that during their final meeting in London she had confided to him that she planned to fly to America with Hinch and once they had landed leave the plane disguised as a boy. *The Australian Women's Weekly* carried a full-page feature on the story, complete with a crudely drawn illustration of Mackay and Hinch in full flying gear and standing next to an aeroplane. The theory must have been painful for both families and came at a time when Millie, who had remarried in 1936, was trying to rebuild her life.

*

The second decade of the twentieth century was awash with ambiguous loss. According to one estimate there were 4.5 million people in Britain alone mourning a close relative after the Great War – nearly ten per cent of the population.[12] This new generation of the bereaved had no idea how to grieve for a loved one who might lie in an unmarked grave or whose earthly body may have been shattered into thousands of atoms by a newly industrialised way of killing. Over 30,000 British and dominion casualties had no known resting place and this brought with it connotations of a paupers' grave, shared with strangers.[13] Worse still, if the deceased had been killed by an explosion, how could their body be resurrected if it was scattered around a foreign field?

Most people could not afford to visit the grave of their son, brother, or husband – only the well-off, like the couple whom Hinch had flown over their son's final resting place, could justify such a luxury. Others took advantage of a service run by travel company Thomas Cook, which started to offer tours of the Western Front. But many more found solace round the Ouija board or behind the drawn curtains of a medium's parlour. By 1919 around 250,000 people in the UK were attending seances.

Sir Arthur Conan Doyle had long been a believer in spiritualism and his enthusiasm deepened after the death of his son Kingsley from influenza, aggravated by his war wounds. Conan Doyle had been following the transatlantic attempt by Mackay and Hinch and in May 1928 he wrote to Millie asking whether she had heard from a medium called Beatrice Egerton who had received a message from Hinch sending Millie his love and reassuring her that all was well with him.[14] Sherlock Holmes's creator was convinced that the message was genuine because Hinch had given the medium the address of the Hinchliffes' solicitor, a fact unknown to her. A second clairvoyant confirmed this message and claimed insider knowledge by pointing out that she knew that Millie was not originally from England and that she had a baby and, maybe, another child.[15] Bad weather, she said, had forced *Endeavour* to head south.[16]

Egerton had, in fact, already contacted Millie but Millie only decided to visit her after Conan Doyle's encouragement. Egerton communicated with the spirits using a Ouija board but did not ask for payment. She wanted to help the bereaved as she herself had been helped after her only son had been killed in the Great War. The message she had received from Hinch was that he had drowned after their plane had been hit by fog, storm, and winds and had gone down 'from great height [sic]'.[17] When asked, Hinch said the plane had crashed off the Leeward Islands, and that he was desperate to speak to his wife.

There were two major errors in the message. The first was that

Hinch and Mackay had, according to Egerton, ended up in the Caribbean, off the islands of Dominica and Martinique, roughly 4,224 miles from Cranwell. The second puzzling detail was that Hinch had misspelt his own surname, adding a 'c' to produce the more common name – 'Hinchcliffe' – and in appending an extra letter unnecessarily extended the medium's already painfully slow journey around the Ouija board. This error was later explained by the confusion he must have been experiencing as he adapted to his new existence in the afterworld.

Millie spoke to Egerton for two hours and left with a recommendation that she should meet with a 'trance medium' because the Ouija board was too slow. It was the equivalent of being told she needed to upgrade from analogue to digital, and one of the best providers at the time was Eileen Garrett.

Garrett was a large, jowly Irish woman with close-cropped hair who was thirty-six when Millie agreed to meet her for the first time at the London Spiritualist Alliance in its grand town house in South Kensington.[18] Garrett's life had been dogged by death: her parents had both died by suicide and she'd lost three children. She joked that her husband had left her because he'd grown tired of sharing their life with ghosts.[19] Once she moved to London, she became friends with writers such as D. H. Lawrence, George Bernard Shaw, H. G. Wells, and Conan Doyle.

Egerton then explained that Garrett's guide was 'an Arab' called Uvanhi (elsewhere spelt 'Uvani') who, when the medium went into a trance, would take over her body. Garrett appeared to fall asleep and after two minutes crossed her arms and bowed her head to Millie before addressing her in English, but with an 'eastern accent'.[20] Millie took shorthand notes as Uvanhi dropped details of their life into the conversation: her name, 'Elise or Elisabeth' and their daughter's, 'Little Joan'; how the person waiting to speak to her had died of congestion of the lungs (drowning) and had flown a plane. He then went on to describe Hinch's final flight and how, at about midnight, the sleet and gale were so severe that a strut broke. Hinch decided to change course to head south, to the islands to the leeward. Millie believed he was referring to the Azores, not the Leeward Islands cited by Egerton. Uvanhi concluded the sitting with:

> Your husband says that you knew he wanted to do it. He was coming to the end of his flying, he could not have flown very much longer, his eyes [sic] were not as good as they used to be and he wanted to give it up, although flying was his life.[21]

The next time Millie went to see Garrett alone and, through Uvanhi, Hinch told her where she would find the shirt studs she'd been looking for. Once a communication had been established spirits often provided practical advice such as where a missing item could be found and Hinch later helped her locate a letter she had misplaced.

On her third sitting on 9 June 1928 Hinch mentioned that he had seen Savile's co-pilot, Hamilton. He said they had had a 'terrible time', that they had turned back and were within sight of Ireland when they struck bad weather and the plane caught fire.[22] As the relationship deepened, Millie became convinced that Hinch was present at their home and she and some visitors heard his footsteps along the corridor and on the stairs.

But Hinch wasn't always right. On 1 August an aviation expert asked two questions which prompted Uvanhi to reply 'Oh, Madame, tell this friend, I am only an Arab and do not know anything about planes.'[23] By way of compensation, Hinch supplied the number CV 11352, which he said identified the two magnetos fitted to *Endeavour*'s engine. However, the magneto manufacturers confirmed that this was not the serial number and did not appear on any part of the plane.

In October she was invited by a well known medium to a house in Harrow. She was one of twelve participants who were told to link hands. The medium insisted he must be tied to a chair. During the hour-long séance Millie heard Hinch's voice and felt something stroke her face. She smelt flowers and experienced them being placed on her knee. She was back again in the early days of their courtship, perhaps she was in the KLM aeroplane, flying over the Dutch tulip fields.[24] At the end of the session her husband urged her to come again and kissed her on the forehead.

Millie started to have private sessions and her contact with Hinch grew into a sort of supernatural courtship. She saw her husband's face at another séance in Harrow on 6 November when he appeared to have brought her flowers that looked so real that she warned him not to tread on them when he placed them on the floor. Edward Carpenter, the influential socialist, writer, vegetarian, and campaigner for homosexual equality who was also a friend of Garrett's, was one of the witnesses who confirmed he had seen the airman.

Millie was convinced that both their daughter, Joan, and their dog Bonzo saw him, but he never appeared to his wife in their home. One day, though, when she was sitting by the fire in the kitchen but not thinking of her husband, Millie saw a small golden aeroplane that flew round the room for about a minute and a half. She believed it had been sent by her husband.[25]

A more tangible piece of evidence appeared at the end of December 1928, and on 1 March 1929 the Air Ministry wrote to Millie to tell her that part of a plane's undercarriage had washed up at County Donegal, northwest Ireland. The wreckage, a tyre and metal wheel well, bore a serial number and address that allowed the Goodrich Rubber company to confirm that this was part of *Endeavour*. Despite this evidence, Millie still believed that the plane had gone down over the Azores and that the Gulf Stream had deposited the wreckage off the coast of Ireland.

She was careful not to mention Mackay in the book she wrote about her experiences, *The Return of Captain Hinchliffe*, published in 1931, following a successful lecture tour about her experiences. On page twelve she writes: 'All reference to the lady in question has been suppressed in deference to the expressed wishes of her family and no allusion to her by name is made in the short description of the preparations for the flight ...'[26]

But Mackay had caught the attention of another spirit guide. On 19 March 1928, less than a week after *Endeavour* had left Cranwell, Sir Oliver Joseph Lodge dictated a memo for the Society for Psychical Research. Lodge was a highly respected physician who became interested in spiritualism after his son, Raymond, was killed in Flanders. Lodge believed that he had been in touch with his son through mediums and wrote about the experience in a bestselling book, *Raymond*, that brought comfort to many enduring a similar grief.

Lodge recorded a message from John King, a spirit guide who was well known in the world of spiritualism for moonlighting between mediums. He was said to be the ghost of Henry Owen Morgan, an English pirate who had plundered Jamaica in the seventeenth century and risen to be its governor.[27] According to legend, he first appeared in 1850 in the flash of Ira Davenport's pistol. Ira and his brother, William, ran a supernatural act in America in the first half of the nineteenth century.

Now, on a Sunday afternoon on 18th March 1928, the medium conveyed John King's insights into the last moment of Mackay and Hinch:

> That when the two left Ireland they ran into a storm, which was like a whirlpool, and had to turn North. Gradually the temperature fell considerably, and the girl became unconscious. The man, in attending to her, lost control of the machine, which turned turtle and dived into the sea. They are now both on the other side, and the girl is asleep. The man has spoken to John

> King and told him that the wreckage could be found if the search were extended further North. He says he could bring them both next Sunday, and possibly Mrs Bailey [Mackay's sister?] will be invited to that appointment.[28]

A scribble in pencil beneath it is hard to decipher but appears to read: 'obtained by Mary W Sunday 18 March 1928 to help her sister who however was not there.' It's difficult not to view John King's message as placing the blame firmly on the female driver.

Wyndham also attended seances in the hope of making contact with his former wife but the voice he heard was always unfamiliar and simply strengthened his conviction that she was still alive. He told a journalist that the couple had made a pact that whoever died first would try to contact the other one. They would be able to identify the deceased by their pet name but when he asked the medium for Mackay's they failed to use the 'Hindu' [sic] word that meant 'my tiny one' and by which he called his former wife.[29]

*

As well as the emotional cost of her husband's loss, Millie had to deal with the all-too-earthly reality that she was short of money. Very short. Hinch, convinced that Millie – whether he made it across the Atlantic or not – would be provided for through his arrangement with Mackay, failed to leave a will. Much more seriously, there was a problem with the £10,000 life insurance he thought she had arranged for him. It seems that the paperwork had been completed and a single premium of £2,700 handed over to the insurance company but Mackay had forgotten to ensure she had sufficient funds in her current account.[30] Put bluntly, in the whir of arrangements surrounding the take-off, her cheque had bounced. But this wasn't just the sort of temporary, public shame most of us have experienced through those two words, 'insufficient funds', but a life-changing catastrophe for Hinch's family. In another version of the oversight, two hours after *Endeavour* took off, a letter arrived for Mackay from the insurance company saying that she must pay an additional \$10,000 if they were to insure Hinch's life.[31]

It came as a huge shock, therefore, when, in July 1928 the Chancellor of the Exchequer, Winston Churchill, announced to the House of Commons that Lord Inchcape had decided to donate the lion's share of Mackay's estate – £500,000 – as a gift to the nation in memory of his daughter. Inchcape hoped the money, which was placed in trust, would be used to reduce the national debt which stood at £7,554,617,647. It was the second half million pounds the chancellor had received that year for this purpose. The first donation had been made by a male donor who wished to remain anonymous.[32] The rest of Mackay's estate passed to the Inchcape family.[33]

When a *Daily Express* reporter relayed the news to Millie, she said it was the first she'd heard of it, adding, 'Nothing has been done to ease the position in regard to my two children and myself.'[34] She said she had written several letters to Lord Inchcape over the past three months, hoping to explain to him the financial arrangement between her husband and Mackay. She sent her final letter by registered post to ensure that it reached him, but she received no reply. As if to highlight the different ways in which the two women were being treated, the *Express* carried a glamorous photo of Mackay smiling with one of her pet dogs above an image of Millie looking serious with her familiar middle parting and with her right hand clasping the earpiece of an old-fashioned 'candlestick' phone; the left hand gripping its stem.

The newspapers worried away at the unfairness of the situation and carried front page news of donations from well-wishers keen to help the Hinchliffe family. Much to Millie's surprise Lady Houston, widow of another shipping tycoon, sent one hundred pounds. Millie had never met her and was delighted by the gift:

'This will relieve my immediate anxieties and make life a little brighter for my two babies and myself.'[35]

Her predicament was raised in the House of Commons and, in reply to a question, Sir Samuel Hoare noted that, since Hinchliffe was not an officer in the RAF reserve, he was not eligible for any support.[36] Eventually, in September 1928, Churchill made a surprise statement. In it he said that Inchcape did not want the fund to be 'the occasion or object of any complaint by other sufferers from the disaster in which his daughter lost her life' and that £10,000 from Inchcape's own money would be given to meet any 'complaint'. In other words, Inchcape had agreed to give Millie the sum.

One paper commented: 'It is impossible not to infer the existence of a feeling of resentment probably associated with a view as to responsibility for the ill-starred adventure.'[37] Millie responded: 'We worked and planned for them [their children] above everything. Now that they are provided for my mind is at rest.'[38]

But Inchcape was troubled by news that Millie was to give a lecture at Caxton Hall in London in which she would describe her supernatural experiences. In a handwritten letter from his home at 4 Seamore Place in Mayfair, he told Churchill on 18 November 1928:

> She has no right to mention Elsie's name without my permission and it will only reopen my poor wife's wound. I don't want to get into correspondence with the woman and I wonder if seeing you gave her £10,000 whether you might try and stop her.[39]

Churchill replied on 21 November saying that he had taken advice and 'Apparently it was quite impossible to stop the lecture wh.[ich] is to be delivered under the auspices of the Stead-Conan Doyle gang.' (W. T. Stead was a popular journalist of the time.) However, Churchill said that the Public Trustee would go through the text and 'cut out everything that might cause you offence or your wife distress. She

[Millie] has promised to abide by these alterations & I hope she will keep her promise, as the Public Trustee feels sure she will.'[40]

*

In May 1930, it was announced that Hinch's estate amounted to just thirty-two pounds (around £1,731.45 in today's money); Mackay's estate, by comparison, was valued at £682,517 (over £36 million).[41]

When the Hinchliffe children grew up, they emigrated to Australia and in 1969, Joan transcribed her father's meticulous logbook, which Hinch had kept up to date until the moment when he left Cranwell with Mackay bound for the USA. It can now be read in the Imperial War Museum in London.[42] This typed version includes a final entry 'compiled from evidence received' – that is, not written at the time or by Hinch.

This posthumous addition we can assume – although this is never made explicit – was written by Millie and explains, without saying how the writer knows this, that *Endeavour* hit bad weather at 10.00 pm and that, when a 'terrible gale' descended, Hinch decided to change direction. The account goes on to describe how the plane went due south but by 1.00 am they knew they could not overcome the weather and tried to head for the Azores 'but had to come down on water at 3.10 am within sight of an island (Azores). Machine was buffeted about. I left machine and tried to swim to land, but failed.'[43]

However, the original, handwritten logbook, which is held in the RAF Museum, Hendon, North London, close to what was then Stag Lane and that is now a teeming part of the capital, offers a final entry that is different in several points.[44] This version, in which the final entry is clearly written in Millie's hand, is less coy about 'the evidence received' and states explicitly: 'The following messages received through Mrs Garrett, Spiritualist Medium, and Mrs Egerton ...'

The original also states that, before they hit bad weather, 'Our spirits were high' and then, once the gale hits, it adds a few technical details: 'Also backfiring through one plug missing ... Gale broke left strut & right strut cracked. Fabric torn.'

It's unclear why Joan decided to omit these details. She leaves in 'But from 1 am on, I knew that everything was finished' but omits 'E. became unconscious.'

From this distance in time we can only guess at her motives for these oversights. Perhaps the family was still mindful of Lord Inchcape's instruction to leave his daughter's name out of any account, or perhaps there was a part of the little girl tucked up in bed waiting for her father to arrive home who resented the role played in his downfall by the rich socialite.

Millie had one final, agonising taste of ambiguous loss when several close members of her family were taken from their homes in the Netherlands during the Second World War and ended their lives at Auschwitz.[45]

PART SIX

Crossing the Atlantic

Flight Checklist: Noteworthy Hair

Captain Hilton Railey first telephoned Amelia Earhart at Denison House, where she was working as a social worker in April 1928, but she was reluctant to meet him in person until he hinted at the role that he was offering her. Even then, she only agreed to visit him in his office if she could bring a senior colleague from Denison with her.

Later that afternoon she probed him for details of the flight and said she didn't like the idea of not taking the controls at some point during the crossing. Railey was excited by her resemblance to Lindbergh and couldn't resist asking her to remove her hat.

'She complied, brushing back her naturally tousled, wind-swept hair, and her laugh was infectious.'[1]

In a later age this might have been a scene from a shampoo advert.

Railey wasn't the only one obsessed with her locks and that word 'tousled' became as strongly associated with her as her habit of wearing trousers. The press frequently asked her to take off her hat and when she visited the UK for the first time Nancy Astor, who, in truth, wasn't a big fan of short hair for women, asked her to remove her closely fitting hat of 'hydrangea blue' at a lunch in her honour.[2] When she complied and revealed her 'Eton-cropped curly hair', she was loudly cheered.[3] At her first press conference in London, wearing borrowed clothes, reporters said it was only her 'unruly mop of curly hair' that made her recognisable.[4]

Putnam wrote to her: 'Your hats! They are a public menace. You should do something about them when you must wear them at all! Some of them are cataclysms!'[5] After her death, he concluded: 'AE's most widely emphasized feature was, I suppose, her hair. Some writer referred to it as "carefully tousled" and, as time went on, and she wore a hat less and less her hair became a sort of hallmark.'[6]

He acknowledged that she had a 'definite inferiority complex about her personal appearance',[7] and he was said to have advised her to close her mouth for photos to hide the prominent gap between her two front teeth.[8]

A handwritten letter from about 1937, when they had been married for six years and he had been her manager since her first attempt on the Atlantic, hints that it was a subject they had discussed. He concludes with the line:

> 'I love you very much and would rather play* and work with you than with anyone I have yet encountered or could in time. Comb that out of your carefully tousled hair.
>
> G.
>
> *open to several interpretations, and applicable to all'[9]

That asterisk is telling. It clearly indicates a meaning known only to them and hints at a more sensual side to a marriage often portrayed as cold or even mercenary. The 'carefully' may also allude to the fact that she used curling tongs to supplement the natural wave in her hair.[10]

Details of her hair varied wildly, depending on the person describing it. Perhaps the most objective version appears in official documents including her Transport Pilot's licence, which was issued on 1 May 1930, when she was 31.[11] It notes she weighs 118 pounds (eight stone, four pounds or fifty-three and a half kilograms), stands five feet eight inches tall, has grey eyes and blonde hair. The accompanying photo is the one most often reproduced in which she's looking off to the side, wearing an unfastened coat and a necktie.

But her hair hadn't always been so boyish. Photos of her as a child show a sweet little girl, first with a bob to just below her ears, later with long blonde hair tamed into a ponytail or plait. In both cases, her hair is adorned with a giant bow that looks like a butterfly had just alighted on her head. As a nurse during the First World War, she wore a scarf over her head and tied at the back. The head covering wasn't enough, though, to supress exuberant curls that escaped from both sides of her face and forehead.

As she became more interested in flying her hairstyle adapted to fit her windswept profession. On the day she approached Neta Snook to teach her to fly, when she was living in California, she wore her hair in a plait coiled around her head. It must have been shortly after that, when she was marching along the road in 'breeks' and a leather coat on her way to or from the airfield, that a car stopped to give her a lift. One of the passengers, a little girl, was excited at the prospect of a female pilot travelling with them and exclaimed: 'But you don't look like an aviatrix. You have long hair.'[12]

Until then Earhart had been secretly trimming inches off her hair but, ironically, avoided a bob in case she was thought 'eccentric'. Since it was unusual for a woman to want to fly, she had to look as 'normal' as possible. For a man, looking 'normal' in an airfield meant short hair and usually being clean-shaven. She snipped away at her locks incrementally, as if reaching the right length was part of the process of becoming a fully-fledged pilot.

Indeed, long hair could be dangerous with so many cylinders pumping away and propellers whirring into action. In April 1927 Anglo-Irish pilot Mary Bailey, who was taught to fly by Heath, slipped on wet grass at Stag Lane and tumbled into a propeller. While she was lucky to escape with her life, she lost a lot of hair and skin, and her family attributed her later violent temper to this head wound.[13]

As well as the obvious risks, part of the decision to avoid a fancy haircut may simply have been that Earhart wanted to spend as much time in the air as possible. She didn't like fuss and noted that another early pilot, Katherine Stinson, who earned her flying licence in 1912, wore a ribbon in her curly hair. Earhart observed that keeping both the curl and the ribbon in place must have been just as arduous as flying 373 miles in one day.[14] Perhaps, too, she was reflecting back to the constraining ribbon of her childhood.

Reporters found it impossible not to comment on her hair and the adjective that hounded her throughout the miles of newspaper columns she generated, and which is forever attached to her name, was 'tousled'. A few accounts sidestepped this adjective with alternatives such as 'a riot of seeming disorder', 'mop of flaxen hair',[15] 'rebellious [hair]',[16] or 'mass of close blond curls'.[17] But the sentiment was the same: there was something titillating and transgressive about her androgenous look.

Other female pilots had hair that stressed their femininity to compensate for their masculine profession: Elsie Mackay's was long, wavy, and jet-black; Ruth Elder was the 'beautiful brunette' who set a trend with her ribbon and Mabel Boll coloured her naturally brown hair to a vampish blonde. A reporter who visited Boll at her New York apartment noted how 'she twists her fingers, with their ponderous diamonds, through the long white hair of Tio, her cavorting Sealyham terrier [a popular breed of the time whose coat could become a mass of ringlets if left untrimmed], or gives her own smooth blonde, bobbed hair small feminine pats'.[18] In France, waiters were less kind and referred to her as 'The Woman with the Silver Wig'.[19] Frances Grayson often wore a demure cloche to hide her hair and Savile took care to colour co-ordinate her flying outfits as a way of making up for the required, unflattering flying helmet.

Earhart could appear lackadaisical about her appearance, at least at the start of her career, because flying was paramount. She became fashionable by default and was completely on trend at a time when flappers were wearing daringly short haircuts. The difference was that bobbed, bleached styles made a woman a slave to the hair saloon whereas Earhart often cut her own hair. She was reported to have visited a barber's and on another occasion asked a cowboy to trim it for her.[20] Few female celebrities of the time were as relaxed about their crowning glory. Silent movie star Mary Pickford, for example, was so anxious about the part her blonde curly hair played in her successful film career, which started before the First World War, that she didn't dare try a shorter style until 1929.[21]

Such was the unease surrounding Earhart's haircut that it was often a shock when she turned out to be much more feminine in person than her image suggested. The *Sioux City Journal* was pleasantly surprised when she visited in 1933:

> She is not especially masculine in appearance, as her pictures frequently indicate. The dark brown of her small brimmed hat and long tailored coat were chosen with feminine regard for her complexion and hair, which has more than a hint of red. Freckles told of the out-of-doors where her many laurels have been won.[22]

Her hair was often described differently by female reporters and if the topic they were writing about was not directly related to aviation. Janet Mabie, for example, made only passing reference in *The Christian Science Monitor*, 29 April 1936, to her 'curly hair that blew in the cold wind' as part of a full-page article about Earhart's appointment as Consultant in Careers for Women at Purdue University.[23]

A reporter from *Tech News* described her 'curled up in a large comfortable chair with her light brown hair in countless little ringlets, the owner of that pleasant voice telling a newspaper correspondent from Toronto her opinion of women in the business and professional world'.[24]

When Earhart expanded on her views that all women should earn their own living and that men should do their share of the housework a female journalist noted: 'She was as boyish as ever, and one reporter, who had interviewed America's first lady of the air about once a year for the last several years, thought she had grown prettier and more attractive year by year.'

Earhart wore a white morning frock that she had designed herself and which 'enhanced her slim beauty and set off to a good advantage her curly, short brown hair, with wind-blown effect, and her cool, blue eyes.'[25] The reporter's description was a long way from the eye and hair colour of Earhart's pilot's licence but the admiration is obvious.

Other observers were deeply troubled by her hair cut. One, anonymous, member of the public felt compelled to send her advice in an undated, handwritten note: 'Dear Amelia, You surely look like a Zuluwoman. Won't you please try to be more cultured by combing your hair before an audience.'[26]

The writer also sent a photo of Earhart in which, ironically, her hair looks neater than in most instances, although the pudding bowl cut does her no favours.

When, in the 1980s, women started to train as astronauts they faced a similar focus on their hairstyles. There was also considerable debate around what NASA should include in a make-up kit for women when they left earth.[27]

Even thousands of miles into space there was no avoiding the newsworthiness of hair. As Hank Hartsfield mounted an IMAX camera on his shoulder to film the interior of *Discovery*'s cabin for a documentary, fellow astronaut Judy Resnik felt her hair being tugged into the camera's drive belt, which had been left uncovered.[28] It was a space-age version of a plane's propeller catching liberated hair – and was only slightly less painful. Eventually the belt jammed when it couldn't consume any more strands and, like a vacuum cleaner that has sucked up too many loose carpet threads, the astronauts had to resort to a solution as rudimentary as scissors to free Resnik. She knew that if word got out that America's second female astronaut had been responsible for disabling a highly expensive piece of kit in this way, it would undermine her achievement. Her colleagues were aware of this danger too and agreed to tell Mission Control only that the camera had 'jammed'.

This wasn't enough, though, to dodge the hair-obsessed media who became mesmerised by Resnik's thick, black curls that floated behind her in the spaceship as if they belonged to a weightless mermaid. When they returned to earth a local newspaper asked if she had any advice about hairstyles for future women in space. Her response was a clipped: 'No advice.'[29]

When Amelia Earhart assumed the form of a Barbie doll in 2018 she was given perfectly coiffured, rich chestnut hair. While the product description focusses on her achievements, her hair continued to cause comment. One purchaser from the UK left a review saying, 'My daughter loves this ... although she was a little surprised by the hair style' and another customer commented that the doll's hair was flatter than in the promotional photos.[30]

Although they didn't have television or the internet to worry about, the first women to fly the Atlantic quickly became aware of how they would be seen by a voracious press. Some, like Ruth Elder and Mabel Boll, realised how, handled with care, a growing mass media could prolong their careers when they were no longer in the skies. Others, like Savile, Mackay, and Grayson, seemed untroubled by how the press reported on their adventures. Amelia Earhart was perhaps the only long-distance female pilot who came close to sticking to the main principles of how she wanted to live her life, regardless of what was expected of her. But that became ever harder the more famous she grew.

CHAPTER NINETEEN

'Violet. Cheerio'

Earhart had not had the chance to fly *Friendship* before they set off from Boston to Newfoundland because she needed to maintain the secrecy surrounding the flight, and to prevent the bid turning into a race with Boll and the young German pilot, Thea Rasche. She had mostly stayed away from East Boston Airport in May 1928 to avoid raising suspicion and had set eyes on the plane only once before they started their journey. When she finally met *Friendship* it was jacked up at a hangar while mechanics and wielders replaced her wheels with pontoons. The plane was painted red and orange, and the reason – to make her easier to spot in the sea – provided a sobering reminder of the peril they faced.

Earhart was fully aware of these dangers and left behind 'popping off' letters for Putnam to give to her parents,[1] both written on 20 May, in pencil, on Denison House headed notepaper:

> Dearest Dad,
>
> Hooray for the last grand adventure! I wish I had won, but it was worthwhile anyway. You know that.
>
> I have no faith we'll meet anywhere again, but I wish we might.

> Anyway, goodbye and good luck to you.
> Affectionately, your doter [sic],
> MILL [short for 'Amelia'][2]

She wrote to her mother saying she was sorry she had to 'pass out of the picture in such a way'. She regretted leaving her without an income and asked her to destroy all her personal writing, 'without examination'. She added: 'Even though I have lost, the adventure was worthwhile. Our family tends to be too secure. My life has really been very happy, and I didn't mind contemplating its end in the midst of that.'[3]

Her will listed her car, a US Treasury bond, and shares in the Kinner Airplane and Dennison Airport Companies. If sold, her assets should clear her debts and leave a small amount for her mother.

Gordon and Stultz had got to know the plane under the guise that they were part of Byrd's forthcoming Antarctic expedition. When Earhart, Stultz, Gordon, and another experienced pilot, J. H. Lewes Gower, who would accompany them as a reserve as far as Newfoundland, finally assembled at the Copley Plaza Hotel in Boston on Sunday 3 June 1928 they switched to a new subterfuge of pretending they were setting off on a fishing trip.

Earhart's first experience of *Friendship*'s capabilities on that very early Sunday morning in Boston wasn't encouraging. The weather seemed perfect for the first stage of their flight north when they boarded a tug to the Jeffrey Yacht Club, where the plane was moored. But the plane just couldn't make it into the air – not even after they had jettisoned six five-gallon tins of fuel. When she twice failed to lift off from the water Gower did the decent thing and, like Captain Oates, but in a less perilous position, gathered his meagre possessions and hitched a lift from a tug who took him back to shore. Just being one body lighter gave *Friendship* the boost she needed and allowed her to escape into the sky despite her five-tonne weight and the added drag of her pontoons.[4]

When, at the third attempt, they left Boston at 7.00 am, Earhart settled into her cramped position in the cabin behind Gordon and Stultz. She reflected that, in more relaxed circumstances, the Fokker seaplane would have been a comfortable way to travel. Now, however, she was forced to squat on the floor next to a cumbersome motion picture camera with her feet on a 'dunnage bag'. The sack was carefully positioned to stop items in the cabin bouncing around inflight, a sort of bigger version of the plastic pellets that spill out of modern mail order packaging. *Friendship* had four wing tanks – twice the usual number for this type of plane – and an additional two tanks that took up the space where passengers would normally have sat.[5] It was such a tight squeeze that Gordon and Stultz had to turn sideways to make their way to the cockpit. Earhart assumed residency between the two tanks so that she could catch some of the warmth that wafted back into her unheated space.

From time to time, Stultz would struggle to the rear to open the hatchway in the floor and peer down at the land and sea below while consulting his navigation instruments on a small table and the drift indicator on the floor. So long as land was in sight, his approach to keeping them on track was similar to that used by any car driver in the days before GPS. Landmarks, such as towns and villages, rivers, churches, and major roads, offered clues that helped him to pinpoint their position on a map. A compass confirmed he was heading in the right direction.

His real skill emerged when they lost sight of the ground, due to bad weather, or if he was flying over a featureless expanse. You don't get much more featureless than the North Atlantic. It was then that he relied on dead reckoning.

Apart from one window and a hatch, the cabin was enclosed, but Earhart still managed to observe the world they were flying over, the shoals of fish, the subtle shading of the sand, and how *Friendship*'s shadow played over the treetops.[6] She imagined the people they were passing and how, despite their remoteness, they would recognise the sound of an aircraft. Later she wrote of the other pilots and passengers who had gone before her – including Lindbergh, Byrd, and Grayson. As she shifted her perch to sit on a can of fuel, she spotted the green 'mottled' shoreline and the 'scudding' clouds they were outpacing.[7]

She was relaxed enough to doze off but awoke to thick fog and a fierce wind. Stultz found a way through and, having circled the town twice, slipped into Halifax, Nova Scotia where the bad weather forced them to stay overnight and robbed them of any chance of secrecy. A policeman who boarded *Friendship* had the 'surprise of his life' when he discovered a woman in the cabin.[8]

When they left Halifax for Trepassey, and what turned into a frustratingly long stay, they passed a steamer and Earhart wondered if the ship knew who they were, adding gnomically, 'I wonder if we know.'[9]

*

Earhart's team's decision to set off from Boston for Newfoundland took Boll by surprise and she was still in New York while *Friendship* was soaring towards Trepassey. It wasn't long, though, before Boll and her crew were doing their best to catch up with their rival. But while *Friendship*'s team was keen to avoid any perception of a competition, the press had different views and did everything they could to stoke up tension between Earhart and Boll with headlines such as 'Girls Prepare for Air Race Over the Atlantic Ocean'. Even *The New York Times* referred to a 'woman's transatlantic derby'.[10] The possibility of the young German pilot, Thea Rasche joining the starting line-up brought further piquancy to the tussle.

In Earhart and Boll reporters had perfectly contrasting combatants. Earhart in her brown 'knickers' and laced up boots, was cool, reserved, quietly engaged to her heating engineer boyfriend, and repeatedly compared to Lindbergh. The 'Queen of Diamonds' in her haute couture outfits excited chatter about former husbands and lovers wherever she went. Earhart was supported by George Palmer Putnam, 'New York publisher and Arctic explorer'. Boll's closest confidant was Charles Levine, and the Atlantic race provided ample opportunity for reporters to air details of their turbulent relationship, such as the $12,000 court case his business, the Charles Albert company, had recently brought against her and then settled.[11] It was only occasionally that a different woman emerged from the cartoon character constructed by most of the press. In Rochester, where she grew up, she was remembered as a 'bright, small, thin little girl, daughter of one of the city's favourite bartenders' who had married Robert Scott when she was eighteen.[12] The *Ottawa Citizen* even carried a photo of her young son, Robert Scott Junior in shirt and tie, as a freshman at the Aquinas [sic] Institute in Rochester. The newspaper reminded its readers that the 'Queen of Diamonds' was officially 'Mrs Robert Scott, wealthy Philadelphia matron in private life'.[13]

Even their planes and destinations seemed to sum up their differences. *Friendship*'s three engines and pontoons appeared to put safety first. Although he was not officially the leader of the expedition, Stultz was a highly experienced pilot. He'd been astute enough to force Frances Grayson to turn back when she'd been intent on ploughing on with her Atlantic bid and his flight to Cuba with Levine and Boll gave him enough of an insight into the character of *Friendship*'s rival to turn down a seat in *Columbia*.

Stultz had one key weakness, as Putnam wrote later:

> The hole in Bill's armour was his tendency to veer off to alcohol to dull progressively the *ennui* of inaction. I suppose no more ironic difficulty could have risen up to plague a girl [Earhart] who never drank herself, hence knew little about drinkers and the technique – if any – of handling them.[14]

Earhart, whose father had also been in thrall to alcohol, later told Putnam that she was on the point of sending for the reserve pilot Lou Gower to replace Stultz. In the end, her sense of justice held out and she felt it would have been unfair to replace him at this last minute and, besides, she didn't want such a move to be interpreted as a sign of weakness or fear.[15]

Boll's inexperienced crew, by comparison, risked cancelling out the advantages of her plane, *Columbia*, which had already crossed the Atlantic and broken the record to Cuba. Her pilot Le Boutellier had a reputation for caution that was bound to put him in conflict with Boll who longed to fly the Atlantic. *Friendship* was weighing up whether to head for Southampton or the Azores; *Columbia* was considering Paris, Vienna, or Rome. Boll's plane was thirty miles per hour faster than Earhart's, which was slowed down by pontoons.

A news agency report summed up the state of play in the headline:

> Woman to fly Ocean
> Miss Earhart, Amateur Aviatrix, Steals March on Others of Sex by Taking Plane up North –
> Mabel Boll Weeps[16]

Levine, full of bravura as usual, put a brave face on the fact that *Friendship* had taken an early lead by leaving before them: 'If they [*Columbia*] get through to Newfoundland all right and get away within six hours of the Fokker the race will be a walk-away.'[17]

But the press was more interested in Boll's disappointment that Stultz didn't want to join her. She had been under the impression that he had accepted her reported $25,000 offer,[18] but Dick Byrd had persuaded him that Earhart's attempt was more likely to succeed.[19] She was depicted as a scorned lover, who was 'surprised and hurt' and who burst into tears once she learnt that he had departed with another woman.[20]

She was forced to call newspapers to discover what her rivals were up to and told reporters: 'I can't understand it. Wilmer [Stultz] was down here only a few days ago and I asked him when he was coming back to fly the *Columbia.* He said in just a few days and that he would be here today for sure.'[21]

Between sobs that were plainly audible to the eager reporter listening at the other end of the line, pencil hovering over notebook, she continued: 'And now he has gone and taken off with this other woman.'

It took a moment for her to compose herself before she continued: 'My car is waiting down here now and I am going right out to Curtiss Field and see if I cannot take off at once.'[22]

But when she arrived at the hangar she found it locked and mechanics estimated it would take two days for the plane to be fit to fly the Atlantic.[23] If she had paused to glance up at the skies she might have spotted Rasche 'stunting' in her new biplane, her backer Mrs James A. Stillman, wife of a retired banker, as her passenger. Rasche's Bellanca was due to be delivered by the end of the week and she aimed to make her Atlantic bid by 1 July.[24]

When Boll's comments were relayed to Stultz as he waited in Trepassey he replied that she had mentioned the possibility of a transatlantic flight in *Columbia* when they had flown to Havana but that he had made no 'definite' promises and not signed a contract. He added provocatively: 'I cannot see what ails her, unless she is displeased with her present pilot.'[25]

The delay gave the press the chance to accentuate Boll's reputation as a ditzy woman who was more interested in fashion than the serious proposition of crossing the Atlantic. According to reporters, Boll whiled away the hours by deciding which items of clothing she should send ahead of her to Paris. Plans about her jewels went 'whizzing around in her blonde head' before she decided to convey her valuables by special messenger on a liner so that she could wear them at the receptions that would inevitably await her.[26]

On Friday 8 June bad weather meant that Boll, having set off from Long Island, was forced to retrace her steps for the first leg of the flight to Maine. Despite evidence to the contrary, newspapers still reported that she had said she would never start a journey on a Friday.

But, despite this inauspicious beginning, Boll's team managed to catch up with Earhart. They left New York in torrential rain that continued until they reached Nova Scotia. Le Boutillier said the weather was the worst he had encountered in his twelve years of flying. Boll wore a fur coat and flying helmet and was squeezed into the space behind a fuel tank. Argles described how, as they neared Newfoundland, she had not been able to hide her excitement that they were on the first leg of their transatlantic crossing.

Later, Boll said that, although the New York newspapers were doing their best to stoke up bitter rivalry between the two teams, this was not the case. Speaking with a graciousness normally not associated with her she added: 'I would like to be the first woman to cross the Atlantic, but if the fates are against us I am satisfied to be the second. I wish Miss Earhart and her companions the best of luck.'[27]

News reached Trepassey that six barrels of aviation fuel had arrived at Harbour Grace airfield.[28] The delivery was made by a truck from St John's and, although the hauliers refused to disclose the name of their customer, it was widely believed that *Columbia* planned to refuel there before heading out across the Atlantic. In Trepassey, a leak had been found in one of the tanks, which would have proved disastrous out at sea, and dealing with it added to the frustration surrounding the weather delays. Next, a hole in one of the pontoons was discovered and plugged.

*

In an era when even busy aerodromes could feel more like muddy fields or dirt tracks, Harbour Grace resembled a lunar scape with its bleakness and pitted surface. Only the previous year the runway had been cleared by hand of tree stumps and boulders, but pilots still had to contend with potholes and scree. When Harry Gatty and Wiley Post landed there at the start of their round-the-world flight in June 1931 they described what awaited pilots: 'Coming in, planes have to drop over a rocky bluff and land with a downhill roll, but after 2,000 feet the runway slopes uphill. Just beyond the end, the ground rises rapidly.'[29]

It's hardly surprising, then, that Boll admitted to being 'a bit nervous' as she peered through *Columbia*'s tiny window to the scrappy landing strip below. The hundreds (some accounts say thousands) of people who turned out to scan the heavens on Tuesday 12 June watched as the aeroplane 'dropped lightly down out of a clear evening sky' at 8.03 pm before bouncing down onto the east end of Harbour Grace's landing field.[30] The 'vivacious "Queen of Diamonds" stepped to the ground fresh and not at all tired' before retiring to a local hotel.[31] *Columbia* was roped off and surrounded by barrels to prevent over-eager crowds getting too close. Her tail was supported by another barrel. Cars parked as near as they could and children, men of all ages, hands in pockets and wearing flat caps, and women in thick coats against the cold came to gawp at this sudden arrival from the United States.[32] While Earhart, Stultz, and Gordon never wandered far from their plane, Boll, Le Boutillier, and Argles took a tour of St John's and were entertained by the Catholic benefit society, the Knights of Columbus.[33] Newfoundland had been turned into 'an arena in which two American women are vieing [sic] for the glory of being the first woman to cross the Atlantic by plane', a Canadian newspaper reported with a mixture of pride and annoyance.[34]

*

On Sunday 17 June Le Boutillier announced that *Columbia* was all set to take off from Harbour Grace the next morning. But news that

Friendship had departed made his words immediately redundant. After a conference with Boll and his co-pilot Argles, he pronounced the weather out in the Atlantic unfavourable and that *Friendship* must be merely circling the coast to study conditions and not heading out across the ocean. *Columbia* would not be 'drawn out' into an attempt.[35] But it quickly became evident this this was not a recce; Earhart and her team were on their way.

'We have a dandy breeze in back of us and we are going in spite of everything,' she is reported as saying. 'I am confident we will make it.'[36]

It was clear that *Friendship* wasn't prepared to risk *Columbia* stealing a march on them and had taken their chance.

In Harbour Grace, Le Boutillier responded that there were two storms out in the Atlantic and it would not be safe to set off: 'My ambition is to be the oldest living aviator. I am not going to take any chances.'[37]

Boll agreed: 'I just can not imagine Stultz taking such a foolhardy jump with a three-cornered gale raging in the Atlantic. I wish them luck, but I think twenty hours' fuel is not sufficient to carry them across.'[38]

In another report, Boll couldn't hide her agitation and that the team was divided over how to respond. Le Boutillier wanted to continue with their bid to fly the Atlantic while other members favoured returning to New York where they would crate the plane back to Europe to try the bid from east to west.[39]

*

Trepassey, Newfoundland, Sunday, 17 June 1928, 11.15 am.

When *Friendship* finally climbed into the sky on that Sunday morning she had left behind any item that could lighten their load. Out went their spare cans of fuel, the motion picture camera, and the boys' thermoses. They had even jettisoned three cushions that softened

Earhart's cabin seat; instead, she nestled into a pile of flying suits.[40]

Earhart had dressed with practicality and economy in mind. She wore high laced boots, brown 'broadcloth breeks', a white silk blouse with a red necktie, a long, 'homely' brown sweater, battered leather coat with plenty of pockets, and a collar that could be buttoned down, a light flying helmet and goggles. Her 'single elegance' was a brown and white silk scarf.[41] When it grew cold each of them put on a heavy fur-lined suit that covered them from head to toe, including their shoes. Earhart's was lent to her by Major Charles Woolley, an Air National Guard pilot, who had no idea it would be flying the Atlantic.[42]

In a small army knapsack, she carried a toothbrush, comb, handkerchiefs, and a tube of cold cream. Layman, the lawyer employed by Earhart's sponsor Amy Guest, had lent her his camera and his wife her wristwatch. Putnam gave her the field glasses he had used on his Arctic trip and a logbook. She also carried a small number of letters and Byrd's book, *Skyward*, to be delivered to Amy Guest. The inscription inside read:

> I am sending you this copy of my first book by the first girl to cross the Atlantic Ocean by air – the very brave Miss Earhart. But for circumstances I well know that it would have been you who would have crossed first. I send you my heartiest congratulations and good wishes. I admire your determination and courage.[43]

As they had done so often, the crew taxi-ed to the end of the harbour so that they were facing into the wind for take-off. Earhart clutched a stopwatch to check their progress, her eyes glued to the air speed indicator.

If they could edge beyond fifty miles per hour they had a chance of lifting the unwieldy machine off the water.

Thirty . . . forty . . . it was almost possible to feel the effort.

'A long pause.

Then the pointer edged towards fifty. Then, fifty-five ... sixty.'[44]

On Sunday morning at 11.15 am, on her fourth attempt, *Friendship* staggered into the air, her two outboard motors sputtering from the seawater that had drenched them.[45]

Earhart had left a telegram to be sent half an hour after their departure. It said simply:

> Violet. Cheerio.
> A.E.[46]

'Violet' was code for 'We are just hoping off.'[47]

CHAPTER TWENTY

Crossing the Atlantic

Over 2,000 miles away, in London's Mayfair, Earhart's sponsor Amy Guest had been pondering the best way for *Friendship* and her crew to arrive in England. She rather liked the idea of the seaplane alighting opposite the Houses of Parliament on the River Thames. She was probably remembering the stylish way Alan Cobham had descended on the capital after his epic 26,000 mile, round-trip to Australia. Cobham, who was currently touring Britain in his seaplane, touched down on 1 October 1926 to create a perfect image of his aircraft on the river in front of Big Ben and Parliament; a giant Union flag fluttering behind him.

But Guest was denied her photogenic finish when the Air Ministry pointed out that it would be safer for *Friendship* to land at Southampton. Since, as she told the press, safety was the 'governing consideration' of the flight she agreed that the plane should aim for the south coast port instead.[1] Amy, whom newspapers tended to refer to as 'Mrs Frederick Guest, wife of the MP for Bristol North' or if they were feeling informal 'wife of the popular Major "Freddie" Guest',[2] added: 'To be truly helpful to the cause of aviation we had to make this adventure as safe as science and human ingenuity would permit. We have spared no expense to bring this about.'[3]

She wasn't shy about sharing the fact that the 'adventure' had cost 'at the very least' £8,000 (about £422,000,000 in today's money). She didn't know the exact figure because the cost had never been an 'important consideration'.[4] Amy and her family were 'deeply interested in the advance of aviation' and hoped the flight would add to public confidence in planes. 'Only such a friendship will permanently outlaw war and make for a federated world closer in understanding and mutual appreciation.'[5] However, mischievous newspapers pointed out that she had never lost 'an almost fanatical devotion to her native land' and that she spent most of her time in the USA.[6]

Amy, her eldest son, Winston, and, almost certainly, her husband Freddie aimed to fly to Southampton to greet *Friendship*. But, when weather continued to delay Earhart's take-off from Trepassey, Amy turned her thoughts, instead, to a ball she was arranging at her mansion, Aldford House. The building in Park Lane, described as 'one of the finest residencies in London' was built by a South African diamond millionaire at a cost 'running into seven figures'.[7] During the First World War Amy allowed the Red Cross to transform it into a hospital where American sailors were carried up its marble staircase to rest in tranquil luxury.

She spent most of the 1928 'season' at Aldford since her daughter, Diana was due to be presented at Court in a rite of passage that was so important to Anglo-Americans. As Earhart and Boll were studying the weather in Newfoundland, Amy was watching the Prince of Wales sweep Diana round the huge double ballroom at her 'brilliant ball'.[8] The prince would one day – briefly – be King Edward VIII before abdicating to spend his life with his American wife, Wallis Simpson. As he had not been to many private dances lately his presence represented quite a coup, although he was outdone for athleticism by the many polo players who, freed from the constraints of their steeds, took to the dancefloor with gusto. The Duke of Gloucester and the French ambassador were among the other glittering guests who helped to give the dull mansion a little sparkle. The house had been transformed for the night into something smelling like a very upmarket florist's: the fireplaces were filled with lilies, and partygoers had to negotiate walls of carnations.

By comparison, Earhart's cramped seat at the back of *Friendship* provided a capsule of sensory deprivation: the drone of the engines, the faint whiff of fuel, the picnic she left untouched, the pile of flying suits in place of cushions, the swirl of Newfoundland fog. Here she sat, in the back of a rattling aeroplane flying towards night and towards a country she had only ever read about. Earhart, who unlike Guest, Boll, Mackay, Grayson, and Savile, had never crossed the Atlantic by ship, was falling completely under the ocean's spell. Her logbook records a series of extraordinarily vivid impressions, of startling colours and preternatural descriptions – as if she was undergoing some sort of psychedelic experience.

What the logbook doesn't mention is the contrast with the weeks running up to the flight. During that short period, she had left her job as a social worker at the Boston Settlement and met the beguiling George Palmer Putnam. Perhaps she was trying to work out how she felt about him and how he compared to her fiancé, Sam Chapman, who was as safe and practical as his job as a heating engineer. She had thrown her lot in with a woman she had never met and who had selected her as someone to epitomise the high ideals of *Friendship*'s voyage. She kept her thoughts about these momentous events to herself.

The logbook records the plane's movement up and down, like a gentle rollercoaster testing its passengers on the foothills before hurling them into the true thrills and spills of the ride. They sail over eastern Newfoundland at 1,000 feet and, as she studies the lakes below her, they form shapes in her imagination: two are gigantic footprints, another looks like a buffalo and a fourth some sort of prehistoric animal. From the air these watery landmarks appear as primeval beasts with 'lumpy paws and flat head' branded into the earth. She sketches the rough outline of a dinosaur and poses the question 'is this a plesiosaurus [sic]'?

They skim the 'fluffy top' of the fog, having 'wobbled' through to 2,500 feet. Stultz predicts the entire journey to England will alternate between stormy patches and moments of calm. Wisps of cloud pass the cabin windows and from time to time the fog obliterates all light. She remembers how Irish fogs are said to hold fairies and little people and is struck by the uniqueness of her bird's eye view of the weather. They climb to 3,000 feet where the sky is intensely blue; when she sees the water it is 'brilliant'.[9]

At first, they are not quite as alone as they imagine. The cheerful red and white lighthouse at Cape Race, Newfoundland, stolidly perched on its lonely rocky outcrop looking out into the gloom they are heading for, sends a radio message to see how they are going. The ship *SS Elmworth* taps out a hello through the fog.

They climb to 5,000 feet to try to escape the fog but, instead, hit flurries of snow. She can glimpse better weather to the right but not straight ahead. The temperature drops to forty-two degrees, but Trepassey has helped her to acclimatise to the cold. She shrugs on Major Woolley's size forty coat to take the edge off the chill.

At 4,000 feet they are flying through the storm, tons of metal shaking and rattling their bones.[10] They are 'bucking' a head wind and rain.[11] It's by far the fiercest storm she's ever experienced in the air – but now she doesn't have the option to abandon the trip and head for home. The sea below is 'fairly placid' but she knows that, from this height, everything looks flat and smooth.

She can see clear sea ahead but the ride between pockets of cloud and sunshine is bumpy. Gordon visits from the cockpit to tell her that there is snow in the air, but she's already spotted it. Then she makes her way forward when he takes the controls and Stultz is advising him on direction. She describes his 'homing pigeon sense of direction'.[12] He tells Gordon to hold to 106 degrees.

The snow has passed. They enter a stretch of sunshine and blue sea before plunging into a world of perpetual cloud but they're flying at 140 miles per hour and the heater from the cockpit pushes the temperature in the cabin up to fifty-two degrees. Perhaps it is this touch of warmth that allows her to doze off and she curls up on Major Woolley's suit for thirty minutes in an attempt to shake off the headache she started the day with and which was so intense at times that she could hardly focus.[13] When she rouses herself all she can see is 'churned mist', startlingly white in the afternoon sun; ahead, the clouds look like a long shoreline. Halfway across the Atlantic she eats one of her original Californian oranges, which has been with her since Boston, nearly a month ago.

She watches the strange world outside the plane as she kneels beside the chart table on the port side. The folding table is where Stultz studies charts and adds calculations to help him dead reckon his way across the ocean. The radio set is next to it. Although it's possible to stand up in the cabin the height of the table means she can only really see outside by leaning on it or kneeling next to it in a cramp-inducing posture.[14]

At 4.15 pm the clouds form mythical creatures that rear their heads towards them and 'wallop' *Friendship* as she finds her way through the fog.[15] The weather hides the shipping lanes beneath. While they may not be visible, the ships can still trace them via the radio. Although Stultz has been complaining that the radio is 'cuckoo' he picks up a message from the British ship, *Rexmore* who gives them their bearings: 48 north 39 west [700 miles east northeast of Newfoundland] 20:45 GMT.[16] The ship would pass on their position to Putnam waiting in New York, who would in turn convey the news back, passed *Friendship* to England.

Glancing out of the window Earhart sees a rainbow, but not the pot-of-gold fairy tale half-circle but a bright circle with a yellow middle and a round grey shadow in the centre, a fainter ring and, if she can believe her eyes, a third 'suggestion' of a circle at its edge.[17] She ponders whether the phenomenon is caused by their 'props' (propellers). The vision would be familiar to today's long-distance pilots but Earhart's wonderment at the sight shows the extent to which she is flying through unchartered territory.

The fog hasn't finished with them, and she begins to experience the full range of its ethereal qualities. She writes of how 'marvellous shapes in white stand out, some trailing shimmering veils' and how the clouds look like icebergs in the distance.[18] She imagines the plane could 'bounce forever on the packed fog'.[19] The highest peaks of the 'fog mountains' are 'tinted pink with the setting sun. The hollows are grey and shadowy'. The pink vastness reminds her of the Mojave Desert in California and inspires her to try to remember three lines of French poetry to suit the moment.

It is about this time that the stodgy, Christmas pudding-like pemmican is passed around. 'What stuff!' she notes.[20] But it is the weather outside her window that is having the greatest effect on her and which seems to foreshadow the experience of the early astronauts when they viewed earth as no one had seen it before.

As she kneels at the chart table, looking north, the sun is 'splashing to oblivion behind the fog, but showing pink glows through apertures in the fog.' She wishes the sun would linger but knows they will soon be 'grey-sheathed'.[21] The exhaust trail is beginning to glow pink.

'Endless foggies. The view is too vast and lovely for words. I think I am happy – sad admission of scant intellectual equipment.'[22]

She takes photos and enjoys 'gulping beauty'. Her position is so uncomfortable that she worries that she's getting housemaid's knee. Given the circumstances, the medical complaint seems ludicrously misnamed.

As they chase the night, Stultz positions a flashlight so that they can better see the all-important compass in the half-light. But the glow stops the radium from doing its job of illuminating the instruments' hands and numbers and it isn't until it is fully dark that the dials glow again.

When darkness is complete, at around 10.00 pm Earhart continues to attend to her logbook by guiding her pencil across the page using the thumb of her left hand to mark the start of each line. She is reluctant to turn on the light in case it dazzles Stultz as he flies the plane, 'every muscle and nerve alert'.[23]

They climb to 9,000 feet to escape the fog and clouds that now take the shape of 'dragons and sea serpents and monstrosities ... silhouetted against the dawn' and which eventually turn into 'homogeneous teddy-bears'. They all comment on these 'grotesques' and how the fog sprouted 'recurrent mountains and valleys and countless landscapes amazingly realistic'.[24] This aerial mirage is so convincing that when land does, finally, appear it takes some minutes for them to trust their own eyes.

But before that moment comes, they start to worry about the two outboard motors, which had picked up water while they flew through clouds.[25] The port motor is coughing and then all three engines give the impression that they are cutting out. 'Sounds rotten on the right,' Earhart notes in her log.

As the radio had been silent since 8.00 pm the previous evening, there is no way to gather information from ships who could have verified their position.[26] Instead, Stultz is flying entirely by instruments.

When morning arrives, they climb to 11,000 feet to try to escape the clouds 'piled in front of her [the plane] like fantastic gobs of mashed potatoes'.[27] But Stultz realises they can't squander any more fuel trying to leave the clouds behind. As they drop to 5,000 feet to clear the water from the motors the pressure makes Earhart's ears hurt – even though she rarely suffers from this sort of pain. Water starts to drip in through the window as it becomes lighter all around them. One motor is still spluttering as they enter storm clouds.

They've reached the point when they should be about to spot Ireland. Their fuel is running low and if they don't make land soon, they will have to ditch in the sea. To save weight, they had left their life jackets and dingy behind.

They suddenly spot, through a gap in the fog, two boats. The sight of the steamer is so surprising that it warrants four exclamation marks in the logbook. It isn't just the relief of knowing they are near human beings after hours trapped in fog and cloud; they are also baffled by the fact that the ships appear to be travelling at right angles to them, whereas they believed they had been following the shipping lanes. The final entry in the logbook reads 'All craft cutting our course. Why?'

Friendship circles what turns out to be an ocean liner, *SS America*, hoping the ship will recognise the manoeuvre as a request for the crew to paint their position on the deck. After all the careful preparations for the crossing what happens next seems to suggest a certain level of panic.

Stultz scribbles a note on a piece of paper and Earhart puts it in a bag with one of her oranges for ballast. She ties everything up with what she admitted is an 'absurd piece of silver cord' and the package is dropped through the hatch in the plane's floor, like an early Christmas present. The missile misses its mark and a second attempt, with the remaining orange, also fails. At least Ruth Elder and her copilot George Haldeman had been better at target practice when they encountered the tanker that saved them in the middle of the Atlantic.

Stultz, Gordon, and Earhart discuss whether or not to try to land next to the ship but the sea is so rough that this seems foolhardy and it would be even more risky to attempt a take-off in such conditions. Instead, Stultz plays with the radio to try to coax some life from it. Before they close the hatch Earhart lies flat on the floor to take a photograph. Then they retrace the twelve-mile detour they had made to reach the ship. They are risking everything on the belief that they really are on track. They have less than one hour of fuel left. Gordon chooses this moment – which Earhart later described as the 'lowest ebb' – to tuck into a sandwich.[28]

The greyness is all around them: they can see only a few miles of water and the mist forces them to fly as low as 500 feet. Thirty minutes later they spot a fishing boat; soon the one vessel has multiplied into a fleet, almost directly below them. They're relieved to see that the boats are all moving in a direction parallel to *Friendship*. The fact that they are fishing boats is also encouraging because it means they must be near land – although they aren't sure which stretch of land – not that it matters.

A blue shadow starts to take shape in front of them. At first it is as ill-defined and wispy as the cloud formations that have haunted most of their Atlantic journey. But, unlike the previous apparitions, it holds its shape and grows larger and more distinct. Gordon studies it and then dares to name it as land.

Stultz yells and Gordon abandons his sandwich and chucks it out of the window. Stultz 'permits himself a smile'.[29] They start to spot islands, then a coastline but visibility is still so poor that they remain unsure exactly where they are. They pootle over what they assume is typical English countryside of hedges, neat fields and tree-lined roads until it is too risky to continue on their meagre fuel reserves.

They circle what looks like an industrial town before alighting on water; they taxi to a buoy about half a mile from shore and Gordon drops down onto the starboard pontoon to tie *Friendship* to it with a rope they have kept for this very moment.

They open the fuselage door and look out on the rainy landscape – which is much like the one they had left twenty hours and forty minutes earlier.[30] They have crossed the Atlantic.

CHAPTER TWENTY-ONE

Grounded: London, June 1928

They had, in fact, flown over the southern tip of Ireland and crossed St George's Channel, which divides Ireland from Wales. This explains why the ships they saw were not following a parallel course.

The coastline they latched on to then took them east in the direction of Swansea, although they didn't know this at the time, towards the relative safety of the Burry Estuary. They flew low over Pembrey, passing Burry Port Lighthouse, a stunted version of Newfoundland's stately red and white lighthouses. The beacon guided ships hauling coal for export away from Welsh mines and around the world. *Friendship* was going in the opposite direction and followed the estuary inland and towards the port of Llanelli. The 'industrial area' they spotted bore witness to the tin, copper, and coal industries that had driven Wales's Victorian expansion as surely as fishing had kept Trepassey alive. They banked over the New Dock area before returning back down the estuary.

The tide was out, exposing large sandbanks, but the village of Pwll, with houses 'dotted on the green hillside' behind it, provided the stretch of water they needed and they alighted at the western end, opposite the former Crown Colliery, near Tyrwaun.[1]

When they touched down it was 12.40 pm local time, Monday 18 June, and they could hear a 'hum of activity' from distant factories.[2] The beach was 'muddy and barren' and three men were working on the railroad track that runs nearby.[3] *Friendship*'s crew waved and shouted at them but it took a while for the men to spot the travellers and to walk towards the beach for a closer look. Earhart wondered if they were finding it difficult to understand their American accents.[4]

The sight of the seaplane was not sufficient to sustain the men's interest, and they returned to their original task. Three or four other onlookers arrived but ignored Gordon's request for a boat. Earhart waved a towel desperately out of the front window and one of the men on the beach took off his coat and waved back, as if they were involved in some friendly game of semaphore.

It was 30 minutes before a small boat arrived and took Stultz ashore to telephone Southampton. Other boats started to collect around *Friendship* and their occupants pressed Earhart for her autograph. While they waited Gordon napped and Earhart considered a sandwich but decided she couldn't face food. Eventually Captain Railey, whom she had last seen in Boston, arrived by seaplane with Captain Bailey from Imperial Airways and Allen Raymond from *The New York Times*, which had bought the rights to the story. As the tide was racing in, they decided to stay the night, rather than press on to Southampton, and were rowed ashore where six policemen had to hold back what had turned into a crowd who had finally woken up to the significance of their arrival. The throng 'pawed and buffeted'[5] the arrivals and nearly 'tore' their clothes off them.[6] It was only when they were given a cup of tea at the offices of Frickers Metal Company, a zinc oxide manufacturer in nearby Burry, that Earhart felt certain that they were in Britain.[7]

It was while they were taking tea that Earhart started to realise that the 'accident of sex', that she happened to be the first woman to cross the Atlantic in a plane, made her 'the chief performer in our particular sideshow'.[8] No matter how often she tried to point out that

Gordon and Stultz had done all the work, she was unable to deflect the attention.

Outside, the crowd was growing restless and twice the crew had to appear on the balcony to wave – like some aerial members of the royal family. The police guarded the works' entrance and initially refused to admit the chairman and members of the Burry Port Urban District Council who had come as the official welcoming party. Local newspaper reporters were said to be 'worst of all ... like wolves trying to fight their way in'.[9] Eventually police reinforcements cleared a way for two cars who took the crew to Ashburnham Hotel. While fans waited outside, they were photographed and interviewed and had their first hot bath since Boston.

When *The New York Times* representative arrived, he sat down at the works typewriter and pounded out his story late into the night. The newspaper had paid $20,000 for the account of the flight.[10] A local policeman stood ready to deliver each section to the post office at Llanelli as it was ripped out of the machine. From here it was wired back to New York.[11]

*

Sitting in *Friendship*, bobbing up and down on the Burry Estuary, wondering if she could face a sandwich, was Earhart's last taste of normality. The next day the crew flew the 190 miles to Southampton; Gordon, who hadn't been allowed to smoke when they were crossing the Atlantic, puffed away in the cabin as he watched the English countryside drift by.[12] The port was the only seaplane base in Britain and in the same part of the country as Frederick Guest's Bristol North constituency. But it was no longer just the three of them; Railey was with them as Earhart's minder and the reporter from *The New York Times* noted her every move and comment.

Amy Guest was waiting for her. Astonishingly, given the part Guest had played in transforming Earhart's life, it was their first meeting and in the photos everyone looks a little awkward. In one, Earhart is at the centre of the line-up clutching a bouquet of roses; Gordon to her right; Stultz on her left. Guest stands at one end, wearing a hat that almost conceals her eyes. Her ample chest seems further inflated with pride and the fact that the mayor of Southampton happened to be a woman made the occasion feel even more of a celebration of what females could achieve. Except that Earhart was acutely aware that Stultz and Gordon were only ever an afterthought in this brouhaha. She took every opportunity to laud their contribution – particularly Stultz's – and replied to a congratulatory telegram from President Coolidge with the message:

> . . . SUCCESS ENTIRELY DUE GREAT SKILL OF MR STULTZ STOP HE WAS ONLY ONE MILE OFF COURSE AT VALENTIA [southwest Ireland] AFTER FLYING BLIND FOR TWO THOUSAND TWO HUNDRED FORTY SIX MILES ...[13]

While Earhart was whisked away to Amy Guest's home in Park Lane, stopping en route to pop in at Winchester Cathedral, the two men faded from view. Occasionally, they pop up, like chauffeurs invited to sit in a corner at a party while their passenger becomes the centre of attention. Once in a while they were asked to say a few words about the crossing and they laid a wreath on Alcock's grave in Manchester, where a small crowd turned out 'by accident' to see them.[14] There's a photo of them taken on 22 June at Ye Olde Cheshire Cheese, on Fleet Street, made famous by its association with Dr Johnson. They look dapper in three-piece suits, complete with flowers in their buttonholes. They're larking around – holding long, clay 'Churchwarden' pipes – and ensconced in a wood-panelled booth; the cutlery suggests they're about to tuck into a fine meal, but they both have a tankard in front of them and with Stultz there is always a worry that the boredom has led him back to alcohol.[15] In another shot they're outside the Albert Memorial in Kensington Gardens, again in suits but less at ease. They're with three other men and standing in front of a polished car. They don't look like they're having much fun.[16] In truth, they didn't enjoy being in the limelight and often made their excuses to leave; as *The New York Times* put it, 'the two airmen, like old war buddies, have been drifting about the town, seeing what they wanted to see and doing what they wanted to do without molestation.'[17] Gordon also used some of his $5,000 earnings (about $92,000 today) to propose over a long-distance telephone call to his girlfriend, Ann Bruce,[18] who lived in Massachusetts.[19] They married on 21 July, a few weeks after his return to the US and 5,000 people attended the ceremony.[20] The bride wore a dress worth $1,000.[21]

One of the perils of being a pioneering airwoman is that you travel light, and Earhart arrived in Burry with the clothes she was standing up in, plus a spare scarf, a toothbrush, and a comb. Such was her fame that the scarf was quickly snatched away by a fan and she believed the toothbrush and comb only survived because they were hidden deep in the crew's communal duffle bag.[22] When Amy Guest landed with her husband at Hamble Aerodrome, near Southampton, she brought Earhart a travelling case with fittings in gold and mother of pearl, plus Parisian gowns and shoes. She emerged after a good night's sleep at the Hyde Park Hotel unrecognisable in her 'fluttering, printed summer dress', which had been borrowed from Mrs Guest. A few reporters commented that it was 'a little large for her in spots'.[23] She also wore a pair of tiny French shoes and silk stockings but no make-up. Later, when they were ensconced in the Guests' Mayfair home representatives from fashionable dress shops visited to kit her out with a new wardrobe.[24] But she has a slightly comic air in most of the photos and it's hard not to imagine that she would have been much happier in breeches. In one photo she stands next to a British policeman and they both look as though they're in fancy dress.

Meanwhile, everyone wanted a piece of Earhart. Astor invited her to her grand home at Cliveden and was keen to find out more about her social work, Lord Lonsdale took her to the Olympic Horse Show, and she lunched with the wife of the American ambassador. The American correspondents arranged an off-the-record luncheon at which she was the only woman. Her two weeks in London was a 'jumble of teas, theaters, speech making, exhibition tennis, polo and Parliament, with hundreds of faces crowded in.'[25] Amy Guest took all three crew members with her to a concert by the Irish tenor John McCormack at the Royal Albert Hall.[26]

Two moments stood out for Earhart. In the first, she visited Toynbee Hall in the East End of London. The ivy-covered building, built in a 'vicarage-gothic style' was created in 1884 and became the model for Denison House and other settlements in the US.[27] The other event that allowed her to indulge her genuine interests, rather than her obligations, was when she met Lady Mary Heath – originally at the Guests' – but later at the conveyor belt of events that were organised for her, including a luncheon given by the British Air League at the glittering Criterion Restaurant off Piccadilly Circus.[28]

Heath was thirty-two and had just returned from a daring solo flight from Cape Town via Cairo to London. She was able to continue a flying career in which she'd pushed the boundaries of what was acceptable for a woman because the year before she had married her second husband, Sir James Heath, a rich ironmaster and colliery owner who was more than forty years her senior. He had bought her the new Avro Avian III she'd flown back from South Africa and provided her with an allowance to keep flying.

When they met at the Guests' home the two women struck up an instant rapport and Earhart was all for heading to Croydon the very next day to try out one of the light Moth aeroplanes that were becoming so popular among female pilots in Britain.[29] But her enthusiastic plan didn't fit in with the busy schedule set out for her and she had to find a more clandestine way to take to the air.

She was still staying with the Guests under a sort of benign house arrest when, on Sunday 24 June, she rose early and slipped out of the grand house and round the corner where a car was waiting for her. She was on her way to Croydon Aerodrome.[30] As she didn't have a British licence, she went up in a dual control aircraft with Heath at her side, although Earhart took the controls for the entire hour and a half. When Amy Guest and Railey discovered she was missing they instigated a frantic search for her and then rushed to Croydon – only to see her land. The flight was reported as a way for Earhart to prove that she could fly a plane, even though she had failed to take the controls over the Atlantic, but she was so impressed by Heath's aeroplane that she decided to buy it and have it shipped back to the USA.[31] One account suggested that the two women pilots had become so close that they arranged that Heath would buy the plane back to use for her own American tour later that year.[32]

As the time drew near to leave England, Stultz expressed concern about the safety of crossing the Atlantic by ship and said he would feel more comfortable in an American liner.[33] His remarks, just as he was discussing the possibility of joining an aerial expedition to Antarctica with Commander Byrd, were greeted with incredulity but the comments brought home the fact that this would be the first time Earhart, Gordon, and Stultz would see at close quarters the vast stretch of water they had crossed so fearlessly by air.

He needn't have worried. They set off on 28 June on the *SS President Roosevelt* of the United States Lines and it was only then that they realised what they had achieved. As Earhart wrote, 'There never had been adequate comprehension of the Atlantic below us.'[34]

In a curious series of coincidences, the *Roosevelt* had relayed some of their radio messages and Captain Fried, whose ship *America* had watched helplessly as their orange-weighted messages had splashed into the sea around them in the last hour of their voyage, had once skippered the *Roosevelt.* Fried determined that ever after if he knew a flight was in progress he would make a point of having the ship's position regularly painted on her hatches to guide any straying pilot.[35]

Boll and her team left Harbour Grace for New York on 21 June. She thanked the people of Newfoundland for their kindness and presented the president of the airfield with a cheque for $500 towards its upkeep. This was in addition to the fees she had paid for its use.[36] An acknowledgement at Purdue University, which houses an extensive Amelia Earhart archive, also suggests that Levine sent a gracious telegram to the crew of *Friendship*.[37]

At Harbour Grace, the airfield's logbook stood ready to be filled in. The neat headings, handwritten in black ink and underlined in red, had been prepared in expectation of the transatlantic crossing:

> 'Time of Departure from Harbour Grace ...'
> 'Destination ...'
> 'Time of Arrival at Destination ...'

But someone had scribbled in pencil: 'returned to New York'.

PART SEVEN

1932, The First Woman to Fly the Atlantic Solo

CHAPTER TWENTY-TWO

Solo

A few months after Earhart had become the first woman to cross the Atlantic in a plane, and after she had been lauded on both sides of the Atlantic, and celebrated with a New York ticker-tape parade, a seventeen-year-old 'girl flyer' momentarily stole the headlines back from her.

Elinor Smith, 'the flying flapper from Freeport', grew up in a family that valued razzamatazz and biplanes in equal measure. Her father was a vaudeville song-and-dance man who had starred as the scarecrow in a touring production of *The Wizard of Oz* and who hated trains so much that he hired pilots to transport him from town to town. Elinor first flew when she was eight, when her father paid for her to be taken up in a joyride over a potato field on Long Island. When she turned fifteen she became one of the youngest pilots to fly solo and a year later she was the youngest licensed female pilot.[1] Her FAI licence qualification was signed by Orville Wright, no less. From then on, she spent most of her free time at Roosevelt Field, wearing her brother's old clothes, and rubbing shoulders with heroes such as Lindbergh.

On Sunday 21 October 1928, and with no opportunity for a practice run, she responded to a bet by preparing to swoop under four of the bridges spanning New York's East River. From 800 feet up in the air, she studied the water sparkling in the autumnal light, the white sails and dark hulls of the ships contrasting with the concrete and glass of Manhattan's skyline. If she was successful, it would be the first time a landplane had managed the feat.

Smith steadied her flimsy, silver and blue Waco biplane with its thirty-foot wingspan as an Atlantic breeze collided with the heat of Brooklyn's packed buildings. She dropped close to the river's surface to head for Queensboro Bridge.[2] She was aiming to sweep through an arch of 900 feet, which was 130 feet tall, but at the last moment she spotted a yacht heading for the same area.[3] She pulled away hurriedly and then approached from the other side of the bridge – this time aiming for a 750 foot gap. But, as she drew nearer, she saw her way cluttered by a 'gaggle of cables' and large wooden blocks, forcing her to drop within ten feet of the water.[4] As she wove through, she glimpsed a Paramount news camera on the bridge and knew her stunt could no longer be kept secret. She would have to explain her recklessness to the Department of Commerce.

The Williamsburg Bridge was next, until 1924 the world's longest suspension bridge, and she dropped to just above stalling speed to allow the plane to weave round boats and barges. She was feeling so confident that she rocked the plane from side to side in salute to the Fox Movietone team.[5] By the time she faced the majestic Manhattan Bridge she could see another crew, probably Pathé, and several onlookers waving madly. Brooklyn Bridge offered her a pathway to fame but, just as she was about to sail under, a tanker, which had been plodding its way out to open sea, and a navy destroyer, which appeared from nowhere, made the channel feel dangerously cramped. Smith put the Waco into a sudden vertical bank and slid through sideways.

The stunt was undoubtedly reckless, but there was no denying the piloting skill needed to thread a plane under four bridges. The achievement gave Smith the publicity and confidence to take on other challenges. The most gruelling of these was the women's world record for endurance flying – a title which, over the course of a few months, was established and then wrenched away from Viola Gentry and Evelyn 'Bobbi' Trout before Smith grasped it in her frozen mittens at the end of January 1929 after thirteen and a half hours in the icy skies. Photographs showed her mother cradling an exhausted Smith in her arms. When she recovered, Smith resumed her more familiar stance, one hand in a pocket, leaning nonchalantly on the fuselage of a plane.

These exploits, together with the achievements of Heath, Thaden, Nichols, and, in 1930, Amy Johnson's solo flight from London to Australia, reminded Earhart and, perhaps more importantly, Putnam that there was a whole squadron of women pilots chasing her. Many of them were much more experienced in the air and much better qualified to snatch the title of first woman to fly the Atlantic solo. It is easy, with hindsight, to assume that Earhart was always destined to become a feminist icon, but this was not the case.

In her memoir, *Aviatrix*, Smith casts Putnam in the role of malevolent fixer – someone who sought out rivals like her and Heath, offered to help them but, once he had wheedled their plans out of them, used his contacts to thwart their efforts. Promising job opportunities evaporated; venues for speaking engagements suddenly found they were double-booked. Smith claimed that Putnam had asked her to act as Earhart's pilot and mechanic in the Women's Derby of 1929 and subsequent tour but that the contract ruled her out of any speaking engagements or writing commissions during the two-year period. She would also have to agree to stand on Earhart's left for photographs so that Earhart's name always appeared first in captions.[6] When Smith declined the offer, Putnam, she claimed, threatened she would never fly professionally again.[7] It's true that Putnam, who married Earhart in 1931, guarded his wife's reputation carefully but this approach does not fit easily with the support Earhart gave other pilots. Nevertheless, being the first woman to fly the Atlantic solo would put an unassailable distance between her and her rivals.

*

The Atlantic represented unfinished business for Earhart. She had become the first woman to cross the ocean in a plane but told Railey in London 'I was just baggage, like a sack of potatoes' and potatoes may have been on her mind after her enforced stay in Trepassey.[8] It was also when she was in England that she received an envelope that she assumed – from the shaky handwriting – was from an elderly person. Inside she found a cutting from *The Church Times* that quoted the *Evening Standard* as saying that her presence aboard *Friendship* added no more to the crossing than if she had been a sheep. Earhart joked that this was the 'zoological last straw' since, after two weeks of eating mutton at Trepassey, she was certain Stultz and Gordon could not have endured sharing the plane with the animal.[9] Nevertheless, the comment meant enough for her to include it in her account of the flight, *20 Hrs., 40 Min.*

When she returned to the USA, she continued to dwell on her contribution. She wrote that her role had been 'slightly below that of the back-seat driver' because she couldn't even shout loud enough to 'annoy' the pilot.[10] What she seemed to have overlooked was that simply being part of the expedition had provided her with invaluable experience: she'd observed the range of weather conditions and how Stultz had responded to them; she knew what it felt like to be running low on gas and to be unsure of where you were; she knew what it was like suddenly to realise that your radio had died on you. All of this made her the ideal candidate to attempt the crossing alone.

Flying offered the degree of adventure that she thrived on. She set her sights on the Atlantic because she wanted to fly, she needed to. In his biography of her, Putnam admitted that he had known ever since *Friendship*'s successful flight that she would repeat the feat – this time sitting alone at its controls.[11] She wrote in *The Fun of It*, which she completed in 1932, that she had wanted to attempt a solo flight ever since the first crossing. 'It was, in a measure, a self-justification – a proving to me, and to anyone else interested, that a woman with adequate experience could do it.'[12]

Putnam and Earhart occasionally skirted round the subject. The topic hung in the air between them – as it might for a couple in which one partner has a hankering to give up their safe profession for something more risky but dare not broach the subject. The prospect finally crystallised over the breakfast table at their home in Rye, on the coast of New York state. Putnam remembered the morning light as 'pearl-coloured and mysterious, with more than a hint of snow'. Earhart lowered her morning paper and said slowly, 'Would you *mind* if I flew the Atlantic?'[13] He felt a clutch at his heart and something close to elation at her spirit of adventure but at the same time knew the question was academic. He had no power to stop her.

The plan moved one step further when Bernt Balchen visited for Sunday lunch in April 1932. They had left the house to play croquet in the garden against a backdrop of sprouting crocuses and elms and oaks coming into bloom. Earhart paused in mid shot and laid down her mallet to tell Balchen that she had something to say to him. The two men put their mallets to one side and the three of them went to sit on a smooth grey rock, from where Earhart asked Balchen three questions. Was she ready to fly the Atlantic? Was her plane? And would he help her? He paused for a minute before answering 'yes' to each query.

The decision remained a tightly guarded secret only shared with Earhart's cousin who happened to be visiting Rye that day, and the team's mechanic, Eddie Gorski, a sharp-featured young man with floppy hair who had worked with Fokker. The secrecy gave Earhart the option to pull out of the attempt without facing a storm of questions from the press or the embarrassment of failure. Keeping the plan under wraps also reduced the risk of a rival, such as Smith, turning the attempt into a race, as Boll had done four years earlier. Instead, a cover story was constructed in which Balchen had leased a plane in preparation for a polar expedition.

Lindbergh's solo crossing of the Atlantic remained the high-water mark of aviation achievement and Earhart and Putnam planned her attempt on the same stretch of water to coincide – exactly – with the fifth anniversary of his flight. She would not, though, be following his route. Instead, she would take the controls at Newfoundland, whereas he had set off from New York and, while she would, like him, *aim* for Paris, it was acknowledged that Britain was a more likely destination. She would be flying the Atlantic solo but not be in the air for as long.

This time she wouldn't be squatting in the back of a converted Fokker F7 but at the controls of a perky, single-engine Lockheed Vega 5B that she named *Little Red Bus*. The aeroplane, which was painted a brilliant scarlet with gold trimmings, seemed to mirror the optimistic eagerness of her pilot. The Vega was introduced in 1927, and its streamlined structure helped it to gain a following among pilots planning speed and distance records. Harry Gatty and Wiley Post flew one across the Atlantic when they set off from Harbour Grace in 1931 to attempt to fly round the world in eight days. Earhart bought hers in 1930 but a 'nose-over' accident meant the fuselage had to be replaced.

The plane was shipped to the former Fokker plant at Teterboro, New Jersey, close to Balchen's home, where it was transformed into an aircraft capable of crossing the Atlantic. The fuselage was strengthened to allow it to hold the necessary extra fuel tanks in the wings and the cabin gutted to make way for a large auxiliary tank. These new tanks increased the plane's capacity to 420 gallons and gave her a range of about 3,200 miles. With twenty gallons of oil, the plane weighed 5,500 pounds. The additional instruments brought home the special challenges of finding your way over miles of featureless ocean: a drift indicator and three compasses (aperiodic, magnetic, and directional gyro).[14] This caution may have been influenced by the problems Australian pilot Charles Kingsford Smith had faced in 1930 when he became disorientated while trying to land at Harbour Grace after crossing the Atlantic from east to west. Kingsford Smith believed the problem was caused by the special properties of Newfoundland fog and that each particle of moisture held in it was charged with electricity. He was convinced that the process of flying through that fog had caused the steel components of his plane to become charged in a way that made them magnetic and which affected the proper working of his compasses.[15]

It was hoped a new supercharged, 500 mile per hour Wasp motor from Pratt &Whitney would give the Vega extra oomph. Major Edwin Aldrin, an accomplished flyer and father of future Apollo XI astronaut, Buzz, supervised the fuelling at Teterboro and at their first stopping point, Saint John in New Brunswick, before the final refuelling at Harbour Grace. His task was to ensure that fuel was consumed at a rate that allowed for weight to be distributed in a way that kept the plane flying at its most efficient.[16] Earhart motored the thirty miles from her home in Rye as often as she could to take the plane up for practice flights. Most of these hours were devoted to 'blind flying' – that is flying solely by her instruments and not relying on what could be seen from the window.

While the preparations gained momentum, a terrible tragedy within the Lindbergh family provided a reminder of the price fame could bring. On Tuesday 1 March someone broke into Charles and Anne's home in New Jersey and between 8.00 and 10.00 pm snatched their twenty-month-old son, Charles. 'Wanted' posters for the little boy carried photos of him and unbearable details such as 'the deep dimple' in the centre of his chin and the fact that he was last seen dressed in his 'one-piece coverall night suit'. On 12 May, a truck driver found the child's body by the side of a nearby road, not far from the family's home. The tragedy and trial consumed the national and international press for several months.

As Earhart threw herself into preparations for her solo flight her thoughts must inevitably have turned to Stultz. The expert pilot, whom she had always insisted was key to guiding them safely across the Atlantic, had been killed after a horrible 'stunting' accident over his hometown of Mineola in July 1929. Two young men from nearby Roslyn whom he had taken up as passengers were killed instantly but Stultz survived long enough to be transported to the nearby hospital where he died on the operating table.

The accident was even more upsetting because reports called into question Stultz's judgement. He shouldn't have been taking passengers up to go stunting from Roosevelt Field and his Waco biplane wasn't strictly big enough to hold two passengers. Moreover, to attempt the 'falling leaf' manoeuvre at 300 feet was seen by experienced pilots as reckless. Distressingly, the two shoes that were found in the wreckage suggested that the passengers at the front of the cockpit had braced themselves against the movement of the daring stunt and in so doing had jammed their feet under the rubber bar. Their actions had locked the controls and made it impossible for Stultz to pull them out of the dive. Stultz was blamed for not having disconnected the dual control system in advance and for not switching the engine off before impact, although, mercifully there was no fire.[17] An autopsy also suggested that Stultz was drunk at the time but the subsequent inquest went some way to squashing the findings and added that several witnesses who had spoken to Stultz before the flight said he showed no sign of being intoxicated. Earhart attended the funeral and was 'visibly affected'.[18]

*

As the anniversary of Lindbergh's flight approached, Earhart's team started to pore over the weather maps and to ask for Kimball's help. They never told him what they were up to but he must surely have had an inkling. On 18 May – two days before planned take-off – a persistent low-pressure area hung over the eastern Atlantic. Earhart was again caught in the agony of waiting. On 19 May she drove to Teterboro to talk things over with Balchen and to fit in a bit of flying. *Little Red Bus* was sitting, expectantly, ready for the off. Earhart arrived at 11.30 am and Gorski told her that Putnam was ringing from Kimball's office where they had just studied the weather reports gathered from ships out at sea, England, and key weather stations in the USA. Visibility between New York and Harbour Grace was perfect and Earhart decided they would set off that afternoon. She sped back to Rye, changed into her jodhpurs, silk shirt, and windbreaker, grabbed her leather flying suit, scarf, toothbrush, thermos bottle, tomato juice, and maps and was back at the airfield at 2.55 pm.[19] By 3.15 pm she was in the air; Balchen flew while Earhart rested in the converted cabin, next to Gorski. Three hours and thirty minutes later they were at St John in New Brunswick. The next day, Friday 20 May they arrived at Harbour Grace at 2.15 pm. The latest reports from Kimball confirmed the weather wasn't perfect but it was good enough.

So it was that Earhart found herself, for the second time, and exactly five years after Lindbergh had made his solo flight, heading for Europe. Four years after she had crossed the Atlantic, she was a different person and one of the most famous women in the world. She'd completed her book, *20 Hrs., 40 Min.*, about the crossing, and begun a series of lecture tours organised by Putnam to publicise it. *Cosmopolitan* had made her its aviation editor and she wrote regular articles about flying. Transcontinental Air Transport and Ludington Lines employed her to encourage women to travel.

She finished third in the first all-female transcontinental air race, the 'Powder Puff Derby' and in 1929 she set the women's flying speed record of 181.18 miles per hour and secured her transport pilot's license. She also bought and became the first woman to fly an autogiro, an ungainly hybrid of plane and helicopter. Although she set several records in it, it was a distraction and didn't attract the same public interest as flying a plane.

Being part of the *Friendship* expedition had given her valuable insights into crossing the Atlantic and she had become a more experienced pilot since sitting, as little more than a passenger, behind Stultz and Gordon. But a crash during a transcontinental flight across the United States by an autogiro in 1931 earned her a reprimand in writing from the Department of Commerce and lingering doubts about just how good a flyer she was bubbled to the surface. Whether these were justified or not, what she couldn't know was how she would handle the loneliness of flying the Atlantic *solo*.

The world was a different place in 1932 too. The Wall Street Crash of 1929 had ushered in the Great Depression and a period of high unemployment, homelessness, and hopelessness. That feeling of despair was keenly felt in Newfoundland and a few weeks before Earhart arrived at Harbour Grace, around 5,000 people marched through the fog to the grand Colonial Building that housed the provincial government in St John's. Here they presented a petition condemning the corruption of their government. The protestors, growing impatient at the slow response to their petition, started to smash windows and attack the building's massive doors. Inside they broke furniture and tried to set fire to the building. The prime minister was forced to flee to his private residence and to resign while the riots continued outside. Police bludgeoned protestors and many innocent bystanders with their batons.[20]

*

If Trepassey was a patch of Ireland, Harbour Grace was reminiscent of Scotland: a watery landscape of mosses and firs, blending greens and browns together with a painterly texture that made the backdrop look like a colourised photograph. But Harbour Grace felt far less remote than Trepassey. In the four years since Boll and her crew had waited to head off over the Atlantic the airfield had attracted so many other pilots that it now believed its own publicity that it was on its way to becoming the pre-eminent airport for transoceanic voyages.

Gatty and Post had described the stretch of land on which the town sits, pointing out into the Atlantic, as a 'hook-like peninsula'. The airfield is perched above the town on Crow Hill and looks out onto Conception Bay – an area of water big enough to hold several islands and to warrant a story about a giant squid supposedly attacking a fishing boat in the nineteenth century.

'One could scarcely imagine a wilder or more beautiful spot,' Gatty and Post wrote. 'The homes and churches of Harbour Grace dotted the steep hillside that extends down to the black deep waters of Conception Bay. Across the short span of water more rugged hills rose.'[21]

The bay was a 'fiord' and Lady Lake, situated to the west of the airstrip and which has an evergreen forest on its far shore, like a huge eye fringed with 'beautiful lashes'.[22]

The airfield itself was a triumph of local initiative and will and, if things had turned out differently, Harbour Grace might have become Newfoundland's international airport. As it was, Gander, 280 kilometres to the northwest, which opened in 1938, and St John's were to share that title.

On 25 July 1927 a public meeting at Harbour Grace's Town Hall established a twenty-one-person committee and local labourers cut an area 4,000 feet in length by 300 feet wide. They cleared rock walls and dug up tree stumps, finally using a heavy roller weighed down with several hundred pounds of iron bars to smooth out the hummocks. Work was finished on 26 August, just in time for the arrival of *Pride of Detroit* whose pilot, William S. Brock was trying to break the round-the-world record.[23] Most of the pilots who used the runway praised its surface and beautiful setting. Gatty and Post described the field as a 'comparatively level spot in that barren, rocky land'.[24] The airstrip is still used by local flying enthusiasts and in the summer it smells of wild flowers, although the birdsong is largely obliterated by the whoosh of the nearby Trans-Canada Highway. The brutal, rocky cliff at one end is a reminder of the effort needed to transform it into a runway.

Earhart left Balchen and Gorski, who appears in film footage manically chewing gum, checking over the plane while she took a nap at Cochrane House, Harbour Grace's hotel. According to Putnam, she had the capacity to fall asleep suddenly and completely, like a child after a long play, no matter what lay ahead of her.[25] An ability to doze before such a momentous event is a rare gift and one shared by astronaut Gordon Cooper who managed to snooze in his seat while waiting for the countdown to blast his Atlas rocket into space in May 1963.[26]

She was woken just after 6.30 pm and strode out onto the desolate airfield, her elbows pinning her mittens to her side and holding her thermos.[27] She signed a few autographs among the crowds and passed her flask filled with soup made by a local woman, Rose Archibald, up to the cockpit. Balchen handed her a telegram from Putnam and gave her a final briefing, going over her course and the weather she could expect. The engine was warming up and 'sang a sweet song of harnessed power, all of its five hundred "horses" ready to go'.[28] A southwest wind played with her hair and the scarf at her neck fluttered frantically. She asked Balchen if he thought she could make it and he replied breezily, 'You bet'.[29] Film shows her looking intently at the sky as if to read what the weather might hold.

*

Pilots who fly solo over long distances say that this moment before they climb into the cockpit holds a special quality. It's when they walk round a plane that they've come to know intimately and which has assumed its own personality. They'll trail their hands over parts that have been given extra attention or which might play up – where a screw has a tendency to work loose or where oil might start to leak. As one twenty-first century pilot, who happened to be female, put it: 'The walk-round is like a meditation. It's not just a walk-round to check the aircraft – which it is – it's also like a reconnection with the aeroplane. You're turning off the outside world, even before you're in the space of the aircraft.'[30]

When it was time to leave, Balchen said simply, 'O.K. So long. Good luck'. She shook hands with him and Gorski and climbed into the aeroplane. She later said that it wasn't that she *wasn't* afraid but that knowing what she was up against in advance had made her reconciled to fear.[31]

For most pilots, settling into the cockpit brings its own rituals, the order in which you check the instruments, whether you have a good luck charm that you touch before you start the engine. Earhart would have ensured everything was as she liked it, that her charts were close by, and she would have made minor adjustments after Balchen had been sitting in the cockpit.

Although the Lockheed Vega cockpit had windows on three sides, they were not large and the side windows in particular offered only a limited view. Even for someone as slim as Earhart, the cockpit was still cramped and a daunting prospect for anyone in the least bit claustrophobic. Eleanor Smith didn't like the Vega because the cockpit was so high off the ground that her legs rested practically under the engine mount, which made it uncomfortable when the engine heated up.[32]

Everything that would keep Earhart alive was below shoulder height: a messy collection of rudder, gear stick, levers, pipes that snaked around the cockpit, and dials. Directly in front of her she could see her all-important Pioneer compass above her bank and turn indicator. To the left she kept an eye on the gauges that told her how her fuel tanks were doing and when to switch tanks. Compared to the blinking lights of a modern plane she had far fewer dials to monitor but each one played its part in guiding her across the Atlantic.

She scanned the instruments and 'mags' (magneto), opened up the throttle, nodded to Balchen and Gorski to remove the chocks. Gorski, in his overalls with the Fokker logo on the back, swung the propeller until the engine caught. And she was off. Despite its weight, *Little Red Bus* moved smoothly along the runway, which stretched like a strip of sticking tape across the plateau, and lifted easily into the air. It was twelve minutes after 7.00 pm. This was it – just *Little Red Bus* and her. Alone, solo.

Long-distance pilot and later yachtsman Francis Chichester, who was the first pilot to fly solo across the Tasman Sea from east to west, said he thought of people tucked up in bed as he flew over them.[33] But Earhart left no record of this sort of daydreaming, unlike the time when she was crossing as a passenger, she had no time to reach for lines of poetry or to find prehistoric shapes in the clouds.

Many solo long-distance pilots have spoken of the loneliness of their pursuit and of how, at some point, they faced their own demons. Chichester wrote of hallucinations, and how he'd imagined he'd seen an airship. He felt 'intensely lonely, and the feeling of solitude intensified at every fresh sight of "land", which turned out to be yet one more illusion or delusion by cloud.'[34] Nearly three decades after his flight, Lindbergh confessed that he had had a supernatural experience twenty-one hours into his crossing, significantly when there was no chance of turning back. Without moving his head, he could see that the fuselage was filled with 'ghostly presences'.[35] These 'phantoms' spoke with human voices and were 'friendly, vapor-like shapes, without substance, able to vanish or appear at will, to pass in and out through the walls of the fuselage as though no walls were there'. This feeling of not being alone has been likened to the experience of the polar explorer Sir Ernest Shackleton who was convinced that an unseen, benign companion walked with him and his companions over the frozen peaks. No member of the group commented on this at the time, but each man later admitted to the same feeling.[36] T. S. Eliot would later describe this sensation as the 'third man'. If Earhart experienced anything like this, she kept it to herself.

She had started with the intention of keeping a log and jotted down: '8:30 – two icebergs'. A few hours out of Harbour Grace she blinked her navigation lights at a small boat but there was no response, and she was probably too high to be noticed.[37]

The first few hours of the flight were plain sailing. The weather was gentle, and the sunset lingered before the moon appeared over a low bank of clouds.[38] She flew at around 12,000 feet.

Then, something happened that she had never experienced in all her twelve years of flying. The hands of the altimeter, the instrument that tells the pilot whether they are skimming the waves or flying high in the sky, started to swing aimlessly around the dial. She knew that there was nothing she could do to fix it and every time she glanced at the airspeed indicator, positioned to her right just above the joystick, she saw the altimeter with its now useless numbers. She had lost one of the key tools she needed to guide her across the Atlantic and, as if to confirm the seriousness of the situation, at about 11.30 pm the moon disappeared behind cloud and the plane hit a storm that buffeted it around for an hour. During this period Earhart drifted off course slightly. She knew there was no point in turning back, especially given how difficult it was to land at Harbour Grace. Manoeuvring the still heavily laden plane over the wall of rock that bookended one end of the runway would have risked 'a crack up, almost certainly'.[39]

When the storm subsided, she flew on through cloud, unsure of her height. The moon peeked through, persuading her she could rise above the cloud, and she climbed for half an hour until the fact that the plane was labouring made her realise that she was picking up ice. Slush appeared on the window and ice crept over the airspeed indicator so that it, too, stopped working properly. She drove the plane lower hoping that this would melt the ice and went as far as being able to see the waves breaking, although, without the altimeter, she couldn't tell exactly how far above the water she was flying. She continued like this until the fog descended and she didn't dare risk flying too close to the water. Instead, she sought a middle ground – at a level when she would escape the ice but not too low that she risked ditching into the waves. Without the altimeter she was flying on guess work. When she tried to gain height, the plane started to ice up and she decided instead to persevere through the 'soup'.[40] She resolved not to peer out of the window but to wait until daylight and to rely on her remaining instruments. The directional gyro to her top left, which needed to be set every fifteen to twenty minutes,[41] proved a 'real life-saver'.[42] It was fixed on true north and south and was more accurate than the Pioneer compass next to it that could be swayed by the Earth's magnetic forces.[43]

Earhart wrote later that flying by instruments can be easier than straining to see an obscured horizon.

> It is a curious fact that our sense of position in space sometimes depends on our being aware of the horizon. A flyer in a fog is just as blind as if he had a bandage tied over his eyes, and his unaided senses may give him the incorrect impressions.[44]

When Gatty and Post crossed the Atlantic from Harbour Grace in their Lockheed Vega, *Winnie Mae*, they too reached a point when they were flying solely by dead reckoning. Dense vapours swirled about the plane and seeped in through cracks around door. When they tried to look out: 'It was just as if somebody had pasted up the window with a grey material. The dim little light in the cabin threw a ghastly orange glow over everything, and shadows danced in the corners.'[45]

Earhart once said that if she had the choice she would rather 'drown than burn'.[46] By dipping close to the waves to avoid the ice she had risked the first fate and, four hours out from Harbour Grace, fire became a threat.

She wished she hadn't spotted the small blue flame while it was still dark because the fire looked fiercer in the gloom. The flame licking through a broken weld in the exhaust manifold wasn't an immediate threat, but she knew that the damage would worsen and worried that the vibration from the pipe might lead to something more serious, such as dislodging a cylinder.[47]

When dawn broke, she found herself suspended between two expanses of cloud. The first was maybe 20,000 feet higher, the lower layer consisted of fluffy white clouds that allowed her a first daylight glimpse of the sea. The white caps indicated a wind from the northwest and suggested that she must be heading for southern Ireland.

But the cotton wool clouds began to condense and to stretch out like a 'vast snow field'. Particles of ice formed on the leading edge of the plane's wings, and she climbed higher. At this height she encountered another bank of cloud and stayed there for about an hour until she emerged again into a corridor above the white snow fields. This time, though, the sun was able to pierce the upper layer and transform the lower cloud into a surface as dazzling as real snow. Even with dark glasses the glare was too much, and she descended through the lower stratum to more subdued lighting.

Reducing her height also gave her the chance to look for passing ships. About one hundred miles from the coast, she spotted a small fishing boat. Its appearance was 'probably more exciting than actually sighting land' and she circled to make sure that someone would know that she had got that far.[48] The vessel let off whistles and some sort of flare, and, although she couldn't hear the whistle, she could see its smoke and steam. It was her first human contact since Newfoundland. She then kept below the low-hanging cloud, even though she was dangerously close to the sea.

The final two hours were the toughest. Other pilots have reported physical discomfort – aching buttocks and burning eyes[49] – but Earhart said she wasn't particularly tired, just worried by the sound of the vibrating manifold, which Putnam later described as 'like a bony hand rattling a door-knob'.[50] When she turned on the reserve tanks she realised they were leaking and made up her mind to land as soon as possible. She adjusted her course to due east, anxious not to miss Ireland's southern tip, although she was probably nearer its central region.[51]

Other pilots have spoken of the difficulty in maintaining self-belief at this crucial moment. Chichester wrote:

> Doubts began to press on me, and tried to panic me; doubts about the accuracy of my drift reading, about the sextant work, about my compass. My neck ached with twisting, as I searched the horizon ... I was attacked by crazy suggestions, one after the other, to change course and fly North or North-East, or South-East. For each of these in turn there was some clear reason why it was my only hope.[52]

Earhart had entered the period of the journey that long-distance swimmers refer to as 'the swimmer's mile' – the final leg of the journey when success or failure may be entirely down to the willpower and skill of the athlete.[53]

As she followed the coast she bounced through thunderstorms. Without the altimeter she was worried that a mountain would suddenly loom out of nowhere in this foreign landscape. For safety's sake she turned north where the weather was calmer. As soon as she found a railway track, like any good American pilot, she followed it in the hope that it would lead to a city and – with any luck – an airport. The first big settlement she came upon was Londonderry in what is now Northern Ireland. She circled it without finding an official airfield but, instead, scouted out nearby pastures, where grazing cattle were startled by her sudden appearance. She was anxious not to land in a bog and eventually found a long, sloping stretch of meadow.[54] It was later reported that she had just one gallon of petrol left but she said it was nearer one hundred and that she had to pay duty on it.[55]

*

There are several versions of what happened next. But in each, as is often the case in moments of great drama, her exchange with the astonished farm worker was as prosaic as if they had just met in the local shop.

He saw the bright red plane in the distance and arrives just as she is climbing down from the cockpit in the clearing at Culmore, close to Ballyarnett Church, which sits in a small wood.

'Where am I?' she asks – probably expecting confirmation of the country or the nearest city.

'In Gallegher's pasture,' he replies.[56]

The farm hand, confused by her flying breeches, shirt, and short hair, is unsure about her gender.

'Have you come far?' he asks with restrained politeness.

'From America,' she replies.[57]

The farm hand, Danny McCallion, later said he was 'dumbfounded' by this reply as he had no idea a woman was trying to fly the Atlantic and he thought that she must be the British pilot, Amy Johnson. When he first noticed the plane approaching he feared it was going to be 'dashed' against the cottage where his brother lived and where a woman (probably his sister-in-law) was standing holding her baby until she took fright and ran for safety[58] but that the pilot had 'manoeuvred very cleverly' and, although doing about sixty to seventy miles per hour, pulled up twelve feet short of a hedge.[59]

Earhart later described a calmer descent and said she taxied to the upper end of a sloping pasture and turned the plane into the shelter of trees. She did, however, admit that she feared she might be shot as she climbed from the plane if the farm hand thought she was a '"smart Alec" from some big town come down to scare the cattle.'[60]

Several local papers recorded her first words as 'Surely this must be the prettiest spot in Ireland!'[61]

She was then passed from pillar to post in a game of Irish hospitality tag. By the time she landed in Northern Ireland, she was parched and McCallion took her first to his home for a cup of tea from where farmer Robert Gallegher appeared to ferry her to his house where she stayed the night.[62]

Her flight made her the first person to cross the Atlantic twice by air nonstop. She had set a record for the fastest Atlantic crossing (thirteen hours and thirty to forty minutes) and the longest distance flown by a woman. Perhaps most significantly, she was only the second person to fly the Atlantic solo. Personally, she had proved to herself that she could fly blind for five hours and 'still get through'.[63]

*

At Harbour Grace, the official responsible for adding the flight details to the Airport Trust Company's logbook Boll had signed four years earlier dusted down their copperplate handwriting to record the details of Earhart's flight.

They noted that she had started from Teterboro and set off for Paris from Harbour Grace at 7.20 pm and reached Londonderry the next day. They stated that she had travelled as far as Newfoundland with Balchen and Gorski and recorded the oil and gas capacity. But, in case anyone reading the book failed to appreciate the magnitude of her achievement, the scribe added: 'This is a remarkable flight as Miss Earhart is first lady pilot to cross Atlantic.' A photo beneath the entry shows her smiling and clutching a flask filled with Rose Archibald's soup.

Earhart's achievement sealed her fate and her legacy. The artist Walter Sickert instantly captured her unique position as someone who drew a crowd but was, at the same time, subsumed by it. His oil painting *Miss Earhart's Arrival 1932* is based on a photo that appeared on the front page of the *Daily Sketch* on 23 May. The pilot is a tiny, ghostly face lost in the multitudes who have swarmed to see her arrive from Ireland in the driving rain at Hanworth Air Park in Middlesex.

The newspaper story was headlined, 'Welcome "Lady Lindy"! Heroine of the Air Reaches London in a Storm' and shows her arrival after Paramount News had flown her from Londonderry to Stanley Park Aerodrome in Blackpool and then on to Hanworth. The same front page carried news that the *Daily Sketch*'s cameraman E. V. Barton and pilot Major I. N. Clarke had been killed when their plane crashed in thick fog on their way home from reporting the story.[64]

On her second trip to London Earhart stayed with the American ambassador and had a private audience with the Prince of Wales. Department store Selfridge's, run by a famous American of the same name, invited her to sign one of its windows with a diamond-pointed pencil and displayed her plane on the shop's ground floor. Back in the USA, President Hoover honoured her at the White House with a gold medal of the National Geographic Society.

The *Daily Sketch* photo, and Sickert's painting of it, is unusual because it focuses on the crowd – the adulation created by a woman who is lost in that adulation. Most other photographs of the time depicted Earhart at the centre of the action, waving from the steps of the Paramount plane, rather than sheltering under its wing. In the painting the eye is naturally drawn to the red coat of one of the onlookers in an otherwise drab colour palette.

The oil picture went on display only seven days after the photo was taken with a sense of urgency that mirrored the crossing itself and was described by the *Daily Mail* as 'stunt painting'.[65] Sickert's use of newspaper cuttings, like the pioneering pilots, was also pushing at the boundaries of what was thought possible.

Sickert had always been fascinated by celebrity, whether murder victims, killers, or actors, and Earhart represented the latest incarnation of that theme. It was this level of celebrity that shaped the rest of her life.

EPILOGUE

Flight Debrief

In 1929, a year after her fruitless visit to Harbour Grace, Boll crossed the Atlantic – but by ship, not plane. She arrived in France to spend time with Levine as he searched for the perfect aircraft in which to tackle the crossing from east to west. They stayed in the fashionable seaside resort of Deauville where British gossip columnists described how she was 'got up to kill' and 'tinkled' with jewels.[1] She may even have been wearing the $18,000 diamond bracelet Levine had bought her but then declined to pay for.[2]

At Deauville, Levine confirmed his pugnacious reputation by slugging Erskine Gwynne, the American founder of a monthly magazine called *The Boulevardier*, in the jaw. Levine was furious at the 'dirty cracks' Gwynne had made at him in the magazine. Society millionaires and sportsmen rushed to separate the pair and when the air cleared, Boll, 'sparkling with diamonds as usual, took Levine's arm and led him away'.[3]

There were rumours that they planned to buy *Friendship*, the plane Stultz, Gordon, and Earhart had first crossed the Atlantic in, and to take off from the long, smooth beach at Deauville.[4] But, in the end, their transatlantic ambitions only got as far as Croydon where they arrived in August with a new Junkers aeroplane, *Queen of the Air*. Here, Bert Acosta, Byrd's transatlantic pilot and mechanic, made it ready for the crossing but the Air Ministry was slow to grant permission and Acosta also had qualms about sharing the ride with Boll.[5]

The idea of the crossing slowly faded and the pair went their separate ways. Both started to appear in the press for reasons other than flying. In 1930 Levine, who had lost most of his fortune in the stock market crash of 1929, was summoned to court in Vienna charged with counterfeiting French currency. Boll confided to a reporter, 'I cannot believe there is anything serious. He told me he wanted to make me a nice present of a sculptural coin containing my portrait.' The journalist described her as 'hollow checked', 'a ghost of her former self'.[6] It was Levine's ever-patient wife, Grace, who put up the bail.[7] The court appearance was one of a string of cases against him and Grace finally sued for divorce in 1932. Two years later Levine tried to take his own life.

By the late 1930s he was beginning to regain his financial feet by making money out of experimental aeroplanes, although he continued to sail close to the law. In 1937 he was convicted on federal charges of smuggling 2,000 pounds of tungsten powder from Canada and spent two years in jail.[8] The FBI investigated him over tax dodging but couldn't make anything stick. In 1942 he was convicted of a more noble form of smuggling when he tried to help a German 'alien' – and concentration camp survivor – across the Mexican border into the USA. After the war he spent some time living on the streets, until an anonymous woman took him in. He died, aged ninety-four, in 1991.[9]

Boll stayed in France for most of the early 1930s and, in 1931, married Count Henri Boleslav de Porcari in Paris.[10] At the time he described himself as a Polish count but when, two years later, they divorced, it emerged that he was an ordinary American, although it seems he was born in a town now part of Poland and became a US citizen in 1926.[11] Three years later, in May 1934, a young admirer, Georges Charlot, twenty-seven, of Dijon, shot himself in the garden of Boll's rented villa in Nice. She discovered him in a pool of blood on her lawn when she returned one night and later arranged for him to be moved to a private hospital. Charlot, a professional dancer had become besotted with her when he met her at a nearby hotel.[12] In newspaper reports of the incident she was still referred to as 'a former showgirl' and 'Queen of Diamonds'.

By 1936 she told a reporter, who visited her in her rose- and lily-filled apartment in the Waldorf-Astoria in New York, that she was 'mentally cured' of flying.[13] It was her first visit to the USA in six months and she described her previous flying obsession as a 'madness' but said she still owned her trademark gold mesh sweater, valued at $100,000, but that she seldom wore it. She remained partial to jewellery, though, and her newest piece was an eye-shaped diamond brooch that she pinned to her right breast and which winked in imitation of its owner when Boll pressed a clasp. She was wearing a forty-eight-carat ring on her right hand and three strings of plump pearls at her throat but preferred not to display too much jewellery because she had been warned that New York was plagued by robbers.

Her final husband was Theodore Cella, a harpist and assistant conductor of the New York Philharmonic Orchestra.[14] They married in 1940 and her son by her first marriage, Robert Scott, lived with them at 240 West Fifty-Ninth Street, until his tragic death in 1942, aged twenty-eight, from appendicitis.[15] Boll died of a stroke in Manhattan, aged fifty-four – or thereabouts – in 1949.[16]

Elder married her fourth husband, George K. Thackery in 1932. A year later she tied the knot with Albert Arnold 'Buddy' Gillespie and they had a son, William, in 1940. Gillespie worked in special effects and won Oscars for *The Wizard of Oz* (1939), *Ben-Hur* (1959), and *Thirty Seconds over Tokyo* (1944). The latter was about an American pilot taking part in the Doolittle Raid, a daring bombing attack on Tokyo and other Japanese cities in 1942, and many of his other films featured pilots.

Elder's final husband was a movie cameraman, Ralph P. King, whom she married in 1945. They were together for eight years until, in 1953, she divorced him for calling her a 'gray-haired old bag'.[17] She was forty-seven and photos of the time show her still wearing an elaborate headdress, although not quite the 'Ruth Ribbon' that had once been her trademark accessory. A year later the press had caught up with her, as it did all her life, and she is shown prim, matronly, and erect at a desk where she worked as a secretary for an aircraft company executive in Culver City. The image was juxtaposed with a photo of her in her flying days of 1927. The caption reads: 'Once "Miss America of Aviation", Ruth Elder Working as Secretary'.[18] The report explained how she had tried writing and then advertising but the agency failed and how she enjoyed her job because it gave her the chance to talk flying. She married King for a second time in 1956 and died in her sleep in 1977 in the San Francisco apartment she shared with him. Her ashes were scattered over the Golden Gate by an Air Force plane.[19]

Her co-pilot, George Haldeman, by comparison, spent his entire career in the air. The year after he and Elder had got as far as the Azores he teamed up with Eddie Stinson, who had designed *American Girl*, to break the world non-refuelled endurance record by spending over fifty-three hours in the air. In the Second World War he led the Federal Aviation Administration in its Test Flight Branch, helping to decide which planes the US Army Air Corps would take to war. By 1977, five years before his death, he had clocked up 34,000 hours in the air.[20]

Unlike Stultz's tragic ending, Slim Gordon enjoyed a long and largely uneventful life. He and the girlfriend he had proposed to via an expensive long-distance phone call from England divorced in 1933. He always believed he didn't earn enough for her – and her $1,000 wedding dress must surely have offered a clue as to her tastes.[21] He gave up flying in 1938 after 'several questionable landings', remarried and in 1941 legally changed the name he was born with – Lewis Elwood Avaritt – to Louis Edward Gordon. He joined TWA Transcontinental as a Senior Mechanic-Maintenance and worked for the company for the next twenty-three years. At his death, in Kansas City, Missouri, in 1964, aged sixty-two, he had reached the position of inspector for TWA.[22] His passing went largely unmarked by the national press.[23]

When an aerial survey of Northwestern Ontario in 1927 discovered several large lakes that didn't appear on modern maps the Department of the Interior decided to use the opportunity to honour the many crews lost trying to cross the Atlantic. Savile is remembered in lakes Wertheim and St Raphael, the latter named after her plane, and her pilots live on in lakes Minchin and Hamilton. Since Savile was heading for Canada's capital of Ottawa the honour feels particularly appropriate. Lakes Grayson, Goldsborough, and Omdahl (sic) remember *Dawn*'s flight. [24]

Mackay is memorialised in a stained-glass window at Glenapp Church in southwest Scotland, near the sinuous roads she used to career around in her silver Rolls-Royce. For several years it was possible to make out her first name in the rhododendrons and azalea bushes planted by her parents to remember her on the hill opposite.[25]

Hinch's widow, Millie, remained convinced that her husband had lost his life, as reported by the spirit guide, near the Azores and left instructions that her ashes should be scattered there. She and her two daughters emigrated to Australia and her granddaughter who, like her mother and aunt, had become a pilot carried out her wish in 1982.[26] At the time of her death, Millie had eleven pounds left of the money given to her by Inchcape.[27]

The George Hotel at Leadenham closed after the COVID pandemic but a story persists that a tall airman wearing a patch over his left eye could sometimes be seen striding over the courtyard on a March evening at twilight.[28]

Amy Guest, who made Earhart's first crossing possible, continued to divide her time between Europe and America. Although their marriage had not always been happy, her husband's death in April

1937 at the age of sixty-one still saddened her. Their son Raymond flew home in a specially chartered plane from Cherbourg to be at his father's side in his final hours at his country home at Sunbury-on-Thames, Middlesex; his siblings Amy and Winston Guest had already arrived by liner from their home in Palm Beach.[29]

By then, Amy's relationship with the Churchills had mellowed and she wrote to thank Winston for his friendship.[30] While her husband was in his final illness she contacted Winston about the passport she gave up when she became an American citizen in 1923. She was worried that someone was using the document to impersonate her and that she might be viewed as a spy. Churchill went out of his way to obtain an official letter to reassure her that there was no danger of this happening.[31]

Amy lived to be eighty-six and died in Geneva. She had an apartment in Manhattan and a summer house on Long Island but spent much of her time in Palm Beach. During the Second World War she handed over her Florida mansion so that sailors could use it to convalesce, just as her London mansion had served injured servicemen in the Great War. All her life she had been fascinated by politics and before the Suez crisis of 1956 she met Israel's prime minister David Ben-Gurion and President Gamal Abdel Nasser of Egypt.[32] The following year a survey by *Fortune* magazine placed her eleventh in a list of the seventy-six richest Americans and estimated her fortune at between $200,000,000 and $400,000,000.[33]

While the Guest money was inherited, Earhart's income had always relied on lecture tours, journalism, and the next flight. Encouraged by Putnam, she tried her hand at fashion design and opened a shop within Macy's department store, but its success was short-lived – although who could resist any garment with a label that incorporated her signature with a red plane soaring across it? In the autumn of 1935, she joined the faculty of Purdue University, where she offered careers advice for women and advised on aeronautics.

In 1934, their family home in Rye burned down and she lost many irreplaceable papers, most painfully, writings from her youth. *Friendship*, which had been her home for twenty hours, forty minutes, suffered a similar fate. Donald Woodward, a millionaire aviation enthusiast from Le Roy in New York state whose father owned the patent for Jell-O, bought the plane from Guest in 1928.[34] Less than a year later he sold the plane to a group of wealthy Argentinians led by José Roger Balet, who hoped to fly her from South America to Spain. But two years later she was used to transport five men from Argentina to Chile in what was said to be an attempt to overturn the government.[35] General Enrique Bravo made her part of the Colombian National Air Force, and she appears to have been destroyed by fire in 1934.[36]

Earhart made several solo flights that proved her Atlantic crossing was no fluke. In 1935, she became the first pilot to fly solo from Hawaii to the American mainland, making her the only person to have flown solo across the Pacific Ocean and the first to have flown alone across both the Atlantic and Pacific Oceans.

Although it is sometimes claimed that GPP was the driving force behind this expedition, a typed letter held in the National Archives in Kew shows how keen she was to make the flight and that she was prepared to play her part in smoothing diplomatic waters to make this possible. The letter, which she wrote in February 1937 to Sir Francis Shelmerdine, Director of Civil Aviation, when they were still planning the westward route, beginning with the Pacific, stressed how her flight had been approved by the US State Department but that she needed permission from the British Government to fly over 'Arabia'. By this she meant the patchwork of territories that is today dominated by Saudi Arabia, the United Arab Emirates, and Yemen.

Shelmerdine had greeted her after her solo flight in 1932 and they had both joined a sailing party in the Channel. She wasn't shy about using that connection and it must have been flattering for Shelmerdine to receive a letter from such a famous woman who was eager to confide her plans in him. She reassured him that she had made many take-offs when *Electra* was full of fuel, that the plane could survive on one engine and that she had already flown 900 miles from St Louis to New York. She concluded: 'This letter then is to request such permission as may be necessary and any special instruction or guidance which it is in order that I should receive. I am deeply grateful for your interest and such cooperation as you may be able to extend.'[37]

The letter was partly successful and he replied that she could fly direct from Aden, in southern Yemen, which was an independent state but which Britain still had some influence over, to Karachi (then in India) but that she must not fly over Muscat, which was part of a sultanate, or over the imamate of Oman – both in the far north of the peninsula – and that she must respect the three-mile exclusion coastal zone in the area. He wished her well for the flight and regretted that she wouldn't be visiting Britain so that they could renew their acquaintance.[38]

A further memo in the files shows that Earhart's representative in London, Viscount Jacques de Sibour, who was Gordon Selfridge's son-in-law, requested the official Resident in the protectorate of Aden should advise on a possible landing place. Shelmerdine, though, had pointed out the considerable risk of touching down on the Arabian coast and the expense and difficulty in launching a rescue operation. De Sibour countered, with great prescience, that the risk was not as great as the danger Earhart faced in what, at this point in time, was the first leg of her flight – the Pacific section, from San Francisco to Honolulu and from there to Fiji.[39]

In the event, this westward route was not tested because, on 20 March 1937, *Electra*, with Earhart at the controls, crashed on take-off from Luke Field, Honolulu, Hawaii on its way to the tiny island of Howland. Accounts differ, but the accident was due either to a wet runway or a blown tyre.

Less than three months later, on 1 June 1937, Earhart resumed her round-the-world bid, but this time flying in the opposite direction due to a seasonal shift in the prevailing winds. She travelled eastbound from Oakland to Miami then on, via Central and South America to Africa and then north towards India, before heading for Singapore and the Pacific. *Electra* had undergone major repairs and there was now just one navigator on board. Harry Manning, who had a much keener understanding of the plane's modern radio direction finder, was no longer available. Instead, the sole responsibility for guiding the plane around the world would rest with Fred Noonan, forty-four, an experienced navigator who had guided Pan American flying boats across the Pacific eighteen times.[40]

A month shy of forty, there was a sense that this was Earhart's last 'stunt' flight before she settled down to a more sedate life of lecturing and working at Purdue University. But, nine years on from her first crossing of an ocean, this was a much more ambitious expedition than any she had taken on and cracks in the pilot-navigator relationship began to appear after they crossed the South Atlantic. Earhart ignored Noonan's advice to turn south in order to reach Dakar, in French West Africa (now Senegal), but, instead, headed north to fly fifty miles along the coast until she realised her mistake.

Over the next few days they sped through the continent of Africa until, on 12 June, they reached the shores of the Red Sea. From here they flew to Karachi (then part of India) and two days later pressed on to Calcutta and Burma (now Myanmar). By 20 June they were at Singapore but stayed several days longer than expected at Surabaya and didn't reach Port Darwin in Australia until 27 June. By the time they arrived at Lae on New Guinea it was 29 June and they had flown a total of 35,405 kilometres (22,000 miles). They still had 11,265 kilometres (7,000 miles) ahead of them to reach Oakland, but before that they had to aim for their next refuelling point of Howland Island, a three-kilometre (two-mile) long sandbar, which was less than a mile wide.[41]

Their destination was 4,113-kilometres (2,556-miles) out in the Pacific.

They left Lae on 2 July, keen to be home in time for 4 July and the extra press attention this date would garner in an expedition that had rarely made the front pages. But Earhart was worried about the weather, which was deteriorating, and there seems also to have been tension between Earhart and Noonan. Earhart hadn't been eating much and was exhausted after a month-long expedition. She may also have been concerned about her own ability to use a radio and the fact that neither she nor Noonan were well-versed in Morse code.

As they left Lae the US Coast Guard cutter, *Itasca*, sat waiting off Howland to help guide them to their destination. But, worryingly, *Electra* wasn't responding to the weather reports *Itasca* sent. Then, just before 3.00 am, the chief radioman on *Itasca* recognised Earhart's voice amid the static. Later he heard KHAQQ (*Electra*'s call letters) and Earhart saying that she would listen at the frequency 3105 kilocycle on the hour and half hour. But when *Itasca* tried to reach her there was no response. Her words came and went over the next few hours, but the conversation was a one-sided monologue fizzing with static. She didn't appear to be able to hear *Itasca*'s responses and this may have been due to a lost antenna. At 7.42 am she said she must be over the cutter, flying at 1,000 feet, but couldn't see the vessel. One radio man thought he heard her say they had only thirty minutes of fuel left. At 8.00 am she said they had heard *Itasca* and asked for a reading. The cutter was now listening on all wavelengths, not just the one she said she had heard *Itasca* on.

At 8.43 am, the voice, sounding distressed, said they were flying along a 'line 157 337' – travelling northwest to southeast on a path that would bisect Howland Island. The problem was that if they failed to see the island they would not know if they'd simply missed it, or whether it lay further ahead. To the northwest they faced thousands of miles of ocean; to the southeast – on the line – lay the uninhabited volcanic atoll of Nikumaroro. Earhart urged *Itasca* to 'Wait'.[42]

And much of the world did wait, its breath held in a communal act of hopefulness that continues today.

As soon as it was realised she was missing, the US government launched a massive search but found no trace of Earhart, Noonan, or their plane. Putnam continued to finance his own investigation until October 1937.

Earhart was declared legally dead in 1939 but theories about how she died have gathered momentum over the years. Some speculation has been so far-fetched as to enter the realm of fantasy – that she was captured by Japanese soldiers, that she was spying for the American government, or that she turned back and resumed her life under an assumed identity.

More plausible and rigorously tested theories at the start of the twenty-first century focus on four areas of evidence: the radio messages sent by *Electra*; a grainy photo of the coastline at Nikumaroro; a pile of bones; and, most convincingly for me, a few items probably belonging to a 1930s castaway.

Nikumaroro has become the focus for the most hi-tech search, led by Bob Ballard, famous for discovering the wreck of the *Titanic*. The tiny speck of coral has gained notoriety as *possibly* Earhart's final resting place because of various clues that seem to point to its location. On the day that Earhart's plane was desperately trying to find Howland, Pan American Airlines and coast guards picked up communication that could only have been transmitted by Earhart's plane because of the unique signal it emitted during the day. These signals, a bit like an aerial 911 or 999 call, were reported to the Navy who plotted the different bearings on a map and found the lines converged at Gardner Island (now Nikumaroro), in the southwestern Pacific republic of Kiribati. At the same time dozens of radio 'hams' in the US, Canada, and the central Pacific, picked up ghostly distress calls from a woman, speaking English and sometimes giving her name as 'Amelia Earhart'.

Many twenty-first century investigators, including The

International Group for Historic Aircraft Recovery (TIGHAR), believe Earhart and Noonan started to send signals when they landed at Nikumaroro.[43] This would have been possible if the plane was not in the water and records suggest the tide was low enough during this time to allow the engine to run and thus to power the radio.

Nikumaroro is four and a half miles long and one and a half miles wide, a sand and coral pincer that surrounds a lagoon that contains no fresh water. The sides of the atoll shelf steeply down to an underwater volcano. The island is covered in coconut trees and thick scrub. When today's Earhart investigators aren't visiting it is ruled by coconut crabs that can be as large as three feet in diameter and which are capable of catching a bird and stripping meat from any carcass they scrabble over.[44] They, too, have played their part in perpetuating the Earhart myth.

A photo, which was taken in October 1937, of the wreck of the British *SS Norwich City*, which sits mouldering off the northwest corner of Nikumaroro has also excited interest because it appears to show an object protruding from the waves. To some observers, this could be *Electra*'s landing gear – a large wheel encased in metal – that might have been knocked off during a forced landing. To others, the fuzzy black area is as murky as the photo of the Loch Ness monster taken about the same time.

In 1940, a Colonial Service officer discovered thirteen bones under a gnarled tree that he thought might belong to Earhart. The bones, which may have been deposited there by feeding coconut crabs, were found near the remains of a campfire. The officer also uncovered two shoes – a man's and a woman's – and a box that had once held a sextant. The bones were sent to Fiji, measured, and then lost until part of a skull and other bones thought to be a woman's were found at the start of the current century.[45] The distinctive gap in Earhart's front teeth and the surgery she had on her nose to relieve her sinus problems seemed to offer the ideal way to determine whether this was, indeed, her skull.

But, so far, the evidence has proved inconclusive, and the bone has degraded to such an extent that DNA analysis has been unsatisfactory. Superimposing an image of the remains of the skull onto a photo of Earhart seemed to match the placement of her eye sockets and bring her eerily into view but this remains an incomplete spectre.

Rather than clinging to the theory of bones or a blurry photo, it seems much more likely that *Electra* ran out of fuel, was swallowed by the ocean and, if she made it to Nikumaroro, was knocked off the sharp coral cliff that surrounds the atoll to bounce down to the seafloor, or if she was heading in the opposite direction, that her aluminium frame casing was eventually pounded into submission and dispersed among the miles of open sea. Except ...

The area, where the bones and objects have been found, called the Seven Site, has become the focus of intense investigation. It shows signs that several campfires were lit and that the castaway(s) ate birds, fish, turtles, and clams. The way that they consumed what was probably their final meals – the fact that they couldn't stomach the fish heads – suggests this was a Westerner and not a pacific islander.

Seven Site gave up other secrets: a metal zipper, which analysis dates from 1933 to 1938 and that appears to have been fairly heavy-duty – the type you would find in a flying jacket or trousers;[46] five glass shards pieced together to form a nearly complete jar, resembling a bottle used to reduce freckles, and another find appears to be a 1930s make-up compact that may have contained rouge.[47] Did they belong to the aviator who was said to be self-conscious about her freckles and who was aware she needed to look presentable for photographers? This is all circumstantial evidence; finding part of the plane, ideally the two Pratt & Whitney Wasp S3H1 engines, would stamp a much more conclusive full stop on the mystery.

Ballard has scoured the area for signs of Earhart using banks of computer screens to survey the ocean floor, powerful drones to take a gull's eye view and remotely operated vehicles (ROVs) that scoop up objects like a grabber at a funfair desperate to seize part of a plane but which are too often disappointed with coral-encrusted shapes that to the over-eager eye morph into aviation debris. As he searched the sea, archaeologists and sniffer dogs hunted the atoll for human remains, wondering whether the grotesque coconut crabs know what happened to Earhart. So far there is no *Titanic*, no ghostly appearance of an object that was clearly a plane.

That moment was said to have arrived in January 2024 when Deep Sea Vision, an ocean exploration company, used sonar imaging to capture the golden outline of what looked like a plane, 4,877m (16,000ft) below the ocean's surface near Howland Island. The image, which appeared like a smudged, Turin-shroud outline, later turned out to be an 'unfortunate rock formation'.[48]

Whatever happened to her, her disappearance has taken the concept of 'ambiguous loss' to a new level, affecting people born after she went missing. Putnam died aged sixty-three, in 1950, and although he was a publisher, explorer, and author of ten books, he would always be best known as 'Amelia Earhart's husband' – a role he fulfilled for six years.[49] The *New York Herald Tribune*'s tribute to her praised her for her ability to find her place in a man's world but at the same time couldn't resist describing her as a 'lovely lady', adding: 'A tall girl, with a brave smile and tawny, tousled hair has gone to join the gallant group of men who have gone down to the sea in ships, and the ghostly gathering in Heaven's Hangar will welcome her as one of their clan.'[50]

Her many solo flights should have been enough to ensure her place in the history books, but legacies don't always work like that. It was undoubtedly her mysterious, to date, unsolved death, that fixed her place in the public imagination. It is this tragic, unfinished ending that helped her to become a feminist icon but also pushed her into a category rife for commercial exploitation. It made her an obvious model for a Barbie doll, dressed in brown, laced boots, flying trousers, leather jacket, her helmet under one arm, goggles round her neck. Her fame also ensured she lived on in Lego form and the Earhart minifigure with moulded plastic, tousle-free hair holding a map of the world next to her *Little Red Bus* was produced to celebrate International Women's Day in 2021.

But it's the artifacts that she touched, wore even, that are most in demand, as if they physically embody her spirit. This is no more evident than in the flying helmet she sported when she first landed at Trepassey, and which fascinated the young Laura Devereaux. The battered piece of leather had been expected to raise $80,000 when it was sold at an online auction in 2022. On the day it fetched $825,000, making it the most valuable piece of Earhart memorabilia to go under the hammer. [51]

*

Today, taking a seat in an aeroplane is always accompanied by a twinge of guilt. Can the litres of toxic aviation fuel expended in a transatlantic flight ever be justified? I'm flying to a part of the world I've only previously visited in my dreams and then I'll be inflicting more damage on the environment by continuing on to Toronto to visit my in-laws for the first time in their home city. Can this combination of research and familial bonding make up for my contribution to the sizzling ozone?

Part of me hopes that the discomfort of the flight will somehow salve my conscience. But, with a fair wind, the journey time from London Gatwick to St John's, Newfoundland is barely five hours – only a little longer than the journey to a summer holiday in the Mediterranean. Like most of the first transatlantic flyers I'm feeling exhausted, but not because my eyes are scratchy with the strain of scouring the sky for signs of land and scanning my instruments to check that all is well, but because I've stayed up late at an anonymous airport hotel to await news of the UK's general election. As my Boeing 737 taxis off, a shiny black Range Rover is sweeping a new prime minister to Buckingham Palace. On my return, less than two weeks later, he will seem as well established as someone who had been in the post for years. Air travel has a strange effect on time.

I've paid extra for an aisle seat and have much more leg room than Amelia Earhart squatting at the back of *Friendship* or Savile in her wicker chair. Nevertheless, the passenger next to me still manspreads his scrawny, tanned legs so that I pivot my body away from him. He's heading home to Newfoundland after a walking holiday just forty-five minutes from my hometown in East Anglia. Next to him, in the window seat, a younger man is returning from the United Arab Emirates. He says it's only possible for him to teach in his lucrative job because he can make regular flights back to his family in St John's. In a way, he's like the early Irish fishermen who left Europe for long stretches of time to harvest the cod of Newfoundland until, in 1992, a moratorium brought an end to that trade and devasted communities like Trepassey. Around us, disgruntled babies mither and parents do their best to placate them. The world is now peppered with so many airports that each has their own, three-letter International Air Transport Association (IATA) Location Identifier. Gatwick is LGW; St John's is YYT. Although light aircraft still use Harbour Grace, it never fulfilled its initial ambitions to be an international airport and has no need for such an acronym.

For weeks before the flight I swipe through my weather app to compare the temperatures in parts of the world where I have emotional connections: my hometown, my favourite places in Italy and France, and in Newfoundland. Cambridge, Pontremoli, Le Havre, Trepassey. The weather in Newfoundland is so often foggy and drizzly that my husband insists that I stop because it's depressing.

The early transatlantic flyers didn't have the luxury of such accurate weather forecasts. Nor did they have today's instant communication that makes the command 'switch to airplane mode' so important as we lift off. I can even pay extra to watch England play live in the football

Euros, but why inflict pain into what promises to be a smooth ride? Unlike Elder, Mackay, Grayson, Boll, Savile, and Earhart I don't have to shout to be heard and, unfortunately, I can make out every word my neighbour says above the white noise of modern air travel. Indeed, such is the smoothness of this journey that there's a temptation to believe that we haven't left the ground at all, that it's all fake and that we're extras in *The Truman Show*.

Except that if I glance across the passengers to my right and through the rectangular window of dazzling blue sky, I know I will glimpse a tiny red plane, rocking slightly under the weight of the extra fuel and travelling in the opposite direction, out across the endless waves towards the distant horizon. That plane, and the planes of all the other pilots who tried to cross the Atlantic – even if they failed, – are the reason I'm here and why passengers of all ages and from around the world are able to fly to meet family and friends. They're the reason politicians can hold face-to-face peace talks and why scientists and activists can gather to strategise about saving the planet. Their flights and the new versions of planes they necessitated made the world a little smaller. They could not have known the environmental havoc they had unwittingly set in motion.

The concept of flying *solo* no longer exists and even a pilot alone in their cockpit is in constant communication with the wider world. Only the woman in the *Little Red Bus* outside my Boeing 737 can appreciate the loneliness and fear explicit in the word 'solo'. I don't know whether the pilot at the controls of the plane that guides us expertly into St John's airport, the most easterly airport in North America, is female. It would be a neat ending if they were, but in a sense that no longer matters – and that's down to the achievement of six remarkable women and their crews.

Acknowledgements

Producing a book is a bit like a transatlantic flight: it requires a lot of planning and considerable faith. I'm grateful to Simon Wright for commissioning *Atlantic Furies* in the first place and, while I was sorry he wasn't able to see the project to lift-off, I feel very fortunate that Laura Ali was there to guide the manuscript through its various stages with great skill, good humour, and efficiency. It was my good fortune, too, that Maria Bedford joined Scribe when she did and I have valued her insight, knowledge, and experience. Thank you to my agent Eleanor Birne for making this all happen.

Unlike the women I've so enjoyed writing about, I am not a natural traveller. I'm even more grateful, then, for the warmth and hospitality of the people I met when I did venture out from behind my desk. *Atlantic Furies* sent me to Canada for the first time and it was a joy to visit my family there. Thank you to Bob and Heather; David, Kim, Caden and Autumn; Bronwen, Eddie, Cole, Lyla, and Luke; Megan, Ayva, Liam and Julian. Thomas, Vic, Max, Kate and Nick, we'll see you next time.

In Newfoundland, Genevieve McCorquodale and Lorne Warr could not have been more welcoming. Their documentary is a mesmerising introduction to a place few people have the chance to visit. The Edge of the Avalon Inn was the ideal base from which to experience food inspired by the sea, while you listen to the local stories shrouded in fog, ever hopeful of spotting whales.

The volunteers at Conception Bay Museum, Harbour Grace, proved the perfect guide to a spot that welcomed so many characters from the world of aviation. The Rooms cultural centre and archives at St John's are not to be missed and the collection at Memorial University of Newfoundland was worth the hurried detour on the way to the airport.

The following have been helpful from afar: Kim Sulik, Archivist/ Records Manager, New York County Surrogate's Court; Purdue University Archives and Special Collections (and in particular Katey Watson); Sikorsky Historical Archives and Schlesinger Library, Harvard Radcliffe Institute.

In the UK, I'm grateful to the British Film Institute (and to Steve Tollervey); the Royal Air Force Museum and the Imperial War Museums and The Churchill Archives. Thank you to the staff at the University of Cambridge Library – whose librarians always manage to hunt down a book, no matter how obscure.

Talking to *real* pilots was a thrill and I'm particularly grateful to Mel Luck and Tony Hoskins. Authors Sîan Evians and Jayne Baldwin have been incredibly generous and, particularly in the case of Jayne, it has been like discovering we share the same close friend – Elsie Mackay. I was grateful to Sara Hillin for giving me access to chapters from her wonderful book, *The Rhetorical Arts of Women in Aviation, 1911–1970*. The Society of Authors has offered invaluable advice and support. Steve and Gabrielle Bennett were again kind enough to provide a blissful retreat in which to finish writing this book. I'm grateful to Faith Evans for her incisive comments on the manuscript.

Thank you to Rosa Kelly for being there all the way and to Jim Kelly – there's no one I'd rather stand next to in the rain watching whales leap into the air.

The extract from *Speaking for Themselves* is reproduced with permission of Curtis Brown, London on behalf of Portland Churchill Ltd © Sir Winston Churchill Archive Trust CAM College. Extracts from correspondence from Winston Churchill is reproduced with permission of Curtis Brown, London on behalf of Portland Churchill Ltd © Winston S.Churchill / Portland Churchill Ltd. My thanks to Lord Inchcape for his permission to quote from the letters of his great-grandfather. I acknowledge the help of the Syndics of Cambridge University Library and the Society for Psychical Research.

Bibliography

Books

Addison, Paul, *Churchill: The Unexpected Hero* (Oxford; New York: Oxford University Press, 2005)

Adams, Lucia, *Wahoga: Bror Blixen in Africa* (Bloomington, IN: AuthorHouse, 2019)

Backus, Jean L., *Letters from Amelia, 1901–1937* (Boston: Beacon Press, 1982)

Baldwin, Jayne, *West over the Waves: The Final Flight of Elsie Mackay* (Carnforth: 2QT Limited (Publishing), 2017)

Barker, Ralph, *Great Mysteries of the Air* (London: Pan Books, 1978)

Berg, A. Scott, *Lindbergh* (London: Pan, 1999)

Blaney, Daniel E., *Old Orchard Beach* (South Carolina: Arcadia Publishing, 2007)

Blixen-Finecke, Bror, translated by Lyon, F. H., *African Hunter*, (New York: St. Martin's Press, 1986)

Boegner, Peggie Phipps & Gachot, Richard, *Halcyon Days: An American Family Through Three Generations* (New York: Old Westbury Gardens Publishers, 1986)

Bolitho, Hector, *James Lyle Mackay, First Earl of Inchcape* (London: John Murray, 1936)

Bond, Michael, *Wayfinding: The Art and Science of How We Find and Lose our Way* (London: Picador, 2020)

Boss, Pauline. *Ambiguous Loss: Learning to Live with Unresolved Grief* (Cambridge, MA: Harvard University Press, 1999)

Brown, Arthur Whitten, Sir, & Bott, Alan (contributor), *Flying the Atlantic in Sixteen Hours With a Discussion of Aircraft in Commerce and Transportation*

(London: Frederick A Stokes, 1920)

Bryson, Bill. *One Summer: America, 1927* (London: Doubleday, 2013)

Chichester, Francis, *The Lonely Sea and the Sky* (London: Hodder and Stoughton, 1964)

Coster, Graham (ed.), *The Wild Blue Yonder, The Picador Book of Aviation* (London: Picador, 1997)

Courtwright, David. T., *Sky as Frontier: Adventure, Aviation, and Empire* (College Station, TX: Texas A&M University Press, 2005)

Currell, Susan, *American Culture in the 1920s* (Edinburgh: Edinburgh University Press, 2009)

Anne, de Courcy, *Husband Hunters: Social Climbing in London and New York* (London: Weidenfeld & Nicolson, 2017)

Denby, Elaine, *Grand Hotels: An Architectural and Social History* (London: Reaktion Books, 1998)

Earhart, Amelia, *20 Hrs., 40 Min., Our Flight in the Friendship* (Reprint: Mansfield Centre: Martino Publishing, 2014)

Earhart, Amelia, *The Fun of It: Random Records of my Own Flying and of Women in Aviation* (Chicago: Academy Chicago Publishers, 1977)

Evans, Siân, *Maiden Voyages: Women and the Golden Age of Transatlantic Travel* (London: Two Roads, 2020)

Fisher, John & Best, Antony (eds.), *On the Fringes of Diplomacy: Influences on British Foreign Policy, 1800-1945* (Farnham: Ashgate, 2011)

Fisher, Paul, *The Grand Affair, John Singer Sargent in His World* (New York: Farrar, Straus and Giroux, 2022)

Fort, Adrian, *Nancy: The Story of Lady Astor* (London: Vintage, 2013)

Garrett, Eileen J., *Many Voices: The Autobiography of a Medium* (London: George Allen & Unwin, 1969)

Gavin, Will, *The Great Atlantic Air Race* (Dublin: The O'Brien Press, 2011)

Gillies, Midge, *Amy Johnson: Queen of the Air* (London: Weidenfeld & Nicolson, 2003)

Gillies, Midge, *Army Wives, From Crimea to Afghanistan: The Real Lives of the Women Behind the Men in Uniform* (London: Aurum, 2016)

Goldstein, Donald & Dillon, Katherine, *Amelia: The Centennial Biography of an Aviation Pioneer* (Washington: Brassey's, 1997)

Grush, Loren, *The Six, The Untold Story of America's First Women Astronauts* (London: Virago, London, 2023)

Hinchliffe, E., *The Return of Captain Hinchliffe, D.F.C., A.F.C.* (London: Psychic Press, 1931)

Hillin, Sara, *The Rhetorical Arts of Women in Aviation, 1911–1970* (Lanham: Lexington Books, 2020)

Hunter, Jack, *A Flight Too Far: The Story of Elsie Mackay of Glenapp* (Stranraer: Stranraer and District Local History Trust, 2008)

Jackson, Joe, *Atlantic Fever: Lindbergh, His Competitors, and the Race to Cross the Atlantic* (New York: Farrar, Straus and Giroux, 2012)

Krakauer, Jon, *Into the Wild* (London: Pan, 2011)

Lindbergh, Charles, *The Spirit of St Louis* (London: John Murray, 1953)

Lindbergh, Reeve (words) & Paparone, Pamela (illustrations), *Nobody Owns the Sky: The Story of "Brave Bessie" Coleman* (London: Walker Books, 1996)

Lockwood, Allison, *Passionate Pilgrims: The American Traveler in Great Britain, 1800-1914* (New York; London: Rutherford: Cornwall Books; Fairleigh Dickinson University Press, 1981)

Lovell, Mary, S., *Amelia Earhart, The Sound of Wings* (London: Abacus, 2009)

Luff, David, *Amy Johnson, 'Enigma in the Sky'* (Shrewsbury: Airlife, 2002)

Mackersey, Ian, *Smithy: The Life of Sir Charles Kingsford Smith* (London: Little, Brown, 1998)

Markham, Beryl, *West with the Night* (London: Virago, 2001)

Montague, Richard, *Oceans, Poles and Airmen: The First Flights over Wide Waters and Desolate Ice* (New York: Random House, 1971)

Montgomery, Maureen E., *'Gilded Prostitution', Status, Money and Transatlantic Marriages, 1870–1914* (London: Routledge, 1989)

Moore, Lucy, *Anything Goes: A Biography of the Roaring Twenties* (London: Atlantic, 2009)

O'Brien, Keith, *Fly Girls: How Five Daring Women Defied All Odds and Made Aviation History* (Boston, New York: Mariner Books, 2019)

Oxford Dictionary of National Biography (online)

Perez, Caroline Criado, *Invisible Women: Exposing Data Bias in a World Designed for Men*, (London: Chatto & Windus, 2019)

Pepper, Terence, *High Society: Photographs, 1897–1914* (London: National Portrait Gallery, 1998)

Purnell, Sonia, *First Lady: The Life and Wars of Clementine Churchill* (London: Aurum, 2015)

Putnam, George Palmer, *Wide Margins: A Publisher's Autobiography* (New York: Harcourt, Brace & Co, 1942)

Putnam, George Palmer, *Soaring Wings: A Biography of Amelia Earhart* (London: Harrap, 1940)

Quinn, Susan, *Eleanor and Hick: The Love Affair that Shaped a First Lady* (London: Penguin, 2017)

Railey, Hilton Howell, *Touch'd with Madness* (New York: Carrick & Evans, 1938)

Rich, Doris L., *Queen Bess: Daredevil Aviator* (Washington: Smithsonian Institution Press, 1993)

Rich, Doris L., *Amelia Earhart: A Biography* (Shrewsbury: Airlife, c1989)

Rooney, David, *The Big Hop: The First Non-Stop Flight Across the Atlantic Ocean and Into the Future* (London: Chatto & Windus, 2025)

Scully, Jeffrey A., *The Old Orchard (Images of America)* (South Carolina: Arcadia, 2003)

Shapiro, Gwen Laurie, *The Aviator and the Showman: Amelia Earhart, George Putnam, and the Marriage That Made an American Icon* (London: Viking, 2025)

Shores, Christopher F., Franks, Norman, & Guest, Russell F., Above the Trenches: A Complete Record of the Fighter Aces and Units of the British Empire Air Forces 1915–1920 (London: Grub Street, 1990)

Smith, Elinor, Aviatrix (New York, London: Harcourt Brace Jovanovich, 1981)

Soames, Mary (edited), *Speaking for Themselves: The Personal Letters of Winston and Clementine Churchill* (London: Doubleday, 1998)

Southern, Snook Neta, *I Taught Amelia to Fly* (New York: Vantage Press, 1974)

Spence, Charles, *Gastrophysics: The New Science of Eating* (London: Penguin, 2017)

Stafford, David, *Oblivion or Glory: 1921 and the Making of Winston Churchill* (New Haven: Yale University Press, 2019)

Strayed, Cheryl, *Wild: A Journey from Lost to Found* (London: Atlantic Books, 2012)

Stout, Glenn, *Young Woman and the Sea: How Trudy Ederle Conquered the English Channel and Inspired the World* (Boston: Houghton Mifflin Harcourt, 2009)

Strickland, Mary Isobel, *Lamp in the Mist: A Biography of Ida Betty Selby Lowndes* (Mary Strickland, 2018)

Vanhoenacker, Mark, *Imagine a City: A Pilot's Love Letter to the World's Greatest Cities* (London: Vintage, 2023)

Vanhoenacker, Mark, *How to Land a Plane* (London: Quercus, 2017)

Wallace, Graham, *The Flight of Alcock & Brown: 14–15 June 1919* (London: Putnam, 1955)

Walker, Mike, *Powder Puff Derby: Petticoat Pilots and Flying Flappers* (Chichester: Wiley, 2003)

Post, Wiley & Gatty, Harold, *Around the World in Eight Days: The Flight of the Winnie Mae*, (London: John Hamilton, 1932)

Ware, Susan, *Still Missing: Amelia Earhart and the Search for Modern Feminism* (New York, London: Norton, New York, 1993)

Winchester, Simon, *Atlantic: A Vast Ocean of a Million Stories* (London: Harper Press, 2010)

Wohl, Robert, *The Spectacle of Flight: Aviation and the Western Imagination, 1920–1950*, (Newhaven, London: Yale University Press, 2005).

Yount, Lisa, *Women Aviators* (New York: Facts on File, c1995)

Fiction

Benson, E. F., *Queen Lucia* (London: Hutchinson, 1920)

Notaro, Laurie, *Crossing the Horizon* (New York: Gallery Books, 2013)

Articles in specialist publications (other newspapers and other publications references can be found in the footnotes)

Erisman, Fred, 'Margery Brown's Air-Age Utopia for American Women', *Utopian*

Studies, 32.3, 2021

Glass, David V., 'Divorce in England and Wales', *The Sociological Review*, a26.3, 1934

Jennings, Richard T., 'Captain Nels O. Monserud and Medical Consideration of the Women Air Force Service Pilots: An Enduring Legacy', *Aerospace Medicine and Human Performance*, 88.5, May 2017, p. 516–7

Moorby, Nicola, '*Miss Earhart's Arrival* 1932 by Walter Richard Sickert', catalogue entry, April 2006, in Helena Bonett, Ysanne Holt, Jennifer Mundy (eds.), *The Camden Town Group in Context*, Tate Research Publication, May 2012

Film and Television Programmes

Amelia Earhart: A Woman in Pants, producers: Roger Maunder, Genevieve McCorquodale, Lorne Warr, 2018

Expedition Amelia, National Geographic, 2019

Thesis

Gils, Bieke, 'Pioneers of Flight: An Analysis of Gender Issues in United States Civilian (Sport) and Commercial Aviation 1920–1940', University of Windsor, Master's thesis, 2009

Notes

Prelude: June 1928

1 Amelia Earhart, *20 Hrs., 40 Min.: Our Flight in the Friendship* (Reprint: Mansfield Centre: Martino Publishing, 2014), p. 70.

2 Lorne Warr, *Amelia Earhart: A Woman in Pants*, (2018).

3 Larry Dohey, 'Amelia Earhart Arrived in Trepassey', Archival Moments (2019), http://archivalmoments.ca/2019/06/04/amelia-earhart-in-trepassey/; This Day in Aviation, '17–18 June 1928', https://www.thisdayinaviation.com/17-june-1928/.

4 *20 Hrs., 40 Min.*, p. 71.

5 Ibid., p. 71.

6 Ibid., p. 71.

7 'Louis Edward Gordon Personal Papers', San Diego Air and Space Museum Library and Archives (SDASM), https://sandiegoairandspace.org/collection/item/louis-edward-gordon-special-collection.

8 *20 Hrs., 40 Min.*, p. 72.

9 Larry Dohey, 'Amelia Earhart Arrived in Trepassey', Archival Moments (2019), http://archivalmoments.ca/2019/06/04/amelia-earhart-in-trepassey/.

10 Lorne Warr, *Amelia Earhart: A Woman in Pants*, (2018).

11 *Bulletin of the American Meteorological Society*, May 1931.

12 *20 Hrs., 40 Min.*, p. 89. Stultz also borrowed trousers so that he could have his suit cleaned and pressed and his shirts laundered. He bought a new tie and socks.

13 Kayla Hertz, 'This Canadian woman's accent sounds straight out of Ireland', *Irish Central* (2024), https://www.irishcentral.com/culture/craic/canadian-

irish-accent. At its peak in the 1770s over 5,000 people, lured by higher wages, left Ireland every spring, and a remarkably high percentage came from one place, Waterford. At first the work was seasonal, but slowly these partial immigrants stopped returning to their roots. Today over 22 per cent of local people can trace their ancestors back to Ireland.

14 *20 Hrs., 40 Min.*, p. 78.

15 Amelia Earhart, *The Fun of It*, (Reprint: London: Arcturus, 2020) p.60.

16 *20 Hrs., 40 Min.*, p.78.

17 *The Fun of It*, p. 60.

18 Larry Dohey, 'Mysterious Iceberg off St. John's', Archival Moments (2018), http://archivalmoments.ca/2018/06/23/mysterious-iceberg-off-st-johns/.

19 London newspaper clipping, 'Transatlantic Girl Flyer Out Shopping in Borrowed Clothes', following Earhart's *Friendship* flight, June 1928, b1f11i20. George Palmer Putnam Collection of Amelia Earhart Papers. Archives and Special Collections, Purdue University.

20 SDASM, Louis Edward Gordon Personal Papers, https://sandiegoairandspace.org/collection/item/louis-edward-gordon-special-collection

21 *The Guardian*, 25 June 1928.

22 Mary S. Lovell, *Amelia Earhart: The Sound of Wings* (London: Abacus, 2009), p.135.

23 Layman, T, David. Letter from David T. Layman (attorney for owner of the *Friendship* plane, Amy Guest), to the crew of the *Friendship*, stating that upon landing in Trepassey, Earhart is to have final say on aircraft, procedures, personnel, and policies for the flight, 18 May 1928 (signed by Earhart); Identification Numbers: MSP9b001f005i001. George Palmer Putnam Collection of Amelia Earhart Papers. Archives and Special Collections, Purdue University.

24 *The New York Times*, 12 April 1949. *Democrat and Chronicle,* 6 March 1928.

25 *Democrat and Chronicle,* 6 March 1928.

26 Passport application describes blue eyes. *TIME*, 18 June 1928 in Will Gavin, *The Great Atlantic Air Race,* (Dublin: The O'Brien Press, Dublin, 2011), p. 72.

27 *Atlanta Constitution*, 17 June 1928.

28 Passenger list, Southampton, Incoming, 1920, Ancestry.com.

29 Passenger List, 1920, to Liverpool, Ancestry.com.

30 *The New York Times* obituary, 12 April 1949.

31 Ibid.

32 *Evening Despatch*, 6 March 1928.

33 *San Francisco Examiner*, 30 August 1931.

34 'Census 1915', *Los Angeles Examiner*, 30 August 1931.

35 Passport application says her hair is brown. *The Midland Reporter*, Mullingar, 10 May 1928. She never explained the scarring on her throat that was said to be from an old burn.

36 *The Midland Reporter*, Mullingar, 10 May 1928.

37 Ibid.

38 *The Oklahoma News*, 20 February 1936.

39 Will Gavin, *The Great Atlantic Air Race*, (Dublin: The O'Brien Press, Dublin, 2011), p. 60.

40 Ibid., p. 72.

41 Pathé news footage, https://www.youtube.com/watch?v=qZaduBSNjNk.

42 *TIME*, 18 June 1928.

43 Ibid.

44 'New York, US, Death Index, 1949–1965', Ancestry.com, https://www.ancestry.com/search/collections/61461/.

45 *San Francisco Examiner*, 30 August 1931. He died in Bogota or Italy, *Belfast News Letter*, 8 June 1928.

46 Ian Mackersey, *Smithy: The Life of Sir Charles Kingsford Smith*, (London: Little, Brown, 1998), p. 241.

47 *The New York Times*, 13 June 1928.

48 *TIME*, 18 June 1928.

Chapter One: The First Attempts

1 Jeff Webb, 'Marconi', Heritage Newfoundland & Labrador (2001), https://www.heritage.nf.ca/articles/society/marconi-guglielmo.php; Diana Lambdin

Meyer, 'Canada's vital role in the communications revolution', BBC (2017), https://www.bbc.com/travel/article/20170831-canadas-vital-role-in-the-communications-revolution; 'Milestones: Reception of Transatlantic Radio Signals, 1901', ETHW (2015), https://ethw.org/Milestones:Reception_of_Transatlantic_Radio_Signals,_1901; Stephen Barnes, 'Marconi, Signal Hill, and the First Transatlantic Wireless Communication', Owlcation (2023), https://owlcation.com/humanities/Marconi-Signal-Hill-and-the-First-Transatlantic-Wireless-Communication#gid=ci02a5fc2b500026b6&pid=marconi-signal-hill-and-the-first-transatlantic-wireless-communication-MTc0NjQ2MTE0NzY1NTE0MTA2.

2 *The Times*, 17 December 1901.

3 It's not the only place to claim this noteworthy event. See Bill Bryson, *One Summer: America, 1927* (London: Doubleday, 2013).

4 Simon Winchester, *Atlantic: A Vast Ocean of a Million Stories* (London: Harper Press, 2010), pp. 132–3.

5 Bill Read, 'The Great Transatlantic Race', Royal Aeronautical Society, (2019), https://www.aerosociety.com/news/the-great-transatlantic-race/.

6 Bryan Swopes, '14–15 June 1919', This Day in Aviation (2024), https://www.thisdayinaviation.com/tag/alcock-and-brown/ [accessed 15 April 2023].

7 Some accounts still report that Alcock and Brown boarded with their two pet kittens, Twinkletoe and Lucky Jim. Arthur Whitten Brown, *Flying the Atlantic in Sixteen Hours With a Discussion of Aircraft in Commerce and Transportation*, (London: Frederick A. Stokes, 1920), p. 32.

8 Graham Wallace, 'Alcock and Brown over the Atlantic', pp. 10–1 in Graham Coster (ed.), *The Wild Blue Yonder: The Picador Book of Aviation* (London: Picador, 1997).

9 *The New York Times*, 16 June 1919, p. 1.

10 Ambrose McEvoy, 'Alcock, Sir John William', *Oxford Dictionary of National Biography* (2004), https://www.oxforddnb.com/display/10.1093/odnb/9780198614128.001.0001/odnb-9780198614128-e-1003676.

11 During the Second World War he trained RAF pilots in engineering and navigation but flying had one last blow to deliver when Brown's son Arthur,

a flight lieutenant, was killed in action on D-day, 1944 at the age of twenty-two. Each year for the remaining four years of his life Brown turned up at the Science Museum in London on the anniversary of his transatlantic crossing to gaze up in a moment of reverie at the plane that had taken the two pilots and Twinkletoe and Lucky Jim across the Atlantic. He died in October 1948 in Swansea, Wales from an accidental overdose of veronal, the first commercially available barbiturate, although the suspicion remains that he may have taken his own life.

12 Sir John Lavery, 'Brown, Sir Arthur Whitten', *Oxford Dictionary of National Biography* (2004), https://www.oxforddnb.com/display/10.1093/odnb/9780198614128.001.0001/odnb-9780198614128-e-1012530; 'R34 – The Record Breaker', Airship Heritage Trust, https://www.airshipsonline.com/airships/r34/R34-Altanticflight.html.

13 The outward flight also had a real cat, Whoopsie (some sources spell the name as 'Wopsie') and the first-ever aerial stowaway, twenty-two-year-old William Ballantyne, who had worked on the ship but been forced to give up his place to an American observer. Charles Woodley, 'The R34 airship', https://www.thehistorypress.co.uk/articles/the-r34-airship/, *The Great Atlantic Air Race*, pp. 27–8.

14 A. Scott Berg, *Lindbergh* (London: Pan, 1999), p. 91.

15 'René Fonck', Britannica Kids, https://kids.britannica.com/students/article/Ren%C3%A9-Fonck/323503 [accessed 15 April 2023]; Robert Wohl, *The Spectacle of Flight: Aviation and the Western Imagination, 1920–1950* (New Haven: Yale University Press, 2005), p. 15.

16 A. Scott Berg, *Lindbergh*, p. 91.

17 *The Great Atlantic Air Race*, pp. 36–7.

18 Ibid., p. 39.

19 Air Mail Act of 1925 (The Kelly Act), https://postalmuseum.si.edu/exhibition/fad-to-fundamental-airmail-in-america-airmail-creates-an-industry-from-public-to-private.

20 *The Spectacle of Flight*, p. 16.

Chapter Two: Girls Will Be Girls

1 George Palmer Putnam, *Soaring Wings: A Biography of Amelia Earhart* (London: Harrap, 1940), p. 44.

2 Neta Snook Southern, *I Taught Amelia Earhart to Fly* (New York: Vintage Press, 1974), pp. 1–2.

3 Ibid., p. 141.

4 Ibid., pp. 106, 116.

5 Ibid., p. 124.

6 'Barnstorming', *Oxford English Dictionary* (2022), https://www.oed.com/dictionary/barnstorming_adj?tl=true.

7 *I Taught Amelia Earhart to Fly*, p. 84.

8 Ibid., p. 89–95.

9 Earhart stood five feet, eight inches according to her Transport Pilot's Licence.

10 Bieke Gils, *Pioneers of Flight: An Analysis of Gender Issues in United States Civilian (Sport) and Commercial Aviation 1920–1940*, (University of Windsor: Master's thesis, 2009), p. 54.

11 Quoted in Fred Erisman, 'Margery Brown's Air-Age Utopia for American Women', *Utopian Studies*, 32.3 (2021), p. 515.

12 *Daily Express,* 15 March 1928.

13 Caroline Criado Perez, *Invisible Women: Exposing Data Bias in a World Designed for Men* (London: Chatto & Windus, 2019), Kindle edition, p. 122.

14 *Amelia Earhart*, p. 17.

15 Ibid., p. 37.

16 'Harriet Quimby', PBS, https://www.pbs.org/wgbh/americanexperience/features/flygirls-harriet-quimby/.

17 'Brooklands Stories: Hilda Hewlett', Brooklands Museum (2021), https://www.brooklandsmuseum.com/explore/stories/brooklands-stories/tales-of-brooklands-hilda-hewlett.

18 Graham Wallace, *The Flight of Alcock & Brown 14–15 June, 1919* (London: Putnam, 1955), p. 69.

19 *Pioneers of Flight: An Analysis of Gender Issues in United States Civilian (Sport) and Commercial Aviation 1920–1940*, p. 10.

20 Keith O'Brien, *Fly Girls: How Five Daring Women Defied All Odds and Made Aviation History* (Boston, New York: Mariner Books, 2019), p.10.

21 'Ruth Nichols', Pioneers of Flight, https://pioneersofflight.si.edu/content/ruth-nichols.

22 *Aeronautic Review* 7.3 (1929), p. 7, quoted in Susan Ware, *Still Missing: Amelia Earhart and the Search for Modern Feminism*, (New York, London: Norton, 1993), p. 91.

23 'Jon Wertheim and Jacob Feldman, 'The Incomparable Life and Mysterious Death of Suzanne Lenglen', *SI* (2019), https://www.si.com/tennis/2019/06/27/suzanne-lenglen-tennis-wimbledon-life-death.

24 *Fly Girls*, p. xii.

25 Theresa Kraus, *They Forged A Path For Us: Getting to Know Some of the Women Aviation Trailblazers*, https://www.faa.gov/sites/faa.gov/files/about/history/pioneers/women_in_aviation_2019.pdf.

26 See Nels O. Monserud in 1945 in a report in the *Air Surgeon's Bulletin. Pioneers of Flight*, p. 65, and 'Captain Nels O. Monserud and Medical Consideration of the Women Air Force Service Pilots And Enduring Legacy' in *Aerospace Medicine and Human Performance* 88.5 (2017), pp. 516–7.

27 Michael Bond, *Wayfinding: The Art and Science of How We Find and Lose our Way* (London: Picador, 2021), p. 122.

28 Loren Grush, *The Six: The Untold Story of America's First Women Astronauts* (London: Virago, 2023), p. 206.

29 *Fly Girls*, pp. 52–5.

30 *Fly Girls*, p. 53.

31 *Amelia Earhart*, p. 50.

Chapter Three: Queen Bess

1 Biographical information from Doris L. Rich, *Queen Bess: Daredevil Aviator* (Washington: Smithsonian Books, 1995). Kindle edition.

2 Sara P. Hillin, *The Rhetorical Arts of Women in Aviation, 1911–1970* (Lanham: Lexington Books, 2019), p. 57, *Queen Bess*, p. 36.

3 *Queen Bess*, p. 52.

4 *New York Times*, 14 August 1922.

5 *Queen Bess*, p. 144.

6 Ibid., p. 46. Passport application.

7 Ibid., p. 123.

8 Ibid., p. 136.

9 Ibid., p. 142.

10 Ibid., p. 57.

11 Sara Hillin, *The Rhetorical Arts of Women in Aviation, 1911–1970* (Lanham: Lexington Books, 2020), pp. 56, 63.

12 Marisa Mathias, 'Mae Jemison', National Women's History Museum (2024), https://www.womenshistory.org/education-resources/biographies/mae-jemison.

Flight Checklist: A Memorable Nickname

1 Lucy Moore, *Anything Goes, A Biography of the Roaring Twenties* (London, Atlantic, 2008), p. 289.

2 *Ottawa Citizen*, 30 August 1926.

3 *Brisbane Courier*, 2 September 1927.

4 *Daily News*, 11 October 1927.

5 A. Scott, Berg, *Lindbergh*, (London: Pan, 1999), p.108.

6 *Lindbergh*, p. 169. The song was played at most receptions he attended after his successful crossing.

7 She is described in this way in many newspapers, e.g. *Albany Ledger*, 28 July 1927.

8 *Amelia Earhart*, p. 205.

9 Glenn Stout, *Young Woman and the Sea: How Trudy Ederle Conquered the English Channel and Inspired the World* (Boston: Houghton Mifflin Harcourt, 2009) Kindle edition, pp. 229, 297.

10 Bill Bryson, *One Summer: America, 1927* (Transworld: London, 2013), p. 442.

11 *Irish Examiner*, 8 August 2014.

12 *One Summer*, p. 444.

13 Lucy Moore, *Anything Goes, A Biography of the Roaring Twenties* (Atlantic Books: London, 2008), p. 26.

14 *One Summer*, p. 441.

15 Ibid., p. 435.

16 *Latrobe Bulletin*, 20 June 1925.

17 *Amelia Earhart*, pp. 92, 206.

18 George Palmer Putnam, *Wide Margins: A Publisher's Autobiography* (New York: Harcourt, Brace and company, 1942), p. 288.

19 *Amelia Earhart*, p. 196.

20 *The Catholic News*, 17 September 1927.

21 *One Summer*, p. 357.

22 *Amelia Earhart*, p. 131.

23 *One Summer*, p. 87.

24 *The Six*, p. 115.

25 *The Idaho Statesman*, 23 August 1932.

26 *Shamokin News-Dispatch*, 6 August 1934.

27 *New York Daily News*, 8 October 1927.

28 *Fly Girls*, p. 52.

29 Dorothy Cochrane and P. Ramirez, 'Breaking Records and Making History Striking Stunts', National Air and Space Museum (2021), https://airandspace.si.edu/stories/editorial/breaking-records-and-making-history-striking-stunts.

30 Marisa Mathias, 'Bessie Colman', National Women's History Museum (2024), https://www.womenshistory.org/education-resources/biographies/bessie-coleman.

31 *The San Francisco Examiner*, 30 August 1931.

32 *The Atlanta Journal*, 12 October 1927.

33 'Rescuing the "Flying Flapper"', Time and Navigation (2013), https://timeandnavigation.si.edu/research/rescuing-the-flying-flapper.

34 Richard Montague, *Oceans, Poles and Airmen: The First Flights Over Wide Waters and Desolate Ice* (London: Random House, 1971), picture section.

35 Richard A. Durose, 'Above & Beyond: Aunt Mildred', *Smithsonian Magazine* (2011), https://www.smithsonianmag.com/air-space-magazine/above-and-

beyond-aunt-mildred-79371463/.

36 *I Taught Amelia Earhart to Fly*, p. 19.

37 *Amelia Earhart*, p. 29.

Chapter Four: Amy Phipps and the Challenges of High Birth

1 *Pittsburgh Post-Gazette,* 20 June 1898.

2 Peggie Phipps Boegner and Richard Gachot, *Halcyon Days: An American Family Through Three Generations* (New York: Old Westbury Gardens Publishers, 1986), p. 13.

3 *Halcyon Days*, p. 16.

4 Ibid., p. 21.

5 Ibid., pp. 169, 171.

6 Ibid., p. 192.

7 *Evening World Herald*, 1 July 1898.

8 Ibid.

9 *Halcyon Days*, p. 192.

10 *Northern Chronicle*, 5 July 1905.

11 *The Queen*, 1 July 1905.

12 J. S. Marcus, 'Florida's Norton Museum acquires John Singer Sargent portrait of socialite who sponsored Amelia Earhart', *The Art Newspaper* (2023), https://www.theartnewspaper.com/2023/04/17/john-singer-sargent-portrait-acquired-norton-musem-amy-phipps-guest.

13 Barbara Ann Levine, *Portrait of Mrs. Phipps and her Grandson Winston*, JSS Gallery (2005), http://jssgallery.org/Paintings/10086.htm.

14 'Florida's Norton Museum acquires John Singer Sargent portrait of socialite who sponsored Amelia Earhart', https://www.theartnewspaper.com/2023/04/17/john-singer-sargent-portrait-acquired-norton-musem-amy-phipps-guest.

15 *Los Angeles Express*, 15 July 1905.

16 Ibid.

17 *Bournemouth Graphic*, 14 June 1906; *Los Angeles Express*, 15 July 1905.

18 Lucia Adams, *Wahoga: Bror Blixen in Africa* (Bloomington: Author House,

2019) and Bror von Blixen-Finecke, *African Hunter* translated by F. H. Lyon, (New York: St. Martin's Press, 1986).

Chapter Five: The Flying Princess

1 Siân Evans, *Maiden Voyages: Women and the Golden Age of Transatlantic Travel* (London: Two Roads, 2020).

2 Allison Lockwood, *Passionate Pilgrims: The American Traveler in Great Britain, 1800-1914*, (Rutherford: Fairleigh Dickinson University Press, 1981), p. 15.

3 Kelly Cooper and Brett Romig, 'John Lewis Peyton: Confederate Abroad', The Home of Civil War History at Virginia Tech (2015), https://civilwar.vt.edu/john-lewis-peyton-a-confederate-abroad/, Quoted in *Passionate Pilgrims*, p. 283.

4 *Passionate Pilgrims*, p. 308.

5 Ibid., p. 299.

6 Ibid., p. 298.

7 *Maiden Voyages*, p. 23.

8 *Times-Dispatch*, 29 January 1913.

9 See also *Eastern Daily Press*, 5 April 1897.

10 *The Gentlewoman*, May 1897. *Truth*, 20 May 1897.

11 *Evening News,* 8 February 1899.

12 Ibid., 4 February 1899.

13 *Weekly Dispatch (London)*, 5 February 1899.

14 Joseph Matthews, 'Walter Burton Harris, Times Correspondent in Morocco', *Journalism & Mass Communication Quarterly* 17.3 (1940) https://journals-sagepub-com.ezp.lib.cam.ac.uk/doi/full/10.1177/107769904001700304.

15 John Fisher and Antony Best (eds.), *On the Fringes of Diplomacy: Influences on British Foreign Policy, 1800–1945* (Farnham: Ashgate, 2011), p. 155.

16 Divorce findings. Harris Savile, Lady Mary Louisa, v. Harris, Walter Burton, court minutes, petition filed 17 June 1905, final decree 13 September 1905.

17 'Spanish–American War and the Philippine–American War, 1898–1902', National Park Service (2023), https://www.nps.gov/goga/learn/

historyculture/spanish-american-war.htm.

18 *The Buckingham Express*, 8 April 1899.

19 'Inflation Calculator', Bank of England, https://www.bankofengland.co.uk/monetary-policy/inflation/inflation-calculator.

20 *The Gentlewoman*, 15 July 1905.

21 *Bradford Daily Telegraph,* 22 February 1911, See https://chater-genealogy.blogspot.com/search/label/Savile for more details of Lady Anne's life.

22 'Self-leveling cot, bunk, couch, and the like, for use of shipboard', Google Patents, https://patents.google.com/patent/US986108.

23 'Great Britain, Royal Aero Club Aviators' Certificates, 1910–1950', Ancestry.com.

24 'Hendon the cradle of aviation', Royal Air Force Museum, https://www.rafmuseum.org.uk/about-us/our-history/hendon-cradle-of-aviation/.

25 *Somerset Guardian*, 29 May 1914.

26 *The Standard*, 4 May 1914.

27 *The Manchester Courier*, 22 May 1914.

28 *Bath Chronicle*, 30 May 1914.

29 Ibid.; *Somerset Guardian*, 29 May 1914, says crossing at average speed of 110–115 miles per hour.

30 *The Mail*, 25 May 1914.

31 *The Manchester Courier*, 22 May 1914.

32 *The Queen*, 20 June 1914.

33 *The Mail (Hull)*, 20 June 1914.

34 *Nottingham Evening Post*, 17 June 1914.

35 *The Standard*, 17 June 1914.

36 *The Leeds Mercury*, 6 October 1917.

37 *Daily Record*, 1 October 1917.

38 *Evening Herald*, Dublin, 5 October 1917.

39 *John Bull*, 13 October 1917.

40 Greig Watson, 'War at Home: William Ding's life and death as a test pilot', *BBC News* (2014), https://www.bbc.co.uk/news/uk-england-26015132; 'William Rowland Ding', Oakwood Church, http://www.oakwoodchurch.

info/ding.html.

41 *Sunday Pictorial*, 7 July 1918, The National Archives: HO 1441/1331/255965.

42 *Ottawa Citizen*, 30 August 1927.

43 *Sunday Pictorial*, 23 August 1925.

44 *The Edinburgh Evening News*, 9 September 1922; *Illustrated London News*, 16 September 1922.

45 *The Times*, 11 September 1922.

46 *Evening Despatch*, 22 August 1925.

47 *The Telegraph*, 24 August 1925

48 *Evening Despatch*, 22 August 1925.

49 *The Shields Daily*, 24 August 1925; *Sunday Pictorial*, 23 August 1925.

Chapter Six: Elsie Mackay: From Interior Designer to Stunt Pilot

1 Jack Hunter, *A Flight Too Far: The Story of Elsie Mackay of Glenapp* (Stanraer: Stranraer and District Local History Trust, 2008), p. 4.

2 Hector Bolitho, *James Lyle Mackay, First Earl of Inchcape* (London: John Murray1936), pp. 43–4.

3 Jayne Baldwin, *West over the Waves: The Final Flight of Elsie Mackay* (Carnforth: 2QT Limited, 2017), p. 8, *Oxford Dictionary of National Biography*.

4 'Glenapp Castle', *The Telegraph*, https://www.telegraph.co.uk/travel/destinations/europe/united-kingdom/scotland/ayrshire/hotels/glenapp-castle-hotel/.

5 James Lyle Mackay, *First Earl of Inchcape*, p. 147.

6 *West over the Waves*, pp. vii, 12, 19; *The New York Times*, 15 March 1928.

7 *Yorkshire Evening Post*, 20 January 1920.

8 *Shields News*, 19 November 1920.

9 *The Tatler*, no. 1399, 18 April 1928, quoted in *Amy Johnson* by Midge Gillies, p. 77.

10 *The Sporting Times*, 29 May 1920.

11 *The People*, 23 September 1917.

12 *The Fun of It*, p. 19.

13 *Essex County Chronicle*, 28 September 1917.

14 *The Sporting Times*, 29 May 1920.

15 *A Flight Too Far*, p. 10.

16 *The Sunday Sun*, 5 February 1922.

17 *The People*, 23 September 1917.

18 Ibid.

19 Ibid.

20 Ibid.

21 Hector Bolitho, *James Lyle Mackay*, p. 195.

22 *Pall Mall Gazette*, 1 February 1922; *The Daily News*, 2 February 1922.

23 *The China Express and Telegraph*, 13 July 1922.

24 *The Cornishman and Cornish Telegraph*, 31 May 1922.

25 *Sunday Pictorial*, 4 June 1922

26 *Daily Mirror*, 31 July 1922.

27 *The Civil & Military Gazette*, 24 December 1922.

28 *A Flight Too Far*, p. 14.

29 *Maiden Voyages*, p. 118.

30 *A Flight Too Far*, p. 16.

31 Pilot's licence, *Daily Mirror*, 23 August 1922.

32 *The Vote*, 8 September 1922.

33 *A Flight Too Far*, p. 17.

34 *The New York Times*, 15 March 1928.

35 Ibid.

36 Ibid.

37 *A Flight Too Far*, p. 18.

38 *Montrose Review*, 3 June 1927.

39 *Lindbergh*, p.147.

40 Ibid., p. 148.

41 Ibid., p. 5.

42 Ibid., p. 5.

43 *The New York Times*, 9 September 1928.

44 Imperial War Museum (IWM) 13905.

45 'UK, Medical and Dental Students Registers, 1882–1937', Ancestry.com, https://www.ancestry.co.uk/search/collections/61100/?srsltid=AfmBOoozap8a-HN-MyWQNOwCuwVNjO0-8DMXoVW58ZUNe3YTk_b03vxs.

46 His father gives his profession in the 1911 census.

47 *West over the Waves*, p. 36.

48 IWM 13905, introduction by Joan Humphrey (née Hinchliffe.)

49 This account from IWM logbook. Other versions say Hinch was injured when attempting to fly a Camel, which was damaged after a forced landing in a cornfield by another pilot, back to base.

50 8 August – logbook, IWM.

51 9 August – logbook, IWM.

52 'Calendar of Prisoners, 1868–1929', Ancestry.com, https://www.ancestry.co.uk/search/collections/61808/?srsltid=AfmBOoqgqU4h4ugBTNrNOm8F5B-M8WSrFkKWdViL4QSDB6b2AOv2XjDy.

53 *West Over the Waves*, p. 39.

54 Christopher F. Shores, Norman Franks, and Russell F. Guest, *Above the Trenches: A Complete Record of the Fighter Aces and Units of the British Empire Air Forces 1915–1920*, (London: Grub Street, 1990), p. 195.

Flight Checklist: A Tendency To Tomboy

1 *Soaring Wings*, p. 18.

2 *The Fun of It*, p. 10.

3 Ibid., p. 12.

4 Ibid., p. 12.

5 *Soaring Wings*, p. 12.

6 *St Louis Globe Democrat*, 14 August 1927.

7 Ibid.

8 Hinchliffe's logbook, RAF Museum, 25 February 1928.

9 *The Richmond River Herald and Northern Districts Advertiser*, 20 March 1928.

10 Ibid.

11 'Amelia Earhart, Biographical Sketch', Purdue Libraries, https://collections.lib.purdue.edu/aearhart/biography.php, *Amelia Earhart*, p.95.

12 Midge Gillies, *Amy Johnson*, (London: Weidenfeld & Nicolson, 2003), p. 72.

13 Heath in *Oxford Dictionary of National Biography* (https://doi-org.ezp.lib.cam.ac.uk/10.1093/ref:odnb/67141); *The Times*, 11 April 1928.

14 *Aeroplane*, 23 May 1928.

Chapter Seven: Frances Grayson and Ruth Elder Square Up

1 'When Penn Station Was a Masterpiece', https://www.nyhistory.org/blogs/penn-station-masterpiece, *The New York Times*, 26 December 1927.

2 *New York Times*, 26 December 1927.

3 US Passport application, 1914–1915 (Roll 0249-Certificates: 301-700), (Ancestry.com).

4 In a 1921 court case over Rosa's will, it was stated that the Spangs had never doubted they were Mabel's parents, *Matter of Spang*, 197 App. Div. 310, 188 N.Y.S. 754 (N.Y. App. Div. 1921).

5 *Pittsburgh Daily Post*, 1 December 1904; *The Pittsburgh Press*, 1 December 1904.

6 *Matter of Spang*, 197 App. Div. 310, 188 N.Y.S. 754 (N.Y. App. Div. 1921).

7 *New York Tribune*, 27 January 1920.

8 *Matter of Spang*, 197 App. Div. 310, 188 N.Y.S. 754 (N.Y. App. Div. 1921); *New York Tribune*, 27 January 1920; *Yonkers Herald*, 1 December 1904.

9 *The New York Times*, 19 January 1905.

10 New York, Episcopal Diocese of New York Church Records, 1767–1970. Extracted Marriage Index, 1866–1937.

11 *Den Danske Pioneer*, 3 December 1931; *The New York Times*, 6 February 1920.

12 *The New York Times*, 6 February 1920.

13 Ibid., 28 May 1921; Ibid., 1 October 1919.

14 Ibid., 23 January 1924

15 Ibid., 29 January 1920.

16 One doctor said she was suffering from dementia and described how she had flirted with him. *The New York Times*, 30 January 1920.

17 Ibid., 29 January 1920.

18 Ibid., 3 February 1920

19 Ibid., 4 February 1920.

20 *Den Danske Pioneer,* 10 March 1938 and 3 December 1931.

21 *The New York Times*, 23 January 1924.

22 *Miami News*, 14 February 1923.

23 Karlebo Local History Association, *Karlebogaard* af Merete Carstens (*Karlebogaard* by Merete Carstens), 2007. https://www.superusers.dk/eventyret-om-karlebogaard/.

24 Passenger list, various, Ancestry.com

25 In newspaper reports of the time, Mabel is sometimes referred to as a 'sportswoman' but with little evidence to support this. *The State*, 3 September 1927; *The Akron Beacon Journal*, 3 September 1927.

26 *Fly Girls*, p.33.

27 *The Akron Beacon Journal*, 3 September 1927; *The Bismarck Tribune*, 3 September 1927.

28 *New York Evening Journal*, undated Sikorsky Collection.

29 https://www.mainehistory.org/maine-connection/worldwide-maine-frances-wilson-grayson-female-aviator/ Maine Historical Society.

30 *The New York Times,* 26 December 1927.

31 Ibid.

32 *The Sun*, 25 April 1915; Marriage, *Fly Girls*, p.34.

33 *The Washington Herald*, 8 July 1915.

34 Passport application.

35 Unidentified cutting, Sikorsky Archive, p. 40 of 'Grayson Data'.

36 *Brooklyn Times*, 11 June 1926.

37 *The New York Times*, 26 December 1927.

38 *Skyways*, January 1988, Sikorsky Archive.

39 *Brooklyn Times*, 5 January 1928.

40 *The State,* 3 September 1927.

41 *Muncie Evening Press*, 7 September 1927; quoted in *Fly Girls*, p. 34; *Skyways*, January 1988, Sikorsky Archive.

42 *The New York Times*, 12 October 1927.

43 1910 and 1920 US Census.

44 *The New York Times*, 12 October 1927.
45 Ibid.
46 Ibid.
47 Ibid.

Chapter Eight: Amy Guest: Thwarted Adventurer

1 *The Times*, 7 August 1908; 1910 and 1920 US Census.
2 *Illustrated London News*, 15 August 1908; 1910 and 1920 US Census.
3 *The Times*, 7 August 1908; Ric Carlyon, 'Churchill and Fire, A Trilogy', *Dispatches* (2023), https://dispatches.co.nz/churchill-and-fire-a-trilogy/.
4 *The Staffordshire Sentinel*, 12 September 1908.
5 *The Queen*, 31 October 1908.
6 *The Nebraska State Journal*, 22 May 1921.
7 Anne de Courcy, *The Husband Hunters*: *Social Climbing in London and New York* (London: Weidenfeld & Nicolson, 2017), introduction.
8 Maureen E. Montgomery, *'Gilded Prostitution', Status, money and transatlantic marriages, 1870–1914*, (London: Routledge, 1989), p. 1.
9 Ibid. p. 138.
10 Ibid. p. 143.
11 *The Husband Hunters*, p. 40.
12 *Gilded Prostitution*, p. 22.
13 Ibid. p. 128.
14 Nancy Astor, *Oxford Dictionary of National Biography* (https://doi-org.ezp.lib.cam.ac.uk/10.1093/ref:odnb/30489).
15 Frederick Guest, *Oxford Dictionary of National Biography*, https://doi-org.ezp.lib.cam.ac.uk/10.1093/ref:odnb/33596.
16 *The Times*, 12 June 1918.
17 Robin Harragin Hussey, 'LONG READ: The Faith that Motivated Nancy Actor', University of Reading (2020), https://research.reading.ac.uk/astor100/long-read-the-faith-that-motivated-nancy-astor-by-robin-harragin-hussey/.
18 *Halcyon Days*, p. 24.

19 E. F. Benson, *Queen Lucia* (London: Hutchinson,1920), p. 68.
20 Dean McCleland, 'Churchill vs Lady Astor: The Age of Classic Insults and Witticisms', *The Casual Observer* (2015), http://thecasualobserver.co.za/churchill-lady-astor-classic-insults-and-witticisms/.
21 'LONG READ: The Faith that Motivated Nancy Astor'.
22 The Churchill Archive (CHAR) 1/73.
23 David Stafford, *Oblivion or Glory: 1921 and the Making of Winston Churchill* (New Haven: Yale University Press, 2019), p. 36.
24 Paul Addison, *Churchill: The Unexpected Hero* (Oxford; New York: Oxford University Press, 2005) p. 48.
25 Ibid., p. 49.
26 Ibid., p. 48.
27 Mary Soames (ed.), *Speaking for Themselves: The Personal Letters of Winston and Clementine Churchill* (London: Doubleday, 1998), p. 244.
28 *New York Times*, 8 December 1936.
29 CHAR 1/299.
30 CHAR 1/298, April 1937.
31 *Halcyon Days*, pp. 218–9.
32 'Mission and History', Old Westbury Gardens, https://www.oldwestburygardens.org/about/#mission-history.
33 *Halcyon Days*, p. 105.
34 Ibid., p. 107.
35 Ibid., p. 192.
36 *Buffalo Evening News*, 12 April 1949.

Flight Checklist: A Well-Packed Picnic Basket

1 *The Mail*, 16 June 1919, p. 6; The ale is mentioned in *The New York Times*, 16 June 1919.
2 *Grantham Journal*, 17 March 1928.
3 *The Roanoke Times, Virginia*, 12 October 1927.
4 *The Sheboygan Press*, 19 October 1927; *Public Opinion*, 18 October 1927; *Brooklyn Times*, 12 October 1927.

5 *The Sheboygan Press*, 19 October 1927; *Public Opinion*, 18 October 1927.
6 *Lindbergh*, p. 92.
7 Ibid., p. 92.
8 Ibid., p. 115
9 Ibid., p. 115.
10 *Salt Lake Tribune*, 24 October 1927.
11 *Times Union*, 7 June 1928.
12 Charles Spencer, *Gastrophysics: The New Science of Eating* (London: Penguin, 2017), Kindle, Chapter 8, 'Airline Food'.
13 *20 Hrs., 40 Min.*, p. 69.
14 Ibid., p. 51–83.
15 Ibid., p. 93.
16 These had become popular during the First World War and a 1916 advert boasted that 10–20 tablets dissolved in the mouth provided the nourishment of an ordinary meal.
17 *Amelia Earhart: A Girl in Pants* (Producers: Roger Maunder, Genevieve McCorquodale, Lorne Warr, 2018).
18 *20 Hrs., 40 Min.*, pp. 98–9.
19 *The Fun of It*, p. 187.
20 *Gastrophysics*, p. 146.
21 Ibid., p. 148.
22 *20 Hrs., 40 Min.*, p. 59.

Chapter Nine: Anne Savile and the 'Superfliers'

1 *Brisbane Courier*, 2 September 1927.
2 *The Times*, 27 July 1927.
3 *Western Daily Press*, 24 August 1927; *New York Times*, 1 September 1927.
4 *The Times*, 27 August 1927.
5 *Olean Times*, 31 August 1927 (Cited from: http://www.militarian.com/threads/lt-col-ffr-minchin-cbe-dso-mc-bar.7729/).
6 *Brisbane Courier*, 2 September 1927.
7 *Olean Times*, 31 August 1927 (Cited from: 'Lt Col FFR Minchin CBE DSO

MC & Bar' in 'Military Biographies' (2009), Militarian, http://www.militarian.com/threads/lt-col-ffr-minchin-cbe-dso-mc-bar.7729/).

8 *The Times*, 26 August 1927. *New York Times*, 26 August 1927 reverses their roles.

9 *The New York Times*, 4 July 1927.

10 Ibid., 24 July 1927.

11 *Daily Mirror*, 19 August 1927.

12 *The New York Times,* 31 August 1927.

13 *Daily Mirror*, 1 September 1927.

14 *Brisbane Courier*, 2 September 1927; *The Times*, 1 September 1927.

15 *The Scotsman*, 1 September 1927.

16 *The New York Times*, 1 September 1927.

17 *The Times*, 1 September 1927.

18 *The Gazette*, 7 May 1928; *Herald and Review*, 6 May 1928. Her devotion to luggage seemed to confirm a story that she had once spent $1,500 on commissioning a plane to transport her trunk from southern Spain to France; *New York Times*, 26 August 1927.

19 *Daily Mirror*, 1 September 1927.

20 *The Times*, 1 September 1927.

21 *The New York Times*, 31 August 1927.

22 *The Times*, 1 September 1927.

23 *The New York Times*, 13 July 1927.

24 *The Times*, 3 September 1927.

25 Ibid.

26 *The Gazette* (Montreal), 3 September 1927.

27 *The New York Times*, 13 July 1927. Another British pilot, Captain Courtenay, planned to cross in a Wal flying boat; *The Times*, 3 September 1927.

28 *The Times*, 1 September 1927.

29 Ibid., 1 and 3 September 1927.

30 Ibid., 5 September 1927.

31 Ibid., 3 September 1927, p. 10.

32 *Birmingham Gazette*, 2 September 1927.

33 *The Times*, 2 September 1927.

34 Ibid.

35 Ibid., 5 September 1927.

36 Ibid., 3 September 1927.

37 *Birmingham Gazette*, 2 September 1927.

38 *The Times*, 5 September 1927.

39 *The New York Times*, 31 August 1927.

40 Ibid., 1 September 1927.

41 Ibid., 2 September 1927.

42 Ibid., 3 September 1927.

43 Ibid.

44 Ibid., 2 September 1927.

45 *Nottingham Journal*, 2 September 1927.

46 *The Times*, 6 September 1927.

47 *The New York Times*, 3 September 1927.

48 *Hull Daily News*, 9 September 1927.

49 *The New York Times*, 7 February 1928.

50 *The Times*, 7 February 1928, 2 and 4 January 1928.

51 *The New York Times*, 1 September 1928.

Chapter Ten: The Flying Matron Versus 'Miss America of the Air'

1 Daniel E. Blaney, *Old Orchard Beach*, (Arcadia Publishing, 2007), p. 65.

2 Ibid., p. 64.

3 Ibid., p. 75.

4 *Biddeford-Saco Journal*, 1 June 1912.

5 *Journal Tribune*, 31 May 1912.

6 Jeffrey Scully, *The Old Orchard (*Arcadia, 2003), Kindle.

7 *Press and Sun-Bulletin*, 3 September 1927.

8 *The Stanford Herald*, 16 September 1927.

9 *The Washington Post*, 16 September 1927.

10 Ibid., 18 September 1927.

11 *The Stanford Herald*, 16 September 1927.

12 Ibid.

13 'Old Orchard Beach: The Dawn' by Frederick R. Hamlen, *The Journal of the Airplane 1920–1940,* No. 5, Jan 1988.

14 *The New York Times*, 25 September 1927.

15 *International Herald Tribune*, 2 September 1927, Sikorsky Archives.

16 'Old Orchard Beach: The Dawn' by Frederick R. Hamlen, *The Journal of the Airplane 1920–1940*, No. 5, Jan 1988.

17 Ibid.

18 *The New York Times*, 26 December 1927.

19 https://timeandnavigation.si.edu/multimedia-asset/pioneer-earth-inductor-compass.

20 'Old Orchard Beach: The Dawn' by Frederick R. Hamlen, *The Journal of the Airplane 1920–1940*, No. 5, Jan 1988.

21 *Daily News*, 11 October 1927.

22 *The New York Times*, 11 October 1927.

23 Ibid., 7 October 1927.

24 *Manchester Guardian*, 12 October 1927.

25 *Brooklyn Times Union*, October 12 1927.

26 *The New York Times*, 12 October 1927.

27 Ibid.; Mascot, *Boston Globe*, 15 October 1927; *Daily News*, 12 October 1927.

28 *New York Times*, 12 October 1927.

29 Ibid.

30 Ibid.

31 Ibid.

32 Ibid.

Chapter Eleven: The Weather Man

1 *Bulletin of the American Meteorological Society*, Vol. 12, May 1931.

2 Ibid.

3 https://web.archive.org/web/20041013235207/http://www.nws.noaa.gov/pa/history/index.php.

4 https://www.weather.gov/timeline.

5 Wiley Post and Harold Gatty, *Around the World in Eight Days: The Flight of the Winnie Mae* (London: John Hamilton, 1932), pp. 58–64.

6 *Time,* 20 April 1931.

7 *Bulletin of the American Meteorological Society*, Vol. 12, May 1931.

8 *Time*, 20 April 1931, p. 44.

9 *Bulletin of American Meteorological Society*, Vol. 25. December 1944.

10 *The New York Times*, 12 October 1927.

11 Ibid., 13 October 1927.

12 Ibid.

13 Ibid., 14 October 1927.

Chapter Twelve: Missing

1 *The New York Times*, 16 October 1927.

2 Ibid.

3 Ibid., 14 October 1927.

4 Ibid., 16 October 1927.

5 Ibid.

6 Ibid., 17 October 1927.

7 Ibid.

8 Ibid.

9 Ibid., 7 and 15 October 1927.

10 *The Kansas City Star*, 16 October 1927. In November their plane was damaged in an attempted take-off to fly to Harbour Grace (*Muncie Evening Press*, 28 November 1927) and the flight abandoned (*The Owensboro Messenger*, 28 December 1927). Although she tried to raise money in 1928 for a second attempted crossing this never materialised.

11 *The New York Times*, 16 October 1927.

12 Ibid.

13 Ibid., 17 October 1927.

14 Ibid.

15 Haldeman and Elder later reacted angrily at the suggestion that she had been on the wing: 'The only time I was on the wings was after the plane landed,' she

told reporters in New York. *The New York Times*, 12 November 1927.

16 *The New York Times*, 14 October 1927.

17 Ibid.

18 'Old Orchard Beach: The Dawn' by Frederick R. Hamlen, *The Journal of the Airplane 1920–1940*, No. 5, Jan 1988.

19 *Daily News*, 11 October 1927, Sikorsky Archives.

20 Ibid.

21 *The New York Times*, 14 October 1927, Sikorsky Archives.

22 Ibid.

23 Ibid.

24 Ibid.

25 Ibid.

26 Ibid., 17 October 1927.

27 Ibid.

28 Ibid., 14 October, 1927.

29 Ibid., 16 October 1927.

30 Ibid., 15 October 1927.

31 Ibid., 14 October, 1927.

Chapter Thirteen: 'A safe and sane flight'

1 'Old Orchard Beach: The Dawn', *The Journal of the Airplane 1920-1940*, No. 5, Jan 1988.

2 *The New York Times*, 17 October 1927.

3 Ibid., 16 October 1927.

4 Ibid., 17 October 1927.

5 Ibid., 18 October 1927.

6 Ibid.

7 *New York Graphic*, 15 October 1927.

8 'Old Orchard Beach: The Dawn' *The Journal of the Airplane 1920-1940*, No. 5, Jan 1988.

9 *The Herald*, 24 October 1927, Sikorsky Archives.

10 *The New York Times (or Journal?* – hard to read*)*, 24 October 1927, Sikorsky

Archives.

11 Ibid.

12 *World*, 24 October 1927.

13 *The New York Times*, 24 October 1927, Sikorsky Archives, p. 41.

14 *The World*, 24 October 1927.

15 *The New York Times (or Journal?* – hard to read), Sikorsky Archives, 26 October 1927.

16 *World*, 24 October 1927.

17 *The New York Times*, 25 October 1927.

18 Ibid., 31 October 1927.

19 *Knickerbocker Press*, 31 October 1927, Sikorsky Archives.

20 Ibid.

21 *The New York Times*, 30 October 1927.

Chapter Fourteen: Winter Comes to Old Orchard

1 *The New York Times*, 24 December 1927.

2 *The Boston Globe*, 24 December 1927.

3 https://www.extremeweatherwatch.com/cities/new-york/year-1927#december.

4 *The New York Times*, 24 December 1927.

5 Ibid., 13 November 1927.

6 Ibid.

7 Ibid.

8 Ibid.

9 Ibid., 19 November 1927.

10 'Col. Bernt Balchen', National Museum of the United States Air Force, https://www.nationalmuseum.af.mil/Visit/Museum-Exhibits/Fact-Sheets/Display/Article/196172/col-bernt-balchen/.

11 *The New York Times*, 3 November 1927.

12 *The Evening Star*, Washington, 8 December 1927.

13 *The New York Times*, 26 December 1927.

14 *The Brooklyn Daily Eagle*, 27 December 1927.

15 *Ottumwa Daily Courier*, 9 January 1903.

16 *The Sioux City Journal*, 25 January 1903.

17 Ibid.

18 *The New York Times*, 26 December 1929.

19 Ibid., 24 December 1927.

20 William Pitt Mason to Mr W. B. Parsons, Superintendent, Bureau of Issue, Equitable Life Assurance Society, 27 January 1928, Surrogate's Court held in and for the Country of New York, Exhibit A, p. 43.

21 *The New York Times*, 24 December 1927.

22 *The Enid Morning News*, 25 December 1927.

23 *The Brooklyn Daily Eagle*, 1 March 1928

24 Quote and description of days before the flight and the take-off from Surrogate's Court, letter from Gertrude J. Goldsborough to W. B. Parsons, Superintendent, Bureau of Issue, Equitable Life Assurance Society, 28 January 1928, Exhibit B.

25 Ibid.; *Brooklyn Daily Eagle*, 1 March 1928.

26 *New York Times*, 25 December 1927.

27 Ibid., 24 & 25 December 1927.

28 *Daily News*, 24 December 1927.

29 *Atlanta Constitution*, 26 December 1927.

30 *The New York Times*, 25 December 1927.

31 Ibid., 27 December 1927.

32 Ibid., 27 December 1927.

33 *Muncie, Evening Press*, 24 December 1927.

34 *The New York Times*, 26 December 1927.

35 Ibid., 25 December 1927.

36 Ibid., 27 December 1927.

37 Ibid.

38 Ibid., 26 December 1927, *Portland Press Herald*, 27 December 1927.

39 *The New York Times*, 25 December 1927.

40 Ibid., 27 December 1927.

41 Ibid.

42 Ibid., 28 December 1927.

43 *Muncie, Evening Press,* 24 December 1927.

44 *The Atlanta Constitution*, 26 December 1927.

45 *The New York Times*, 25 December 1927.

46 Ibid., 25 December 1927.

47 Ibid.

48 Ibid.

49 Ibid., 26 December 1927.

50 *Brooklyn Times Union*, 20 May 1929.

51 *Baraboo News Republic*, 21 May 1929.

52 *The New York Times*, 26 December 1927.

53 Ibid., 27 December 1927; *Portland Press Herald*, 27 December 1927.

54 *The New York Times*, 25 December 1927.

55 *Brooklyn Daily Eagle*, 1 March 1928.

56 Ibid.

57 Ibid.

58 Ibid.

59 Surrogate's Court held in and for the Country of New York, p. 2 and Exhibit 'G' File Number: A1928–463.

60 Surrogate's Court, File Number: A1928–463.

61 Surrogate's Court, letter from Gertrude J. Goldsborough to W. B. Parsons, Superintendent, Bureau of Issue, Equitable Life Assurance Society, 28 January 1928, Exhibit B.

Flight Checklist: A Handle on Husbands

1 *Hamilton Evening Journal*, 21 April 1928, and other syndicated outlets.

2 Ibid.

3 *Brooklyn Times Union*, 4 January,1928.

4 *The New York Times*, 24 June 1928.

5 Ibid., 7 September 1928.

6 *Harrisburg, Pennsylvania*, 12 December 1928

7 *Chicago Tribune*, 18 March 1928.

8 *The New York Times*, 12 November 1927.
9 Ibid.
10 Ibid.
11 Ibid.
12 Ibid.
13 Ibid.
14 'Ladies Home Journal' in *Baltimore Sun* Obits, August 1937; *Chicago Tribune*, 13 November 1927.
15 *Chicago Tribune*, 13 November 1927.
16 *Washington Post*, 13 November 1927.
17 *Chicago Tribune*, 16 November 1927.
18 *Brooklyn Times*, 4 January 1928.
19 *Chicago Tribune*, 4 December 1927.
20 Ibid.
21 Ibid., 18 March 1928.
22 *Washington Post*, 6 September 1928.
23 *Chicago Tribune*, 7 September 1928.
24 Ibid.
25 *Washington Post*, 11 September 1928.
26 *Chicago Tribune*, 18 September 1928.
27 *The New York Times*, 13 April 1929.
28 Ibid., 13 May 1930.
29 *Chicago Tribune*, 30 August 1929.
30 *The New York Times,* 15 November 1932.
31 *The San Francisco Examiner*, 24 November 1929.
32 *Brooklyn Daily Eagle*, 27 December 1927; *New York Times*, 26 December 1927.
33 *The New York Times*, 12 April 1949.
34 *The Atlanta Constitution*, 17 June 1928.
35 *The New York Times*, 12 April 1949; *San Francisco Examiner*, 30 August 1931.
36 David V. Glass, 'Divorce in England and Wales', *The Sociological Review* a26.3, 1934.

37 'Divorces since 1900', UK Parliament, https://www.parliament.uk/business/publications/research/olympic-britain/housing-and-home-life/split-pairs/.

38 National Archives, https://www.nationalarchives.gov.uk/help-with-your-research/research-guides/divorce/.

39 'Divorce rates data, 1858 to now: how has it changed?', *The Guardian*, https://www.theguardian.com/news/datablog/2010/jan/28/divorce-rates-marriage-ons.

40 Frank Olito, 'How the divorce rate has changed over the last 150 years', *Business Insider* (2019), https://www.businessinsider.com/divorce-rate-changes-over-time-2019-1?r=US&IR=T#the-divorce-rate-decreased-in-the-50s-as-american-ideals-changed-8.

41 https://web.archive.org/web/20200523111412/https://www.radcliffe.harvard.edu/schlesinger-library/item/amelia-earharts-weiu-employment-reference-front-and-back-august-19-1926.

42 Tom Verde, 'Amelia Earhart's "Secret" Connecticut Wedding', *CT Insider* (2015), https://www.ctinsider.com/connecticutmagazine/news-people/article/Amelia-Earhart-s-Secret-Connecticut-Wedding-17041926.php.

43 Ibid.

44 Jean L. Backus, *Letters from Amelia, 1901–1937*, e-book, 34 per cent; In *Soaring Wings*, p. 76, GP said 'twice at least' she refused the idea of marriage, but he may also have been referring to her engagement to Sam.

45 'Amelia Earhart's "Secret" Connecticut Wedding'.

46 *Soaring Wings*, p. 77.

47 Earhart, Amelia. Letter to George Palmer Putnam, 1937. b7f149i1. George Palmer Putnam Collection of Amelia Earhart Papers. Archives and Special Collections, Purdue University. Amelia Earhart Papers. Typed version: Purdue ID No. b7f150i1.

48 Earhart, Amelia. Notes, personal musings on marriage, undated. b6f127il. George Palmer Putnam Collection of Amelia Earhart Papers. Archives and Special Collections, Purdue University.

49 'Putnam, George Palmer, 1887–1950', https://archives.lib.purdue.edu/agents/people/1288.

Chapter Fifteen: Limbering up: Boll and Earhart in Cuba and Boston

1 'Cuba weather', Met Office, https://www.metoffice.gov.uk/weather/travel/holiday-weather/americas/caribbean/cuba.
2 'Here's What Happened the Last Time a US President Visited Cuba', *ABC News* (2016), https://abcnews.go.com/International/happened-time-us-president-visited-cuba/story?id=27689730.
3 *Western Mail*, 1 September 1927.
4 *The New York Times*, 20 September 1927.
5 Ibid., 6 March 1928.
6 *Evening Despatch*, 6 March 1928.
7 Ibid.
8 *Democrat and Chronicle*, 6 March 1928.
9 *Evening Despatch*, 6 March 1928 – £800.
10 *Times Herald*, 7 March 1928.
11 Ibid.
12 Appointment Bureau, Amelia Earhart, typed letter, signed and employment record, 1926. Additional records of the Women's Educational and Industrial Union, 1877–1977, 81-M237--82-M11: M-89: Vt-12, 212., Carton: 11. Schlesinger Library, Harvard Radcliffe Institute.
13 *The Fun of It*, p. 47.
14 Ibid., p. 49.
15 Ibid., p. *50.*
16 *The New York Times*, 26 March 1928.

Chapter Sixteen: Hinch and Mackay

1 RAF Museum AC86/74/3/2, collection of transcripts taken from published articles, relating to the career of Capt. Walter George Raymond (Ray) Hinchliffe, 1917–1928.
2 *West over the Waves*, p. 43.
3 IWM logbook and *West over the Waves*. p. 43.
4 A note in the original logbook from Joan identifies the handwriting as her

mother's from about 28 April 1921.

5 Unidentified cutting in logbook.

6 RAFM, AC86/74/3/5.

7 IWM, logbook, 31 July 1927.

8 Ibid.

9 *New York Times*, 9 September 1928.

10 IWM, logbook, 30 August 1927.

11 British Film Institute, 625952A.

12 *The New York Times*, 18 September 1927.

13 Ibid.

14 IWM, logbook, 23 September 1927.

15 Ibid., 4 October 1927.

16 *West Over the Waves*, p. 48.

17 *The New York Times*, 9 September 1928.

18 RAFM unidentified cutting.

19 *The New York Times*, 11 September 1927.

20 Ibid., 9 September 1928.

21 1921 passport.

22 Elaine Denby, *Grand Hotels: An Architectural and Social History*, pp. 236–40.

23 *Daily Express*, 16 March 1928.

24 *A Flight Too Far*, p. 19; *New York Times*, 9 September 1928 says $50,000.

25 *The New York Times*, 14 December 1927.

26 *West over the Waves*, postscript, The Stinson Detroiter, p. 140,

27 *West over the Waves*, p. 68.

Chapter Seventeen: 'The most secret flight in the history of aviation'

1 It sold 1,184,150 copies in February, a figure calculated without 'resorting' to coupon competitions. *Daily Express*, 8 March 1928. For comparable figures today see Charlotte Tobitt, 'Newspaper ABCs: Daily Mirror drops below print circulation of 200,000', *Press Gazette*, https://pressgazette.co.uk/media-

audience-and-business-data/media_metrics/most-popular-newspapers-uk-abc-monthly-circulation-figures-2/.

2 *Daily Express*, 8 March 1928.

3 Ibid., 14 March 1928.

4 *Yorkshire Evening Post*, 8 March 1928.

5 *Daily Express*, 9 March 1928.

6 Ibid.

7 *New York Times*, 9 September 1927.

8 RAFM, logbook.

9 *The New York Times*, 9 September 1928.

10 Hinchliffe's logbook, held at RAF Museum. Copy at IWM.

11 IWM logbook.

12 https://www1.camra.org.uk/pubs/george-hotel-leadenham-191975

13 *Grantham Journal*, 17 March 1928.

14 *Daily Chronicle*, 15 March 1926

15 *Daily Express*, 16 March 1928.

16 *Grantham Journal*, 17 March 1928 'efforts were made by a close relative to influence Miss Mackay to abandon the idea of the flight'; *West over the Waves*, p. 78.

17 *The Courier and Advertiser*, 15 March 1928.

18 'Picture House', Cinema Treasures, https://cinematreasures.org/theaters/18202.

19 *Hull Daily Mail*, 17 March 1928 described as a 'recent convert', while the *Westminster Gazette*, 21 March 1928 said she converted at least ten years earlier.

20 *Daily Express*, 15 March 1918.

21 *The Daily Chronicle*, 15 March 1928.

22 *Daily Express*, 15 March 1928.

23 *Civil & Military Gazette*, 19 March 1928; *Hull Daily Mail*, 17 March 1928.

24 *Hull Daily Mail*, 17 March 1928.

25 *Daily Express*, 15 March 1928.

26 Ibid.

27 *Daily Mirror,* 14 March 1928.

28 *Daily Express*, 15 March 1928.

29 Ibid., 17 March 1928.

30 Ibid., 19 March 1928.

31 Ibid., 14 March 1928.

32 *Daily Mirror*, 14 March 1928.

33 *Daily Express*, 14 March 1928.

34 IWM Catalogue number 8512-01.

Chapter Eighteen: Ambiguous Loss

1 Pauline Boss, Ambiguous Loss, https://www.ambiguousloss.com/about/leading-therapist/, See Pauline Boss, *Ambiguous Loss: Learning to Live with Unresolved Grief* (Harvard University Press, 1999).

2 Emilie Hinchliffe, *The Return of Captain Hinchliffe*, (London: Psychic Press, 1931), p.18.

3 *The Courier and Advertiser*, 15 March 1928.

4 *Daily News*, 23 March 1928.

5 *Birmingham Gazette*, 16 March 1928.

6 *The Courier and Advertiser*, 15 March 1928.

7 *The People*, 15 April 1928.

8 *The New York Times*, 2 and 3 August 1928.

9 *The Indiana Gazette*, 29 January 1929.

10 *The Edinburgh Evening News*, 9 May 1928.

11 *The Australian Women's Weekly*, 27 August 1938.

12 Midge Gillies, *Army Wives From Crimea to Afghanistan: The Real Lives of the Women Behind the Men in Uniform* (London: Aurum, 2016), p. 138.

13 Ibid., pp. 143, 148.

14 *The Return of Captain Hinchliffe*, p. 21.

15 Ibid., p. 21.

16 Ibid., p. 22.

17 Ibid., p. 23.

18 'The History of the College of Psychic Studies', College of Psychic Studies,

https://www.collegeofpsychicstudies.co.uk/about-us/our-heritage/.

19 Eileen J. Garrett, *Many Voices: The Autobiography of a Medium* (London: George Allen & Unwin, 1969), p. 6.

20 *The Return of Captain Hinchliffe*, p. 27.

21 Ibid., p. 32.

22 Ibid., p. 43.

23 Ibid., p. 47.

24 Ibid., p. 50.

25 *Daily News and Westminster Gazette*, 23 November 1928.

26 *The Return of Captain Hinchliffe*, p. 12.

27 https://occult-world.com/john-and-katie-king.

28 Cambridge University Library, Sir Oliver Lodge: Correspondence And Papers within Society for Psychical Research collection, Reference Code: GBR/0012/MS SPR/35/1128, https://archivesearch.lib.cam.ac.uk/repositories/2/archival_objects/631832.

29 *The Australian Women's Weekly*, 27 August 1938.

30 *A Flight Too Far*, p. 29; *New York Times*, 9 September 1928.

31 *The New York Times*, 9 September 1928.

32 *Western Daily Mail*, 4 July 1928.

33 *Daily Express*, 4 July 1928.

34 Ibid.

35 Ibid., 6 July 1928.

36 Ibid., 12 July 1928.

37 *The Courier and Advertiser*, 1 August 1928.

38 *Daily Express*, 18 September 1928.

39 CHAR 1/200.

40 CHAR 1/200.

41 *Lincolnshire Standard & Boston Guardian*, 3 May 1930; *Yorkshire Post*, 28 April 1930.

42 IWM 13905.

43 Ibid.

44 RAF AC86/74/1/7 Aircraft logbook for Stinson SM-1 Detroiter X4183

Endeavour, February 1928–13 March 1928.

45 Arolsen Archives, https://collections.arolsen-archives.org/en/search/person/82492072?s=Sara%20Gallizien&t=248928&p=0.

Flight Checklist: Noteworthy Hair

1 Hilton Howell Railey, *Touch'd with Madness* (New York: Carrick & Evans, 1938), p. 103.

2 Adrian Fort, *Nancy: The Story of Lady Astor* (London: Vintage, 2013), p. 56, 'At that time women were treated with a respect and courtesy they probably forfeited when they cut off their hair and their skirts.'

3 *Daily Mirror*, 7 July 1928.

4 Amelia Earhart scrapbook 9; 'Miss Earhart Is Dinner Guest As She Ends Visit to City'; 1932–1933, AESB009. George Palmer Putnam Collection of Amelia Earhart Papers. Archives and Special Collections, Purdue University.

5 *Soaring Wings*, p. 79.

6 Ibid., p. 91.

7 Ibid., p. 90.

8 *Aviatrix*, p. 70.

9 Letter, George Palmer Putnam to Amelia Earhart, circa 1937 [?], b7f155i3. George Palmer Putnam Collection of Amelia Earhart Papers. Archives and Special Collections, Purdue University.

10 Doris L. Rich, *Amelia Earhart: A Biography* (Shrewsbury: Airlife, c1989), p. 32.

11 Transport pilot's licence, 1 May 1930, blf2i2. George Palmer Putnam Collection of Amelia Earhart Papers. Archives and Special Collections, Purdue University.

12 *The Fun of it,* p. 24.

13 *Amy Johnson*, p. 78; Liz Evers, 'Bailey, Mary ('Lady Bailey') (née Westenra)', *Dictionary of Irish Biography*, https://www.dib.ie/biography/bailey-mary-lady-bailey-nee-westenra-a10296.

14 *The Fun of It*, p. 166.

15 *Time*, 20 April 1931; *Still Missing*, pp. 19, 160.

16 *Still Missing*, p.160.

17 *The New York Times*, 7 July 1928.

18 *The Midland Reporter*, Mullingar, 10 May 1928.

19 Ibid.

20 *Anything Goes*, p. 70 and *Still Missing*, pp. 160, 270.

21 *Anything Goes*, p. 83.

22 Amelia Earhart scrapbook 13, 1932-1935, AESB013, George Palmer Putnam Collection of Amelia Earhart Papers. Archives and Special Collections, Purdue University; *The Sioux City Journal*, 7 October, 1933; Amelia Earhart scrapbook 13.

23 Scrapbook number 15 kept by Amelia Earhart and George Palmer Putnam, ca. 1930s, AESB015, George Palmer Putnam Collection of Amelia Earhart Papers. Archives and Special Collections, Purdue University.

24 *Tech News,* Technical High School, Springfield, Mass., 14 December 1932. Purdue, Scrapbook 10, AESB010. George Palmer Putnam Collection of Amelia Earhart Papers. Archives and Special Collections, Purdue University.

25 Amelia Earhart scrapbook 11, *Columbus Citizen*, 12 January 1934, AESB011. George Palmer Putnam Collection of Amelia Earhart Papers. Archives and Special Collections, Purdue University.

26 Handwritten note written to Amelia Earhart by an anonymous individual, b7fl63il. George Palmer Putnam Collection of Amelia Earhart Papers, Archives and Special Collections, Purdue University.

27 *The Six*, p. 205.

28 Ibid., pp. 255–7.

29 Ibid., p. 261.

30 Customer review, Amazon, https://www.amazon.co.uk/Barbie-Collector-FJH64-Inspiring-Earhart/dp/B076Q6YJ2V.

Chapter Nineteen: 'Violet. Cheerio.'

1 *Soaring Wings*, p. 60.

2 'Popping Off Letter', Letter, Amelia Earhart to her father Edwin S. Earhart,1928, b7f146i1. George Palmer Putnam Collection of Amelia Earhart

Papers. Archives and Special Collections, Purdue University.

3 Letter, 20 May 1928, Boston, Mass., to Mrs. E.S. Earhart, Medford, Mass., b7f145i3. George Palmer Putnam Collection of Amelia Earhart Papers. Archives and Special Collections, Purdue University.

4 *The Fun of It,* p. 54.

5 *20 Hrs., 40 Min.*, p. 55.

6 Ibid., pp. 60–1.

7 Ibid.

8 Ibid., p. 63.

9 Ibid., p. 68.

10 *The New York Times*, 13 June 1928.

11 *Passaic Daily Herald*, 5 June 1928.

12 *Sunday News*, 10 June 1928.

13 *The Ottawa Citizen*, 13 June 1928.

14 *Soaring Wings*, p. 64.

15 Ibid., p. 65.

16 *Wilkes-Barre Times Leader*, 4 June 1928.

17 *The New York Times*, 13 June 1928.

18 *The New York Times*, 28 March 1928.

19 *Soaring Wings*, p. 64.

20 *Wilkes-Barre Times Leader*, 4 June 1928.

21 Ibid.

22 Ibid.

23 Ibid.

24 Ibid.

25 *Brooklyn Times Union*, 9 June 1928.

26 *Sunday News*, 10 June 1928.

27 *The New York Times*, 3 June 1928.

28 *The Boston Globe*, 8 June 1928.

29 *Around the World in Eight Days*, p. 84.

30 *The Gazette*, 13 June 1928.

31 Ibid.

32 *The Great Atlantic Air Race*, pp. 62–3.

33 Ibid., p. 72.

34 *The Gazette*, 13 June 1928.

35 *The Knoxville Journal*, 18 June 1928.

36 *The San Francisco Examiner*, 18 June 1928.

37 Ibid.

38 Ibid.

39 *The Province*, 18 June 1928.

40 *20 Hrs., 40 Min.*, p. 91.

41 Ibid., p. 48.

42 Ibid., p. 49.

43 Ibid., p. 50.

44 *The Fun of It*, p. 62.

45 Ibid.

46 *20 Hrs., 40 Min.*, p. 93.

47 Ibid.

Chapter Twenty: Crossing the Atlantic

1 *Taunton Courier, Bristol and Exeter Journal* and *Western Advertiser*, 13 June 1928.

2 *Manchester Evening News*, 18 June 1928.

3 *Taunton Courier, Bristol and Exeter Journal and Western Advertiser*, 13 June 1928.

4 Ibid.

5 *The Derry Daily Telegraph*, 5 June 1928.

6 *Manchester Evening News*, 18 June 1928.

7 Library of Congress, https://www.loc.gov/item/2017675682/.

8 *Western Mail*, 15 June 1928.

9 All descriptions from this paragraph from *20 Hrs., 40 Min.*, p. 94.

10 Ibid., p. 95.

11 Ibid., p. 96.

12 Ibid., p. 97.

13 Ibid., p. 98.
14 Ibid., pp. 101–2.
15 Ibid., p. 99.
16 Howell Rees, 'Pioneer of Aviation', *The Bônau Cabbage Patch* (2004), http://www.pwllmag.co.uk/spdf/spdf1.pdf.
17 *20 Hrs., 40 Min.*, p. 99.
18 Ibid., p. 100.
19 Ibid., p. 100.
20 Ibid., Logbook.
21 Ibid., p. 101.
22 Ibid., Logbook.
23 Ibid., p. 104.
24 Ibid., p. 105.
25 Ibid., p. 104.
26 *For the Fun of It*, p. 65.
27 *For the Fun of It*, p. 64.
28 *20 Hrs., 40 Min.*, p. 111.
29 Ibid., p. 112.
30 The time became the title of Earhart's subsequent book about the journey, but it was closer to 20 hrs 49 minutes.

Chapter Twenty-One: Grounded: London, June 1928

1 *20 Hrs., 40 Min.*, p. 114.
2 Ibid.
3 Ibid.
4 *The Fun of It*, p. 69.
5 *Touch'd with Madness*, p. 106.
6 *20 Hrs., 40 Min.*, p. 115; see also 'Pioneer of Aviation' http://www.pwllmag.co.uk/spdf/spdf1.pdf.
7 'Pembrey Copper Works; Imperial Smelting Corporation Ltd; Frickers Metal Company, Pembrey', Coflein, https://coflein.gov.uk/en/site/34047/.
8 *20 Hrs., 40 Min.*, p. 115.

9 'Pioneer of Aviation', http://www.pwllmag.co.uk/spdf/spdf1.pdf.

10 *Still Missing*, p. 110.

11 'Pioneer of Aviation', http://www.pwllmag.co.uk/spdf/spdf1.pdf.

12 *The New York Times*, 21 June 1928.

13 Amelia Earhart, typed note to President Calvin Coolidge, thank you from the crew of the *Friendship*, ca.1928. b1f8i1. George Palmer Putnam Collection of Amelia Earhart Papers. Archives and Special Collections, Purdue University.

14 *Guardian*, 25 June 1928.

15 Louis E. 'Slim' Gordon, Special Collection Photo, Catalog #:09_01524, https://www.flickr.com/photos/sdasmarchives/.

16 Ibid.

17 *The New York Times*, 21 June, 1928.

18 SDASM, https://sandiegoairandspace.org/collection/item/louis-edward-gordon-special-collection. He was contracted through Mechanical Science Corporation for $5,000. The money was deposited with R. E. Byrd at Byrd Antarctic Expedition and held for payment when the contract was fulfilled.

19 *The New York Times*, 25 June 1928. Stultz earned a $20,000 bonus, Mike Hall, 'Amelia Earhart Memorabilia: 7 Historic Items, Just Collecting (2021), https://www.justcollecting.com/blogs/news/amelia-earhart-memorabilia-7-historic-items.

20 *The Boston Globe*, 21 September 1933.

21 *The York Dispatch*, 21 July 1928.

22 *The Fun of It*, p. 71.

23 London newspaper clipping, 'Transatlantic Girl Flyer Out Shopping in Borrowed Clothes', following Earhart's *Friendship* flight, June 1928, b1f11i20. George Palmer Putnam Collection of Amelia Earhart Papers. Archives and Special Collections, Purdue University.

24 *The New York Times*, 19 June 1928.

25 *The Fun of It*, p. 72.

26 *Liverpool Daily Post*, 25 June 1928.

27 'The Settlement Houses', *Stories of London*, https://stories-of-london.org/settlement-houses-1/.

28 *Daily Express*, 25 June 1928.

29 *The New York Times,* 21 June 1928.

30 Ibid., 25 June 1928.

31 *Edinburgh Evening News*, 25 June 1928.

32 *Birmingham Daily Gazette*, 27 June 1928.

33 *New York Times*, 21 June 1928.

34 *20 Hrs., 40 Min.*, p. 119.

35 Ibid., p. 120.

36 *The Guardian* (Bay Roberts, Newfoundland), 22 June 1928.

37 Crew of the *Friendship* cablegram to Charles A. Levine, acknowledgement of his cable, ca. 1928, b1f8i12, George Palmer Putnam Collection of Amelia Earhart Papers. Archives and Special Collections, Purdue University.

Chapter Twenty-Two: Solo

1 *The New York Times*, 29 March 2010; Elinor Smith, *Aviatrix* (New York: Harcourt Brace Jovanovich, 1981), p. xii.

2 Andrew Cafourek, 'Know Your Landmarks: Bridges of the East River', Become a New Yorker, (2013), https://becomeanewyorker.com/know-your-landmarks-bridges-of-the-east-river/.

3 *Aviatrix*, p. 13.

4 Ibid., p. 131.

5 Ibid., p. 14.

6 Ibid., p. 100.

7 Ibid., p. 101.

8 *Touch'd with Madness*, p.106; Donald Goldstein and Katherine Dillon, *Amelia: The Centennial Biography of an Aviation Pioneer,* (London: Brassey's, 1997), p. 54.

9 *20 Hrs., 40 Min.*, p. 172.

10 *The American Magazine*, August 1932.

11 *Soaring Wings*, p. 97.

12 *The Fun of It*, p. 181.

13 *Soaring Wings*, p. 98.

14 *The Fun of It*, p. 182.

15 *Smithy*, p. 241.

16 'Amelia Earhart', Forney Museum, https://www.forneymuseum.org/News_AmeliaEarhart_2.html.

17 *The New York Times,* 2 July 1929.

18 *Brooklyn Daily Eagle,* 3 July 1929.

19 *The Fun of it*, p. 184; *Soaring Wings*, p. 103.

20 *D32,* TV programme, The Rooms, St John's, Newfoundland.

21 *Around the World in Eight Days*, p. 93.

22 Ibid., pp. 83–4.

23 Notice board Conception Bay Museum, Harbour Grace, Newfoundland.

24 *Around the World in Eight Days*, p. 84.

25 *Soaring Wings*, p. 104.

26 Ben Evans, 'The Right Man: Remember Gordon Cooper's Day– Long Mercury, 55 Years On', AmericaSpace (2018), https://www.americaspace.com/2018/05/13/the-right-man-remembering-gordon-coopers-day-long-mercury-mission-55-years-on/.

27 *Soaring Wings*, p. 104.

28 'Courage' by Amelia Earhart, September 193?? [unreadable], Memorial University of Newfoundland, unidentified cutting.

29 Jean L. Backus, 'I came from America', Chapter 13, *Letters from Amelia.*

30 Interview with Mel Luck.

31 *Daily News*, 21 June 1932.

32 *Aviatrix*, p. 108.

33 Francis Chichester, *The Lonely Sea and the Sky* (London: Hodder and Stoughton, 1964), p. 114.

34 Ibid., p. 165.

35 Charles Lindbergh, *Spirit of St Louis*, (London: John Murray, 1953), pp. 389–90, *Lindbergh*, p. 124.

36 'Sir Ernest Shackleton and T S Eliot's "third man"', Royal Scottish Geographical Society (2023), https://www.rsgs.org/blog/sir-ernest-shackleton-and-t-s-eliots-third-man.

37 *National Geographic* 62.3 (1932), p. 363.

38 *The Fun of It*, p. 184.

39 *New York Sun*, 21 June 1932.

40 *The Fun of It*, p. 185.

41 *National Geographic* 62.3 (1932), p. 365.

42 *The Fun of It*, p. 185.

43 Dorothy Cochrane, 'Inside Amelia Earhart's Lockheed Vega', National Air and Space Museum (2019), https://airandspace.si.edu/stories/editorial/inside-amelia-earharts-lockheed-vega.

44 *National Geographic* 62.3 (1932), p. 365.

45 *Around the World in Eight Days*, p. 99.

46 *Daily News*, 21 June 1932.

47 Ibid.

48 *National Geographic* 62.3 (1932), p. 367.

49 *The Lonely Sea*, p. 83.

50 *Soaring Wings*, p. 106.

51 *The Fun of It*, p. 186.

52 *The Lonely Sea*, p. 217.

53 *Young Woman and the Sea*, p. 103

54 *Daily News*, 21 June 1932.

55 Ibid.

56 Various spellings of his name exist.

57 *Amelia Earhart*, pp. 214–5.

58 *Larne Times*, 28 May 1932.

59 *Western Daily Press*, Bristol, and *Bristol Mirror*, 23 May 1932; *Larne Times*, 28 May 1932.

60 *National Geographic* 62.3 (1932), p. 363.

61 *Irish Independent*, 23 May 1932; *Larne Times*, 28 May 1932.

62 *Amelia Earhart*, pp. 214–5.

63 *Daily News*, 21 June 1932.

64 Nicola Moorby, '*Miss Earhart's Arrival* 1932 by Walter Richard Sickert', catalogue entry, April 2006, in Helena Bonett, Ysanne Holt, Jennifer Mundy

(eds.), *The Camden Town Group in Context*, Tate Research Publication, May 2012.

65 P. G. Konody, 'Painting of Miss Earhart', *Daily Mail*, 31 May 1932.

Epilogue: Flight Debrief

1 *The Leeds Mercury*, 14 August 1928.

2 *Daily News* 16 June 1929.

3 *The New York Times*, 31 July 1928.

4 *The Daily News and Westminster Gazette*, 6 August 1928.

5 *Passaic Daily News*, 31 August 1928; *The Marion Star*, 21 August 1928; *San Francisco Examiner*, 30 August 1931.

6 *Leicester Evening Mail*, 19 November 1930.

7 *San Francisco Examiner*, 30 August, 1931.

8 Joe Jackson, *Atlantic Fever: Lindbergh, His Competitors, and the Race to Cross the Atlantic* (New York: Farrar, Straus and Giroux, 2013), p. 505.

9 *Atlantic Fever*; see also, *Washington Jewish Week*, 2 January 1992, 'Charles Levine', Yiddish Radio Project, www.yiddishradioproject.com; *The New York Times*, 18 December, 1991. https://storycorps.org/stories/levine-and-his-flying-machine/.

10 *The New York Times*, 16 April 1931. Later in 1930 a judgment of $1,232 was filed against Boll for three months' rent on a maisonette at West Fiftieth Street. She did not appear in court and claimed she had given up the apartment.

11 *The New York Times*, 19 August 1931.

12 Ibid., 16 May 1934; *The Tenessean*, 16 May 1934.

13 *The Oklahoma News*, 20 February 1936.

14 *The New York Times*, 31 January 1940.

15 Ibid., 16 January 1942.

16 Ibid., 12 April 1949.

17 *Los Angeles Times*, 20 February 1953.

18 *The Gazette*, 26 June 1955.

19 *Press-Telegram* (Long Beach, California), 11 October 1977.

20 Laurie Notaro, *Crossing the Horizon: A Novel* (New York: Gallery Books,

2016), Author's Note, p. 442

21 *The York Dispatch*, 21 July 1928.

22 Descriptive Finding Guide for the Louis E. Gordon Personal Papers SDASM. SC.10058, San Diego Air & Space Museum Library and Archives.

23 *The Daily Sentinel*, 13 January 1964; *The Kansas City Star*, 11 January 1964.

24 *The Ottawa Journal*, 13 January 1928.

25 *West over the Waves*, p. 120.

26 *Crossing the Horizon*, p. 442.

27 Ibid.

28 'All about The George Hotel & It's History', The George Hotel, https://web.archive.org/web/20150402092521/http:/www.thegeorgeatleadenham.co.uk/aboutus.shtml.

29 *The Times*, 29 April 1937.

30 CHAR 1/299.

31 CHAR 1/300, 7 October 1937, CHAR 1/298.

32 *The New York Times*, 8 October 1959.

33 Ibid., 28 October, 1957.

34 *The Buffalo News*, 23 January 1929; *Democrat and Chronicle*, 24 October 1992.

35 *Des Moines Tribune*, 23 September 1930; *New York Times*, 24 September 1930.

36 '17–18 June 1928', https://www.thisdayinaviation.com/17-june-1928/.

37 TNA: AVIA 2/1082.

38 Ibid.

39 Ibid.

40 *The New York Times*, 19 July 1937.

41 'Amelia Earhart', National Air and Space Museum, https://airandspace.si.edu/explore/stories/amelia-earhart.

42 Rachel Hartigan, 'Exclusive: Inside the Search for Amelia Earhart's Airplane', *National Geographic* (2019), https://www.nationalgeographic.com/culture/article/inside-search-for-amelia-earhart-airplane.

43 Rossella Lorenzai, 'Credible Amelia Earhart radio signals were ignored as bogus', *NBC News* (2012), https://www.nbcnews.com/id/wbna47653021.

44 'Nikumaroro Atoll', Earth Observatory, https://earthobservatory.nasa.gov/images/91889/nikumaroro-atoll.

45 Rachel Hartigan, 'Why This Island Is at the Center of the Search for Amelia Earhart', *National Geographic* (2017), https://www.nationalgeographic.com/adventure/article/amelia-earhart-search-island-dogs.

46 Thomas L. Allison, 'Report: Zipper Slider', The Earhart Project, (2008), https://tighar.org/Projects/Earhart/Archives/Expeditions/NikuV/Analysis_and_Reports/Zipper/Zipper.html.

47 Rossella Lorenzi, 'Has aviator Amelia Earhart's beauty case been found?', *NBC News* (2021), https://www.nbcnews.com/id/wbna48178295.

48 Ellen Wexler, 'Reseachers Thought They Found Amelia Earhart's Missing Plane. It Turned Out to Be a Plane-Shaped Pile of Rocks', *Smithsonian Magazine* (2024), https://www.smithsonianmag.com/smart-news/researchers-thought-they-found-amelia-earharts-missing-plane-it-turned-out-to-be-a-plane-shaped-pile-of-rocks-180985603/.

49 *The New York Times,* 5 January 1950.

50 Richards Vidmer in *Herald Tribune*, quoted in *Honolulu Star-Advertiser*, 16 August 1937.

51 Downhome, www.downhomelife.com, June 2023.

Index

Abbott, Robert, 41–3
Acosta, Bert, 316
Advisory Committee of Pilots, 83
Aero Digest, 124
Aeroplane, The, 220
African Americans, 38–46
Aga Khan, 61
Ailsa Craig, 79
Air Board, 72
Air Commerce Act, 154
air crashes, casualty figures, 34
Air Ministry, 19, 87, 134, 178, 220, 242, 272
Air National Guard, 270
Airco DH6, 29
aircraft names, 50–1
Albert, Prince, 67
Albert Memorial, 285
Alcock John, 4, 18–19, 30, 88–9, 122, 284
alcohol prohibition, 23, 49, 161, 173, 207–8
Aldford House, 273
Alexandra, Queen, 61
altitude records, 95
ambiguous loss, 234–5, 248, 328
  and First World War, 238–9
America, 21
American Civil War, 57, 64, 153
American Girl, 50, 145–51, 154–61, 163, 226, 318
American heiresses, 112–16
Amundsen, Roald, 175–6, 188
Ancker, Aage, 103–4
Ancker, Mabel, 101–5, 107, 119, 144–6, 167, 169, 174, 181–3, 186
Ancker-Grayson Aircraft Corporation, 107
Antarctica, 200–1, 261, 287
Archibald, Rose, 304, 312
Arctic Circle, 178
Arenzen, Father, 230–1, 235
Argles, Arthur, 268–9
Army and Navy Gazette, 68
Astor, Nancy, 92, 113–14, 116
Astor, Waldorf, 114, 253
Atlantic Ocean, scientific understanding of, 17–18
Austen, Jane, 111
Australian Women's Weekly, 237–8
autogiros, 301–3
Avro Avian, 286

Bache, Lieutenant Albert, 202
Bailey, Captain, 282
Bailey, Lady Mary, 37, 95, 255–6
Baker, Josephine, 41
Balchen, Bernt, 175–6, 297–8, 301,

304–6, 312
Baldwin, Stanley, 84
Balet, José Roger, 321
Ballard, Bob, 325, 327
Barbie dolls, 45, 259, 328
barnstorming, 26–7, 47
Barton, E. V., 313
baseball, 49–50
Bauer, Dr Louis, 35
Bean, Sawney, 78
Beatty School, 70–1
Bedford, Duchess of, 37, 93
Beekman Street Hospital, 174
Beeman, Edwin M., 43
Bellanca monoplane, 209, 266
Ben-Gurion, David, 320
Ben-Hur, 317
Bennett, Floyd, 21–2
Benson, E. F., 115
Bertaud, Lloyd, 23
Binney, Dorothy, 204
Black Bart, 4
Blériot aeroplanes, 31
Blixen, Baron Bror, 63
Blue Ridge Mountains, 195–6, 199
Boegner, Peggie Phipps, 59
Boll, Mabel, 9–15, 22, 37, 45, 50–2, 65, 95–6, 108, 120, 177, 256, 259, 274, 312, 331
  Cuba flight, 208–10, 264–6
  and Hinch, 212, 219, 221–2, 225
  later life, 315–17
  marriages, 202–4, 316–17
  and provisions, 124
  race with Earhart, 260, 263–8, 288, 298
  wealth, 11–12
  and weather, 152–4, 212, 273
Boston and Maine Railroad, 143
Boulevardier, The, 315
Brancker, Sir William Sefton, 118, 215
Bravo, General Enrique, 321
'Bright Young Things', 120
British Air League, 83, 286
Brock, William, 226, 303
Brooklands aerodrome, 85, 226
Brooklyn Bridge, 294
Brown, John Whitten, 4, 18–19, 30, 88–9, 122, 160
Brown, Margery, 27–9, 34
  'What Men Flyers Think of Women Pilots', 28
Bruce, Ann, 285
Buchan, John, 78
Bulwer-Lytton, Sir Edward, 57
Burley House fire, 110–11
Burry Port, 281–3, 285
Byrd, Marie, 128
Byrd, Commander Richard E., 21–2, 128, 153, 175, 200–1, 204, 261, 263, 265, 270, 287

Cabbage Island, 167
Cairo, 70, 94, 217, 224, 286
Calais, 69–71
Camel aeroplanes, 87
Camp, Walter Chauncey, Jr, 201, 203
Canadian Department of the Interior, 319
Canadian National Railways, 138
Canuck training plane, 26–7
Cap Gris-Nez, 75
Cape Cod, 174, 180–2, 188–90
Cape Race, 7–8, 17, 138, 275
Cape Town, 94, 286
Capone, Al, 49

Cardiff, Archbishop of, 133
Carnegie, Andrew, 58, 61
Carnegie Steel Company, 58
Carpenter, Edward, 242
Cartier jewellers, 11
Cather, Willa, 90
Catholic News, 141
Cavendish Hotel, 120
Caxton Hall, 246
Cella, Theodore, 317
Chamberlain, Joseph, 114
Chamberlin, Clarence, 23, 163, 173, 176, 183, 217
  Cuba flight, 208–9
Chambers, Dorothea Lambert, 34
Chapman, Sam, 204, 211, 274
Charlot, Georges, 316–17
Chicago Daily Tribune, 199
Chicago Defender, 39–41, 45
Chicago Herald, 41
Chichester, Sir Francis, 306, 310
Childs' restaurants, 12
Christian Science, 107, 115–17
Christian Science Monitor, 257
Church Times, 296
Churchill, Clementine, 111, 117–18
Churchill, Winston, 10, 110–11, 113–14, 116–18, 245–6, 320
civil aviation, 34–5, 94–5, 154
Clarke, Major I. N., 313
Coast Tire and Rubber Company, 42
Cobham, Sir Alan, 84, 272
coconut crabs, 326
coffee, 127
Coleman, Bessie, 38–46, 52
Coleman, John, 40–1
Coleman, Walter, 40
Coleman School of Aeronautics, 43
Coli, François, 22–3
Colombian National Air Force, 321
Columbia, 12–14, 22, 50–1, 217–18, 263–9
  Cuba flight, 208–10, 265
Columbia Aircraft Company, 12
Columbus, Christopher, 169
Comeau, Captain, 189–90
Conan Doyle, Sir Arthur, 239–40, 246
Cook, Thomas, 239
Coolidge, Calvin, 33, 207–8, 210, 284
Coolidge, Grace, 169, 207
Cooper, Gordon, 304
Copley Plaza Hotel, 125
Cornell, Edward, 108
Cosmopolitan, 45, 301
Cramp, Charlie, 215
Cranwell aerodrome, 217–19, 223, 225, 227, 229, 231–2, 240, 243, 247
Crawley, George A., 119
Criado Perez, Caroline, 29
Crome, Johann, 103
Cromwell, Oliver, 111
Crosson, Marvel, 35
Croydon aerodrome, 74–5, 84, 167, 215–17, 220, 227, 286–7, 315
Cuba, 11, 13, 207–10, 264–6
  War of Independence, 60–1, 63, 68
Curtiss aeroplanes, 4, 22, 32, 42–3
Curtiss Field, 22, 28, 42, 106, 146, 175–6, 182, 222, 266
Curtiss Flying School, 26
Curtiss Flying Service, 181

Daily Express, 223–5, 233, 236, 245
Daily Mail, 18, 20, 70, 216, 313
Daily News, 235
Daily Record, 72

Daily Sketch, 312
Daimler, 215
Davenport, Ira and William, 243
Davenport Aviation School, 52
Davis, Noel, 21
Dawn, 50, 144–7, 160–2, 164–72, 174–90, 202, 236–7, 319
dead reckoning, 177, 262, 276, 308
Deep Sea Vision, 328
Delhi Durbar, 62
Denmark, Queen of, 169
Dennison Aircraft Corporation, 92, 261
Devereaux, Fannie, 6–8
Devereaux, Laura, 6–8, 329
Dillens, Lilli, 159
Dilworth, Liza, 43
Ding, William Rowland, 69–71, 73
Discovery space shuttle, 258
divorce, 202–3
Dole, James, 52
Dole Trans-Pacific Air Race, 52
Dolly Sisters, 12
Doolittle Raid, 317
Doran, Mildred, 52, 141
Dorner-Wahl aeroplanes, 176
Drouhin, Bertaud, 217

Earhart, Amelia, 13–15, 22, 33–4, 36–8, 45–6, 50, 52–3, 65, 90–4, 108, 149, 177
  Amelia Earhart Strasse, 45
  appearance, 253–9
  arrival in London and return to America, 284–8
  Barbie doll, 45, 259, 328
  cigarette endorsement, 206
  and fashion design, 320
  final flight, 320–9
  first meeting with Amy Guest, 283–4, 319
  first woman to cross Atlantic, 282–3
  Friendship flight, 3–10, 152, 260–84, 315, 330
  The Fun of It, 297
  Lego figure, 329
  Little Red Bus flight, 295–314, 331
  loses altimeter and airspeed indicator, 307–8, 310
  marriage, 203–6
  meeting with Snook, 25–7
  nicknames, 48, 53
  and nursing, 30, 80, 255
  and provisions, 125–8
  Sickert painting, 313–14
  and social work, 173, 210–12, 253, 274, 286
  and Stultz's death, 300
  Transport Pilot's licence, 254–5
  20 Hrs., 40 Min., 125, 296, 301
  and weather, 152–3, 273, 296, 300, 324
  and women's careers, 257–8, 320
Earhart, Muriel, 90–1, 93
earth induction compass, 147
École d'Aviation des Frères Caudron, 41
Eddy, Mary Baker, 115
Ederle, Gertrude, 32–4, 48, 164
Edison Electric, 204
Edward (VII), Prince of Wales, 63, 69
Edward (VIII), Prince of Wales, 273, 313
Egerton, Beatrice, 239–41, 247
Elder, Ruth, 14, 33–4, 37, 45, 50, 65, 95, 119, 152, 168, 178, 226, 256,

259, 279, 331
American Girl flight, 145–51, 154–61, 163
and Frances Grayson, 107–9
later life, 317–18
marriages, 195–201, 203–4, 317–18
and provisions, 122–3, 149
'Ruth's Ribbon', 52, 108, 318
Electra, 322–7
Eliot, T. S., 307
Ellis Island, 173
Endeavour, 223–33, 239, 241–3, 245, 247
Endeavour space shuttle, 46
endurance flying record, 295
enemy aliens, 71–3
English Channel, 16, 30, 69–70, 75, 83, 133, 321
first woman to swim, 32–3, 48, 164
Evans, G. H., 189
Evening News, 67
Evening Standard, 296
Evening World Herald, 60
Everett, Edgcumbe, 69

Fairchild seaplane, 36
'falling leaf' manoeuvre, 300
Fédération Aéronautique Internationale (FAI), 30
Felsch, 'Happy', 49
Finch, George, 110
First World War, 9, 12, 20, 22, 25, 30–2, 34, 40, 42, 51, 75, 80, 85, 93, 95, 107, 147, 175, 201–4, 255, 257, 273, 320
and ambiguous loss, 238–9
and enemy aliens, 71–3
'Fly Girls', 51
flying boats, 4, 32, 162, 166, 187, 323
flying by instruments, 9, 150, 156, 177, 278, 299, 308
flying circuses, 22, 30, 32, 37, 42
'flying flappers', 48, 52, 83, 293
Fokker, Anthony, 42
Fokker aeroplanes, 3, 50, 134, 298
Fokker company, 297–8, 306
Fonck, René, 20–1, 123
Fortune magazine, 320
Fox, Miss I. F., 235
Frankfurt Airport, 45
Frickers Metal Company, 282
Fried, Captain, 287–8
Friendship, 3–10, 14, 22, 25, 50, 152, 260–83, 288, 296–7, 302, 315, 320–1, 330
frozen-water skiing, 74

Gallegher, Robert, 311–12
Gandil, 'Chick', 49
Garrett, Eileen, 240–2, 247
Gatty, Harold, 154, 268, 298, 303, 308
Gellibrand, Miss, 117
Gentry, Viola, 295
George V, King, 70, 84
George Hotel, Leadenham, 319
Gilded Age, 198
'Gilded Prostitution', 112
Gillespie, Albert Arnold ('Buddy'), 317
Gillespie, John, 225
Gillespie, William, 317
'Glamornauts', 51
Glenapp Church, 319
Gloucester, Duke of, 273
Glynn, Elinor, 50–1
Goldsborough, Brice ('Goldy'), 47, 146–7, 162, 165–71, 175–85,

188–9, 236, 319
Goldsborough, Frank, 179, 181, 185, 190
Goldsborough, Gertrude, 179–82, 185, 188–90
Goodrich Rubber company, 242
Goos, Captain, 158–9
Gordon, Louis 'Slim', 5–9, 47, 125–6, 261–2, 268, 275, 279–80, 282–5, 287, 296, 302, 315, 318–19
Gorski, Eddie, 297, 301, 304–6, 312
Gotha bombers, 87
Gower, J. H. Lewes, 261, 265
Grafton Galleries, 69
Grainger, Dorothy, 233
Grand Banks, 149
Grant, Captain Hugh A., 183
Grant, Ulysses S., 153
Grayson, Dr Cary T., 106
Grayson, Frances Wilson, 9, 14, 37, 45, 47, 50, 52, 65, 95, 105–9, 119, 149, 151, 256, 259, 263, 274, 319, 331
  and acting, 106
  and *American Girl* flight, 160–1
  and Christian Science, 107, 116–17
  Dawn flights and disappearance, 144–7, 160–2, 164–72, 174–90, 202, 236–7, 264
  meeting with Mabel Ancker, 101–2
  her pistol, 178–9, 187–9
  and Ruth Elder, 107–9
  and weather, 152, 229
Grayson, John Brady, 106, 202
Great Circle, 144
Great Coup, The, 79
Great Depression, 302
Great Western Railway, 77
Guest, Amy Phipps, 37, 50, 57–66, 68, 75, 79, 90, 92, 94, 110–21, 204
  and Christian Science, 115–16
  and *Friendship* flight, 10, 270, 272–4, 280, 283–7
  later life, 319–20
  and nursing, 57, 60–1
  and Red Cross hospital, 114–15
Guest, Diana, 119, 273, 320
Guest, Frederick ('Freddie'), 10, 61–3, 94, 110–11, 114–15, 117–18, 120, 272–3, 283, 286–7, 319
Guest, Raymond, 119, 320
Guest, Winston, 118–19, 273, 320
Gulf of Saint Lawrence, 138
Gulf Stream, 6
Gwynne, Erskine, 315

hairstyles, 253–7
Haldeman, George, 122, 145–50, 154–5, 157–61, 163, 168, 196, 198, 279, 318
hallucinations, 306–7
Hamble aerodrome, 285
Hamilton, Barbara, 139, 141
Hamilton, Captain Leslie, 47, 74–5, 133–5, 138–9, 236–7, 241, 319
Handley Page biplane, 70
Hanworth Air Park, 313
Harbour Grace, 10, 13–14, 22, 127, 138, 177, 180, 226, 267–9, 288, 298–9, 301–4, 307–9, 312, 315, 330
Harcourt, Sir William, 114
Harris, Walter Burton, 67
Hart, Richard ('Two Gun'), 49
Hartsfield, Hank, 258
Harvey, Captain, 137
Hay, Will, 237
Hazzard, Robert, 144

Heath, Sir James, 94
Heath, Lady Mary, 37, 94–5, 201, 255, 286–7, 295
Athletics for Women and Girls, 95
Hendon, Stag Lane aerodrome, 69–71, 83–4, 87, 216, 227, 247, 255
Herne, Captain, E. C. D., 83–4
Hewlett, Hilda, 31, 83
Hinchliffe, Captain Walter ('Hinch'), 47, 85–9, 134, 138, 212–22
and ambiguous loss, 234–48
arrangement with Mackay, 221–2
and Boll, 212, 219, 221–2, 225
Endeavour flight and disappearance, 223–33
financial legacy, 244–7
and Levine, 217–20, 222, 227
life insurance, 221, 244–5
Hinchliffe, Emilie ('Millie'), 214–15, 217, 220–1, 228–9, 233–6, 239–48, 319
Hinchliffe, Joan, 85, 216–17, 233, 240, 242, 247–8
Hinchliffe, Mr and Mrs, 235–6
Hoare, Sir Samuel, 215, 227, 246
Holy Roman Empire, 66
Hoover, Herbert, 313
hormones, 36
hot air balloons, 18
Houston, Lady, 245
Howland Island, 323, 325, 328

Illustrated London News, The, 111
Imperial Airways, 88, 217, 219–20, 222, 282
Inchcape, James Mackay, Lord, 76–8, 80–2, 223, 233, 236, 245–6, 248
inflatable suits, 158
International Air Transport Association (IATA), 330
International Commission for Air Navigation, 94–5
International Group for Historic Aircraft Recovery, The (TIGHAR), 325–6
International Women's Day, 329
Iowa State Fair, 30
Irish News, 164
'it girls', 50–1

Jackson, 'Shoeless Joe', 50
Jeffrey Yacht Club, 261
Jemison, Mae, 46
Jenkins, Rev. Shulford, 195–6, 199
Jerome, Jennie, 113
Jodhpur, Rani of, 215
John Bull, 73
Johnson, Amy, 53, 295, 311
Johnson, Samuel, 284
Johnson-Wreford, Anthony, 221
Jones, Harr M., 144
Journal of Aviation Medicine, 35

Kemp, George, 15, 17
Keystone Pathfinder biplane, 21
Kimball, James H. ('Doc'), 125, 152–6, 178, 183, 209, 300–1
Kinkade, T. Harold ('Doc'), 161–2, 166–7, 171–2
King, John, 243–4
King, Ralph P., 318
King's Cup race, 74, 133
Kingsford Smith, Charles, 299
Kinner, Winfield 'Bert', 27
Kinner Airplane Company, 261
Kinner Airport, 24

KLM, 88, 214, 242
Knights of Columbus, 268
Koehler, Fred, 177, 184, 189, 236

Lake Goldsborough, 319
Lake Grayson, 319
Lake Hamilton, 319
Lake Michigan, 40
Lake Minchin, 319
Lake Omdahl, 319
Lake St Raphael, 319
Lake Wertheim, 319
Lascelles, Viscount, 224
Latrobe Bulletin, 50
Lawrence, D. H., 240
Lawrence, T. E., 229
Le Bourget, 23, 84–5, 94, 175, 216–17, 220
Le Boutillier, Oliver, 14, 265, 267–9
Le Crotoy, 41
League for Fostering Genius, 164
Lee, Harper, 90
Lenglen, Suzanne, 33–4
Levine, Charles, 12–13, 23, 50–1, 134, 138, 163, 173, 202, 264–5, 288
  Cuba flight, 208–10, 264
  and Hinch, 217–20, 222, 227
  later life, 315–16
Levine, Grace, 208, 316
Lewis, Rosa, 120
Lhasa, 63, 121
Libinski (mechanic), 162
Life Guards, 62
Lillie, Beatrice, 215
Lindbergh, Charles (senior), 22
Lindbergh, Charles, 4, 12, 22–3, 28, 30, 37, 84–5, 105–7, 120, 144, 150, 163, 196, 208, 210, 217, 226, 293
  child's abduction and murder, 299
  and Earhart, 153, 253, 263–4, 298, 300
  and earth induction compass, 147
  hallucinations, 306
  nicknames, 47–8
  and provisions, 123–4
  We, 204
  and weather, 152–3
Little Red Bus, 50, 295–314, 329, 331
Lloyd George, David, 115, 117
Lockheed Vega, 50, 298–9, 305, 308
Lodge, Raymond, 243
Lodge, Sir Oliver Joseph, 243
London Ritz, 221
London Spiritualist Alliance, 240
Londonderry, 310
Long, Helen, 60
Lonsdale, Lord, 112, 286
looping the loop, 31–2, 43, 73, 87
Los Angeles airship, 182
Los Angeles Express, 62
Louis of Loewenstein-Wertheim, Prince, 66
Love's Greatest Mistake, 230
Löwenstein-Wertheim-Freudenberg, Ludwig, 66–8, 202
Lucky Strike cigarettes, 206
Ludington Lines, 301
Lufthansa, 174
Lynd, Robert and Helen, 106

Mabie, Janet, 257
McArdle, T. H., 108
McCallion, Danny, 311–12
McCormack, John, 286
Machado y Morales, General Gerardo, 208

McIntosh, Captain Robert, 134, 210
Mackay, Hon. Elsie, 14, 29, 37, 45, 47, 52, 65, 76, 78–86, 88, 90, 92–3, 95, 149, 256, 259, 274, 331
  and acting, 82
  and ambiguous loss, 234–48
  arrangement with Hinch, 212, 221–2
  Endeavour flight and disappearance, 223–33
  marriage, 80–2
  memorial, 319
  and nursing, 79–80
  and provisions, 122
Mackay, Margaret, 230, 235
Mackenzie King, William Lyon, 141
McPhetridge, Louise, *see* Thaden, Louise
Macy's department store, 320
Madison Square Garden, 12
magnesium flares, 31
Mail, The, 122
mail flights, 30–1
Malaysian Airlines Flight 370, 234
Manchester Guardian, 148
Manhattan Bridge, 294
Manning, Harry, 323
Mara, William, 222, 225
Marconi, Guglielmo, 15–18
Markievicz, Constance, 116
Marlborough, Duke of, 114
Marlborough House Set, 69
Marsalis, Frances, 51–2
Martin, Bradley, 119
Mary, Princess, 224
Mary, Queen, 69
Matrimonial Causes Act, 203
Mensink, H., 214
menstrual cycles, 35–6
messages in bottles, 237
Mexborough, Earl of, 66–8, 72, 134, 141
Miller, General Marcus, 68
Minchin, Lieutenant Colonel Frederick, 133–5, 137–9, 236–7, 319
Mizen Head, 232
Moody, Claude Emmett, 196
Morgan, Henry Owen, 243
Morse Code, 16–17, 324
Moth aeroplanes, 286
Muncie Evening Press, 180
Muncie Star, 181

NASA, 36, 51, 258
Nasser, Gamal Abdel, 320
National Aeronautic Association, 211
National Playground Association, 212
navigation, and menstrual cycle, 35–6
navigation flares, 149
Nebraska State Journal, 112
Negro Tri-State Fair, 42
Negro Welfare League, 43–4
New York County Surrogate Court, 188–9
New York Daily News, 52
New York Herald Tribune, 328
New York Philharmonic Orchestra, 317
New York Times, 42, 68, 83, 141, 147, 151, 163–4, 176, 182, 189, 201, 204, 208, 263, 282–3, 285
New York World's Fair, 33
Nichols, Ruth, 31–2, 36, 52, 164, 212, 295
nicknames, 47–53
Nikumaroro, 324–7

Nile Valley, 93–4
Ninety-Nines, 28, 46, 212
Noonan, Fred, 323–6
Norge dirigible, 176
North Pole, 21
Northcliffe, Lord, 18, 20
Northesk, Earl of, 74
Norwegian Naval Air Force, 175
Now, Clara, 51
Nungesser, Charles, 22–3
nursing, 30, 57, 60–1, 72, 79–80, 119, 255

Odescalchi, Prince, 74
Oelrich, Marjorie ('Bubbes'), 198
Oiseau Blanc, 22
Old Orchard Beach, 142–4, 147, 151, 160–1, 165–6, 168, 170, 172, 184–5, 209, 229
Olympia Horse Show, 286
Olympic Congress, 95
Omdal, Lieutenant Oskar, 176–8, 180, 183–4, 188, 190, 236, 319
Orteig, Raymond, 20, 23, 52
Other Wise Man, The, 173
Ottawa, 134, 136–7, 139, 319
Ottawa Citizen, 264

P&O, 65, 76, 224, 237
Palladium Tire Manufacturing Company, 135, 141
Palomar Park, 42–3
Pan American, 323, 325
Panama Canal, 198
Pankhurst, Emmeline, 70
parachuting, 43–4
Paramount News, 313
Paris Aeronautical Exhibition, 19
Paris Olympics (1924), 33
Paterson, Jane, 77
Pathé News, 42
pemmican, 124, 126
Penn Station, 101, 106
Pennsylvania Railroad, 50
Philippine-American War, 68, 202
Phipps, Henry, 57–9
Phipps, John ('Jay'), 61, 119–20
Phipps, Margarita ('Dita'), 119
Pickford, Mary, 257
Pinedo, Francesco di, 4
Pioneer compass, 305, 308
Pioneer Instrument Company, 147
Pittsburgh Post-Gazette, 57
Playfair, Sir Lyon, 114
Plunkett and Leader solicitors, 67
Poor Persons' Procedure, 203
Porcari, Count Henri Boleslav de, 316
Post, Wiley, 154, 268, 298, 303, 308
'Powder Puff Derby', 35, 201, 301
Pratt & Whitney Wasp engines, 299, 327
Pride of Detroit, 303
provisions, 122–8
Public Trustee, 246–7
Purdue University, 257, 288, 320, 323
Putnam, George Palmer, 46, 50, 204–6, 254, 264–5, 270, 274
  and Earhart's final flight, 320–1, 325, 328
  and Earhart's solo flight, 295, 297–8, 301, 304, 310

Queen, The, 112
Queen of the Air, 316
Queensboro Bridge, 294
Quimby, Harriet, 30–1, 70, 83

R34 airship, 19–20, 136
radio, 15–16, 146–7
RAF, 136, 214, 246
Railey, Captain Hilton, 212, 253, 282, 287
Railwaymen's Union, 215
Rainey, Ma, 51
Rasche, Thea, 37, 45, 48, 164, 260, 263, 266
Raymond, Allen, 282
Red Cross, 273
Reichsbank, 216
Reisner, Rev. Dr Christian F., 164
Resnik, Judy, 258–9
Ride, Sally, 36
Ries, Sophie, 229, 233, 236
Risberg, 'Swede', 50
RMS *Aquitania*, 197
RMS *Majestic*, 82, 174, 197
RMS *Mauretania*, 155
RMS *Titanic*, 8, 17, 29, 31, 325, 328
RMS *Viceroy of India*, 83
'Roaring Twenties', 48–9
Rocha, Hernando, 11, 13
Rogers, Harry, 32
Rogers, Will, 164
roller-skating, 69
Rolls-Royce cars, 11, 78–9, 93, 319
Roosevelt, Eleanor, 164
Roosevelt Field, 21–2, 123, 143, 145, 151, 161, 177–8, 208, 293
Rose Ann Belliveau (schooner), 189–90
Rossetti, Christina, 25
Rover (yacht), 78, 82
Royal Aero Club, 85
Royal Flying Corps, 80
Royal Naval Air Service (RNAS), 86
Royal Naval Reserve, 187
Royal Navy Meteorological Department, 183
Ruth, 'Babe', 49

S-35 biplane, 21
S-4 submarine, 173–4, 178, 181
Sable Island, 170, 181–2, 187
sabotage, 35, 44
St Claire, Mary, 237–8
St George's Channel, 281
St Inglevert, 75
St John's, 4, 8, 13–15, 18, 138, 267–8, 302–3, 329–31
St Moritz, 74
St Raphael, 50, 134–41, 236–7
Salem Harbour, 237
San Francisco Examiner, 201
Sargent, John Singer, 61–2, 114, 119
Sassoon, Sir Edward and Lady, 112
Savile, Lady Anne, 14, 37, 45, 47, 50, 52, 66–76, 90, 93–4, 146, 149, 202, 208, 232, 241, 256, 259, 274, 319, 330–1
  alien status and nationalisation, 71–3
  and provisions, 122
  St Raphael flight and disappearance, 134–41, 236–7
Savile, Lady Mary Louisa, 67–8
Savoy Hotel, 11, 208
Schlee, Edward, 226
Scott, Robert, 11, 264, 317
Scott, Sir Walter, 78
seances and spiritualism, 239–44, 246
seasickness, 66, 83, 135
Second World War, 35, 203, 248, 318, 320
Selfridge, Harry Gordon, 12, 322

Seven Site, 327
Shackleton, Sir Ernest, 306–7
Shaffer, Annie Childs, 58
Shaw, George Bernard, 240
Shelmerdine, Sir Francis, 321–2
Sibour, Viscount Jacques de, 322
Sickert, Walter, 313–14
Signal Hill, 15–17
Sikorsky, Igor, 107, 165, 167, 172, 183
Sikorsky amphibian, 50, 105, 145, 186
Sikorsky company, 162, 166
Simpson, Wallis, 273
Sinclair, Gordon, 225, 229, 231–3, 236
Sioux City Journal, 257
Smith, Elinor, 293–5, 298, 305
Smith, F. E., 110–11
Smithsonian Institution, 153
Snook, Anita ('Neta'), 24–8, 36, 52–3, 255
Society for Psychical Research, 243
Spang, Charles, 102–3
Spang, Rosa, 102–3
speed records, 36, 301
Spirit of St Louis, 22–3, 85, 144
SS *Albertic*, 187
SS *America*, 279, 287
SS *American Banker*, 155
SS *Barendrecht*, 157–9
SS *Beothic*, 138
SS *Blijidendijk*, 138
SS *City of New York*, 65
SS *Coahoma County*, 170
SS *Elmworth*, 275
SS *Homeric*, 155
SS *Ile de France*, 155
SS *Josiah Macey*, 138
SS *Leviathan*, 155
SS *Luchana*, 168
SS *Norwich City*, 326
SS *President Roosevelt*, 287–8
SS *Rexmore*, 276
SS *Ryndam*, 155
Stanley Park aerodrome, 313
Stead, W. T., 112, 246
Stewart, Major Oliver, 79
Stillman, Anne ('Fifi'), 37
Stillman, Mrs James A., 266
Stinson, Eddie, 318
Stinson, Katherine, 31, 256
Stinson Aircraft Company, 178
Stinson Detroiter monoplane, 50, 146, 181, 222, 225–6
Stoner, Winifred Sackville, 164
Stultz, Wilmer ('Bill'), 5–9, 13, 47, 125–6, 261–6, 268–9, 275–80, 283–5, 287, 296, 302, 315
  and alcohol, 9, 208, 264–5, 285, 300
  Cuba flight, 208–10, 264–6
  and *Dawn* flights, 146–7, 161–2, 165, 167–72, 175, 179, 183–4, 189, 264
  death, 300, 318
Suez Canal, 77
Suez Crisis, 320
Summers, Captain F. F., 187
Sun of David, The, 82
swimming, 32–3, 48

Tasman Sea, 306
Tatler, The, 79
Taylor, Dorothy, 87
Tech News, 257
tennis, 33–4
Thackery, George K., 317
Thaden, Louise, 36–7, 51–2, 295
Thibodeau, Louis, 189

Thirty Seconds over Tokyo, 317
Thompson, General John Taliaferro, 49
Tichenor, Frank, 124
Tidal Wave, The, 82
Time magazine, 14
Times, The, 17, 67, 74, 94, 136, 140
Times-Dispatch, 66
Tommy guns, 49
Toynbee Hall, 286
transatlantic sea travel, 64–6, 83, 135, 274, 287
transcontinental air race (1929), 35, 38
Transcontinental Air Transport, 301
Travel Air Corporation, 36
Treaty of Paris, 68
Trepassey, 3–8, 10, 17, 138, 142, 204, 263, 266–7, 269, 273, 275, 281, 296, 302–3, 329–30
  and provisions, 125–7
Trout, Evelyn ('Bobbi'), 295
Truth, Sojourner, 45
Tsen-Li Ching, Lieutenant Commander, 86
TWA, 318–19

Union Iron Mills, 58
United States Line, 287
US Airforce, 29–30
US Army Air Corps, 9, 318
US Army Signal Service Corps, 153
US Coast Guard, 174
  Itasca cutter, 324
US Department of Agriculture, 154
US Department of Commerce, 294, 302
US Federal Aviation Administration, 318
US Naval Air Corps, 21
US Navy, 115
US Postal Department, 45
US Postal Service, 31
US State Department, 321
US War Department, 13
US Weather Bureau, 153–4, 178, 182, 186
USS *Mahan*, 181
USS *Texas*, 207

Vanderbilt, Consuelo, 114
Vanderbilt, W. K. ('Anna'), 112
Vaughan, Fr Bernard, 73
Very pistols, 149
Vickers aeroplanes, 18–19
Vickers company, 226
Victoria, Queen, 67
Vikings, 18, 175
Virgin Mary, 8
Vote, The, 83
Waco biplanes, 294, 300
Waco company, 108
Wall Street Crash, 302, 316
War Brides, 106
Washington Post, 198
Waugh, Evelyn, 120
Wells, H. G., 240
Wheeling Aero Exhibit Company, 108
White Star Line, 82, 187
Wies, George, 181
Williams, 'Lefty', 50
Williamsburg Bridge, 294
Wills, William D., 43–4
Wilson, Andrew, 106, 180–1
Wilson, Frances, 52
Wilson, John A., 140
Wilson, Minnie, 106
Wilson, Woodrow, 106

Wimbledon tennis tournament, 33–4
Wimborne, Lord and Lady, 61
Winchester Cathedral, 284
Wings, 51
Winnie Mae, 308
Winston, William, 181
Wizard of Oz, The, 293, 317
Womack, Lyle, 145, 163, 196–201
Women's Amateur Athletic Association (WAAA), 95
Women's Derby, 295
Women's Educational and Industrial Union, 210
Woodward, Donald, 321
Woolley, Major Charles, 270, 275–6
Wooster, Stanton, 21
Wright, Orville, 293
Wright Aeronautical Company, 177, 184
Wright Bellanca, 50
Wright Whirlwind engines, 145, 166, 177, 226, 236–7
Wyndham, Captain Dennis, 80–2, 237–8, 244

Ye Olde Cheshire Cheese, Fleet Street, 284
YMCA, 43
Yorkshire Evening Post, 224
Younghusband, Sir Francis, 63

zeppelins, 18
Ziegfeld Follies, 198
ZR3 airship, 136
Zwölf Uhr Blatt, 164